George Gunton

Principles of Social Economics

Inductively considered and practically applied, with criticisms on correct theories

George Gunton

Principles of Social Economics
Inductively considered and practically applied, with criticisms on correct theories

ISBN/EAN: 9783337311766

Printed in Europe, USA, Canada, Australia, Japan

Cover: Foto ©Suzi / pixelio.de

More available books at **www.hansebooks.com**

PRINCIPLES

OF

SOCIAL ECONOMICS

INDUCTIVELY CONSIDERED AND
PRACTICALLY APPLIED

WITH

CRITICISMS ON CURRENT THEORIES

.

BY

GEORGE GUNTON

AUTHOR OF "WEALTH AND PROGRESS"

———

G. P. PUTNAM'S SONS

NEW YORK   LONDON
27 WEST TWENTY-THIRD ST.   27 KING WILLIAM ST., STRAND

𝕿𝖍𝖊 𝕶𝖓𝖎𝖈𝖐𝖊𝖗𝖇𝖔𝖈𝖐𝖊𝖗 𝕻𝖗𝖊𝖘𝖘

1891

TO MY WIFE

WITHOUT WHOSE INSPIRATION AND AID THIS BOOK
COULD NOT HAVE BEEN WRITTEN.

PREFACE.

IF there is one subject that should be more attractive to the student and more inspiring to the citizen than another, it is that of social economics, because it deals directly and exclusively with the influences and conditions which control all human welfare. It is through a knowledge of the principles and laws of human economics that we are enabled to make nature contribute to man's comfort and luxury by substituting abundance for poverty, freedom for slavery, peace for war, intelligence and morality for ignorance and brutality ; in short, a civilization of democracy and culture for one of despotism and degradation. Whenever the science which should furnish the key to nature's bounties and the light to human progress becomes unattractive to the student and repulsive to the average citizen, we may be assured that there is something fundamentally amiss with the conception and treatment of the subject.

This is precisely the case with political economy to-day. Instead of being the beacon-light of industrial and social affairs,—the source to which all may turn for safe instruction and hopeful guidance,—it is the "dismal science" which students avoid, statesmen and capitalists disregard, citizens ignore, and laborers discredit. Why is a science so dreary and pessimistic, which by its very nature should be fascinating and hopeful? The obvious answer is, that it fails to fulfill its function as a science of industrial welfare and social advancement. On nearly all fundamental questions affecting the production and distribution of wealth its doctrines are both uncertain and inconsistent. The popular theory of wages has been exploded by experience, and the current doctrines of value, interest, and profit have for generations been subjects of perplexing controversy between experts and sources of utter bewilderment to students. This is mainly due to the fact that the accepted theories belong to the hand-labor conditions of the seventeenth and eighteenth centuries, which have very little relation to the factory conditions of the nineteenth century. Nor should this be a matter of surprise, since it is entirely consistent with the law of industrial evolution. In its development society has assumed several distinct and essentially different industrial phases, which have each changed the economic structure of society, shifting the centre of industrial movement and the point of view of economic study.

Under feudalism, for instance, the land-owning class was the centre of all social and industrial movement. Economic policy therefore was considered from the standpoint of a land-owning class.

With the development of manufacture and trade however, came a radical change in economic relations. Serfs became wage receivers, and the cultivation of the land passed to tenant farmers, which change transferred the distribution of wealth from the domain of authority, to that of economic law. By this transition the social basis of industrial prosperity was broadened, and the centre of economic movement was shifted from the industries required to supply the needs of a small land-owning class to those required to supply the demands of a relatively large commercial class, whose interests were more varied and extensive. In proportion as new conditions developed, the narrow paternal policy which was adapted to the old régime became inimical to the welfare of the community, and a reconstruction of economic doctrine from a new point of view became necessary. The efforts of two centuries to supply this need culminated in the " Wealth of Nations," which really marks the advent of middle-class political economy, whose influence has practically moulded the economic thought of the present century.

For the same reason that under feudalism every thing was viewed from the standpoint of the land-owner, every thing was now considered from the standpoint of the manufacturer and merchant, whose income was derived from trade.

How to promote sales became the fundamental idea of what has been well named the "Commodities School" of political economy. To sell extensively necessitated producing cheaply. And since wages formed the greater part of the cost of production, it appeared from the "commodities" point of view to be as necessary to obtain cheap labor as cheap raw material, and for the same reason. Consequently it became a cardinal doctrine of the "Commodities School" that large profits depend upon low wages. "It has been my endeavor to show throughout this work," says Ricardo, "that the ratio of profits can never be increased but by a fall in wages." In the days of hand labor and small factories, when the consumption of the upper and middle classes furnished a sufficient market for products, this cheap-labor policy was successful in giving profits.

But this very success led to the development of large factories, which were destined again to revolutionize the economic structure of society. For since these large enterprises required a more extensive market for their success than any possible increase in the consumption of wealth by the upper and middle classes could furnish, the habitual demands of the masses for the first time necessarily became the foundation of industrial prosperity. Therefore *it is in the needs of the masses that the economics of the future must be studied and statesmanship determined.*

To such a change of industrial relations Adam Smith and his followers were altogether oblivious; their conception of industrial evolution was too limited to enable them to anticipate it, and their purely "commodities" point of view prevented them from observing it. They saw the importance of the factory as a means of making wealth cheap, but they did not see the economic importance of making man dear. Having failed to recognize the laborer as the great factor in a market whose consuming power must be increased, they continued to treat him only as a productive force in the factory, whose cost should be reduced, on the theory as Mill puts it, that "profits depend upon wages, rising as wages fall and falling as wages rise."

Thus through an effort to apply erroneous ante-factory theories to factory conditions political economy has for three quarters of a century been made a gospel of cheap labor and an enemy of social advance.

The growing incompetency of political economy to deal with modern conditions has begun to be recognized by inductive economists, and during the last twenty years an increasing departure from economic orthodoxy has been manifest among the younger economists of Europe and this country, which is now developing to the proportions of a new school.

In breaking from the hard and narrow lines established by the doctrines of early English economists, the " New School " has already rendered an important service to economic science, by making respectable the re-discussion of the fundamental principles governing industrial relations and political policy, in the light of modern knowledge.

Thus far, however, its work has been critical rather than constructive. It has contributed far more to break up the old than to establish a new body of economic doctrine. Although the English theory of wages has been repudiated and the doctrine of *laissez faire* rejected by them, no approximately adequate explanation of wage phenomena has been furnished, nor any affirmative principle of public policy suggested.

In the following pages I have endeavored to discuss the principles of social economics from the nineteenth century point of view. If the facts of modern experience are to be the court of final appeal, the great fundamental fact to be recognized in our society is *the democratic basis of industry*.

The factory system has made the use of natural forces (steam, electricity, etc.) necessary to successful industrial enterprise. Nature is intensely democratic. She will only work cheaply when she is serving a large number. Kings and aristocracies may command the unpaid service of slaves, but natural forces will work efficiently only for the million. Millionaires could not travel by steam or communicate by electricity if millions of workmen did not use the same methods. In short, the success of all machine-using industries now primarily depends on the extent to which their products are consumed by the masses. Therefore the prosperity of the community in general and capitalists in particular depends upon increasing the wants and elevating the social life and character of the laboring classes. Considered from this standpoint, the whole subject of economics assumes a new and altogether more rational and humane aspect. It ceases to be a mere "science of wealth," subordinating producers to the product, and becomes a science of human welfare, making the social life of the producers the end to which the creation of commodities is the great means. In other words, it is transformed from a dismal science of pessimism and despair, which complacently sees the masses crowded to the verge of starvation, into a science of optimism and hope; which bears a message of prosperity and progress to the whole of humanity.

Besides giving economic science a humane, hopeful aspect hitherto conspicuously wanting, this change in the point of view makes it integral, harmonious, and intelligible. Much that has been involved in confusion becomes simple and clear; much that has been mistakenly regarded as unjust and oppressive enough to warrant revolution, becomes obviously beneficent and progressive ; and much that has been dolefully taught as axiomatic truth is seen to be manifest error.

Moreover, when we change our point of view from commodities to men, and make the laborer the initial point of observation, the questions of production and distribution become susceptible of discussion in terms intelligible to ordinary minds. We then find value or price assuming a human basis, and commodities are seen to be dear or cheap not as they will exchange for more or less gold, but as they will exchange for more or less of labor, *as economic equivalents.* With this idea of value the theory of supply and demand of which Malthusianism and the wage-fund fallacy are a natural outcome, is incompatible. The ratio in which a given quantity of cloth or shoes is the economic equivalent of a day's labor can no more be determined by the mere fact of the quantity of cloth or the number of laborers, than can the moral quality of a robbery by the number of thieves. The only basis upon which two things can be economic equivalents of each other is the substantial equality of their cost of production. Upon no other principle can exchanges be economic, equitable, and mutually advantageous.

The principle of cost, governed as it is by the cost of the dearest portion of the economic supply of any commodity, furnishes a keystone to the arch of economic science. It supplies the basis for a consistent body of economic doctrine capable of explaining the phenomena of wages, rent, interest, and profit upon one general principle of universal application—namely, the law of economic price and its corollary, the law of economic surplus. Instead of a system of "*commodity*" economics which justifies human degradation as a means of cheapening wealth, we have a system of *social* economics, which shows that the most effective means of promoting the industrial welfare of society on a strictly equitable basis, must be sought in influences which develop the wants, and elevate the social life and character of the masses. Here then we have a sound, economic, and broad social basis for intelligent, humane, and progressive statesmanship, which shall promote individuality without incurring the follies of *laissez faire,* and utilize the educational and protective functions of the state without incurring the dangers of paternalism.

NEW YORK CITY, January, 1891.

CONTENTS.

PART I.

THE PRINCIPLES OF SOCIAL PROGRESS.

CHAPTER I.

SOCIAL PROGRESS.

CHAPTER II.

THE LAW OF SOCIAL PROGRESS.

xi

CHAPTER III

THE CAUSE OF SOCIAL PROGRESS.

CHAPTER IV.

VERIFICATION OF THE LAW OF SOCIAL PROGRESS.

CHAPTER V.

THE RISE AND SOCIAL POWER OF FREE CITIES AS VERIFYING THE LAW OF SOCIAL PROGRESS.

CHAPTER VI.

THE FALL OF THE FREE CITIES AND ITS EFFECT UPON SOCIAL PROGRESS.

CHAPTER VII.

THE LAW OF SOCIAL PROGRESS AS VERIFIED IN THE PROGRESS OF POLITICAL
AND RELIGIOUS FREEDOM.

PART II.

THE PRINCIPLES OF ECONOMIC PRODUCTION.

CHAPTER I.

WEALTH AND THE LAW OF ITS PRODUCTION.

CHAPTER II.

ECONOMIC VALUE.

CHAPTER III.

DEMAND AND SUPPLY NOT THE LAW OF ECONOMIC PRICES.

CHAPTER IV.

THE LAW OF ECONOMIC PRICES.

CHAPTER V.

THE LAW OF THE COST OF PRODUCTION.

CHAPTER VI.

MONEY AND ITS ECONOMIC FUNCTION.

PART III.

THE PRINCIPLES OF ECONOMIC DISTRIBUTION.

CHAPTER I.

THE DISTRIBUTION OF WEALTH.

CHAPTER II.

SOME RECENT THEORIES OF WAGES CONSIDERED.

CHAPTER III.

· THE LAW OF WAGES.

CHAPTER IV.

RENT, ITS ECONOMIC LAW AND CAUSE.

CHAPTER V.

THE LAW OF INTEREST.

CHAPTER VI.

THE LAW OF PROFIT.

PART IV.

THE PRINCIPLES OF PRACTICAL STATESMANSHIP.

CHAPTER I.

LAISSEZ FAIRE AS A GUIDING PRINCIPLE IN PUBLIC POLICY.

CHAPTER II.

THE STATE ; OR, THE NATURE AND FUNCTION OF GOVERNMENT.

CHAPTER III

THE PRINCIPLE OF INTERNATIONAL TRADE.

CHAPTER IV.

THE PRINCIPLES OF ECONOMIC TAXATION.

CHAPTER V.

BUSINESS DEPRESSIONS.

CHAPTER VI.

COMBINATION OF CAPITAL.

CHAPTER VII.

COMBINATION OF LABOR.

SUMMARY AND CONCLUSION.

PART I.

THE PRINCIPLES OF SOCIAL PROGRESS.

Principles of Social Economics.

CHAPTER I.

SOCIAL PROGRESS.

Section I.—*The Nature and Meaning of Social Progress.*

The promotion of social progress may be regarded as the primary object of all human institutions. The wisdom or unwisdom of any form of government, political and industrial policy, or moral code—regardless of climate, country, or civilization—depends upon whether or not it tends to promote the social progress of the people. When we can furnish an adequate explanation of the law of social progress we shall be in a position to.explain why the march of civilization has been so marked and continuous in some countries and so retarded in others ; why nations once the most advanced are now greatly in the rear ; why the ancients made such progress in art and philosophy, while they lacked simple contrivances with which to procure the common comforts and decencies of daily life ; why general poverty, religious, social, and political despotism prevail in some countries, while comparative abundance with religious freedom and political democracy obtain in others. "The law of prog-- ress," says Fiske,[1] "when discovered, will be found to be the law of history. The great fact to be explained is either the presence or the absence of progress, and when we have formulated the character of progress and the conditions essential to it, we have the key to the history of the stationary as well as of the progressive nations. When we are able to show why the latter

[1] "Cosmic Philosophy," vol. ii., pp. 195, 196.

3

have advanced, the same general principle will enable us to show why the former have not advanced." Indeed, to explain the nature, law, and cause of social progress is not only to lay the foundation for the science of social economics, but it is also to furnish the key to social philosophy, and thereby to establish a rational basis for statesmanship and social reform. This involves, first of all, the consideration of what constitutes progress. Unless we understand what social progress is, there can be no intelligent consideration of the law and cause of its development, and hence no approximately correct science, either of economics or of government, is possible.

Progress is commonly regarded as synonymous with improvement. This expression confounds the process with the product. It states what progress *does* rather than what it *is*. If asked what constitutes the progress of the plant, it would not be correct to say the flowers, buds, and foliage. Their condition correctly indicates the state of the plant's progress, but they no more constitute the progress than the apple constitutes the tree, or the barometer the storm. The progress of the plant consists of a series of changes that take place in its organization before the flower appears, and of which it is the result. So, too, of improvement. While progress usually implies a change for the better, the improvement is not the progress, but the result of it ; it is the change of form or condition which precedes and produces the improvement. Although all progress is simply change, all change is not necessarily progress. It may be retrogression. What then are the distinguishing characteristics of the changes which constitute progress ? Fortunately science has furnished the answer to this question, so far as physical development is concerned. The investigations of Linnæus, Wolf, Goethe, Schelling, Von Baer, Darwin, and others have established the fact that the growth or progress of organisms, both vegetable and animal, consists of a series of structural changes from a relatively simple to a relatively complex state of organization. For more than half a century this definition of progress has so completely stood the test of verification that it has become an accepted scientific truth, and now both plants and animals are classified in the scale of development according to the simplicity or complexity of their organization.

If we examine the history of social institutions we shall find that this distinguishing characteristic of progress is equally true of society. Although the precise forms of the earliest phases of social life are difficult to determine, modern investigation has proved beyond question that society in its primitive stages was a homogeneous aggregate of human beings without industrial specialization or social or political individuality, and that all progress from that time to this has been a movement towards a greater complexity of life and definiteness of individual, social, and political functions. Progress in general, therefore, may be defined as a tendency to change from a relatively simple to a relatively complex organization.

Although this movement from the simple to the complex is the distinguishing characteristic of all progress, the form it assumes in physical and social phenomena is very different. In all the phases of physical development the tendency is to produce a greater perfection, individuality, and freedom of the organism,— the highest type of which is *man*. Society is not an individual organism, but an association of individual organisms. Social development, therefore, does not consist in organic differentiation, but in the differentiation of the social environment of individuals.

In considering social advancement, therefore, we are concerned only with social phenomena ; that is to say, with the influences which affect the material, political, and moral condition of man in society ; nor are we called upon to deal with the origin of the elements in his social character, but only with the development of their expression.

The phenomena of society may be classified as social and economic ; the former relates to man's political and ethical life, and the latter to his industrial efforts. In order to correctly understand progress in society, it will be necessary briefly to consider the historic tendency of these two phases separately.

SECTION II.—*The Historic Tendency of Social Progress.*

Although the genesis of man is still an unsettled question, the fact that he once existed as a mere physical being scarcely superior to the lower animals is conclusively established.[1]

[1] The wild men in the interior of Borneo are described by Dalton as living : " absolutely in a state of nature, who neither cultivate the ground nor live in

Recent investigations have shown that primitive man was so devoid of social life and character as to neither cook his food nor build himself a hut to live in. In many instances the institution of marriage was entirely unknown ; in others the conjugal ties were so slender that they existed only until the birth of the child.[1] The interminable struggle for life against the elements, wild beasts, and his fellows, made man's localization necessary, and brought him into social and personal relations that gradually assumed a more permanent or tribal character. This may properly be said to constitute the first stage of social existence— the jelly-fish period of society. Here the social homogeneity was such that every thing was owned in common—even wives and children. Authorities agree that "the primitive condition of man socially was one where every man and woman were regarded as equally married to one another," and "any woman who attempted to resist the marriage privileges claimed by any member of the tribe was liable to severe punishment."[2] The child had no particular father or mother, but belonged to the tribe.[3]

The struggle for existence being now between tribes, war was the chief occupation, and those who were most proficient and brave as warriors naturally became the most honored and influential leaders of the tribe. One of the chief characteristics of tribal warfare was that the will of the victor became the law of the vanquished. Accordingly, if the chief desired to take a

huts, who neither eat rice nor salt, and who do not associate with each other, but rove about some woods like wild beasts ; the sexes meet in the jungle, or the man carries away a woman from some campong. When the children are old enough to shift for themselves, they separate, neither one afterwards thinking of the other. At night they sleep under some large trees, the branches of which hang low." Sir John Lubbock's "Origin of Civilization," pp. 5, 6 ; *Ibid.*, chapter iii. See also Lichtenstein's "Travels in South Africa," p. 137 ; "Expedition to Borneo," vol. ii., p. 10 ; Lubbock's "Prehistoric Times," pp. 563–5, 595, 596 ; Lyell's "Antiquity of Man," pp. 377–80 ; Sproat's "Scenes and Studies of Savage Life," p. 120 ; Dubois' "Description of the People of India," p. 3 ; "Transactions Ethnological Society," new series, vol. iii., p. 248.

[1] Lubbock's "Origin of Civilization," pp. 53–57. See also Sir Edward Belcher's "Transactions Ethnological Society," vol. v., p. 45 ; Starke's "Primitive Family," pp. 82–84.

[2] Lubbock's "Origin of Civilization," p. 67 ; Starke's "Primitive Family," p. 245 ; McLennan's "Primitive Marriages," pp. 229, 230.

[3] Lubbock's "Origin of Civilization," p. 71.

woman from among his war captives, he could have the exclusive use and enjoyment of her as against any and all other members of the tribe.[1] This instituted a departure from tribal homogeneity which naturally led first to a certain degree of personal domestic exclusiveness, then to individual marriages, and finally to the family group. Thus, through the gradual process of social differentiation and integration, society was slowly transformed from a simple homogeneous mass, in which the tribal aggregate was the only unit, into a relatively complex social organization with the family as the unit, possessing definite social functions, rights, and powers. It should be remembered, however, that this social individuation conferred no rights or powers upon the individual, but only upon the family.[2] Indeed, it is a universal law in society that the exercise of social rights extends only with the growth of the social unit. Hence, when the family became the unit, it acquired all the social rights and powers of the unit. But all rights absolutely stopped at this point. The individual members of the family acquired no more social recognition by this change than had been previously accorded to the individual members of the tribe. The family was recognized solely through its male head, whose power was absolute, even to life and death.

With the settlement of the family came the necessity of cultivating the lands. This led to the substitution of an agricultural for a pastoral life, and the right of private for public ownership in land and its products.[3]

Another feature of this *régime* was the practice of enlarging the family by enforced or voluntary adoption ; those entering the family by this means were kinsmen ;—a fiction that nothing but

[1] " A war captive, however, was in a peculiar position ; the tribe had no rights to her ; her capturer might have killed her if he chose ; if he preferred to keep her alive he was at liberty to do so ; he did as he liked, and the tribe was no sufferer." Sir John Lubbock's " Origin of Civilization," p. 71 ; also McLennan's " Primitive Marriages," pp. 43, 44.

[2] " At the outset, the peculiarities of law in its most ancient state lead us irresistibly to the conclusion that it took precisely the same view of the family group which is taken of individual men by the system of rights and duties now prevalent throughout Europe."—Maine's " Ancient Law," p. 129. " But ancient law, it must again be repeated, knows next to nothing of Individuals. It is concerned not with Individuals, but with Families ; not with single human beings, but with groups."—*Ibid.*, p. 250. " Village Communities," p. 10.

[3] Maine's " Early History of Institutions," pp. 1, 2, 73-79.

the absolute authority of the head of the family could have established. In this way the simple primitive family made up of blood
relations, was expanded into the patriarchal family, held together
by the tie of a mythical kinship.[1] Greater sacredness of, and
protection to, life and property came with this higher state of
organization, and "marriage by capture" gave place to marriage
by purchase, transferring the selection of a wife from the muscu-
lar authority of the savage suitor, to the civil authority of the
parent.[2]

These social relations continued theoretically until the Christian era, and practically until the middle of the sixth century.
From the time of the Twelve Tables, B.C., 450, to that of
the Justinian Code, progress was very tardy, but tended towards a further differentiation of the social polity in the direction of substituting the individual for the family as the social
unit. This movement, which is most distinctly indicated by
the innovations made upon the domain of *patria potestas* (the
authority of the father over the person and property of his de-
scendants), though imperceptible during the latter four hundred
years of the Republic, began to show itself in the early days of
the Empire.

If we pass from the ancient to the modern world, where social
progress has been more marked, we shall find that its movement
has been everywhere distinguished by the same general characteristics. During the savage struggle for imperial supremacy
which covered the face of Europe for nearly four hundred years
after the fall of the Western Empire, in which all permanent
authority and recognized law were practically abolished,[3] the patriarchal system virtually disappeared and society reorganized into
the feudal system. Social institutions then assumed a different aspect. Instead of being composed of family groups, held together

---

[1] We must look on the family as constantly enlarged by the adoption of
strangers within its circle, and we must try to regard the fiction of adoption as
so closely simulating the reality of kinship that neither law nor opinion makes
the slightest difference between a real and an adoptive connection."—Maine's
"Ancient Law," p. 128. See also "Early History of Institutions," p. 310 ;
"Village Communities," p. 115 ; Lubbock's "Origin of Civilization."

[2] Maine's "Ancient Law," pp. 119-133 ; *cf.* Lubbock's "Origin of Civilization," p. 52 ; "Fiske's "Cosmic Philosophy," vol. ii., pp. 220, 221.

[3] Guizot's "History of Civilization," pp. 6, 69 ; also Hallam's "History of
the Middle Ages," vol. i., p. 92.

by a mythical kinship under parental despotism, subject to imperial absolutism, society consisted of manorial or baronial groups,
held together by mutual dependence upon the land-owner, who,
while giving nominal allegiance to the king, was practically independent of him.[1] The individual instead of the family was the
social unit, and industrial interest instead of kinship was the
cohesive principle in society[2] ; land, or wealth, instead of birth,
became the basis of rank and authority.[3]

No sooner had feudalism become the settled order of society
than the process of further social differentiation set in. One of
the earliest evidences of this was the localization of the serfs
on the estates of the respective barons, and their division into
classes as "hinds" and "artificers." By this division of labor
the former became permanently ruralized, and the latter centralized, into groups whose history is that of modern civilization.
During the tenth century these groups grew into permanent towns
and became the centres of trade and industry. As they increased
in population and wealth they grew in social activity, intelligence,
and power ; and hence became the permanent source of the
further division of labor, the specialization of social and religious
functions, and of personal and political rights.

By the middle of the eleventh century we find the burghers
asserting their right to the ownership of property, and forcibly
resisting the efforts of the barons to despoil them. Early in the
twelfth century the towns began to obtain the right of local self-
government. During the thirteenth and fourteenth centuries the
serf was differentiated from the lord's estate, and became an
economic and social individual. The separation of political institutions from the authority of the Church, and the power of
Parliament over the Crown were also positively asserted during
this period.

---

[1] " The kingdom was as a great fief, or rather as a bundle of fiefs, and the
king little more than one of a number of feudal nobles, differing rather in dig-
nity than in power from some of the rest."—Hallam's " History of the Middle
Ages," vol. i., p. 136.

[2] " It was feudalism which for the first time linked personal duties, and by
consequence personal rights, to the ownership of land."—Maine's " Ancient
Law," p. 102.

[3] Hallam's " Middle Ages," vol. i., p. 88; also *ibid.*, p. 122, and Guizot's
" History of Civilization," p. 67.

This was followed in the fifteenth and sixteenth centuries by a general breaking up of the feudal system and a new formation of social institutions. Throughout Europe the political elements integrated into definite nations.[1] The gentry and inferior nobility, who were economically and socially segregated from their class, and the superior artisans who, by the growth of manufacture and trade in the Free Towns, had become " master artificers," formed a new social stratum—the mercantile or middle class— which henceforth became the enterprising and progressive element in society. With the rise of this class came a new era in civilization. Under its influence industrial, political, and religious institutions were revolutionized. In this period the discovery of America and the passage to India by the Cape of Good Hope, and the use of the mariner's compass were consummated ; painting with oil and the manufacture of paper from linen were invented ; the right of private judgment in religion and the supremacy of parliamentary government were permanently established. From this came the use of steam, the invention of the spinning-jenny and the power-loom, and the establishment of the factory system, the railroad, steamship, and telegraph, with their natural accompaniments—the daily press, cheap books, and popular education.

As the outgrowth of these movements slavery has been abolished from Christendom and the principle of civil and religious freedom for the individual, without regard to caste, color, race, or sex, has been established in the most advanced countries, and is destined to be extended to the whole human race.

Thus the universal tendency of progress in society is to increase the power, rights, and freedom of the individual, and diminish the arbitrary control of collective authority.

SECTION III.—*Historic Tendency of Economic Progress.*

Upon the principle that all progress is governed by one general law, it is commonly supposed that progress must assume the same form in economics that it does in society and politics. Consequently, because social progress tends toward greater democracy of administration, it is held that industrial progress

---

[1] Guizot's " History of Civilization," chap. xi.

must be in the direction of the public administration of industry. A little reflection will show this to be a mistake. Although industrial progress has a tendency toward greater specialization, the form it assumes differs from that in social and political institutions, as much as progress in the latter differs from that in physical phenomena.

The essential difference between political and industrial institutions is that the utility of the former consists in their harmonious adaptation to the social habits and character of the people, whereas the utility of industrial institutions consists in their economic efficiency—their capacity of furnishing wealth cheaply. Since social institutions will necessarily more completely reflect the desire and character of the people in proportion as the masses participate in their construction, it follows that progress in society is a tendency towards democracy of administration of political and social affairs. With economics the case is different. No advantage can accrue to the laborer or the community by any change of industrial institutions which does not enable the laborer to obtain more wealth for a day's work. Whether industry is conducted on the democratic town-meeting plan, or by a few private individuals, cannot possibly affect the welfare of the community, except as it promotes that end. Unless democracy of ' industrial administration would cheapen wealth, it would be a burden upon the community, without any compensating advantage, since it would involve the care of management without any beneficial result.

A brief survey of the history of industrial progress will show that the increasing efficiency of productive methods, and hence the improvement of the means of getting a living, has two characteristics. One is the division and concentration of labor power, the other is the increase and social diffusion of political power. The former tends to specialize and limit the laborer's economic function, the latter tends to generalize and extend his social function. Thus, as the laborer's industrial individuality diminishes, the influence of his social and political individuality increases.

Primitive industry, like primitive society, was very simple and homogeneous. Every one performed practically all kinds of labor with equal proficiency. Progress from that point to the

present has been a continuous tendency toward a greater division, and specialization of labor and concentration of capital.
The tendency of this movement has ever been to differentiate
productive force into numerous portions, integrating the laborer
and machinery upon special branches, every one of which is
dependent not only upon the action of the others, but upon the
united action of the whole.   Thus industrial differentiation, instead of increasing, tends to diminish the economic individuality
of the laborer.   It is because of this tendency to make the laborer
an almost automatic part of a highly complex productive machine, that the present industrial system is regarded as inimical to
his social freedom.   Those who take this view, and they are very
numerous, lay great stress upon the fact that the laborer is an
employé.   To them the very stipulation of income means limitation of freedom.   Of all the objections urged against the wages
system, this is probably the most universal, and is regarded as
the most fundamental.   They think the only conditions under
which social freedom is possible, is where the laborers employ
themselves.   The fallacy in this position arises from a misconception of the idea of freedom.   Freedom is not a mere theoretic
form, but a sturdy fact.   It does not consist in the formal permission, but in the actual power, to go or to do.   Nothing can
give social and political freedom but wealth ; the freedom that
wealth affords does not depend upon whether the laborer works
for himself or for another, but it depends entirely upon how much
wealth he receives.   There is no power in nature, society, or
government that can make a poor man free.   Poverty is social
weakness ; it is the source of slavery, and the background of
despotism.

Social well-being consists not so much in doing, as in having.
In proportion as man's energies are expended in obtaining a living,
the possibilities of his social, intellectual, and moral life and development are restricted.   In order, then, to maximize man's
social individuality, it is necessary to minimize the expenditure
of his physical energy.   This is precisely what the division of
labor, the concentration of capital, and the development of the
factory system promote.

The de-individualization of the laborer as a producer promotes
his social advancement in many ways.   In the first place, it makes

the wages or stipulated-income system necessary. In proportion as the income of any class becomes stipulated, it becomes less contingent. To the extent that this occurs, material subsistence becomes more certain, which is the first step toward social and intellectual development. So long as the laborer's living is uncertain, he is in a more or less constant state of anxiety and suspense, which tends to make progress in the higher phases of social life impossible.

Another beneficial feature of this tendency is that it concentrates the laborers, and specializes their occupations. By this means they are not only forced into closer and more frequent intercourse with each other, but it also increases their mutual interdependence. The material condition of the masses cannot be improved, nor can their political freedom or social character be developed, by any thing which does not increase the economic interdependence of the people, and weld them together in social classes. In proportion as this process of social differentiation increases, interests and sympathies broaden, altruism is developed, and the welfare of all becomes identical with that of each. Nothing so surely aids social advancement as that which makes it necessary for millions to rise together. No industrial system, no civilization, no religion even is worth sustaining which only saves a few.

Another feature of the wages system is the tendency to promote more constant employment. There is no fact more conclusively established in the history of industrial progress than that the concentration of capital in fixed plants and large enterprises makes a marked increase in the permanence of employment. As industrial establishments increase in size, constant employment of capital becomes necessary. The loss involved in the short stoppage of a large factory will soon be more than equal to the profit of a year's business. Whatever increases permanence in the use of capital necessarily increases the constancy of employment. Thus, as the factory methods develop, the capitalist has to pay the penalty for enforced idleness through loss or bankruptcy ; and hence permanent employment becomes one of the features of the industrial expertness of capitalistic management. Under the individual or self-employing *régime* this was not the case. When the hand weaver failed to sell his cloth or make a living, he could starve, beg, go to jail, or die, as the case might be. His poverty involved nobody else, while under the wages system the great capitalist, nay, the whole community, is involved with the enforced idleness of the laborer.

Accordingly, the world over, we find that permanence of employment increases and enforced idleness diminishes where the wages system is most developed and capital most concentrated. This is clearly shown by the currents of emigration. People always leave those localities and countries where employment is the most precarious and least remunerative, and move towards those where it is most permanent and best rewarded. Hence the tendency of emigration is always from those countries where the wages system and factory methods are least developed, to those where they are most highly developed. It is from China, Bohemia, Austria, Italy, Germany, and Ireland, towards England and America, that laborers emigrate, and not from England or America to Continental Europe and Asia.

The industrial system, which tends to socialize the laborer, increase the economic interdependence of the capitalist, consumer, and workman, and make the material well-being of the masses the basis of business success, necessarily possesses all the possibilities of an ever-advancing civilization. Progress in politics and society, therefore, may be defined as the tendency to increase the sovereignty of the individual and diminish the arbitrary authority of the state by establishing greater democracy of administration. In economics it may be defined as the tendency to centralize industrial administration and responsibility, de-individualize the laborer as a producer and socialize the results in better and cheaper products.

CHAPTER II.

THE LAW OF SOCIAL PROGRESS.

SECTION I.—*The Elements of Social Progress.*

IN the preceding chapter two facts were established. First, that social progress is the movement of society toward the realization of the highest material, intellectual, and moral possibilities in human life; *i.e.*, toward the plane of greater human well-being. Second, that this progressive movement consists in a series of changes from a relatively simple to a relatively complex state of social organization. We now come to the consideration of the law by which this movement takes place ; that is to say, the order in which the different phases of social phenomena are developed. These may be grouped under three general heads, as the material, the intellectual, and the moral. The material element in social progress is not merely that which relates to man's physical necessities, but every thing that relates to his wants and desires, of whatever kind,—the gratification of which involves the production of wealth. These will be found to include, not only the necessities for food and shelter, but those for education, art, travel, intellectual and moral culture, and even religion. In fact, there are no desires of which man is capable whose gratification does not directly or indirectly necessitate the production of wealth. The material element in social progress, therefore, includes every thing which relates to the gratification of human wants, desires, and aspirations. The intellectual element is that which relates to man's capacity to acquire and apply knowledge ; it is the analyzing, reasoning, judging, and directing element. Morality simply relates to the quality of

15

human conduct. We designate conduct as moral or immoral according as it directly or indirectly tends to promote or retard social *well-being* or *human happiness.*

While these phenomena are distinct in their character they are inseparable in their relation ; hence no differentiation can result in permanent integration and specialization which does not find expression in all these phases of social life.[1] If the development of any one of these elements should be promoted at the expense of the rest, it must necessarily fail of its function because not one of them can permanently exist without the sustaining influence of the others. The increased production and accumulation of wealth, for example, could not continue without the increase of intelligence to devise the means necessary to produce it, and a corresponding advance in the social integrity to sustain it. A general advancement of intelligence is impossible without the relative elimination of poverty and vice ; and no considerable advance in ethics can take place without a previous increase in material well-being.

SECTION II.—*The Natural Order of Social Progress.*

Although the various elements of social development are inseparably connected with, and constantly act and react upon each other, one of them must necessarily sustain the initiative relation to the others, or no movement could take place. Which of these occupies that position? The answer to this question must explain the relative position these elements occupy in the scale of development and the historic order of their appearance, —both of which are indicated by their functional relations.

Morality, being the quality of conduct, necessarily arises from motives, decisions, and actions, and hence must be a resultant of the other elements. Morality is the fruit and not the root ; it is the objective point towards which progress tends, and consequently is the last to be developed.[2] The intellect, as already explained, is the reasoning, analyzing, judging faculty ; its function consists exclusively in adapting means to an end. It occupies the position of servant and guide to the other faculties.

[1] "The progress of society is not moral progress, or intellectual progress, or material progress ; but it is the combination of all the three."—Fiske's "Cosmic Philosophy," vol. ii., p. 245.

[2] Ward's "Dynamic Sociology," vol. i., p. 216.

Human activities are never exerted except for the gratification of some desire, want, sympathy, sentiment, or ambition arising in the feelings. Intellectual or physical effort put forth without some motive or desire would be senseless.[1] Of necessity, therefore, the material element in social progress is first in the scale of development and supplies the motive which calls the intellect into activity. All the inventions and discoveries in manufacture, science, and literature, all the doctrines of economics, ethics, politics, and religion have been produced by the intellect in its effort to gratify the desires. These efforts have been perpetuated or abandoned in proportion as they were found, by experience, to be favorable or unfavorable to human well-being.

Clearly, therefore, the natural order of the various elements in social development is : the material, the intellectual, the moral ; the material being the basis or motor force, the intellectual the means, and the moral the result.[2]

Although the fact that progress of society has always been in the ascending order—from the material to the moral—has been generally recognized as a matter of history, it has been almost uniformly ignored as a principle in social philosophy.

There appears to have been an undefined apprehension that to permanently regard the material as the preponderating element in human progress is to belittle the influence exercised by the intellect upon the advance of civilization. This is a mistake. The danger of inverting the order of its operation is what is most likely to occur. It is precisely at this point that some of the most fatal errors have entered the popular theories. The best writers agree that in the early stages of social growth the material element is first in order and influence, but seeing that the material conditions and moral character advance more rapidly as the

---

[1] Comte's "Positive Philosophy," pp. 384-500.

[2] "The same may be said of all the so-called virtues—honesty, benevolence, justice, etc. These qualities are the result of his civilization. His moral nature has sprung from his rational faculties, and may be traced back to its origin in sympathy : at first confined to his immediate companions or offspring ; thence gradually extended to embrace his own clan ; then his particular tribe, race, or country ; then, to a limited degree, the whole human race ; and lastly, as exhibiting the highest type, and quite rare even among the most civilized, made to comprehend the lower brute creation in one beneficent scheme of morals."—Ward's "Dynamic Sociology," vol. i., p. 461.

2

intellect develops, they appear to assume that the order of progress changes and the intellectual instead of the material element
becomes the dominating influence in social progress. Even
Comte says : " If our affective faculties were subordinated to the
intellectual, all idea of improving the social organism would be
senseless. . . . For our affective faculties must preponderate,
not only to rouse the reason from its natural lethargy, but to give
a permanent aim and direction to its activity,—without which it
would be ever lost in vague, abstract speculation."[1] After
having thus affirmed the truth of the ascending order, he says :
" This is the natural order . . . whereas the reverse is the
rational one and that which gains upon the other in proportion
as the intellect assumes a larger share in the human evolution."[2]
Thus, according to Comte, upon the dawn of the human intellect,
the natural order became irrational. Buckle, Draper, and Guizot
all take practically the same position. Though they do not go
through the same course of reasoning that M. Comte does, they
act upon the same conclusions. They all admit that material
conditions must precede intellectual and moral development, and
then insist that the intellect is the source of human progress.[3]

For the assumption that the order of evolution is thus reversed
by the accession of the intellect there is no warrant either in reason or fact. That the material element in progress is greatly
accelerated by the reflex action of the intellect, and the intellectual by the moral, and that progress is greatly enhanced thereby,
is unquestionable. But that in no way implies any change in the
law of social movement. The fact that the intellect fills a much
larger sphere in human life than it once did, does not tend to show
that it has in any way changed its relative position. The difference in the activities of man in modern civilized society and
those of his savage ancestors simply represents the difference in
the quality and quantity of his desires. The intellect, by the
very nature of its function, is not a propelling, but a guiding
element. It is the servant and not the master of human wants.

[1] " Positive Philosophy," p. 500. American edition.
[2] *Ibid.*, pp. 685, 686.
[3] Buckle's " History of Civilization," vol. i., pp. 30, 31 ; *cf.* also pp. 242
and 509 ; Draper's " Intellectual Development of Europe," p. 591 ; Guizot's
" History of Civilization," pp. 66, 84, 85, and 230.

The operation of this principle is clearly illustrated in the social effect of the discovery of the mariner's compass, the art of printing, the use of gunpowder, etc. It was not until some considerable portion of mankind desired the products of other nations that navigation became necessary and the mariner's compass could be of service to man, while gunpowder and printing, having been invented before the desire for them was developed, had to wait thousands of years before they could exercise any influence upon civilization.[1] Although our acquisitions in science, art, labor-saving inventions, etc., are the work of the intellect, it is only when those achievements minister to human wants that its activities tend to promote human progress.

It is true, however, that the influence of a new acquisition by the intellect seldom fully expands itself in the satisfaction of the wants to which it directly relates, but it frequently exercises a reflex influence, the tendency of which is to again increase the desire and consequently still further stimulate its own activity. For example, the art of printing not only increased the number of books sufficiently to supply those who had already acquired a positive desire for reading, but it so cheapened them as to put them within the reach of a large class to whom such a luxury had previously been impossible,—thereby greatly increasing the desire for, as well as the possibilities of, obtaining knowledge. Again, when the power-loom and the spinning-jenny were invented, they not only enabled the manufacturers to supply the increasing demand for cotton cloth, but they so reduced its price that it could become an article of common use among the masses. This fact naturally soon gave rise to such desires for other and superior fabrics that the result was to ultimately revolutionize the industrial system of all Europe.

It is therefore not true that the natural order of social evolution is changed by the development of the intellect. To whatever extent the sphere and activities of the intellect may be increased, its relative position and function must, by the very nature of its constitution, remain the same.

A similar error prevails in regard to the position of ethics in social progress. Because personal morality, commercial integrity, industrial equity, and social harmony are seen to increase

[1] See Part II., chapter i.

as the altruistic feelings advance in society, it is held that altruism and egoism are essentially antagonistic to each other. Egoism is a term usually employed as relating to self, and altruism as relating to others ; hence all actions and feelings are regarded as egoistic in proportion as they tend to promote the welfare of self to the exclusion of others ; and conversely they are altruistic in proportion as they tend to promote the well-being of others to the exclusion of self.

From this position it has been consistently inferred that self-interest is inimical to the well-being of society. The natural effect of such a conclusion is to create an aversion to all industrial institutions in which this principle is recognized and to stimulate the demand for a reconstruction of society on a so-called altruistic basis. This reasoning involves a misconception of the terms egoism and altruism and their logical relation to each other. It is a radical error to regard altruism as anti-egoistic,—or even non-egoistic, in its influence. To injure or ignore the well-being of self is to destroy the first essential condition for promoting the welfare of others. We can only be helpful to others in proportion as we are well provided for ourselves.[1] The poor, the weak, and the inferior are always a burden rather than a help to their friends.

Egoism may be defined as relating to the welfare of self ; and altruism as relating to the welfare of *self and others.* The basis of true altruism is successful egoism. Altruism differs from egoism, not in being opposed, or even indifferent to, the interests of self, but only in embracing the interests of others besides self. Thus all real altruism is highly egoistic, though all egoism is not altruistic. All conduct may be called relatively altruistic according as it benefits more than one, and relatively egoistic as it benefits less than all. It is a mistake, therefore, to conclude that altruistic conduct in society can be increased only as the principle of self-interest is diminished.

There is, moreover, unconscious and conscious altruism. The

[1] " The acts required for continued self-preservation, including the enjoyment of benefits achieved by such acts, are the first requisites to universal welfare. Unless each duly cares for himself his care for all others is ended by death ; and if each thus dies there remains no other to be cared for. This permanent supremacy of egoism over altruism, made manifest by contemplating existing life, is further made manifest by contemplating life in the course of evolution." —Spencer, " Data of Ethics," pp. 187, 188.

former is altruistic conduct prompted by egoistic motives ; the latter is that inspired by altruistic motives.   In the progress of society unconscious altruism precedes and tends to develop conscious altruism.   Much the larger portion of the altruistic conduct in the world to-day is of the unconscious class.   The great improvements in manufacture and commerce that' have put so many luxuries and refinements within the reach of the average citizen have, for the most part, been created by egoistic motives. It is because the industrial policy of the employing class has been dominated too much by the idea of benefiting self to the exclusion of others that it has received so many disastrous checks. We shall hereafter see that industrial depressions, bankruptcies, enforced idleness, and their accompanying evils, are the economic penalty for ignoring the interests of others in the efforts to benefit self.   Those who are excluded from the benefits we enjoy become a menace to our well-being and a hindrance to our progress ; and conversely, the more completely the welfare of others becomes identical with our own the more is our own increased. Altruism, then, is not opposed to egoism ; it is simply a higher phase of it.   Obviously, altruism—the highest form of ethical conduct—is the consequence of broadening the egoistic activities of the material and intellectual elements, and hence is necessarily last in the order of development.   We are therefore warranted in concluding that the progress of society toward greater complexity of organization, in which the necessity of physical effort is diminished, intellectual power and personal freedom increased, and moral character elevated, is always in the ascending order from the material to the intellectual and moral ;—the material being the basis, the intellectual the means, and the moral qualities the result.

What then are the influences by which exclusive egoism is transformed into all inclusive altruism, and savagery is converted into civilization ?   To answer this question is to explain the *cause* of social progress and will be the subject of the next chapter.

CHAPTER III.

THE CAUSE OF SOCIAL PROGRESS.

It is not enough to known what progress is, or even to know the law of progress ; but the *cause* of progress must also be understood before a true system of social philosophy can be established. We have seen : (1) that social progress consists in changes of man's social polity, or institutions, and not in his physical organism ; (2) that while all progress is change, only those changes are progressive which tend to further social differentiation ; (3) that while there can be no social progress without differentiation, only that differentiation is progressive which results in new integrations and greater complexity of social relations.

What then is the force which produces the changes that result in integrating differentiation ? If we examine the history of social institutions from their simplest beginnings, or trace them from their most complex stages back to the earliest times, we shall find that every change in the polity of society—whether intellectual, political, moral, or religious—has been brought about by man's conscious effort to adapt social institutions to his own needs and desires. Social institutions are established by man exclusively for men. It may be said that the changes in social institutions are the work of the human intellect ; that, where man's social wants are the most numerous his physical and intellectual activities are the most varied and all phases of social institutions are the most highly differentiated. In the last analysis the proximate cause of social progress is human wants.

In the first place, it will be observed that all desires, of whatever character, are simply states of feeling, the distinguishing characteristics of which are pleasure and pain. In proportion as

pleasure exceeds pain in human experience happiness prevails
and life becomes attractive and desirable ; and conversely, as pain
exceeds pleasure misery prevails and life becomes undesirable.
These antithetical states are completely represented in the terms,
want and *satisfaction.* Want is pain ; satisfaction is pleasure ;
and the extent to which the latter exceeds the former is the true
measure of happiness. To increase the proportion of pleasure
to pain, therefore, is the primary purpose of all human effort and
the immediate cause of social differentiation. Although all effort
is exerted for the gratification of some desire, there are many
desires that fail to call forth sufficient effort for their satisfaction.
Effectual desires are those which incite the necessary activity for
their gratification ; those which fail to call out such effort are ineffectual. Only effectual desires cause progress. Why are some
desires effectual and others ineffectual ? it may be asked. Upon
what principle is effort expended for the satisfaction of some
wants and not for others ? A moment's consideration will show
that this is all determined by the relative degree of pain and
pleasure involved. Hence, the gratification of any given desire
must finally turn upon the choice between a relatively painful
want and a relatively painful effort, the decision always being in
favor of the minimum pain. If this be true, it follows that human
wants are not only the cause of social progress, but that advancement toward a higher plane of happiness can only take place on
the egoistic principle of obtaining the maximum pleasure for the
minimum pain.

It thus appears that self-interest in man is not an evil element,
as we have been taught to consider it, but that the principle of
egoism affords the basis of, and inspiration to, social development. Man in his most primitive state was exclusively egoistic
in his desires and in his conduct. Altruism was not visible in
any thing that he did. Having no social or physical interest in
his fellow-man, there was no more economic or ethical reason,
why he should not steal from, or even kill and eat, him, than
that the lion should not devour the lamb.

As his wants became more numerous the efforts to satisfy them
became more burdensome, and the contest between want and
effort began. The want must remain ungratified or a means of
gratifying it less painful than the want itself must be devised. This

could only be accomplished by inventing labor-saving contrivances ; and invention is exclusively the function of the mind. The greater the demand for this mental activity the more rapidly are the intellectual faculties developed, and the more easily are wants gratified. It was precisely upon this principle that the crude tomahawk, bow and arrow, and canoe were first employed, and the division of labor became a necessity. With the division and specialization of labor, exchange of products became indispensable to the gratification of wants, and some degree of intercourse having been established, a beginning of confidence became inevitable. As the wants of men increased, and they became more dependent upon each other for the means of satisfying them, they naturally became more settled and social in their mode of life, and as soon as the crudest form of association became necessary, altruistic conduct began. The fact that association arose from self-interest made it indispensable that the advantages should be mutual to some extent. Thus from purely egoistic motives it became absolutely necessary that the efforts to benefit self should be so directed as to confer some benefit upon others.

Through this closer social contact wants became still more varied and efforts more specialized ; intellectual activity increased and individuality grew more pronounced. When, from these influences, exclusive family relations, with the permanent care of offspring, developed, and the private ownership of property became customary, it was obvious that one of two things must occur,—either the security of life and property must be increased, or these complex social relations must be abandoned ; otherwise the danger to life and property would neutralize all the new advantages. Thus a certain degree of morality became indispensable to self-interest, and the murder, theft, and treachery which a more simple life induced, having proved injurious to all and permanently beneficial to none, were pronounced capital offences. The more closely we consider history in this light, the more clearly it appears that the same principle applies to the whole moral code. Just as fast as the quality of an action becomes uniformly recognized it is designated moral or immoral, and passes from the sphere of conscious expediency to that of moral principle.

In this way virtue tends to perpetuate itself, while vice or immorality tends to its own elimination. The object of intellectual activity being to serve the desire for happiness, it is necessarily employed in devising means for eliminating the painful without reducing the pleasurable experiences, and it is only as this eliminating process takes place that new social integrations become permanent and the best results of progress are secured. This principle applies to all phases of human conduct. All the improvements in medicines, ethics, politics, and economics are the direct results of this eliminating process.

It may be urged that the altruism, or morality, thus evolved from egoistic motives, is only of the unconscious kind, and is very different from the conscious altruistic feeling which we recognize in the highest moral characters. If we pursue the enquiry a little further we shall see that volitional altruism is but a higher phase of the unconscious expedient. The same principle which leads men to repeat the conduct that produces beneficial results, also leads them to have a common interest in, admiration for, and sympathy with, those identified with such beneficial efforts.

It should be remembered, however, that social progress is not a simple, direct movement, but a resultant of the action and reaction of a variety of social currents, and that with each successive increase in the social complexity the influences affecting their differentiation become more subtle and involved.

The increasingly frequent personal intercourse which inevitably arises from more complex social relations, and the greater identity of interests, naturally tends to promote a greater reciprocation of sympathetic feelings. It is a universal principle in sociology that the more frequently we repeat acts which command our own and others' approval, the more they tend to become habitual and automatic ; and in proportion as any conduct tends to become an unconscious part of daily life, it forms a fixed element of social character. Accordingly, in the most advanced countries, where the wants and desires of the people are the most numerous 'and their industrial and social relations the most complex, we find the greatest degree of honor, virtue, integrity, fair dealing, general honesty, and public and private justice ; in short, the highest phase of moral conduct. To such an extent is this true that contracts, sometimes covering millions of dollars, are daily made between parties in New York, London, Paris, etc., who never saw each other. Should either party violate such obligation, the law—which expresses the moral character in the respective countries—would enforce its fulfilment, and the civilized world even sanctions warfare when nations violate their treaties with each other.

The transfer of conduct from a basis of conscious utility to that of moral principle is but another step in social evolution ; the essential difference being direct and indirect experience. When we act upon the abstract principle of right and wrong we are simply basing our conduct upon generalizations drawn from the repeated experiences of others. We accept it as a dogmatic principle only because its expediency has been previously demonstrated.

Nor is this all. The influences which are thus elevating individual egoism into moral principle are also simultaneously tending to expand and intensify sympathetic, altruistic feeling. In proportion as the influence of man's egoism becomes indirect, and that of his altruism direct, he becomes more sensitive to the feelings of others and less absorbed in his own ; so that, instead of regarding the misery of others with indifference, as formerly, a comparatively slight unhappiness becomes the source of great pain to him, and often the incentive to his highest action. Hence we see that, whereas man could once kill and feed upon his fellows, to-day the advanced races regard injury to another as equal to harm inflicted upon themselves.

Viewing the subject in all its phases, we see that in every direction the increase of egoistic wants is the real source of social progress. It develops the activity of the intellect ; this in turn differentiates the social environment ; engrafts virtue into character ; transforms conscious egoism and unconscious altruism into unconscious egoism and conscious altruism ; elevates utility into morality, and makes moral principle, instead of individual interest, the basis of social conduct. Thus, as man's intellect is called into activity by the differentiation of his desires, so is his moral character developed by the differentiation of his interests.

CHAPTER IV.

THE VERIFICATION OF THE LAW OF SOCIAL PROGRESS.

ACCORDING to the theory of social progress presented in the preceding chapters the development of man's social wants, and the consequent increase in the general consumption of wealth, is the necessary precursor of social, intellectual, and moral advancement. If this doctrine is correct we may always expect to find the highest state of civilization, and the most complete social, political, and religious freedom, in those countries where the material well-being of the masses is the most marked and continuous. And conversely, wherever the development of social wants have been the most restricted, we may equally expect to find the greatest intellectual and moral stagnation, and social, political, and religious despotism.

The operation of this law is as universal as the human race. History is replete with the evidence that social, political, and religious freedom is everywhere large or limited, the intellectual and moral character high or low, in proportion as the general consumption of wealth by the masses is great or small. The history of India and China, for instance, reveals to us peoples whose simple habits of life induce very few wants, and those chiefly of a physical character which are easily supplied. Their food consists chiefly of rice, ragi, or millet, with a little seasoning. Their houses are mainly fragile huts which may keep out the rays of the sun, but seldom afford much protection against wind and rain. The furniture and clothing of the common people are equally simple and meagre, being confined to the limited uses which a rice-diet and a ten-cent-a-day social life make necessary.

Although the political institutions of·the two countries are in many respects essentially different, the economic and social conditions of the people are practically the same. What law and caste has done towards stereotyping the industrial and social degradation of the laboring classes in Hindostan, custom has just as firmly established in China. The natural result of these conditions is the arrest of material and social progress in those countries. If we can accept the testimony of modern travellers, the people of India and China are in substantially the same state of mental and moral degradation that they were in nearly three thousand years ago.[1]

In Egypt the industrial and social systems were very similar to those in India and China, and their influence upon civilization was substantially the same. Dates composed the staple food of the common people. The poverty of the masses in ancient Egypt may be inferred from the fact that the children of the lower classes went entirely naked, and that to bring up a child to maturity did not cost more than twenty drachmas, or thirteen shillings of English money,[2] *i.e.*, about three dollars and a quarter. The social and political servitude of the lower classes is shown by the fact that they were prohibited by law and custom from owning land, participating in public affairs, or even choosing their own occupation.[3]

So far as data are obtainable, a similar set of facts present

---

[1] "The nations of Europe have very little idea of the actual condition of the inhabitants of Hindostan. They are more wretchedly poor than we have any notion of."—"Transactions of Asiatic Society," vol. i., p. 482. "From the earliest period to which our knowledge of India extends, an immense majority of the people, pinched by the most galling poverty, . . . crouching before their superiors in abject submission, and only fit either to be made slaves themselves or to be led to battle to make slaves of others."—Buckle's "History of Civilization," vol. i., p. 53. "It is remarkable how little the people of Asiatic countries have to do in the revolution of their governments. They are never guided by any great and common impulse of feeling, and take no part in events the most interesting and important to their country and their own posterity."—"Journal of Asiatic Society," vol. i., p. 250. See also Alison's "History of Europe," vol. x., pp. 419, 420.

[2] Buckle's "History of Civilization," vol. i., p. 63.

[3] "If any artisan meddled with political affairs, or engaged in any other employment than the one in which he had been brought up, a severe punishment was inflicted upon him."—Wilkinson's "Ancient Egyptians," vol. ii., pp. 8, 9.

themselves in the much-lauded early civilization of South America. The leading features of the industrial and social system in ancient Mexico and Peru were similar to those of China, India, and Egypt ; and consequently their influences upon human progress were substantially the same. What rice was to the inhabitants of India and China, and dates to those of Egypt, maize and bananas were to the people of Mexico and Peru. Here too, poverty, ignorance, and servitude, with all their attendant evils, were the direful lot of the laboring classes.[1]

The history of ancient Rome and Greece presents a similar picture, although the setting is somewhat different. These two countries differed from each other in some respects ; their climate, religion, political institutions and literature were unlike those of India, China, Egypt, and early America in many important particulars ; but in one fundamental respect they were all substantially the same—namely, the material and social condition of the people.

The great mass of the people in Greece and Rome were miserably poor and the very few were enormously rich. Despite the progress of art, philosophy, and jurisprudence, the social contempt in which the industrial classes were held by their superiors was as intense as that exhibited by the ruling classes of Asia, Africa, and America.

Slavery was so thoroughly rooted in the social system of Greece that it was not only sustained by those who had a mercenary interest in the traffic, but the philosophers—before whose wisdom we of the nineteenth century are asked to bow—defended it as being in accordance with natural law. Xenophon, a disciple of Socrates, in expressing his contempt for the laboring classes, declared : " The manual arts are infamous and unworthy of a citizen." Even Plato introduced slaves into his ideal republic. Nor did the scientific mind of Aristotle emancipate him from the iniquitous idea. Speaking of laborers, he says : " These indi-

[1] " They (the masses) had nothing that deserved to be called property. They could follow no craft, could arrange no labor, no amusement, but such as was specially provided by law. They could not change their residence or dress without a license from the government. They could not even exercise the freedom which is conceded to the most abject in other countries—that of selecting their own wives."—Prescott's " History of Peru," vol. i., p. 159. See also Draper's " Intellectual Development of Europe," p. 461.

viduals are destined by nature to slavery because there is nothing better for them to obey. It is clear, then, that some men are free by nature and others are slaves ; and in the case of the latter, the lot of slavery is both advantageous and just."

The inability of the learned and high-minded philosophers of Greece, who were too pure to participate in politics or trade, to conceive of the possibility of a social state without slavery attests conclusively how permanently and universally the social degradation of the common people must have been established.

Under Rome we find the same arrogant contempt for industry among the rich, and the same general ignorance among the masses. According to Gibbon, "slaves were so numerous in Rome that the authorities dared not permit them to wear a peculiar habit for fear that they might become dangerous by discovering their own numbers and strength." Athenæus boldly asserts that he knew very many Romans who possessed, not for use but ostentation, ten and even twenty thousand slaves.[1]

We are told that "in Italy itself the consumption of life was so great that there was no possibility of the slaves by birth meeting the requirement, and supply of others by war became necessary."[2]

It will thus be seen that the chief social characteristic of ancient civilizations was the opulence, arrogance, and despotism of rulers, and general poverty, ignorance, and servitude among the masses. Consequently all the forces that naturally tend to promote civilization were limited to a small exclusive class, while those influences which tend to retard progress were in constant and general operation among the great mass of the people. Although wealth, learning, and culture are the most powerful agents in promoting human progress, it should always be remembered that the potency of their influence depends entirely upon the extent and constancy of their operation. It is not surprising therefore that the learning and philosophy of Greece and Rome, like the wealth of Asia and Africa, tended to increase the power of the rulers rather than to develop the social character of the common people.

It is true that modern civilization owes more to the learning and philosophy of Athens, and the jurisprudence of Rome, than it

---

[1] Gibbon's "Decline and Fall of the Roman Empire," vol. i., p. 52 ; note, 59 ; *ibid.*, vol. i., p. 51.

[2] Draper's "Intellectual Development of Europe," p. 184.

does to the wealth and art of India and Egypt ; but this is not due so much to the superior influence which they exercised in their *own* time as to the fact that Greek philosophy and Roman law were committed to parchment, and thereby preserved until a sufficiently large portion of the race reached the advancement necessary to appropriate it. . And long it had to wait for that period to arrive ; it was seventeen centuries after the time of Socrates, Plato, and Aristotle that Greek literature began to exercise any influence upon human progress ; indeed, it was not until a thousand years after the government of Greece and Rome had passed away, and the slavery they had bequeathed to the race overthrown, that—through the influence developed by the Free Cities of Europe—the laboring classes for the first time became active social factors, and a broader field prepared in which the seed of Athenian philosophy could germinate.[1]

Therefore, so far as advancing the civilization—improving the social condition of the masses—of its own period is concerned, the philosophy of Greece and Rome did no more than the pyramids of Egypt, or the palaces of Peru.

It was because the refining elements of these civilizations were not rooted in the industrial and social character of the common people, but represented only the glitter of a small class sustained by the power of the army, that their decay and fall was inevitable. When circumstances arose which forced them to contend with foreign enemies and civil strife, their seeming strength vanished and their real weakness was revealed. The defeat of the army was the fall of their power ; with the military support taken from under the government nothing remained to prevent it from

[1] Draper thinks the revival of Greek may be dated from the close of the fourteenth century, at which time Chrysoloras taught it in Italy. Although this isolated spark appeared in 1395, and some Greek manuscripts (including those of Plato and Pindar) were brought into Italy a few years later, it cannot be said that there was any perceptible restoration of, and much less any social influence from, Greek literature until after the capture of Constantinople by the Turks in 1453. This, it will be remembered, was fully a century and a half after the Free Cities had obtained the material prosperity and political freedom which made them leading factors in the social and industrial life of Europe ; more than a century after the discovery of gunpowder ; nineteen years after the insurrection of Wat Tyler in England ; thirty-seven years after the revolt of the Hussites in Bohemia ; and eight years after the discovery of the art of printing.

falling to the level of the real character of the people—which was *barbarism.*

It was a mistake to assume, as Draper and others have done, that the decay of these civilizations was the natural result of social ripeness and old age. Such was far from being the case ; they all died (socially speaking) in their very babyhood. Not one of them arose above the plane of chattel slavery and hand labor ; they did not even reach the point of having chimneys, or glass windows, in the houses of their most favored classes,[1] —and certainly much intellectual and moral light cannot be expected to enter the minds and characters of a people when sunlight never enter their dwellings.

The commonly accepted notion that the overthrow of these ancient governments was the destruction of superior civilizations is erroneous. When Rome conquered Greece and subjugated all Europe, as well as Egypt and Asia Minor,—or when the barbarians sacked Rome,—they did not destroy high civilizations, but rather reduced the political institutions of the time to the level of the general industrial and social character they had created. Had the material conditions and social character of the Roman people in the fifth century been equal to that of the burgesses of the fourteenth, neither the defeat of the army nor the fall of the empire could have reduced them to barbarism ; but slaves—the chief social product of Rome—were good material for barbarian rule. Human progress was not arrested because Rome fell, but *Rome fell because human progress had been arrested.*

[1] Chimneys and glass windows did not come into use until the middle of the fourteenth century.

CHAPTER V.

THE RISE AND SOCIAL POWER OF THE FREE CITIES.

If we pass from the ancient to the modern world we shall find that, so far as the same causes have been in operation, the same social effects have been produced ; namely, that intellectual and moral development, and civil and religious liberty, have always followed the line of the material prosperity of the masses, and *vice versa.*

The first five centuries of the history of Europe after the fall of the Western Empire compose the midnight darkness of social chaos. Indeed, the only approach to orderly government within that period was during the reign of Charlemagne. After his death the empire soon resolved itself into the elements from which it was constructed, and all law, authority, and regular government again disappeared.

After protracted but futile struggles for political and territorial supremacy, powerful chiefs began to settle upon their domains with their retainers, and there assumed all the functions of military chiefs, civil magistrates, and political sovereigns over their vassals. Thus, before the close of the ninth century, the feudal system—which during the tenth, eleventh, and twelfth centuries governed all Europe—slowly emerged from barbarism.

Feudalism sustained the same relation to barbarism that barbarism did to Romanism.—not that it was superior to it, but that it was the natural outcome of it. Both barbarism and feudalism were simply the means of adapting the external machinery of society to the internal character of the people. As the vast empire of Rome became reduced to wandering tribes and petty

3

kingdoms because it had failed to develop the industrial and social character of the masses, so, for the same reason, in the tenth century authority was transferred from petty kings to feudal lords; society was reduced to its lowest terms, and political rights and social privileges were absorbed by industrial conditions,—he who offered the means of a living commanding complete political, military, and social allegiance.

Under this *régime* all who were not noble were servile ; the extent of servitude was in accordance with the degree of poverty; the very poor were slaves. " Artisans and free husbandmen," says Hallam, "were often compelled to exchange their liberty for bread. In seasons also of famine, and they were not infrequent, many freemen sold themselves into slavery . . . others became slaves, as the more fortunate men became vassals, to a powerful lord for the sake of his protection." [1]

Guizot observed : " No sooner was society a little settled under the feudal system than the proprietors of fiefs began to feel new wants, and to acquire a certain degree of taste for improvement and melioration ; this gave rise to some little commerce and industry in the towns of their domains ; wealth and population increased within them—slowly for certain, but still they increased." [2]

With the concentration of the serfs in the towns the seed of social development was planted.   The influence of the industrial, social, and religious intercourse thus created, though meagre and crude, perceptibly affected the wants and character of the laborers and taught them to produce, and also to consume, wealth.

This first real step towards progress and freedom became too pronounced to be mistaken by the middle of the eleventh century, and finally grew too powerful to be arrested until it had overthrown the feudal system and laid the foundation of a higher civilization.   As the towns increased more rapidly in population and prosperity, they naturally developed a spirit of independence. This tended to excite the jealousy of the barons, who regarded the burghers as serfs having no rights that they were bound to respect, and they therefore increased their exactions and en-

[1] " Middle Ages," vol. i., pp. 121, 122.
[2] " History of Civilization," p. 157 ; also *ibid.*, p. 101.

deavored to rob and plunder them at every opportunity.' "The exactions," says Guizot, "of the proprietors of fiefs upon the burgesses were redoubled at the end of the tenth century. Whenever the lord of the domain by which the city was girt felt a desire to increase his wealth he gratified his avarice at the expense of the citizens . . . merchants on returning from their trading rounds could not with safety return to the city. Every avenue was taken possession of by the lord of the domain and his vassals." Man will seldom take much risk to obtain advantages he has never possessed, but he will risk every thing, often against great odds, to defend and sustain those he has already enjoyed. So the burghers, having had a taste of wealth and social freedom, slight indeed though it was, were ready to risk their all to retain these benefits.

Despite the constant efforts of the lords to check the power and progress of the burghers by greater exactions and open robbery, we are told that : " The towns became continually richer . . . the consciousness that they could not be individually despoiled of their possessions, like the villains of the country around, inspired an industry and perseverance which all the rapacity of the Norman kings and barons was unable to overcome."²

The opposition of the burghers to the harassing policy of the barons at length became so strong that the barons were compelled to abandon the effort to exact tribute from each individual burgher at will, and agreed to accept a specific amount from the whole town, to be paid as a yearly rent. To secure this rent the baron surrendered every other claim which he might have, either upon the town or its individual inhabitants. "The town was then said to be affirmed, or let in fee-farm, to the burgesses and their successors forever."³ This rent, when once fixed, was perpetual, and could not be increased by the lord,—however populous or rich the town might become,—nor could any new tax be imposed upon it without the consent of the burghers. This was really the first victory for liberty ever known by, and for, the laboring classes.

¹ " History of Civilization," p. 158 ; Hallam's " Middle Ages," vol. i., pp. 365, 366, and Wade's " History of the Working Classes," p. 9.

² Hallam's " Middle Ages," vol. ii., p. 78.

³ Hallam's " Middle Ages," vol. i., p. 78.

But, instead of being the end, this was only the beginning of
the struggle, for what the lords could no longer take by tallage
they endeavored to obtain by force.[1] In order, therefore, to
maintain their existence and the little freedom they had acquired, the towns were forced into open hostility to the barons.
To sustain themselves in this struggle we are told that : " Every
citizen was bound by oath to stand by the common cause against
all aggressors, and this obligation was abundantly fulfilled.   In
order to swell their numbers, it became the practice to admit all
who came to reside within their walls to the rights of burgher-
ship, even though they were villains, appurtenant to the soil of a
master, from whom they had escaped."[2]   Thus the towns not
only protected the prosperity and promoted the progress of
those who lived within them, but they offered protection and
freedom to all who would flee from the clutches of the feudal
masters.   Guizot assures us that : " It was not merely the lower
orders, such as serfs, villains, and so on, that sought this protection, but frequently men of considerable rank and wealth, who
might chance to be proscribed.   .   .   .   Refugees of this sort,"
he adds, " had, in my opinion, a considerable influence upon the
progress of the cities ; they introduced into them, besides their
wealth, elements of a population superior to the great mass of
the inhabitants."[3]

By these means, together with the industrial and social influences before referred to, the towns continued to grow in
wealth, population, and power, and before the close of the
eleventh century they were in general rebellion against the
barons.[4]   Although the revolt was local, and spontaneous in
its origin, it was universal and simultaneous in its movement.
The same general causes were everywhere in operation, and
consequently the same general effect was produced.[5]

---

[1] " Wealth of Nations," Book III., chap. iii., p. 306.
[2] Hallam's " Middle Ages," vol. i., p. 170.
[3] " History of Civilization," p. 157.
[4] Guizot's " History of Civilization," p. 161.
[5] " The situation of all the towns being nearly the same, they were all liable
to the same danger ; a prey to the same disaster.   Having acquired similar
means of resistance and defence, they made use of those means at nearly the
same time."—Guizot's " History of Civilization," p. 161.

When the open rupture between the towns and their lords took place, the king, though not necessarily an active partisan, was always a deeply interested party. Adam Smith says : " The burghers naturally hated and feared the lords ; the king hated and feared them too ; but, though perhaps he might despise, he had no reason to either hate or fear, the burghers. Mutual interest, therefore, disposed them to support the king, and the king to support them against the lords. They were the enemies of his enemies, and it was his interest to render them as secure and independent of those enemies as he could " [1] ; accordingly, in their struggles with the barons, the towns frequently called upon the king for aid and support in protecting the rights and privileges which the lords had previously sworn to grant them.

This appeal was generally responded to, at least so far as the king could know that his own power and interest would be promoted thereby. By this means, in the eleventh century, the towns began to obtain charters giving them special commercial privileges,[2] and early in the twelfth century they obtained charters which secured to them, besides commercial privileges, the right of self-government.[3] By these charters the towns were practically transformed into little republics. They were better able than ever before to effectually offer an asylum to overpowered lords, and freedom to the enslaved and degraded serfs who might take refuge within their walls. These Free Cities, therefore, natu-

---

[1] "Wealth of Nations," Book III., pp. 306, 307.

[2] "From the time of William Rufus" (1087 to 1100), says Hallam, "there was no reign in which charters were not granted to different towns, of exemptions from tolls on rivers and at markets, those lighter manacles of feudal tyranny ; or of commercial franchises ; or of immunity from the ordinary jurisdiction ; or, lastly, of internal self-regulation."—" Middle Ages," vol. ii., p. 78.

[3] According to Hallam, the city of Leon received its municipal charter from Alfonso V., of Spain, as early as 1020. The city of London, from Henry I., in 1101, and those of Noyon, St. Quenton, Laon, and Amiens, by Louis VI., of France, about 1110. "The privileges conferred by these charters," says this writer, "were surprisingly extensive. . . . They (the burgesses) were made capable of possessing common property, and authorized to use a common seal as the symbol of their incorporation."—" Middle Ages," vol. i., pp. 166–169. "It is certain," says the same writer (vol. i., p. 190), "that before the death of Henry V., in 1125, almost all the cities of Lombardy, and many of those of Tuscany, were accustomed to elect their own magistrates, and to act as independent communities in waging war and in domestic government."

rally attracted to themselves the most industrious and energetic portion of the population, and consequently, during the twelfth and thirteenth centuries, became the centres of wealth, population, and progress.

In 1164, the Lombard cities formed a league to defend their rights and liberties against the attacks of Frederic Barbarossa, who two years before, attacked and pillaged the city of Milan, the most populous and powerful of their number. The war into which they entered lasted thirteen years, and ended with the famous " Peace of Constance " (1183), which, we are told, " established the Lombard republics in real independence."[1] By 1188 the cities of Spain acquired the right of representation in the national legislature. In 1214 Magna Charta declared the old and new privileges of English cities to be inviolable (this was reconfirmed thirty-two times before the middle of the next century), and in 1265 the burghers, or inhabitants of the free cities, obtained representation in Parliament.

About the middle of the thirteenth century, the Free Cities of Germany, in order to protect their rights and property against the rapacity of the barons, formed the famous Hanseatic League (which was a confederacy of eighty of the most powerful cities), and sixty other cities banded themselves together as the League of the Rhine.[2]

It will thus be observed that, through their material or industrial prosperity, social intercourse, and political activity, the Free Cities gave birth to human freedom and became the nurseries of modern progress[3]; and that in those countries where the Free Cities never existed, such as China, Hindostan, and Egypt, civilization has been most stationary.

[1] Hallam's " Middle Ages," vol. i., p. 196.
[2] *Ibid.*, p. 367 ; *cf. ibid.*, vol. ii., p. 271.
[3] " Order and good government, and along with them the liberty and security of individuals, were, in this manner, established in cities, at a time when the occupiers of land in the country were exposed to every sort of violence."—Smith's " Wealth of Nations," Book III., chapter iii., p. 308.

CHAPTER VI.

THE FALL OF THE FREE CITIES AND ITS EFFECT
UPON SOCIAL PROGRESS.

IT is not necessary to our present purpose to discuss the causes which led to the fall of the Free Cities, but merely to indicate, by a brief notice, the general relation which they sustain to social progress. The important fact everywhere observable is, that although the fall of the Free Cities in different countries was not simultaneous, nor the causes identical, the bad effect upon the material prosperity of the people and the progress of social, political, and religious freedom was substantially the same.

In Spain charters were granted to the towns early in the eleventh century (1020),[1] and before the close of the twelfth they were admitted to representation in the Cortes. The peculiar feature of the history of Spain during the Middle Ages is the fact that for nearly eight centuries she was engaged in religious war. The early charters of Spain, unlike those of France, England, and Germany, were granted more for the purpose of inducing the burghers to defend the country against the Moors, than to enable them to protect themselves against the exactions of the barons.[2] This perpetual religious war served to keep the importance of the clergy and the king constantly before the

[1] " The earliest instance of the erection of a community is (in Spain) in 1020, when Alfonso V., in the cortes at Leon, established the privileges of that city, with a regular code of laws by which its magistrates should be governed." —Hallam's " Middle Ages," vol. i., p. 303.

[2] " Instead of purchasing their immunities, and almost their personal freedom, at the hands of a master, the burgesses of Castilian towns were invested with civil rights and extensive property on the more liberal condition of protecting their country."—Hallam's " Middle Ages," vol. i., p. 303.

people, the former to teach the true faith, the latter to extirpate the heretics. The Christians being more devoted to the killing of heretics than to the production of wealth, manufacturing and commercial industries were, for the most part, carried on by the Mohammedans.[1] Therefore, when the Moors were driven out of Spain, and their industrial centres deserted, the last prop to her material prosperity was destroyed. Buckle pointedly observes[2]: "There was no one to fill their place; arts and manufactures either degenerated or were entirely lost."

The city of Seville, which before the expulsion of the Mohammedans contained sixteen thousand looms and gave employment to thirty out of fifty persons, only employed three hundred looms after that event. During the same period the fifty woollen-factories of Toledo were reduced to thirteen, and her silk trade, which had given employment to over thirty-eight thousand persons, was entirely destroyed.

The poverty and wretchedness which followed this decay of the Christian and the violent overthrow of the Moorish Cities of Spain are almost indescribable,[3] and with this industrial degeneracy the social progress of the burghers was soon arrested.

By the close of the fifteenth century their representation in the Cortes, and with it their industrial and social freedom, was practically extinct.[4] From this time Spain rapidly declined, and soon fell from the position of one of the strongest to that of one of the weakest nations in Europe—a fall she has never since recovered.

In Italy the Free Cities fell from a different set of causes, but the effect of their fall upon progress was essentially the same in kind, if not in degree. As already stated, the Lombard Cities began to acquire wealth and freedom in the eleventh century, and before the close of the twelfth they became recognized, independent republics. Upon the same principle that the increase of wealth which precedes the development of wants leads

---

[1] Buckle's "History of Civilization," vol. ii., p. 52.   [2] *Ibid.*

[3] Mahon's "Spain under Charles II.," pp. 138–140.

[4] "At the cortes of Burgos, in 1315, we find one hundred and ninety-two representatives from more than ninety towns. . . . by the year 1480 only seventeen cities retained the privilege of representation."—Hallam's "History of the Middle Ages," vol. i., p. 314.

to waste, the increase of freedom and power that precede the development of social character necessary to their wise use, naturally lead to maladministration, and tend to promote anarchy rather than the advancement of a higher civilization.

Thus it was with the Free Cities of Italy. They acquired political power too suddenly ; their form of government was republican before their character had become democratic. In short, their external power and prominence were more the result of political despotism than social development. Accordingly after their great victory over Barbarossa in 1183, they soon became the victims of internal feuds. Having no foreign enemy to encounter, they turned their swords upon one another, which was more fatal to their prosperity, power, and freedom than all the attacks of a foreign foe.[1] Weakened by the factious war among themselves, they soon became an easy prey to monarchy. By the middle of the thirteenth century (1233) they had fallen into the hands of a monkish usurper, Vicenza, and by the close of the century they were forced, with little difficulty, to submit to the yoke of a despotic monarchy. So completely did the loss of their freedom follow that of their material prosperity that, "before the middle of the fourteenth century, at the latest, all those cities which had spurned at the faintest mark of submission to the emperors, lost even the recollections of self-goverment, and were bequeathed, like undoubted patrimony, among the children of their new lords."

Although brought about by very different causes, the fall of the free cities in Italy, as in Spain, arrested the material prosperity of that country, and consequently its social progress and political and religious freedom were greatly retarded.

The history of the Free Cities of Germany was somewhat different from that of Spain and Italy. In Germany the rapacity of the barons and petty princes partook more of the character of common highwaymen than in any other country. So universally was this the case among the rural nobles that it became customary for them to build their castles upon inaccessible hills where they could command the public highways. As an evidence of the prevalence of this practice, Hallam relates the story, told by a

---

[1] "For revenge, she threw away the pearl of great price, and sacrificed even the recollections of liberty."—Hallam's "Middle Ages," vol. i., p. 198.

contemporary writer, of an archbishop who built a fortress of this kind. No legal provision having been made for him, he was asked by the governor "how he was to maintain himself," to which he replied that "his castle was situated near the junction of four roads."

As a means of protection against the "robber barons," the cities allied themselves with the emperors, and the emperors, in order to obtain assistance against the petty princes, willingly patronized the cities. German cities were not entirely free from the internal jealousies which were so fatal to those of Italy, but the constant danger from the barons made some degree of united action necessary to their existence. Thus the Hanseatic Union and the League of the Rhine were formed ; the first about 1250, and the latter in 1255. These two organizations comprised, at the time, over a hundred and thirty cities leagued together to defend themselves against the nobility, just as those of Italy were leagued against Frederick I. By this means the German cities escaped the fate of those in Lombardy ; but in their very escape they became the victims of influences which were scarcely less fatal in their results, though more gradual in their operation. Through their almost constant alliance with the emperor they naturally became more and more under his influence and control ; and although they did not become imperial strongholds, they ceased to be democratic nurseries. Guizot has well observed : "They preserved their privileges, but they remained confined to the inside of their walls. Within these, democratic organization was shut up and arrested ; if we walk abroad over the face of the country, we find no resemblance of it."[1] Thus, while they retained their external form until after the close of the sixteenth century, at the close of the fifteenth their power as harbingers of industrial and political freedom was practically destroyed.

If we turn to France, a similar picture presents itself ; although the local causes were different, the general result was substantially the same. France was the birthplace of feudalism, and it is therefore not surprising that the feudal system should have taken deeper root in that country than in any other. While it was a fundamental principle of feudalism that the lord should be

[1] "History of Civilization," p. 223.

supreme on his own domain, in no country was baronial sovereignty so absolute, in theory and practice, as in France. There the lord possessed all the powers that were invested in the king. He even had the right to declare war against the king himself. In many countries this practice was more or less indulged in, but in France it was laid down as one of the legal rights of the lord. By this means the feudal nobility in France were equal in strength to all other elements combined. Although the French kings, in order to strengthen their own hands, granted very liberal charters, they were mainly confined to the towns on the royal domains and those of the weaker nobility in the south of France. Consequently, when the struggle between the barons and the cities came, the power of the former proved too much for the latter, and the cities fell.[1]

With the fall of the Free Cities the feudal system was reestablished, and many of its odious features continued down to the French Revolution.   .

Passing from the Continent to England, we shall find that, while the general appearance of the movement was very similar, the essential features, and therefore their effect upon civilization, were very different. The Free Cities in England, like those on the Continent, were the birthplaces of material prosperity and the nurseries of civilization ; but in England no elements were strong enough to suppress them. Neither the king nor the Church, as in Spain ; nor internal strife and usurpation, as in Italy ; nor baronial weakness and imperial strength, as in Germany ; nor the feebleness of royalty and the power of Feudalism, as in France, were sufficient to prevail against the cities of England.

From the fifth to the eleventh century there was very little difference in the social state of the various countries in Europe ; if any thing, England was probably less advanced than some of the rest. About the middle of the eleventh century, however, an event occurred in England which produced an arbitrary and radical change. When William, Duke of Normandy, decided to present a forceful claim to the English throne, he promised to

---

[1] " And so it was in France. The towns, with few exceptions, fell at the first shock ; and the cities lost their municipal privileges, which, not being grafted on the national character, it was.found impossible to preserve."—Buckle's " History of Civilization," vol. i., p. 449.

freely distribute the wealth and land of England among his followers in order to induce them to enter more heartily into the struggle, and he was as good as his word.

He had no sooner obtained possession of the British Government, such as it was, than he proceeded to dispossess the Britons of all political power and to confiscate their property,—both of which he divided among his Norman followers.[1] In this redistribution of wealth and power, William never lost sight of the main object of the conquest,—his own power and aggrandizement,—and hence, in making his grants, he was always careful to exact the fullest ackowledgment of his own supreme authority.

The feudal system in England was thus arbitrarily reconstructed, and, so far as the nobles were concerned, on a more limited basis than that which obtained upon the Continent. For instance, the most powerful of the English barons never acquired such sovereign privileges as the right of coining money in their own name ; the right to forbid the circulation of the royal money upon their own domains ; exemption from all public tribute except feudal aids ; the right of waging private wars, even against the king, etc.[2] The power of the Norman barons in England being thus limited, the contest for supremacy between feudalism and monarchy was more evenly balanced. Under these conditions the opportunity for the growth and safety of the towns was naturally great. Consequently, we find that, while the English towns did not rise to opulence as suddenly as the Italian cities, they made gradual progress toward wealth, power, and freedom.

In order to weaken the barons, and in the hope of strengthening his own hand, the king granted charters to the towns, exempting them from, and protecting them against, the exactions of the barons. Another beneficial effect of "that vigorous prerogative of the Norman monarchs which kept down the feudal aristocracy" was, that, because of the inability of the barons to

---

[1] " This exclusion of the English from political privileges," says Hallam, "was accomplished with such a confiscation of property as never perhaps has proceeded from any government not avowedly founding its title upon the sword. In twenty years from the accession of William almost the whole soil of England had been divided among foreigners."—" Middle Ages," vol. ii., p. 27.

[2] See Hallam's " Middle Ages," vol. i., p. 127 ; also Buckle's " History of Civilization," vol. i., p. 445.

cope single-handed against the king, it became necessary for them to include the rights and privileges of the burghers (whom they hated) with their own.

It was by this means that, under the leadership of Stephen Laughton and the Earl of Pembroke, the Magna Charta was wrung from that rapacious and treacherous coward, King John, in 1215. This declared that : "The charter of the city of London, and of all the towns and boroughs, is inviolable ; no freeman shall be taken or imprisoned, or be deprived of his freehold liberties ; or free customs ; or be outlawed ; or exiled ; or any otherwise destroyed but by lawful judgment of his peers, or by the law of the land." The great charter of rights extended as much protection to the burghers against the violence and oppression of the barons as it did to the barons against the oppressions of the king, and in order to secure the privileges thus obtained subsequent kings were forced to solemnly ratify this great charter [1] thirty-two different times. In the same way, fifty years later, the burghers obtained the right of popular representation in Parliament. It was in the protracted struggle between the confederate barons and Henry III. that, in order to secure the favor of the burghers and thereby strengthen the hands of the barons against the king, the Earl of Leicester, on the 12th of December, 1264, issued writs to all the sheriffs, directing them to return to parliament "two citizens for every city and borough, in addition to the knights of the county." [2] Nearly all the charters that were granted to the towns after the reign of John gave them complete municipal independence, including the right to make their own laws, elect their own magistrates and judges, levy their own taxes, etc.

With these powers the Free Towns could offer protection and citizenship to all who would reside within their walls. Villeins were declared free, and endowed with the free rights of citizenship, who fled to the chartered towns and continued residents for a year and a day. [3] This obviously tended to increase the power

[1] See Buckle's "History of Civilization," vol. i., pp. 446, 447 ; also Hallam's "History of the Middle Ages," vol. ii., pp. 73, 83.

[2] Hallam's "Middle Ages," vol. ii., p. 73.

[3] *Ibid.*, p. 203. See also Wade's "History of England," p. 9.

of the towns and the number of freemen, and at the same time to diminish the power of the Lords, as is abundantly shown by the petitions sent to Parliament by the lords, praying : " that the villeins might not put their children to school . . . for the honor of all freemen in the kingdom " ; and complaining : "that villeins fly to cities and boroughs, whence their masters cannot recover them ; and, if they attempt it, are hindered by the people ; and prayed that the lords might seize their villeins in such places without regard to the franchises hereof." [1] The result was that the lords were compelled to be more generous in their treatment of villeins in order to prevent them from running away to the towns,[2] and consequently, by the last quarter of the thirteenth century their condition had become greatly modified. Instead of being inseparable parts of the lord's estate, the villeins were now bound only to perform certain specified services, known as "labor rents," for which they were allowed to possess the land they lived upon, or work for wages the remainder of the time as "free laborers for another lord." [3] By the close of the reign of Edward II. (1327) labor rents had almost entirely disappeared [4] ; and before the middle of the reign of Edward III. the villeins, for the most part, had become wage-laborers,[5] and feudalism, as an industrial system, was practically overthrown. The effect of these influences upon the industrial condition of the masses is further seen in the fact that, early in the fourteenth century, not only artisans but farm laborers began to demand higher wages. Rogers informs us that, at the close of the famine in 1321, wages rose "from 23 to 30 per cent., fully 20 per cent. of which became permanent," [6] and thirty years later (1350) they rose again from 50 to 100 per cent.[7] This marked increase in

---

[1] See Eden's "State of the Poor," vol. i., pp. 3, 4 ; also Hallam's " Middle Ages," vol. ii., p. 207.

[2] " It was natural that the country people, or uplandish folk, as they were called, should repine at the exclusion from that enjoyment of competence and security for the fruits of their labor, which the inhabitants of the towns so fully possessed."—Hallam's " Middle Ages," vol. ii., pp. 204, 205.

[3] Hallam's " Middle Ages," vol. ii., p. 202.

[4] Rogers' " Six Centuries of Work and Wages in England," p. 218.

[5] Hallam's " Middle Ages," vol. ii., p. 204.

[6] " Six Centuries of Work and Wages," pp. 218, 237.

[7] *Ibid.*, p. 237.

wages was not the result of temporary causes, such as famine, black death, etc., but the natural effect of the period in which English commerce and manufacture took their first great start.[1] It was in 1431 that Edward III., the "father of English commerce," induced Flemish manufacturers to settle in England, promising them that "they should feed on fat beef and mutton till nothing but fullness should stint their stomachs."

The increasing wealth and comfort of the laboring classes during this period is further shown by the constant complaints of contemporary writers about "the extravagance and vanity of the common people," and the frequent petitions to Parliament complaining that "the masters were obliged to give their servants and laborers great wages to prevent their running away to towns where they became artificers, clerks, etc., to the great detriment of agriculture." Thus the natural prosperity which had its rise in the towns during the twelfth and thirteenth centuries extended, in the fourteenth, to the farm laborers in the rural country and consummated the fall of feudalism.

Thus the towns in England gradually rose from industrial to commercial, and from commercial to political, importance. As their wealth did not precede their wants, each addition to their privileges was an increase of their power, and their influence upon freedom and progress extended beyond their own walls. Consequently, although their struggles were severe, they survived until they had overthrown feudalism, transferred the slavery of villeinage into wage-labor, securely established popular representation, and laid the foundation for the religious reformation in the sixteenth, the political revolution in the seventeenth, and the industrial revolution in the eighteenth and nineteenth centuries.

It is a great mistake to conclude, as Fiske[2] and other eminent writers appear to have done, that this is due to some inherent superiority in the English race. A careful consideration of the fundamental causes which underlie and promote social development will show that, while the political and religious institutions of a country are determined by the character of its people, the character is mainly determined by the industrial and social environment. Therefore,

---

[1] *Cf.* "Wealth and Progress," pp. 110–131.

[2] "American Political Ideas," chap. iii.

the cause of the superiority of the English over the Spanish, Italian, and German institutions in the seventeenth, eighteenth, and nineteenth centuries is not to be found in any inherent quality in the English race, but in the difference of its industrial and social conditions in the thirteenth, fourteenth, and fifteenth centuries. Manufacture and trade became more profitable than agriculture, and therefore naturally attracted to themselves the more intelligent and ambitious. By this means, during the fifteenth and sixteenth centuries there arose a middle or commercial class, whose increase in wealth and influence was such that early in the seventeenth century it began to rival the landed aristocracy.[1] Before the close of the seventeenth century the aggregate income of the manufacturers and merchants was more than equal to that of the nobility, and by the end of the eighteenth century the middle class had become the dominant power in society.

[1] " In the course of the sixteenth century the commercial prosperity of England had increased with amazing rapidity, while during the same time much territorial wealth, much baronial property, had changed hands."—Guizot's " History of Civilization," p. 271.

CHAPTER VII.

THE PROGRESS OF POLITICAL AND RELIGIOUS FREEDOM.

If we examine the progress of political and religious freedom we shall find that it has always followed the line of the material prosperity of the masses, rising where that rose, falling where it fell, and becoming permanent only where industrial improvement had been general and continuous. England was the only country in which the Free Towns were not overpowered by either the Church, the Monarchy, or the Barons, and consequently it was the only country in which social and political progress was not arrested.

The Cortes of Spain, the States-General of France, and the Republics of Italy rose and passed away, scarcely leaving their imprint upon the national character, while the English House of Commons has ever stood out as a conspicuous feature of modern civilization. " No great measure," says Guizot,[1] " which has truly had any influence upon society in France, no important reform either in the general legislation or administration, ever emanated from the States-General. . . . The Cortes of Portugal and Spain afford the same general result. . . . The Cortes, like the States-General of France, has been an accident in history, and never a system—never a political organization or regular means of government. . . . The lot of England has been different. . . . The Commons obtained in England a power much superior to those on the continent, a power really capable of influencing the government of the country. In the fourteenth century, the character of the English parliament was already

---

[1] " History of Civilization," pp. 225–7.

formed. . . . The attempt to bring together the various elements of society, and to form them into one body politic, one true
state or commonwealth, *did succeed in England while it failed in
every part of the Continent."*

What was true of municipal privileges and political representation was equally true of religious liberty. In the fourteenth
century, when, on the Continent, the masses were losing their
political rights and society was gravitating towards civil and religious despotism, the people of England were steadily advancing
towards still more freedom.

The increasing prosperity of the towns from the reign of Henry
III. to the middle of the reign of Edward III.—during which
time villeinage had been transferred into wage-labor, and the last
thirty years (1321–1351) of which had witnessed a general and
permanent rise of wages—greatly developed the social and intellectual character of the people,[1] and made the successful advent
of Wicliff and Wat Tyler possible. Whatever may have been
the influences that induced Wicliff to openly renounce the
authority of the pope, denounce the usurpations of the Roman
Church, stigmatize the friars as its political and financial emissaries, and insist upon the right of the laity to read and interpret
the Bible—which he subsequently translated into English,—the
effect of his teachings upon the community ultimately depended
upon the character of the people.[2] Had Wicliff lived before,
instead of after, the Free Cities, his own fate, as well as the
influence of his doctrine, would probably have been entirely
different.

This is well illustrated by the fate of the Hussites in Bohemia
some forty years later. When John Huss, through the treachery

[1] " A silent alteration had been wrought in the condition and character of the
lower classes during the reign of Edward III. This was the effect of increased
knowledge and refinement, which had been making a considerable progress for
full half a century, though they did not readily permeate the cold region of
poverty and ignorance."—Hallam's " Middle Ages," vol. ii., p. 204.

[2] As Buckle truly says : "Although the origin of a new opinion may be due to
a single man, the result which the new opinion produces will depend on the condition of the people among whom it is propagated. If a religion or a philosophy
is too much in advance of a nation it can do no present service, but must bide
its time until the minds of men are ripe for its reception."—" History of Civilization," vol. i., p. 186.

(or weakness) of Emperor Sigismund, was sent to the stake (1416) for advocating the doctrines of Wicliff, his followers flew to arms under the leadership of one John Zisca, who, though totally blind, proved to be almost a second Hannibal. At the death of Zisca, however, the Hussites fell to pieces ; in less than twenty years after the death of Huss they were suppressed ; and by the middle of the century the movement was practically obliterated.[1] Thus the agitation of Huss in Bohemia only continued during the life of its originators, and died without leaving any lasting impression on the character of the people, while that of Wicliff permeated the whole community to such an extent that, it was said, every third man was a Lollard. Wicliff's Bible created such a desire for reading, especially among the middle classes, that, by the middle of the fifteenth century, the art of printing—which had been waiting a thousand years for a book-reading civilization—became a success, and by its aid the country became ripe for the great religious reformation early in the sixteenth century. Nor can the difference in the fate of this movement in England and Bohemia be attributed to any difference in the quality of the leaders or the tenets of the creeds. Both Wicliff and Huss represented leading universities, and both promulgated essentially the same doctrine. The only differences that existed were in the condition and character of the people.

The same is true of the Wat Tyler insurrection in 1381. Unquestionably the " groat-tax "[2] was the immediate cause of the discontent among the peasants, and the killing of the tax-collector by Tyler, for the assault upon his daughter, was the special fact which caused the uprising and put Wat Tyler at its head ; but the reforms that were demanded, and the permanent effect of the movement upon the community, depended upon the character of those who took part in it and were influenced by it. Despite the fact that Tyler was treacherously slain, the other leaders all sub-

[1] " I cannot assign any beneficial results to the schism of the Hussites, at least its immediate results, in the country where it appeared."—Hallam's " Middle Ages," vol. ii., p. 324.

[2] A groat is fourpence (eight cents). The groat-tax was a tax of three groats a year levied upon every person in the kingdom, male and female, over fourteen years of age. It was the refusal of Tyler's daughter, under fourteen years of age, that led to the assault, for which Wat Tyler struck the collector dead at a blow.

sequently hanged, and the declaration of the Lords and Commons in Parliament that they would never concede to the demand— "if it would save them from all perishing together in one day,"— the insurgents finally obtained all that they claimed. The poll-tax was never collected, and, we are told, "the English laborer for a century or more became virtually free and constantly prosperous." [1]

If we compare the Insurrection in England with the Jacquerie in France, twenty-three years earlier (1358), or with the Peasant War in Germany, one hundred and forty-four years later (1525), the case is even more striking than that of Huss and Wicliff. In each of these countries the revolt was a spontaneous uprising of the people to demand a reform in their industrial and social conditions. There was one important difference, however : the Jacquerie and the Peasant War were preceded by a long period of the direst poverty and galling degradation, while the rising in England was preceded by more than a century of almost continuous prosperity and growing freedom. Nothing is so effective in producing weak character as poverty ; and, for the same reason that empty stomachs make poor soldiers, empty characters make poor reformers.

The Jacquerie and Peasant War were desperate outbursts of long pent-up degradation and despair. The struggles of the people were fierce, but their defeat was overwhelming, and they were hurled back into poverty and subjected to a despotism as oppressive as that against which they had rebelled. The English uprising, on the contrary, being the natural outcome of previous material progress, led on to still greater prosperity and a higher civilization, which laid the foundation for the success of the great event of the sixteenth century—the religious revolution known as the Reformation.

The Reformation was really a social movement. It was the first struggle of the middle class for freedom—of which the new religious doctrines were more the consequence than the cause. Wicliff's first protest was not against the unsoundness of the spiritual teachings of the Church, but against the social injustice of its temporal exactions, which were declared by Parliament to amount " to five times as much as the taxes levied by the king." [2]

---

[1] Rogers' " Six Centuries of Work and Wages in England," p. 271.
[2] Draper's " Intellectual Development of Europe," pp. 397–434.

When he denounced the friars as financial emissaries of the pope, and advocated the heavy taxation of the monasteries, telling the king that "to prohibit the transmission of English money into Roman coffers was not only justifiable but a public duty,".he was simply holding up the hands of Edward and his Parliament against the outrageous demand of the pope for the arrears of tribute—promised in a moment of humiliation by the weak and cowardly King John.   His subsequent revolt against the theological dogma of the Church was the natural sequence of this opposition to her temporal usurpations.

Again, in the sixteenth century, Luther did not raise his first opposition against the doctrines of the Church, but against her unscrupulous methods of exhorting tribute from the people.   His first public movement (1517) was the posting upon the doors of the cathedral at Wittenberg of ninety-five objections to the practice of selling indulgences.   It was not until he had been reprimanded by the pope, and afterwards ordered to publicly retract his utterances against the traffic, and finally condemned as a heretic, that he challenged the religious doctrines of the Church. Finding himself in a deadly conflict with the papal authority on temporal matters, he became defiant on spiritual matters also, and in 1520 publicly committed the books of the canon law and the bull of excommunication to the flames.

In England the Reformation came into active existence in a very similar way.   By the first quarter of the sixteenth century the usurpation of temporal power and the extortion of money from the people by the clergy had become a public scandal.   In 1529 the House of Commons declared, in a formal petition to the king, "that the house of convocation made laws without the consent or knowledge of the people ; that such laws were never published in the English language, and that, nevertheless, men were daily punished under them without ever having had an opportunity to eschew the penalties . . . that poor men were harassed without cause in the spiritual courts for the mere purpose of extortion, and exorbitant fees were exacted from them without cause ; and that bishops illegally imprisoned, sometimes for a year or more, persons in their jails without informing them of the cause of their imprisonment or the name of their accuser." In their defence against these charges the bishops declared : "that canon law was superior to the laws of the realm ; that the punishment inflicted upon laymen had been for the health of their souls ; and that, generally, saints may claim powers to which common men are not entitled."

The determination of the Commons to curtail the temporal power of the clergy at this period is shown by the number of laws that were passed for that purpose, among which was the "Clergy Discipline Act." Thus, when it became necessary for Henry VIII. to depose the pope in order to obtain Anne Boleyn, and subsequently to dispossess the clergy of their wealth in order to retain his newly acquired authority over the Church, he was, for social reasons, readily sustained by the Commons and the middle class in his confiscation policy.

The Reformation was to the middle classes of the sixteenth century what the movements of Wicliff and Wat Tyler were to the peasantry of the fourteenth. It attained higher intellectual and moral results because it was based upon higher material and social conditions. Although Protestantism spread over nearly all Europe, it failed to produce any permanent effect in those countries where the Free Cities had been overthrown and the material progress of the masses had been arrested. Thus, in Spain and Italy, where the Free Cities had been most thoroughly suppressed, the influence of the Reformation was the most fleeting. In the former country it was entirely stamped out in ten years,[1] and in the latter it was suppressed before it could take root among the people.[2] Although its struggle for a foothold was longer and fiercer in France, its extinction was hardly less complete. In Germany, where the Free Cities continued to a much later date, its influence, though more general and lasting, did not become permanent. It was only in England and Switzerland, where the Free Cities were never entirely conquered, that the Reformation became permanently established.

If we pass from the sixteenth to the seventeenth century we shall find that the march of progress was in accordance with the same general principles. It was the same character, produced by the same general causes, that revolted against the usurpations and oppressions of the Church in 1529, and finally took off the head of Charles I. in 1649. In short, for the same reason that

---

[1] Buckle's " History of Civilization," vol. ii., p. 19.
[2] Guizot's " History of Civilization," p. 260.

the Reformation in the sixteenth century succeeded in establishing the right of private judgment in England—while it failed on the Continent—the political revolution in the seventeenth century established popular constitutional government in the same country—while it utterly failed in France.[1] To use the eloquent language of Professor Fiske : "The close of the seventeenth century, which marks the culmination of the Asiaticizing tendency in Europe, saw despotism, both political and religious, firmly established in France and Spain and Italy and in half of Germany ; while the rest of Germany seemed to have exhausted itself in the attempt to throw off the incubus. But in England this same epoch saw freedom, both political and religious, established on so firm a foundation as never again to be shaken, never again with impunity to be threatened, so long as the language of Locke and Milton and Sydney shall remain a living speech on the lips of men."[2].

It is equally obvious, from the industrial history of the period, that when, from causes elsewhere explained,[3] the material progress of the laboring classes was arrested in the middle of the fifteenth century, their march towards freedom was also arrested. It was only that small portion of laborers who passed into the ranks of the middle or capitalist class in the fifteenth, who went on to freedom in the sixteenth and seventeenth centuries. The history of the Poor-laws, the Act of Settlement, and the Allowance system, clearly show the condition of the masses had not been improved from the middle of the fifteenth to that of the eighteenth century, and also that their liberties were not enhanced by the Reformation, the Commonwealth, or the Revolution of 1688.[4] It

---

[1] The difference in the condition and character of the English and French Revolutions is clearly presented by Buckle in " History of Civilization," vol. i., chapter x. ; and even Guizot, the French historian, in discussing the English Revolution, exclaims : " How came it to pass that this struggle took place in England sooner than anywhere else ? How happened it that the revolution of a political character coincided here with those of a moral character sooner than they did on the Continent ?"—" History of Civilization," p. 270.

[2] " American Political Ideas," p. 119.

[3] See " Wealth and Progress," pp. 132–144.

[4] " The eager spirits who crowded the House of Commons, the mounted yeomen who rode with Hampden, the men who fought and won Marston Moor, and Naseby, thought no more of the peasant and the workman, had no more care

was the commercial prosperity of England, during the first half
of the eighteenth century, that made it possible to produce
wealth cheaper by machinery than by hand labor. This led to
the organization of the factory system, which, during the first
quarter of the present century, entirely changed the economic
condition of the English laborer, and has since revolutionized
the industrial system of all Christendom. The factory system
broke up the isolated and non-socializing system of domestic industry, and it brought the laborers into closer and more frequent
intercourse with one another, socially as well as industrially.
The influence of this upon the wants and habits and consequently
upon the material condition of the masses, is shown by the rise
of wages during the first twenty years of the present century.
During the next twenty years the improved condition of the
masses was still more marked, for during that time there was a
pronounced fall in prices as well as a distinct rise in money
wages.[1] The influence of this material prosperity upon the
political freedom of the laboring classes is manifest from the
liberal legislation that has followed from 1825 to the present
time. Previous to this time industrial legislation, from the
" Statute of Laborers " (1350), was directed to keeping down
wages and restricting the social opportunities of the masses. Now
for the first time in history the power of government was directly
exercised on the side of the laboring classes. In 1819 the first
law was enacted restricting the hours that women and children

for bettering him, than the Irish patriots of 1782 cared for the kernes and
cottiers on whose labor they lived. . . . The great Revolution which established
the authority of Parliament, put an end to arbitrary power, and relieved the con-
sciences of those who could not accord themselves to the worship of the English Church, brought no liberty to the peasant and artisan. It stereotyped their
servitude. . . . Laborers had ceased to be factors in political action, and
were simply ignored for a century or more. . . . All this too was done when the
patriots and placemen chattered about liberty and arbitrary administration, and
fine ladies and gentlemen talked about the rights of man."—Thorold Rogers'
" Six Centuries of Work and Wages," pp. 432–434.

[1] According to Thorold Rogers, wages from 1800 to 1820 were 55.25 pence
per day, while from 1821 to 1840 they were 62.75, and during the former
period a given quantity of seven of the chief necessaries of life cost 232.5
shillings, while in the latter they only cost 146.35 shillings.—" Six Centuries
of Work and Wages in England," p. 504. *Cf.* Tooke's " History of Prices,"
vol. i., pp. 329, 330.

should be employed in factories. In 1824 the laws, which for nearly five centuries had made it a penal offence for workingmen to organize for the promotion of their own interest, were repealed ; as was also the Quarter-Sessions Assessment Act.[1] In 1825, 1831, 1833, 1844, 1847, 1874, and 1882, important laws were enacted reducing the hours of labor, by instalments, from fourteen to nine and a half hours per day ; also providing compulsory education for all working children under fourteen years of age ; superior sanitary regulations for all factories and workshops ; proper protection against dangerous machinery ; making the employer responsible for injury to laborers, etc. Through the constantly increasing influence of the growing intelligence and social character of the laboring classes upon public opinion, the right to vote was extended, in 1832, 1867, and 1884, from the middle to the laboring classes ; the last instalment making the agricultural laborer politically (at least on election day) the equal of the Duke of Westminster. It was during this period also that religious tests for holding government offices were abolished ; that Catholics (1828) and Jews (1845) were admitted to representation in Parliament and permitted to enter the universities ; that tithes were commuted and church rates were abolished ; that the great Chartist movement[2] was inaugurated ; that the conspiracy laws were repealed ; that stamps on newspapers were abolished ; and a free press and free speech were established. Thus, in the same way and for the same reason that the civil and religious liberty acquired by the middle classes in the six-

---

[1] See Rogers' " Work and Wages," p. 438.

[2] Macaulay clearly saw the historical error of ascribing our industrial and social progress to our political institutions, and says : " I am perfectly aware of the immense progress which your country has made and is making in population and wealth. I know that the laborer with you has large wages, abundant food, and the means of giving some education to his children. But I see no reason for attributing these things to the policy of Jefferson. . . . You will, I am sure, acknowledge that the progress which you are now making is only a continuation of the progress which you have been making ever since the middle of the seventeenth century. It therefore seems to me quite clear that the facts which you cite to prove the excellence of purely democratic institutions, ought to be ascribed not to those institutions, but to causes which operated in America long before your Declaration of Independence."—Macaulay's letter on Randall's " Life of Jefferson," Oct. 9, 1858.

teenth and seventeenth centuries was the fruition of the material progress of the fourteenth and fifteenth centuries, the social, religious, and political freedom obtained by the masses in the nineteenth century is the result of the material prosperity which made the use of steam, the spinning-jenny, the power-loom, and the factory system possible.

If we pass from Europe to America we shall find that social progress has taken place in the order and in accordance with the same general principle as in England. The most superficial acquaintance with the history of the United States is sufficient to show that our republican institutions are the consequence, and not the cause, of our material prosperity. The Republic was born of the social and intellectual character growing out of a long period of previous industrial prosperity, and this prosperity was due to causes long ante-dating the slightest observable democratic tendency in our political institutions.

The comparative prosperity which prevailed in the American Colonies for three quarters of a century immediately preceding the Revolution is shown by the fact that wages were most of the time one third higher, and the price of provisions very much lower, here than in England. In describing the industrial condition of the American people during that period, Adam Smith says: "Labor is there so well rewarded, that a numerous family of children, instead of being a burden, is a source of opulence and prosperity to the parents. The labor of each child, before it can leave the house, is computed to be worth a hundred pounds clear gain to them." In 1770 the wages of carpenters, masons, etc., in London (which is always twenty-five to thirty per cent. higher than in the country), were two shillings and six pence a day,[1] while at the same date in New York, ship carpenters received "six shillings and six pence sterling, and journeymen tailors two shillings and ten pence sterling"[2]; and, adds the same writer, "the price of provisions is everywhere in North America much lower than in England."

This industrial prosperity made the development of the social and intellectual character of the people inevitable. Consequently

[1] These prices were paid at Greenwich Hospital from 1830 to 1770, and are taken from the records of that institution.

[2] Smith's "Wealth of Nations," Book I., chapter viii., p. 54.

the necessary intelligence and force of character had been created to successfully resist the permanent adoption of the Stamp Act (1765), and it was repealed the next year. The opposition to this measure did not arise from the poverty or hardship it entailed upon the people, but from the injustice of the principle it involved. The same year in which the Stamp Act was repealed in England the "Declaratory Act" was adopted, insisting that the king and Parliament "had the absolute right to make laws binding the colonies and the American people in all things whatsoever." The endeavor to enforce this principle rekindled the flame of resistance in this country and gave rise to the effective cry that "taxation without representation is robbery." This led (1767) to the policy of excluding (boycotting) English goods,—which resulted (1770) in the throwing of tea into Boston Harbor,—and finally culminated (1776) in the Declaration of Independence, a successful revolution, and the establishment of the Republic. Thus, instead of the Revolution being a desperate struggle against industrial degradation, it was a bold, high-minded assertion of political principles, sustained by the superior character consequent upon the previous industrial prosperity. This explains the important difference between the character and result of the French and American Revolutions.

For a century previous to their great Revolution the people of France were in a state of almost indescribable poverty and social degradation, and their struggle was for material existence only. The natural consequence was that they were much more barbarous in their methods and the effects were much less beneficial on this account. The American Revolution resulted in establishing the most liberal and democratic republic the world has ever seen, while that of France did little more than exchange one despot for another. Our Republic was not only born of industrial prosperity, but its success and permanence are due to the same cause. The industrial prosperity of our people during the first seventeen or twenty years of the Republic was phenomenal. By the end of the first decade our exports had risen from nineteen to ninety-four millions of dollars and the revenue had increased from five to thirteen millions. Nor was this prosperity in any sense due to our republican institutions ; it was the result of causes which operated exclusively in Europe. During the first quarter of a century after the outbreak of the French Revolution (1789 to 1815) events in Europe almost uninterruptedly conspired to promote the industrial prosperity of the young Republic.

The French, English, Dutch, Spanish, and Portuguese merchantmen were practically driven from the seas by the campaigns of Napoleon. The United States was in an excellent condition to supply vessels to take their places and her neutrality secured her the opportunity. By this means the Republic obtained, for the time being, a practical monopoly of the ocean freight of the world. All that was necessary for the small capitalist of America to do, in order to rapidly acquire wealth, was to obtain a cargo of American products at normal prices and sail to the West Indies, or to Europe, under the American flag. For several years Europe was supplied with American produce ; Russia, Sweden, Germany, and even England often availed themselves of the service of the American merchants for exchange and freight. The effect upon the trade and industry of the Republic may be seen from the fact that, in 1789 the aggregate capacity of American shipping was only 21,000 tons, while in 1808 it had increased to 110,000 tons.

Another European influence which greatly contributed to the growth of American industry was the discovery of the spinning-jenny and the power-loom (1767–1785), and the inauguration of the factory system in England, which created a great demand for American cotton.

In 1791, the entire cotton crop of America was only 2,000,000 pounds, and by the close of the century the annual product was over 48,000,000 pounds. In 1795, the English consumption of American cotton was 5,000,000 pounds ; in 1820 it was 90,000,000 pounds ; in 1840 it was 488,000,000 pounds ; and by 1860 it was over 1,100,000,000 pounds a year. This prosperity was the one great fact which saved the Republic from going to pieces under the terrible strain to which it was subjected by foreign wars and internal dissensions during the first years of its history.

Therefore, instead of attributing our remarkable industrial prosperity and superior civilization to our republican institutions, as is the custom of our statesmen, journalists, and public teachers generally, the truth is that our republican institutions are the natural result of industrial prosperity and consequent superior civilization.

PART II

THE PRINCIPLES OF ECONOMIC PRODUCTION.

CHAPTER I.

WEALTH AND THE LAW OF ITS PRODUCTION.

SECTION I.—*The Nature and Meaning of Wealth.*

IN considering the laws which govern the economic production of wealth, it will be necessary to explain : (1) wealth, (2) production, (3) the necessary factors in production, (4) the economic importance of these factors, (5) the principle upon which they become active in production.

Unfortunately the term wealth has no uniformly accepted signification. There is no general agreement, even among the best writers, as to what the word wealth means. John Stuart Mill, after saying, "Every one has a notion sufficiently correct for common purposes of what is meant by wealth," within his first two chapters gives several definitions of wealth, all of which are essentially different. For example, he says[1] : "Every thing forms therefore a part of wealth which has a power of purchasing"; and adds[2] : "In the wealth of mankind nothing is included which does not of itself answer some purpose of utility or pleasure." But many things have "a power of purchasing" which in themselves "answer no purpose of utility or pleasure." A dollar bill, a bank check, a mortgage deed, a trade privilege, etc., in themselves "answer" no "purpose of utility or pleasure," but they constantly have a "power of purchasing." In fact, it is only because they can be exchanged for things that will in them· selves "answer some purpose of utility or pleasure" that any one cares to possess them. Again he says[3] : "It is essential to the idea of wealth to be susceptible of accumulation." Services are

[1] "Principles of Political Economy," vol. i., p. 24.
[2] *Ibid*, pp. 24, 25.   [3] *Ibid.*, p. 75.

63

obviously incapable of being accumulated. The products of labor may be stored up, but not so of labor itself. To-day's service, whether of the highest functionary or of the lowest laborer, must be used to-day or it is lost forever; hence, according to this definition, labor cannot be wealth,—although it is about the only "power of purchasing" the masses possess. Again he says[1]: "The skill and the energy and perseverance of the artisans of a country are reckoned part of its wealth no less than their tools and machinery." And on the next page he throws this into confusion by saying[2]: "I shall therefore in this treatise, when speaking of wealth, understand by it only what is called material wealth." With such conflicting definitions as these from Mill, it can hardly be a matter of surprise that confusion should pervade the writings of less able thinkers and more careless writers.

Walker says[3]: "Wealth comprises all articles of value and nothing else." If this definition is correct, then that of Marshall,[4] which includes "human faculties, habits—physical, mental, and moral," as wealth, cannot be accepted, because the essential condition of value is exchange, which involves transferableness. Human faculties and habits are inseparable attributes of individual character, and are absolutely non-transferable, and consequently cannot have value. We can influence others by our faculties and habits, but we can no more transfer them to another than we can give him the color of our hair. To treat human faculties as wealth is to confound wealth with man. Moral and mental qualities indicate rather what a man is than what he has. To thus confound wealth with man tends to increase the confusion, rather than to clarify the conception, of both wealth and its relation to man.

Such is the confusion on this point that some writers have questioned the wisdom of using the term wealth. Perry actually proposes to expunge it from the economic vocabulary,[5] and recommends as a substitute the word property; but it is difficult to see in what sense this would be an improvement. It is as necessary to clearly define the meaning of the word property

---

[1] "Principles of Political Economy," vol. i., p. 75.
[2] *Ibid.*, p. 76.
[3] "Political Economy," p. 5.
[4] "Economics of Industry," p. 6.
[5] "Political Economy," p. 98.

as it is the term wealth, and all the difficulties which beset the use of the former term would be associated with the latter. "That is property," says Perry,[1] "which can be bought and sold." But would it not be just as easy, simple, and correct to say—that is wealth which can be bought and sold ? Manifestly, nothing would be gained to the science by merely substituting the word property for wealth.

Popular phrase is always the most direct avenue to the public mind, and hence should never be abandoned except a manifestly greater directness of expression and clearness of thought can be obtained by so doing. Common language has universally appropriated the term wealth to convey the idea of something which gratifies human wants. Nor does there appear to be any scientific necessity for employing a new word to express that idea. All that is required for the purposes of correct reasoning and clear statement is, that the term shall be so defined as to express all that is included in the idea, without embracing any thing inconsistent with it.

If we examine the characteristic attributes of wealth, we shall find that such a definition is not only possible, but entirely feasible. In the first place, wealth is essentially a social phenomenon ; nothing can be wealth which is not subject to, and conditioned by, social influences. In other words, wealth must be something peculiar to man as a social being, as well as a mere animal organism. Therefore, whatever exists as the result of purely cosmic influences, whether chemical, mineral, vegetable, or animal, cannot be wealth until it comes within the pale of social influences. Second, in order to constitute an object wealth, it must possess the capacity of gratifying some human want or desire. In other words, it must possess utility. Third, it must be socially appropriable ; that is to say, it must be capable of being adapted to the exigencies of social life, and hence must be transferable,— susceptible of exchange. Fourth, in order to possess these qualities, it must have an objective existence ; that is to say, it must be something external to man—a part of his environment.

Therefore, for an object to be wealth it must be at once social, useful, transferable, and material. There are many things which possess some of these qualities, but lack others, and hence can-

[1] "Political Economy," p. 99.

not be classed as wealth. Thus, for example, the sun, air, gravitation, and other forces are useful and objective, but they are
neither social nor transferable ; that is to say, they are the
product of automatic cosmical, instead of social, forces, and
hence are equally in the possession of all without effort. Thus
they are not only independent of social influences, but they are
unappropriable, and consequently incapable of exchange.

Man's physical and mental faculties, and also his moral qualities, are highly useful to himself and to society : they are subject
to, and regulated by, social influences, but they have no objective
existence, and hence cannot be transferable. They may be
higher and better than wealth, but they are not wealth, because
they lack one of the essential attributes of wealth. In short, they
are attributes of man's character and not the external objects with
which he gratifies his wants and desires.

While this view of wealth excludes the personal qualities which
orthodox economists have included—without being able to give
a sufficient reason for so doing—it includes other things which
they excluded. They have made it "essential to the idea of
wealth to be susceptible of accumulation."[1] Hence they have
concluded that all the efforts of teachers, ministers, lecturers,
singers, actors, showmen, etc., are non-productive[2]—because
what they produce cannot be accumulated ; that is, it cannot be
stored up and subsequently enjoyed or exchanged. This has
led to that erroneous doctrine of unproductive labor which pervades so much of English economic literature. It is not necessary to constitute an object wealth that it shall be able to maintain all the attributes of wealth for an extended period. If an
object has all the qualities and fills all the functions of wealth at
any one time, it is wealth. An object is not precluded from being
wealth to-day, because it fails to fill that function to-morrow, or
next month, or next year. That is simply a question of degree
of durability, and not a question as to wealth *per se.*

The product of the minister, the musician, the lecturer, the
actor, etc., in the form of a sermon, song, lecture, or drama, fills

---

[1] Mill's " Principles of Political Economy," vol. i., chap. iii.

[2] "Wealth of Nations," Book II., chap. iii. Mill's " Principles of Political
Economy," vol. i., pp. 77, 78. Marshall's "Economics of Industry," pp. 18,
19.

all the functions of wealth. It is social, because it is entirely the product of human influences. It is useful, because it gratifies human wants and desires. It is transferable, because it is capable of being distributed to an unlimited number of people. It is objective, because it exists entirely in the environment of those who produce it and those who receive it. It is not capable of being redistributed, because it loses all its wealth attributes within a few seconds after its production. But, as before remarked, that is simply a question of duration. The susceptibility to re-distribution is not a necessary quality of wealth, it is only a quality of some kinds of wealth. Therefore we may say that the product of this class is not only wealth, but much of it is vastly more socializing and civilizing in its influences than many forms of wealth which are susceptible of redistribution, long duration, and extensive accumulation.

Wealth, then, must have an objective materiality and possess potential transferable utility—the actualization of which is dependent upon social or human forces ; or, to be more specific, the term wealth includes every thing capable of serving human wants and desires, the utility of which is the result of human effort.

An able critic, to whom this chapter was submitted in manuscript asks : "If a shower of manna fell from Heaven, or an island of coral rose from the sea, or a spring of healing mineral water started from the hill, or the sea washed up a mountain of pearls, would they not be wealth?" Certainly not, they would possess some of the qualities of wealth, they would have objective materiality and they would be appropriable, but they would possess only potential utility—to actualize which would require the human effort necessary to put them into the possession of those whose wants they would supply. Until utility is actualized, it is as though it did not exist. The vast coal-beds of China are not wealth to the Chinese, and the gold in California and the iron in Pennsylvania was not wealth to the roving Indians. Natural or cosmic forces alone can never produce wealth. The most they ever do is to make the production of wealth by man possible. Therefore, *every thing may be regarded as wealth, the utility of which is actualized by human effort.*

SECTION II.—*Production and Producers—Their Economic Meaning.*

The terms production and producers have been scarcely more fortunate in their treatment at the hands of the economists than has wealth. While nearly all writers use them, they seem to take the liberty of expanding or contracting their signification at will. The French physiocrats limited the term production to efforts devoted to the cultivation of land—that is, extracting material commodities from the earth. All efforts devoted to manufacture, transportation, and commerce were regarded by them as unproductive labor.

Adam Smith vigorously attacked this idea as being too narrow.[1] With great force and clearness he showed that efforts devoted to manufacture, transportation, and all the various phases of trade and commerce are as truly productive as are those applied to agriculture ; but he insisted that armies, navies, courts, and government officials, together with all intellectual and literary efforts, were non-productive and a burden upon "the produce of other men's labor."[2]

Mill, who modernized Adam Smith, extends this definition sufficiently to make it include government officials in the productive class, on the ground that : "The labor of officers of government in affording the protection which, in some manner or other, is indispensable to the prosperity of industry, must be classed as productive even of material wealth."[3] Beyond this, however, he adheres to the definition of Adam Smith, and classes all efforts as unproductive that do not produce wealth which can be literally accumulated and inventoried. "All labor," he says,[4] "according to our present definition, must be classed as unproductive which terminates in a permanent benefit, however important, provided that an increase of material products form no part of that benefit. . . . Unproductive may be as useful as productive labor; it may be more useful even in point of permanent advantage. . . . In any case society or mankind grow no richer by it, but poorer."

To say the least, this definition of production is very confusing. For while it recognizes the creation of utility as essential

---

[1] "Wealth of Nations," Book IV., ch. ix.   [2] *Ibid.* Book II., ch. iii.
[3] Mill's "Principles of Political Economy," vol. i., p. 76.
[4] *Ibid.*, pp. 77, 78.

to production, it declares a large class of efforts unproductive which produce the highest kind of utility. The efforts of ministers, lecturers, actors, musicians, and their class, not only create utility, but the kind of utility they produce serves a very high order of human desires ; indeed, they are the most effective of all kinds of effort in producing the new wants which form the very basis for the production of material things. If the efforts of government officials are productive because they tend to increase the security of property, and thereby indirectly aid in the gratification of human wants, surely the efforts of the intellectual classes, which directly serve a much higher class of wants, are still more entitled to that designation.

Moreover, if the philosophers, scientists, and teachers were mere economic parasites on society, and did not increase enjoyable utility, the tendency of progress would be to eliminate them from social life. The fact is exactly the reverse. The more society becomes acquainted with the influences which promote the gratification of its desires, the more this class is increased. A definition according to which politicians, soldiers, policemen, and jailers are productive helpers to society, and scientists, philosophers, poets, teachers, ministers, actors, and musicians are unproductive burdens, should carry with it its own condemnation. To assume that mere parasitic influences increase as the knowledge of the means of gratifying human desires becomes more perfect, is a violation of the fundamental idea of production, and contrary to the whole principle of self-interest underlying all economic movement.

There are others who, while extending the definition of wealth to the products of those workers whose efforts do not increase the actual quantity of things, limit the term production to those efforts which are put forth for pay. Thus any effort is unproductive, however much utility it may produce, if the product is not offered for sale. "*A producer,*" says Perry,[1] "*is any person who gets any thing ready to sell and sells it.*" "One of my boys," he adds,[2] "is now playing the piano in the parlor. It is effort for him—irksome effort, but as he has no intention to ever sell his skill on that instrument it cannot be called productive effort. It is effort put forth for altogether other than commercial reasons.

---

[1] "Political Economy," p. 166. [2] *Ibid.*, p. 167.

The effort of his music-teacher, however, who comes here to give him lessons, is productive effort, inasmuch as it is put forth solely with reference to a sale."

According to this definition, whether a given class of effort is productive or unproductive does not depend upon whether it creates utility, but whether or not it is sold. Thus, if a person raises his own provisions, or makes his own clothes, he is not a producer ; and if an artist paints a picture, or a poet composes a song, or a musician plays Beethoven's Ninth Symphony for his own, or his friend's, instruction without pay, it would be unproductive. But if they charged for it, then it would be productive.

The estimation in which a doctrine should be held which teaches that those who supply their own wants, or gratuitously help to supply those of others, are non-producers, is obvious. The idea so prevalent in the public mind, and especially among the wage-workers, that middle-men are non-producers, and that interest, profits, and rent are robbery, is a legitimate part of the self-contradictory doctrine of non-productive useful effort.

If we accept the definition of wealth stated in the last section, we shall see that all efforts are properly productive which directly or indirectly tend to impart to matter any of the attributes, or surround it with any of the conditions, which make it available for human wants and desires. The desires which induce pay for the services of the actor or musician, minister, lecturer, scientist or statesman, are as purely economic as those which make it profitable for the farmer to raise wheat and wool, or the miller and manufacturer to prepare them for final use. It is fallacious to the last degree to assume that, because the results of any intellectual effort cannot be measured by inches or pounds, they are unproductive.

Much of the plausibility of this popular error arises from viewing the question in its most complex aspect, thus making the inter-relation of the various efforts more difficult to observe. If we examine the process of production in its simplest stages, we shall soon see that the doctrine of unproductive labor is an attempt to deal with an economic myth.

For example, let us take the production of flour. In the simplest stages of society we find that man plants and harvests the wheat, grinds it into flour, and eats it all himself. When the process is complete the wheat has filled the function for which it was produced, it has gratified human want. In this case it was produced and consumed by the same person. Clearly, there were no parasites here ; all that was produced belonged to him who produced it. Every thing that was necessary to obtain the bread in this case was a part of its production.

Let us suppose that man begins to produce flour for his neighbor, and the neighbor to produce shoes for him. By this slight degree of specialization of effort, the process becomes a little more involved. It is now necessary for him to take the flour to his neighbor, and for his neighbor to bring the shoes to him. This is clearly as much a part of the production as it was to take it from his own field to his hut. But suppose that another man will agree to devote his whole time to carrying the flour and allow the first man to devote his time exclusively to raising and grinding it ; the process will now become still more involved, while it will only cover the same article as before. If the new man receives a portion of the flour for his part of the process, will he be a parasite upon the man who raises and grinds it, or upon the distant consumer who receives it ? Certainly not ! The second man simply does a part of the work that the first man has previously done, and by this division of labor they are able to produce more. If we follow the process a little further, we find the man who carries the flour devising means to transport it in large quantities—instead of taking it in small quantities to suit the individual consumer ; but in order to make the flour available to individual consumers, he has to divide it into small quantities to suit their convenience. At this juncture a fourth man enters, and volunteers to receive it in bulk, and to deliver it to the consumers in convenient quantities to suit their wants. Here the process becomes still more complex, but nothing is added. The fourth man requires a part of the flour for what he does, but this is not an added burden to the man who grows the wheat, or to those who use it, because the only reason he does what the other man formerly did is because he can do it cheaper than the other could. Indeed, the only reason any one is permitted to enter the process at any stage is because it is seen that, by this means, each can obtain more of the aggregate utility for less effort and sacrifice.

If we follow the process until a million men are added, the same will be true in every stage. If, at any time, the added man results in lessening the relative utility which accrues to any of the existing producers, they will return to the previous method of production and do without him. Thus the wholesaler, the drummer, the retailer, the shipper, the banker, or broker, all fill a useful function in the process of producing the flour. Until they can do this no one will employ them ; and just as soon as they cease to do it every one is interested in eliminating them.

Again, as the process increases in complexity, new elements arise. As wealth is produced on a larger scale it is necessarily held in large quantities at the factories, and at the various wholesale and retail depots on its way to the consumer. With this increased accumulation of commodities the risks of loss, by fire and other causes, necessarily increase. Hence, in order to secure their safe delivery to the consumer (without which the whole process would be void), it is necessary to have policemen to guard them from thieves and incendiaries—another differentiation, which involves legislators, courts of justice, lawyers, etc. At last, in order to further protect the aggregate community against dangers of molestation by foreign countries, and for the protection of trade between countries (at least, until the moral quality of the race is more highly developed), an army and navy are necessary—the administration of which makes a general government indispensable.

Thus we see that not only are ministers, singers, actors, etc., productive factors in the community, but the policemen, lawyers, doctors, judges, soldiers, sailors, and statesmen are also producers. In other words, every thing that promotes the raising of wheat in Dakota, or its safe delivery as flour into the pantry of the consumer, or in any way aids in compassing the satisfaction of any other human want—physical, mental, moral, political, esthetic, or religious,—is properly production.

SECTION III.—*The Necessary Factors in Production and Their Relative Economic Efficiency.*

The factors which participate in the production of wealth may be briefly stated as Land, Labor, and Natural Forces. By the first is meant the earth's surface ; the second, human energy ;

and the third, cosmic forces—including all natural agencies outside of man and land. Land may be regarded as representing passive material, and the other two as the active forces which operate upon it in producing wealth.

Without the presence of all these factors wealth cannot be obtained. They are equally essential to the simplest and to the most complex methods of production. Land being the passive element, the only factors which actively participate in production are the human and the natural forces. It may be remarked, however, that there are some natural forces—such as the light and heat of the sun, gravitation, atmospheric air, etc.—that are gratuitous, being ever present and ever active, even under the simplest conditions of land-labor. But there are certain other natural forces—such as steam, electricity, coal, wood, iron, etc.—which, as factors in production, are not gratuitous. For instance, steam can only be made to do service in production when it is confined in a boiler and applied to an engine ; and this makes the use of coal, iron, and other materials necessary. This, in turn, cannot be accomplished without a considerable amount of skill and energy having been previously devoted to the construction of engine, boilers, etc. The wealth thus employed is distinguished from that which is used for the direct gratification of human wants, and is called capital.

This brings us to another economic term which has been subjected to a great variety of definitions. Capital is generally used to express the means employed in production, but because man's faculties are constantly employed in the production of wealth, some writers have included them in the term capital. Hence we frequently hear such expressions as : "The laborer's skill is his capital." [1] It would be difficult to conceive of a more misleading

---

[1] "Capital may be said to be any thing which a man can trade with or which he can turn to the purposes of profit, or which helps him to gain an income—any property or quality he possesses which enables him to increase his wealth. . . . Thus the tools of an artisan, together with his skill and industry, form his capital ; the education and books and skill of a physician and lawyer are their capital."—Macleod's "Elements of Political Economy," p. 70. "Personal wealth consists of those human energies, faculties, and habits, physical, mental, and moral. . . . Almost all personal wealth is or may be personal capital."—Marshall's "Economics of Industry," pp. 6 and 20. See also "Wealth of Nations," Book II., chap. i.

expression. Instead of giving any definite meaning to the term capital, it deprives it of all special significance and makes capital and labor synonymous, hence rendering the discussion of their relation logically impossible.

It is equally misleading to speak of capital as "stored up labor" —a mode of speech commonly indulged in. Labor is human energy, and, as we have elsewhere shown,[1] can never be stored up in any thing but a human being, and only to a very limited extent there. It is because the laborer cannot store his labor—because he can never sell more than one day's service in a day ; and because, if he does not sell to-day's labor to-day, it is lost forever, that enforced idleness has such terrors for him. Nor can he store up his labor in external objects. When he devotes his energies to producing an article he does not *impart* his labor *to* it, but he *expends* his labor *upon* it, and as human force it is gone forever. Wealth and capital in every form and under all conditions are something outside of and subservient to man, but can never be a part of him.

There are two states in which wealth may exist : that of being produced, and that of being consumed. It can also fill two functions : that of serving human wants, and that of aiding in production. Hence wealth may be properly divided into two classes : consumable wealth, and productive wealth. It is the latter kind only which can properly be called capital.

It is held by some that, as land is a means of producing wealth, it is capital.[2] There is a certain amount of plausibility in this ; but it should be remembered that land does not necessarily possess any of the qualities of either enjoyable or productive wealth. It is only when labor, or capital and labor, are devoted to it that it can either serve human wants or assist in producing consumable commodities. It is true that, when land has by this means become wealth, it may also become the means of procuring more wealth, and in that sense fill the function of capital.

It may be asked, however, if all other wealth becomes capital

---

[1] "Wealth and Progress," pp. 17, 18.

[2] "By much the largest part of all salable land is nothing more nor less than capital. Capital is some product reserved as a means of further production ; and valuable land is always a product of labor and previous capital and is generally reserved for use in future production and so is capital under the definition."— Perry's " Political Economy," p. 283.

by virtue of aiding in production, why is not all productive land capital for the same reason? Strictly speaking, so far as land directly serves human wants, it is consumable wealth, and so far as it aids in production, it is instrumental wealth, or capital. By making this technical distinction and treating certain kinds of land as capital we should probably add to the confusion, rather than to the clearness, of economic discussion.

Therefore,—while admitting that it might be technically correct to regard land, under certain conditions, as capital, and the returns from it as profits,—for the sake of avoiding any unnecessary confusion, I shall follow the example of Mill [1] and use the term capital as expressing all instrumental wealth, outside of land, the returns from which are interest and profit ; and all wealth invested in and inseparable from land will be regarded as land, and the returns from it as rent.

There is an additional advantage in this use of the term capital in the fact that it is the only wealth, distinct from land, that can be employed in harnessing the reluctant natural forces, such as steam, electricity, etc., to the production of wealth. With this use of the term capital, it will be strictly correct to treat the use of reluctant natural forces in production as synonymous with capital, because they never participate in production except by the use of capital. And, as the substitution of natural for human forces in the productive process is the essential wealth-cheapening feature in economic progress, we shall continue to regard the factors in production as Land, Labor, and Natural Forces (capital).

Which of these three factors then is the most effective in producing wealth ?—which of them is capable of contributing the greatest amount of productive force at the least cost ? The hand is the slowest, and, judged by its results, the most expensive instrument that can be used in the production of wealth. Hence we find that, other things being equal, machine-made products are always cheaper than hand-made products, and the difference in their cost is proportionate to the relative difference in which human and natural forces (capital) participated in their production. How, or upon what principle then, natural forces can be made to save human labor in producing the world's wealth is the question next to be considered.

---

[1] " Principles of Political Economy," vol. i., p. 526.

SECTION IV.—*The Principles upon Which Natural Forces Save Human Labor in Production.*

We have seen that human effort is devoted to production upon the principle of obtaining the maximum enjoyable result for the minimum painful effort. Indeed upon no other principle can the net amount of happiness—*i. e.*, the proportion of pleasure to pain in human experience, be permanently increased. While most civilized people would prefer that the condition of the laborer should be easy and pleasant, and his wages high, very few are willing to give a fraction more for their commodities in order to make such things possible.

That which undersells always supplants that which is undersold, and just as fast as any product can be undersold will the methods used in its production be driven out of use. Consequently the only basis upon which natural forces can supersede human labor as factors in production is that they produce wealth more cheaply.[1] In other words, *the use of capital and improved methods in the production of wealth is ultimately determined by its capacity to yield increasing returns.* This brings us to the question of what makes increasing returns possible.

The fact that wealth can be produced more cheaply by natural forces than by hand labor is recognized by all classes of economic writers. But why the use of natural forces in production is feasible at one time and place and not at another—upon what principle hand labor as a productive force was cheaper than machinery in the ninth century, and machinery became cheaper than hand labor in the nineteenth century, and why machinery will yield increasing returns in America and Europe to-day,

---

[1] By cheapness and dearness is not meant merely the amount of money that is given for a commodity. An article may be and often is cheaper at one time and place at twenty cents than at five cents at another. Shoes, for example, would be very much dearer at fifty cents a pair in China than at a dollar a pair in America. For the simple reason that in order to obtain a pair of shoes at fifty cents the laborer in China would have to give more than a whole week's labor, while the laborer in America would purchase a pair at a dollar with less than one day's work. That is to say, he could give twice as much money for the shoes and still obtain them for less than one sixth of the labor the Chinaman could. Thus a thing is really cheap or dear, not according as it will exchange for a large or small quantity of money, but solely according to the ratio in which it will directly and indirectly exchange for a given quantity of labor.

while it fails to do so in Asia and Africa, the current doctrines of political economy fail to explain. Yet this is one of the most important problems which it is the special function of economic science to solve. To make natural forces cheaper than human labor, as a means of production, is to make wealth cheaper than poverty, and civilization cheaper than barbarism. Therefore, to explain how increasing returns, and hence the successful use of machinery, can be made possible, is primarily to solve the problem of economic production. Because reluctant, natural forces only aid in producing wealth when they are harnessed to the process by capital, it is assumed that capital is the cause of the successful use of improved methods of production. And because capital is wealth which might have been used for personal gratification, instead of being devoted to production, it is concluded that it is the result of painful abstinence.

Adam Smith was never tired of singing the praises of parsimony. Indeed, with him, to save wealth was one of the highest virtues ; while to consume it, except in the meagerest manner, was a social vice. He even went so far as to declare[1] that prosperous manufacturing villages had become "idle and poor in consequence of a great lord's having taken up his residence in their neighborhood," because of his extravagant consumption. There is probably no one thing that the great Scotchman said which has been more generally accepted than that parsimonious abstinence increases prosperity, and liberal consumption leads to idleness and poverty.

Mill emphasized and elaborated this idea even more than did Dr. Smith. He regarded capital as the alpha and omega of industrial employment, and abstinence from consumption as the source of capital, and hence the initial cause of prosperity.[2] This notion is still held by the most modern writers in England and this country. "Capital," says Prof. Walker, "arises solely out of saving. It stands for self-denial and abstinence." It is not difficult to see how this view, which makes capital the immediate,

---

[1] See "Wealth of Nations," Book II., ch. iii.

[2] "While on the one hand industry is limited by capital" so "on the other hand every increase of capital gives or is capable of giving additional employment to industry, and this without assignable limit."—Mill's "Principles of Political Economy," vol. i., p. 98.

and sacrifice and self-denial the initial, cause of prosperity, has given rise to the idea that industrial progress is mainly due to the social martyrdom of the capitalist class, to whom the laborers are under eternal obligation.

This is truly a most convenient and flattering estimate for the successful classes, especially when they are called upon to face the less fortunate masses in time of adversity. The natural outcome of this is the general disposition to repress, rather than to encourage, any movement towards multiplying the wants and desires,—hence, increasing the consumption of wealth among the mass of the people, and "living simply as our fathers did," is commonly held up as the evidence of superior character.

A doctrine which makes parsimonious simplicity of life a social virtue, and regards capital as the cause of industrial progress, is an economic inversion no less inimical to the development of the true principles of social economics than is the socialistic doctrine that regards the laborer as the sole producer of wealth and the capitalist as an economic robber.

A very little examination of the subject will show that, while the use of capital is indispensable to, it is not the cause of, the employment of wealth-cheapening methods in production. On the contrary, capital in its very nature can never be any thing but an economic instrument, the successful use of which has been made possible by previously existing conditions. It is one of the characteristic features of economic production that the superiority of the natural over human forces consists in their capacity to produce a much larger quantity at the same cost, and not in their capacity to produce a small quantity at a less cost. Therefore, if only the traditional quantity of the produce can be utilized (consumed), the new method cannot be successfully employed because it cannot produce that small quantity any cheaper than it can be obtained by existing methods ; and hence fails to yield increasing returns. The first condition, then, necessary to the successful use of natural forces is a sufficiently enlarged market to utilize the increased product resulting from the improved methods.

No amount of increase in the use of capital, then, can cheapen wealth and add to the well-being of the community unless it is accompanied by a larger demand for commodities—an increased

consumption of wealth by the people. Thus, instead of parsimony, on the part of the great body of consumers, promoting the
use of capital in production and the growth of industrial prosperity in the community, it tends to prevent it.

Nor is the claim that capital is created by self-sacrifice any
more correct. It is true that capital consists of wealth which
might have been consumed by its owner for personal gratification.
Capital may be, and doubtless is sometimes, the result of painful
abstinence, but the painful abstinence is always exercised upon
the same principle, and from the same motive, that painful effort
is exerted—namely, that a still more painful desire may be gratified ; in other words, that a greater amount of pleasurable gratification may ultimately be derived from the investment of wealth
in productive enterprise than would be obtained from its immediate consumption. It is therefore no more correct to say that
capital is the result of abstinence than it is to call labor philanthropy. Abstinence—which represents painful self-denial—is
undertaken for the identical reason that labor—painful effort—is
expended. The object of both is to obtain more in gratification
than they give in sacrifice. But even this only applies to capital
in its most primitive stages. It is more than probable that not
one per cent. of the world's present capital is the result of any
such personal abstinence.

While original investments are savings and perhaps the result of
some self-denial, they are always undertaken in the belief that subsequent capital will be the automatic product of the first, and will come
without any personal self-denial. It is not true, then, in any real
sense, to say that capital is created by self-sacrifice, as, even in
its abstinence stage, it is simply the result of enduring a small
amount of pain in order to obtain a large amount of pleasure,
which is the purest self-interest and has no element of real sacrifice in it.

Moreover, as the capital-creating abstinence is always based
upon the hope of future gains, it will only be undertaken in proportion to the probability of its successful investment ; and its
successful investment in production depends upon the possibility
of its yielding increasing returns ; this in turn depends upon the
extent of the market, or the increased consuming capacity of the
community. Thus it is that neither the creation nor the success-

6

ful use of capital is promoted by parsimonious social simplicity, but, on the contrary, they both primarily depend upon advancing social complexity. Capital is the effect, rather than the cause, of social progress, and instead of the masses being indebted to the employing class for their prosperity, it is the social progress of the community which has made the existence and success of the capitalist possible.

It is a universal fact in history that where the social life is the simplest, the wants the fewest, and the consumption of wealth *per capita* the smallest, the use of capital in production is the least.

Thus the real reason why there are practically no capitalists among the Esquimaux and Patagonians—and very few in India and China—is because there is no economic use for them ; and there is no use for them because, as a factor in production, human labor is cheaper there than natural forces. The wants, social habits, and demands of the masses, are too simple in those countries to furnish a market for a sufficiently increased quantity of wealth to make increasing returns possible, and the use of capital profitable.

SECTION V.—*Social Consumption the Basis of Economic Production.*

We are now in a position to affirm the seemingly paradoxical propositions : that consumption is the immediate cause of, and regulating influence in, production ; that, not only the quantity and quality of wealth produced, but also the methods employed, the cost of its production, and consequently its price to the consumer, are finally determined by consumption ; and that wealth becomes cheap as man becomes dear.

Nor is the reason difficult to understand, if we constantly view man and his wants as the source and end of economic movement. When we fully recognize that the progress of society consists in the differentiation of man's social relations, and that every differentiation in the social polity is simply an effort to better adapt his social environment to the more complete gratification of his wants, much of the difficulty surrounding the subject of economic production has been overcome. This being true, it follows that the amount and direction of man's effort is finally governed by his wants. Therefore the quantity and quality of wealth permanently produced at any given time under normal conditions will ultimately be determined by the effectual desires and wants of the community.

As elsewhere explained,[1] the difference between effectual and ineffectual desires is the difference in their power to induce the necessary effort for their gratification. Thus, desires become economically effectual just in proportion as they grow in intensity and their non-gratification inflicts more pain than is involved in the labor necessary to satisfy them. This explains why we see in some individuals, classes, and countries, a willingness to put forth great effort, and take great risk, in order to obtain things which others, while they might gladly receive, would do practically nothing to obtain.

How, it may be asked, is this relation between desire and effort, consumption and production, to be ascertained? How, for instance, do the producers know when the desires—or wants—of the consumers have reached the economic—or effectual—degree of intensity? The answer is : by the willingness of the consumer to give the necessary effort, or its equivalent, to procure the satisfaction of his wants.

For the same reason that economic wants, or demands, can only be recognized by the willingness to exert the necessary amount of effort for their gratification, to-morrow's effectual demands can only be estimated by the knowledge of to-day's consumption. If more of a given kind of wealth is wanted to-day than was produced, and this want is accompanied by a willingness to give the necessary effort, or its equivalent, to produce it, a greater quantity of the commodity will be produced to-morrow. And conversely, if more of a particular commodity is produced to-day than is effectually demanded, it will not all be consumed ; and in proportion as yesterday's production exceeds to-day's consumption, will to-morrow's production be limited. Although desire is the initial cause of production, its effective intensity and extent are economically measured by and registered in actual consumption. Consumption being the only economic measure of want, it is the real basis and final regulator of production. Simple as this truth is, it is far from being generally understood ; indeed, the reverse view is commonly held. Because wealth

---

[1] Part I., ch. iii., p. 23.

cannot be consumed until it is produced, it is contended that consumption must be determined by production. It is of course true that we cannot consume unless we produce, but it does not follow, on that account, that production sustains the causal relation to consumption. Although we must produce before we consume, we do not consume because we produce; but we always produce because we consume, or that we may consume. Chronologically, production precedes consumption, but economically consumption precedes production and is the cause of it.

If bows and arrows, tomahawks, spinning-wheels, or hand-looms were extensively manufactured in this country to-day, that would not cause them to come into general use again, nor would it have the slightest influence in that direction. Whenever a commodity is produced in advance of the effectual desire for it, loss, and perhaps bankruptcy, is the result. Were this otherwise, industrial depressions would be impossible, because an accumulation of products, or what is called over-production, could not occur. The mere fact of the goods being produced would, in that case, be a sufficient cause to create an effectual demand for them, and this, everybody knows, is not the case.

In order fully to understand the economic influence of consumption upon production, it is necessary to consider the subject in its qualitative as well as its quantitative aspect. The consumption, or effectual demand, is determined, as we have seen, by the established wants of the community. These wants are of two kinds—*physical* and *social.* The former are mainly inherent, and comprise those wants which relate to physical ·sustenance, such as food, clothing, and shelter. Social wants are mainly acquired, and comprise the tastes and desires that arise from the quickening influences of social intercourse ; these are luxuries at first, but by frequent repetition finally become necessities of social life. These two classes of wants have distinctive characteristics, are increased by different influences, and have an entirely different effect upon production.

Physical wants alone, of which food comprises the major part, cannot be increased in each individual to any considerable extent. The stomach of the savage will consume as much as that of civilized man ; hence the effectual demand, through this class of wants, can only increase in about the same ratio as the population. Moreover, these wants are mainly supplied by agricultural products which involve isolating and non-socializing occupations.

There are many reasons why an increase of consumption from the mere increase of population would not promote the use of improved methods of production. It is characteristic of the use of improved methods that they are wealth-cheapening only in proportion as they are labor-saving. Unless the discharged laborers can be re-employed, idleness—the worst of social evils—will be increased. Therefore labor-discharging improvements can only be economically successful when they are accompanied by new employment-creating conditions, which an increase of the simple physical wants can never supply.

It will readily be observed that, when an enlarged demand for commodities is entirely due to the increase of population, every discharged laborer involves a corresponding diminution of the market, thereby destroying the wealth-cheapening effect of the new methods. Consequently, all that is gained by the labor-saving process is lost by the increased idleness and contracted consumption. Thus it is that natural forces cannot be profitably employed in production except when the market for their products increases faster than the population, *i.e.*, increases *per capita* of the population.

Social wants are essentially different in all their characteristics. They are the result of social, rather than cosmic, influences. They can be increased indefinitely in each individual, and can consequently be multiplied much faster than the population. They also furnish the demand for distinctively manufactured products, and so necessitate concentrated and socializing occupations.

These features tend to promote the use of natural forces in several ways. Every addition to the number of social wants increases the quantity, and often the variety, of commodities each individual consumes. This necessarily increases the demand for products faster than the number of laborers, and with the growth of this demand the difficulty of supplying it is increased in two ways. (1) Just as the number of wants in each individual increases, the possibility of supplying them by hand-labor diminishes. (2) In proportion as the consumption of wealth by the laborer increases, the cost of his living, and consequently that of his labor, is correspondingly raised and the price of the product advanced. Since an attempt to supply the increased social wants by existing methods involves a corresponding increase of irksome labor, it neutralizes the advantage derived from the satisfaction of the new desires.   Obviously, in this case, the new wants will be abandoned unless they can be supplied cheaper, *i.e.*, with less labor, and this can only be accomplished by making natural forces do a portion of the work.

When this point is reached all the conditions for utilizing improved methods are present.   The new wants not only enlarge the established demand, but they create a market for a greater variety of products, the manufacture of which creates employment for the laborers who have been discharged by the improved methods.

Thus it is that, when wants multiply more rapidly than laborers increase in number, labor-saving methods do not create enforced idleness, as in the case of purely physical wants, because the same influences which compel them to discharge laborers in one industry create new employments for them in another.   By this means the cost of producing each article is diminished and the price to the consumer is thereby lowered, so that, when the demand for commodities is increased by the multiplication of social wants, it not only makes the use of improved methods *necessary*, but it also introduces new employment-creating conditions which make them economically *possible*.   Manifestly, therefore, natural forces become cheaper than human labor, only when the demand for commodities is enlarged by an increase in the *social*, rather than in the *physical*, wants of the people.

It is not enough, however, that this increase of social wants take place in a small class ; to be effective it must be general. Nature is very democratic—she will not work cheaply for the few. Steam and electricity can only be harnessed to production when their services are required to satisfy the numerous social wants, per capita, of large numbers of people ; consequently, the social consumption of the most opulent aristocracy is as impotent to furnish profitable employment for steam-driven machinery as is the meagre fare of a servile peasantry.   Nor is the reason for this difficult to understand if we remember that capital can only be economically employed when it is cheaper than labor as a productive force. There are but two ways in which this can be brought about—either by reducing the cost of employing capital or by increasing the cost of employing labor. The cost of using capital can only be diminished by increasing the market for its products, in order that it may produce on a large scale. The cost of using labor can only be increased by enlarging the consumption and raising the wages of the laborer. Neither of these conditions can be furnished by an increase in the consumption of a small non-laboring class. An increase in the wants of such a class, though relatively very great, could not furnish a sufficiently extensive market to sustain the production of any commodity by factory methods ; and it could exercise no influence in advancing wages, because the increased consumption does not enter into the life, and therefore affect the price, of the laborer. The chief economy in the use of capital being in the extent of its ability to save labor, the lower the wages the smaller the chances of its success—because the cheaper the man the less there is to be gained by saving his labor ;—consequently the necessarily limited market that the wants of a small class could supply would not guarantee a sufficient prospect of increasing returns, to warrant the investment of capital required for the adoption of steam-driven machinery.

An increase in the social wants, and consequent consumption of wealth by the laboring classes, would furnish both of the essential conditions referred to. (1) Because they are so numerous that a slight increase in their consumption, per capita, would be an immense addition to the market, and at once warrant the production of commodities on an increasingly large scale. (2) Because the enlarged market, being due to the increased consumption by the laborers, raises the price of their labor, and consequently that of the commodities they produce—thereby making the use of labor-saving methods indispensable in order to keep these commodities salable. Every fall in prices from such causes extends the market still further, by putting the products within the reach of a larger class of consumers. Therefore, the truly civilizing consumption is that which results from the increased social wants of the masses ; for, by simultaneously

increasing wages and reducing prices, it both raises man to
the appropriation of wealth, and places wealth within the reach
of man.

A clear understanding of this principle will enable us to
explain why the upper classes in ancient civilizations, with all
their pomp, ostentation and almost profligate consumption of
wealth, could not employ machinery ; why men were cheaper
than machinery in the ninth century, as factors in production ;
and why machinery is so much cheaper than men in the nineteenth.
We find to-day, the world over, that the use of steam-driven
machinery is the most general, wealth is the most abundant, and
social development and political freedom the most advanced,
where the *social wants* of the masses are the most numerous and
the general rate of wages is the highest.

In the light of this law we are also able to comprehend why, in
the evolution of society, such great advances were made in philosophy and the fine arts before any of the simpler, though
equally important, mechanical contrivances—*i.e.*, the use of
steam, electricity, etc.—were discovered. We can understand,
for instance, why men could learn the courses of the stars and
the revolutions of the planets before they knew how to make
a good wagon-wheel ; why they could build a Chinese wall, or
an Egyptian pyramid, before they could make a common plough ;
why, they could construct the Parthenon and the Colosseum
before they knew enough to build a saw-mill, use movable types,
or invent sewing-machines.

The fact that the ancients excelled in sculpture, painting,
music, etc., while we are devoted to producing common conveniences and the decencies of every-day life, is frequently alluded
to as evidence that ancient civilizations were superior to our own.
This is a great mistake, the character of a civilization is not indicated by the individual accomplishment of a few, but by the
social condition of the great mass of the people. The error of
considering the earlier civilizations as superior to the present is
mainly due to the failure to recognize the difference in the
economic and social influences which determine the success of
various discoveries, inventions, or attainments.

These achievements may be divided into two classes. One includes all those which can be accomplished by hand labor, and

whose utility does not consist in their capacity to cheapen wealth, or their success depend upon the extent of appreciation among the common people. The other embraces those acquisitions whose utility consists in their ability to economize labor, and whose success depends upon the extent to which their results are consumed by the masses. For example, the discoveries of Euclid and Archimedes in mathematics ; those of Hipparchus, Al Batain, Copernicus, Kepler, Galileo, and Newton in astronomy ; the accomplishments of Phidias, Scopas, Niccolo, and Ghiberti in sculpture ; those of Leonardo da Vinci, Michael Angelo, and Raphael in painting ; and in poetry, oratory, and the drama, the efforts of Homer, Cicero, and Shakespeare, were almost exclusively the result of the individual genius producing them. The success or failure of their undertakings did not depend, in any appreciable degree, upon the material and social condition of the common people ; all they required in that direction was the patronage of a king, a pope, or a very limited aristocracy.

With the mechanical contrivances of the eighteenth and nineteenth centuries, which have revolutionized the social condition of the civilized world, this has not been the case. The utility of movable types, of the printing-press, the spinning-jenny and the power-loom, the railroad, the telegraph, and the thousand other modern labor-saving contrivances, has consisted in the extent of their capacity to save human labor in its efforts to procure the necessities and conveniences of social life ; and the success of these contrivances has entirely depended upon the extent to which their results have been demanded by the masses. If books had not been more generally read in the sixteenth, seventeenth, and eighteenth centuries than in the sixth, seventh, and eighth, Gutenberg's invention of the art of printing, in 1440, would have been as useless as it was when discovered in China two thousand years before. Upon the same principle that to set up and print a single copy of the " Wealth of Nations " to-day would cost $1,000 (while if fifty thousand were printed they could be sold at $1.00 each), the small number of books that were then demanded could be copied cheaper by hand than they could have been printed ; but when the masses began to use books, printing became cheaper than copying.

So long as the consumption of cotton and woollen cloth, silks, laces, and carpets, and the multitude of various commodities produced from wood, tin, iron, brass, silver, gold, etc., was confined to the aristocracy, the small quantity required could be produced by hand-labor cheaper than by steam-power ; but when the millions began to use these things, the factory became cheaper than hand labor.

If travel and transportation were limited to the upper classes, the discoveries of Stephenson and Fulton would be as useless to mankind as a machine to send water down hill. If none but millionaires patronized the steam-cars in New York City, it would cost more to ride on the elevated railroad than in a private carriage ; but now that five hundred thousand people use it daily, every one can ride on it for a little over half a cent a mile.

This is why an emperor of China could build a thirteen-hundred-mile wall, while he could not ride on a railroad. Rome could build the aqueducts, but she could not carry a newspaper three thousand miles for a cent. Euclid could develop the science of geometry, and Michael Angelo could paint the " Last Judgment," but they could not make steel pens or parlor matches. Copernicus and Kepler could discover the course of the planets, and Newton the law of gravitation, but they could not make a type-writer, or publish a daily paper for one cent a copy.

Had the ruling classes used their power as much to develop the social wants and character of the masses as they did to repress them, so that the printing-press and factory would have preceded the Pyramids and the Colosseum, those monuments of human slavery could never have been erected ; and the increased social susceptibility of the common people to the elevating influences of art, poetry, learning, and philosophy, might, and probably would, have saved those, so-called, civilizations from premature decay, and enabled the human race to avoid that historic nightmare, the " Dark Ages," by sustaining a continuous, progressive civilization.

The more thoroughly we investigate the history of the industrial development of society, the more completely is the truth of the conclusions arrived at in the preceding pages of this chapter established. These may be briefly summarized as follows :

(1) That all wealth is produced for the gratification of human wants.

(2) That the active factors in production are, human forces

and natural forces ; the former being represented by labor, and the latter by capital.

(3) That the cost of production, and consequently the price of commodities, diminishes in proportion as natural forces preponderate over human forces in the process of production.

(4) That labor-saving appliances can only be successfully employed in production when they yield increasing returns to the capital invested.

(5) That capital will only yield increasing returns when it can be employed cheaper than labor.

(6) That labor-saving appliances can only become cheaper than hand labor when they can produce in large quantities.   -

(7) That the possibility of producing on a large scale depends entirely upon the market being extended more rapidly than laborers increase in number—*i.e.*, an increase in the consumption of wealth, per capita, of the population.

(8) That such an extension of the market can only result from an increase in the social wants of the masses, which under modern conditions is synonymous with a rise in the general rate of wages.

It may therefore be laid down, as a universal principle in social economics, that the labor-saving and wealth-cheapening capacity of natural forces can only be utilized as the social consumption of the laboring classes is increased.   In other words, *things* can be cheapened only as *man* becomes dear ; and to increase the influences which develop the social wants and raise the wages of the laborer is to make wealth cheaper than poverty, and civilization cheaper than barbarism.

CHAPTER II.

ECONOMIC VALUE.

SECTION I.—*Definition of Value.*

IT is doubtful if there is a term in the vocabulary of economics about which there is such a lack of clear understanding as the word value. In popular phrase it has often a very elastic signification. It is sometimes used to indicate that which we give for things ; and it is quite frequently employed without any relation to exchange—as if it represented some inherent quality residing in the thing itself without regard to its relation to other things. For instance, we often hear such expressions as the value of pure air ; the value of sunlight ; the value of genius, of virtue, of religion, of esthetics, of culture, etc. To give the word such a broad meaning is to deprive it of all specific significance as a scientific term.

Although the necessity of avoiding this loose metamorphical use of the word has been generally recognized by leading economists, they have continued to employ it with such a variety of import as to leave its real meaning scarcely less obscure.

In almost every treatise on this subject we find such expressions as : natural value ; market value ; use value ; exchange value, etc. Very frequently the effect of this indefinite use of the word is to confound value with wealth. Much of this confusion has its rise in that often quoted statement of Adam Smith in which he says : " The word value, it is to be observed, has two different meanings, and sometimes expresses the utility of some particular object, and sometimes the power of purchasing other goods which the possession of that object conveys. The one may be called *value in use*, and the other, *value in exchange*. The things which have the greatest value in use frequently have little or no value in exchange ; and, on the contrary, those which have the greatest value in exchange have frequently little or no value in use." [1] It would be difficult to find a statement that is more misleading, or one which has been more generally accepted than this. To use the word value to " express the utility of a particular object " is entirely incorrect.

Dr. Smith, or his disciples, would probably tell us that this is value in use. Such an expression is a misnomer. A thing may be important, or even indispensable in use—as in the case of the air and the sun,—but it cannot possibly be *valuable* in use. What is really referred to here is utility and not value. The difference between utility and value is fundamental : the former is the qual-ity of a thing ; while the latter is the relation, or proportion, between things. ' Such a view confounds the ratio of exchange with the cause of the exchange, and is fatal to any clear reason-ing on the subject.

There is no scientific reason for using the word value to express utility under any circumstances ; or for accompanying it with qualifying expressions to indicate the *kind* of value. There are no *kinds* of value. The term should never be used to express qualities, but only the exchange relation of quantities. With this definition both terms assume a distinctive meaning and one which their use will always convey without qualification. Utility then, in economic science, always means the quality of a thing which makes it desirable, and for which something will be voluntarily given in exchange ; and value simply expresses the ratio in which the things are exchanged. [2]

In order to avoid any misuse of the term value, as here defined, it should ever be remembered that it is purely an economic phrase, and relates exclusively to social phenomena. There can no more

---

[1] " Wealth of Nations," Book I., ch. iv., p. 21.

[2] Value in exchange expresses nothing but a ratio, and the term should not be used in any other sense. To speak simply of the value of an ounce of gold is as absurd as to speak of a ratio of the number seventeen. What is the ratio of the number seventeen ? The question admits of no answer, for there must be another num-ber named in order to make a ratio ; and the ratio will differ according to the number suggested. What is the value of iron compared with that of gold ? is an intelligible question. The answer consists in stating the ratio of the quantities exchanged."—Stanley Jevons' " Theory of Political Economy," p. 84.

be value without society than there can be ratio with a single thing; the very idea implies a contradiction in terms. Value not only expresses the ratio of exchange but the ratio of *economic* exchange. An economic exchange must be mutually advantageous; hence it must be an equitable exchange in which each gives an equivalent for what he gets. Exchanges in which one gains only by another's loss are highly uneconomic, inequitable, and socially injurious, and tend to extinguish themselves by the injury which they inflict. Economic value is indicated only by exchange relations which tend to perpetuate themselves by promoting general industrial and social well-being. I shall define value, therefore, as the ratio in which different quantities of the various kinds of wealth and service will exchange as economic equivalents.

In order that any object, or service, may have value according to this definition, it must be capable of being exchanged, and of satisfying the motives for exchange. To do this three conditions are necessary. (1) It must have utility; it must have the capacity to serve some human purpose, or no one would care to possess it. (2) Its utility must depend upon human effort; if it were gratuitously supplied by nature, all could have it free, and however useful or desirable an object may be no one will give any thing in exchange for it if they can obtain it for nothing. (3) It must be transferable; no matter how useful an article may be, or how difficult to obtain, or how much labor may be devoted to its production, unless it can be transferred it is incapable of being exchanged, and no one will give any thing for that which they can never possess. When these conditions are all present at once, profitable exchange, and therefore economic value, becomes possible.

Section II.—*The Relation of Value and Price.*

John Stuart Mill considers that a clear understanding of economic principles requires that a discrimination be made between value and price. The former he defines as the ratio in which commodities will exchange for one another; the latter, that in which they will exchange for money.[1] In order to maintain this distinction he adds to the already confusingly numerous kinds of value, the phrase, "money-value," which has been accepted by all

---

[1] "Principles of Political Economy," vol. i., p. 538.

leading writers since his time.' This expression, however, like Adam Smith's "value-in-use," and Ricardo's "natural-value," tends to befog rather than to clarify the subject.

A little consideration will show that there is no more scientific necessity for saying money-value than there is for saying wheat-value, potato value, cloth-value, or mutton-value. If the word price were used in these cases it would convey precisely the same meaning. Price, like value, expresses the ratio of exchange and nothing else. Whether the exchange is commodities for commodities, services for services, services for commodities, commodities for money, or money for labor, makes no real difference. The proportion in which either exchanges for the other indicates the value of each ; and equally so is the price of a thing indicated by that which is given for it. Indeed, we have the explicit authority of Mill himself for saying that "when goods are exchanged for money they are the price of the money, just as much as the money is the price of the goods."'

Obviously, then, the distinction between value and price is as unnecessary as the use of exchange-value and natural-value is misleading. Even admitting that price expresses only the ratio in which things or services exchange for money, since all exchanges are now constructed in terms of money, price and value are economically equivalent terms.

The distinction between price and wages, however, is somewhat different. Popular phrase has always expressed the value of commodities and services in different terms ; value or price having been used in the case of commodities and wages in the case of labor. Although there may be no real technical necessity for making this discrimination, its adoption does not lessen the clearness of statement, and its abolition would tend to confuse, rather than to clarify, the mind of the student. If it could be shown that, in the strictest sense, price, value, and wages all have the same meaning, it would certainly be a matter of doubtful expediency to attempt to employ them as interchangeable terms. For while it might not be especially inconvenient to call wages the value, or price, of labor, it would be decidedly novel, and not

---

[1] " I have used the word price as signifying the money-value of goods."— Walker's "Political Economy," p. 135.

[2] " Principles of Political Economy," Vol. II., Book III., ch. viii., sec. 2.

a little misleading, to speak of the wages of potatoes, pumpkins, or pine-apples.

The unnecessary distinction between value and price has not been limited to mere nomenclature, but it has been carried to the actual sphere of economic movement.

The accepted expounders of political economy emphatically deny the possibility of a general rise or fall of *values*, declaring it to be " a contradiction in terms." Then, almost in the next breath, they insist that a general rise or fall of prices can, and frequently does, take place.[1] If every thing cannot rise or fall in *value* simultaneously, how can the *price* of every thing do so? The usual reply, that *price* is simply the ratio in which things will exchange for money, is wholly inadequate to explain this difference. For instance, if the proportion in which commodities will exchange for money were increased, that would, of course, be a fall in the price of the commodities ; but it would also be, as Mill has clearly shown,[2] a rise in the price of money to exactly the same extent. .On the other hand, if the ratio in which money and other commodities would exchange for wheat were increased, that would be a rise in the value of wheat and a fall in the value of money and all other commodities. Manifestly, the rise of *value* in the one case would be just as general as was the rise of *price* in the other case. It is just as impossible to have a rise in *price* without a relative fall in the price of some one or more of the factors to the exchange, as it is to have a rise of value in one or more commodities without a corresponding fall in some others. There are absolutely no conditions, actual or conceivable, in which a variation of prices is possible, which would not make a similar variation of values equally so. The fact that the word *price* relates to the ratio in which commodities exchange for money is of no more importance, either in theory or practice, than if it referred to the ratio in which money and other products exchanged for

---

[1] " Though there is no such thing as a general rise of values, there *is* such a thing as a general rise of prices."—Mill's " Principles of Political Economy," Vol. I., Book III., chap. iv., sec. 2, p. 565. " While a general rise or a general fall of values is a contradiction in terms, a general rise or a general fall in prices is a perfectly possible, as indeed it is a not uncommon event."—Cairnes : " Some Leading Principles of Political Economy," p. 12.

[2] " Principles of Political Economy," Vol. II., Book III., chap. viii., sec. 2.

cotton, coal, or corn ; because the price or value of mony is governed, as we shall hereafter see, by exactly the same influences as is every thing else for which it will be received in exchange. Evidently there is no good reason for creating a distinction between value and price, and the accepted dogma that "though there is no such thing as a general rise of values, there is such a thing as a general rise of prices," is both confusing in theory and fallacious in fact.

SECTION III.—*Is a General Rise or Fall in the Value or Price of Commodities Possible ?*

Two points in relation to value are now clear : (1) that it expresses nothing but the ratio of exchange ; (2) that for all the purposes of economic science, value and price are equivalent terms,—hence any movement of one is equally possible to the other. From this it follows that if "a general rise or fall in the value of commodities is impossible," then there can never be a general rise or fall of prices ; and conversely, if there can be a general rise or fall in the price of commodities, there may be a general rise or fall in their value. That there can be a general rise or fall in the price of commodities our economists all admit ; and that there has been a general fall in the *value* of commodities is demonstrated by the most obvious facts in modern industrial history. Since value and price are of synonymous import, and a general movement in the value of commodities can and does occur, an explanation of this phenomenon, consistent with the idea that value simply expresses the ratio of exchange, may properly be demanded. The difficulty hitherto experienced in dealing with the question of value has arisen from the mistaken point of view from which the subject has been considered. The error lies in regarding value as a physical instead of a social phenomenon ; and, consequently, in treating it as if it referred only to the exchange relation of things to things, instead of the relation of things to man. There are no economic exchanges in which wealth constitutes all the elements ; for man—human service—is always the principal factor. All exchanges are made by man and for man—the object always being to gratify some desire for which he must, directly or indirectly, render service. In the last analysis exchange will always be found to consist in giving service for gratification—*i.e.*, labor for wealth, though nominally different qualities of wealth are being exchanged.

When we say the price of a commodity has risen or fallen because it will exchange for a larger or smaller amount of gold, the statement would have no significance but for the fact that the variation in the ratio in which the commodities exchange for gold indirectly expresses that in which they will exchange for labor. The rise in the value of commodities means that the articles referred to have become dearer—more difficult for man to obtain —or it means nothing. Wheat cannot be either dear or cheap to potatoes or to gold, any more than shoes can be dear or cheap to fishes. The value of wheat may be high *as compared* with that of potatoes or gold, but it is not high *to* those articles. It is only high *to* man. Nor is it high to him because it will exchange for a larger quantity of things, but solely because it will exchange for a larger quantity of his labor. Therefore, when we speak of a rise or fall in the value of commodities we always mean, directly or indirectly, an increase or diminution in the ratio in which commodities will exchange for labor.

When we once clearly recognize that it is the exchange relation of wealth to man that is to be considered, and not merely the relation of things to each other, much of the difficulty connected with this subject disappears. The hitherto inexplicable phenomenon—of a general rise and fall in the value of commodities—now becomes both possible and entirely rational. It will readily be seen that while all commodities cannot simultaneously rise and fall in their relation to each other, they can all do so in their relation to labor. And since, ultimately, it is only to the extent that the ratio varies in which commodities exchange for labor that their value can rise or fall, it is just as possible for the value of all articles to rise and fall together as it is for any portion of them to do so.

There is another phase of this subject that has been a constant source of perplexing controversy, but which, from this point of view, becomes easy and simple of explanation. It has been held by many able writers that, because value expresses simply a relation, when two commodities vary in the ratio in which they will exchange for each other we cannot strictly say that the one has risen or that the other has fallen in value, but that both have risen and fallen in relation to each other. If, for example, two bushels of potatoes would exchange for one bushel of wheat last year, and one bushel of wheat will exchange for three bushels of potatoes this year, they hold that it is just as correct to say that the value of the wheat has risen as it is to say the value of the potatoes has fallen ; that it is simply a variation in their exchange relations,—the fall in the one case implying a rise in the other, and *vice versa.* This kind of reasoning is very perplexing ; it logically forbids us to speak of the rise or fall in the value of commodities by depriving the expression of all real significance regarding the object to which it refers. But when we consider the question from the point of view that value finally expresses the exchange relation, not of things to things, but of things to man, we have no difficulty in deciding whether the value of the potatoes has fallen or that of the wheat has risen. Then the statement that the value of a given commodity has increased or decreased is strictly correct, and conveys a specific idea regarding a particular object. It always indicates the variation in the exchange relation of that commodity to labor.

It is therefore not correct to say, with Mill, Cairnes, and others, that a fall in the value of potatoes as compared to that of wheat necessarily implies a rise in the value of the wheat. On the contrary, there may be a simultaneous rise or fall in the value of all commodities, or the value of the various commodities may rise or fall in different degrees, or the value of some of them may rise or fall, while that of the others remains entirely unchanged.

To illustrate this point more fully, let us suppose that a day's labor will exchange for one bushel of wheat, or for two bushels of potatoes. In this case the wheat will exchange for the potatoes in the ratio of one to two, while it will exchange for a day's labor in the ratio of one to one. The wheat is now twice as dear, per bushel, as the potatoes. Suppose that another year a day's labor will exchange for three bushels of potatoes, but it continues to exchange evenly for one bushel of wheat. Of course, under such conditions, the wheat will exchange for potatoes in the ratio of one to three, instead of one to two as before. Obviously the value of the potatoes will fall one third, because one third more of them can be obtained for a day's work. It cannot be said in this latter case that the fall in the value of the potatoes implies

9

a rise in that of the wheat, because a day's labor continues to exchange for exactly the same amount of wheat as before. Clearly, therefore, the value of the wheat remains unchanged while that of the potatoes falls one third. Nor does the value of the potatoes fall merely, as compared with, or in relation to, that of the wheat, but they become one third cheaper absolutely without any regard to the wheat whatever.

We may be reminded that the price of labor varies in different countries, industries, and localities. But that fact in no way alters the case ; whether the laborer gets fifty cents or five dollars a day makes no real difference in the operation of the principle. If one day's labor of the fifty-cent man will exchange for ten pounds of flour, or two pounds of butter, then that of the five-dollar man will command a hundred pounds of flour, or twenty pounds of butter. Any variation in the ratio in which the flour or butter will exchange for a day's service of either of these laborers will obtain with all laborers, and hence will constitute a change in the value of those commodities to that extent. But no variation in the ratio in which flour or butter will exchange for any or all other commodities—including silver or gold (which are likewise commodities), will make the slightest change in their value, unless it alters the proportion in which they will exchange for labor.

Therefore it is incorrect to say "a fall in the value of one or more commodities necessarily implies a rise in that of all other commodities, and *vice versa.*" On the contrary, there may, as we have seen in the case of the potatoes and wheat, be a rise or fall in the value of one or more articles in the market without any change in that of the others. But while it is not true that a fall in the value of one or more commodities necessarily implies a rise of that in all others, it is true that a fall in the value of any or all commodities implies a rise in the value of services, and *vice versa.* The reason for this difference is easily understood. It is simply because, ultimately, value, as applied to commodities, expresses nothing but the ratio in which they will exchange for labor, and no amount of increase in the intricate complexity of the process of exchange can alter this fact in the slightest degree.

It will thus be seen that, when we change our point of view and regard man and his desires as the centre of all economic movement,—treating value as a social phenomenon and using the term exclusively to express the exchange relation of things to man,— the whole subject appears in a new light. Then the perplexing distinctions between the numerous kinds of value, and between value and price, and the difference in the possibility of values undergoing the same general rise or fall as prices, all become unnecessary.

The term value being used solely to express the ratio of exchange, *i.e.*, the proportion in which man will give service for wealth or gratification,—it will always convey the same idea and never be misunderstood. And if we regard the word utility as expressing simply the want-gratifying qualities of any portion of man's environment, its meaning is at once simple, definite, and unmistakable. Thus understood, utility and value both become distinctive, intelligible terms—the former expressing the quality for which things are desired by man, and the latter the propor‧ tion in which he will give his service in exchange for them. With these definitions it is scientifically correct to say the value or price of any or all commodities may rise or fall separately or simultaneously. Indeed, were it otherwise, social progress would be impossible, because it is only in proportion as wealth in general becomes cheaper that human well-being can be increased.

In order to furnish a scientific basis for increasing the ratio in which labor exchanges for wealth in accordance with the unconscious operation of social law, it is necessary, first of all, to understand the principle upon which different quantities of the various kinds of wealth and service become economic equivalents. This will explain the law of economic value and will next occupy our attention.

CHAPTER III.

DEMAND AND SUPPLY NOT THE LAW OF ECONOMIC PRICES.

Section I.—*The Doctrine Stated.*

MILL says : " A writer does but half his duty by stating his own doctrines if he does not also examine, and to the best of his ability judge, those of other thinkers." While this is true of all questions in economics, it is especially true of the doctrine of prices. No treatment of that subject can be complete which does not consider the claims of the theory of supply and demand—a theory which is practically universal. Although the question of prices has never been free from controversy since the time of Adam Smith, scarcely a book on economics has been published subsequent to "Wealth of Nations" in which the ratio between supply and demand has not, expressly or tacitly, been accepted as the law of prices.[1]

This doctrine affirms : (1) That under free competition (*i.e.,* in the absence of arbitrary barriers) there cannot be two prices for the same commodity in the same market. (2) That when the supply and the demand are equal the price is the exact equivalent of the cost of production. (3) That the price rises as the demand exceeds the supply, and falls as the supply exceeds the demand ; and, " the rise or fall continues until the demand and the supply are again equal to one another." In order to sustain

---

[1] Perry's "Political Economy," p. 211. Mill's "Principles of Political Economy," Vol. I., Book III., ch. ii., p. 252. Price's "Practical Political Economy," p. 188. Jevons' "Theory of Political Economy," p. 6. (Preface). MacLeod's "Elements of Political Economy," p. 111. Cairnes' "Leading Principles of Political Economy," p. 183.

this claim, two propositions must be established : (*a*) that the value of all commodities and services always rises and falls as the demand exceeds or falls short of the supply ; which movement " continues until the demand and the supply are equal " ; (*b*) that the variation in the price is produced by the alternation in the ratio of the demand and supply. Unless these postulates can be sustained, the doctrine of demand and supply must be rejected as inadequate to furnish a scientific law of value. Although this doctrine has always been held to apply to both commodities and labor, in order to simplify the discussion we will consider it in relation to these factors separately, taking commodities first.

In the seventeenth century, Gregory King observed that the price of commodities varied with the demand and supply as follows :

A decrease in the supply of :

1 tenth raises the price above the common rate	3	tenths.
2 tenths " " " " " " "	8	tenths.
3 tenths " " " " " " "	1-6	tenths.
4 tenths " " " " " " "	2-8	tenths.
5 tenths " " " " " " "	4-5	tenths.

Despite the modifying effect of the "cost of production," introduced by Smith and Ricardo, this scale of variation in prices, which was based entirely upon agricultural products, has been practically accepted as the law of *all* prices ever since. Even Thorold Rogers repeats this formula in his latest work, with emphatic indorsement as " one of the most important generalizations in statistics, and applicable to all values whatever." [1]

The reason the early writers upon this subject confined their studies chiefly to agricultural products is not difficult to understand. During the time of Gregory King and even down to the nineteenth century, agricultural products constituted the chief articles of consumption for the great mass of the community. During the present century, and especially the last fifty years, this has been greatly changed. The proportion in which manufactured, as compared with agricultural, products enter into the daily consumption, is steadily increasing as civilization

[1] " Eonomic Interpretation of History," p. 55 (1888). Jevons reaffirms it in his " theory of Political Economy," pp. 168–171.

advances.   Consequently if the agricultural hypothesis furnishes the true law of prices, it must be applicable to the prices of manufactured as well as agricultural products.

Of course the true law of prices must explain the movement of all prices, but no hypothesis can be assumed to do so merely because it affords a seeming explanation of one class of prices. The recognition of this fact is especially important in this connection because the production of manufactured and agricultural commodities is frequently affected by widely different influences.   In agriculture the quantity and quality of products are often largely determined by purely cosmical forces—the operation of which is entirely outside the domain of economic law,—while, in manufacture, nearly all the influences affecting production are economic and social.   Consequently we may naturally expect to find any theory constructed upon purely agricultural data to be inadequate to explain the prices of manufactured products.

It is undoubtedly true that the price of wheat, potatoes, apples, peaches, or any other farm or garden product tends to rise or fall with the relative increase or diminution of the demand or the supply.   The fact that the price of wheat will rise with a failure of the crop and fall with an abundant yield may be counted upon as unmistakably as any other fact in nature.   It is also true that in all such cases the rise or fall in the price continues until the demand and supply are approximately equal.   Nor is there any doubt that this rise or fall in the price of agricultural products indicates a corresponding change in the ratio in which they will exchange as economic equivalents.   So far as agricultural products are concerned, therefore, the facts seem to accord with the theory.[1]

Let us now see how the case stands with the price of manufactured products.   According to this hypothesis, whenever the quantity of cotton cloth, shoes, or other manufactured commodities is greater than the quantity effectually demanded, the price

[1] This will be true, however, only so far as the variation in the demand and supply is due to cosmical influences, such as favorable or unfavorable seasons. But if the over-supply should be due to the cultivation of a larger number of acres under traditional conditions this would not occur, and any fall in the price would involve loss or bankruptcy to the farmer.

of the article will fall, and the fall will continue until the demand and the supply are equal.' If this theory were correct, there could never be what is called, "an over-production," at least, until the quantity of cloth, shoes, etc., was so great that they could not be consumed at any price. Because, it will be remembered, if the supply more than equals the demand the price will fall to "the point which equalizes the demand and the supply,"'— which must be the point at which all the product can be sold. As a matter of fact, this is what almost never occurs under such circumstances. There is probably no large manufacturing and commercial centre in the world in which the supply of a large number of commodities is not greatly in excess of the demand. And yet the price does not continuously fall, but in a very large majority of such cases remains practically steady for years together.

Industrial depressions are specifically cases of this kind. The characteristic feature of an industrial depression is that manufactured commodities are produced in greater quantities than they can be sold. The expression "over-production" simply means that the supply is in excess of the demand. Instead of the movement of prices under these conditions being that which is predicated by the demand-and-supply theory, it is entirely different. There is a tendency to equalize the demand and supply, but it is brought about by an entirely different process than the fall in prices ; as laid down in the popular theory.

The first symptoms of an over-production, or excess of supply, is the difficulty in selling the entire product. This will generally be followed by an increased competition among the manufacturers and merchants—especially those who have large margins —and will tend to reduce the price toward the point at which they can barely sell without loss—which point is nearly always reached long before the demand and supply are equalized. Here, however, an entirely different movement sets in and the fall is transferred from the price to the quantity of the commodity. Instead of the price continuing to decline until an equilibrium between demand and supply is reached, the fall in price is arrested at the no-profit point, and the decline in the amount of sales commences. As the sales fall off warehouses are filled,

---

¹ "Principles of Political Economy," vol. i., pp. 551, 552.
² *Ibid.*, p. 550.

profits shrink, and the incentives to produce are diminished ; hence the supply is curtailed to prevent further loss. Thus, instead of the demand and the supply being equalized by a continuous fall in the price and larger sales, that result is reached by lessening production—which involves the closing of factories, enforced idleness of laborers, and sometimes the bankruptcy of manufacturers and merchants.[1] It will be seen, therefore, that the equilibrium between demand and supply is reached—if reached at all—by reducing the supply to the dimensions of the demand at *paying prices*, and not by lowering the prices to that of demand and supply. Moreover, if the price of commodities under these conditions continued to fall until the demand and the supply were equalized, as in agriculture, it would not be, as in that case, an exchange of economic equivalents, but it would be a highly uneconomic exchange, involving continuous loss, and probably ruin, to the producers.

Were the conditions reversed the same principle would govern the movement of the phenomenon. If the demand for shoes greatly exceeded the supply, the demand and supply would not be equalized by the increased price, but by an increase in the supply. It is exactly under such conditions that new factories, with improved methods, come into existence. This gives more employment to labor ; enlarges the market ; cheapens the cost of production ; and tends to make profitable sales at lower prices possible. Thus it is clear that the price does not necessarily fall when the supply exceeds the demand, nor rise when the demand exceeds the supply. This much of the fallacy of the demand-and-supply theory was evidently clear to Ricardo, who probably had more glimpses of fundamental truth in economics than any other writer of this century. He says[2] : " Diminish the cost of production of hats, and their price will ultimately fall to their new natural price, although the demand shall be doubled, trebled, or quadrupled. Diminish the cost of subsistence of men, by diminishing the natural price of the food and clothing by which life is sustained, and wages will ultimately fall, notwithstanding that the demand for laborers may very greatly increase."

[1] This is equally true of agriculture where the increased supply or over-production is due to increased investment instead of gratuitous natural forces.

[2] " Principles of Political Economy and Taxation," ch. xxx., p. 232.

There is still another important fact that here presents itself for the demand- and- supply theory to explain. If the value of commodities is governed by the ratio between the demand and the supply, why has the value of manufactured articles steadily fallen during the present century, in some cases sixty and seventy per cent., while the value of farm and garden products has generally risen, and in some cases very considerably. It cannot be because the relative demand for agricultural products, as compared with the supply, has been greater than that for manufactured commodities, because, in that case, the profits of agriculture would have been greater during the period than those of manufacture and trade, whereas the reverse is true. For the same reason the fall in the price of manufactured articles cannot be attributed to the excess of supply as compared with agriculture. Now, if the normal price of commodities were governed by the ratio between demand and supply, this phenomenon would be an economic impossibility. Nor can it be objected that the fall in the price of manufactured articles is like that in the auction sale, —at the expense of the seller. The manufacturers of cotton cloth, who to-day sell their product at four cents a yard, are economically as well off as were those who received eighteen or twenty cents a yard a hundred years ago. In other words, to give twenty yards of cotton cloth for one dollar to-day is just as equitable an exchange of economic equivalents as it was to obtain a dollar for six yards in 1820. This is not the exception, but the rule, and represents the normal economic movement in modern society ; clearly therefore the theory of demand and supply is wholly inadequate to explain the movement in the economic price of commodities.

SECTION II.—*Does the Price of Labor Obey the Law of Demand and Supply ?*

In the case of labor the failure of this theory will be found to be no less conspicuous. If the doctrine were true, that wages always fall when the supply of labor is in excess of the demand, enforced idleness or able-bodied pauperism would be impossible, as we have elsewhere pointed out.[1] In that case, as soon as un-

---

[1] " Wealth and Progress," Part II., ch. i., sec. i.

employed laborers appeared wages would begin to fall, and the fall would continue until all the laborers were employed at some price, that being the only point at which the demand and the supply could be equalized. So far from this being the rule, there is not a country in all the world in which it ever occurred. There may have been times and places when laborers were all employed, but this was never accomplished by the lowering of wages. History does not afford a single instance of abolishing enforced idleness, and reducing able-bodied pauperism, by that means. Such a phenomenon is an economic impossibility. Every fall of wages tends to lessen the general consumption of wealth, and thereby diminish rather than increase the employment of labor. As a matter of fact, wages do not fall ; any thing like a general fall of real wages is practically an unknown phenomenon.

It is one of the distinguishing characteristics of the history of industrial evolution that, since the dawn of the wage-system, neither royal authority, civil law, religious dogma, or any other industrial or social pressure, has been able to permanently force the price of labor below the point that has once been generally established in a community, although the supply has frequently been greatly in excess of the demand. The statistics of able-bodied pauperism, and the history of poor-law legislation, furnish abundant evidence of the over-supply of labor during the last three hundred years. The same fact is clearly shown in the economic literature of the period, which abounds with the discussion of the pauper problem. It was the alarming extent to which the supply of labor was continuously in excess of the demand, which gave rise to the Malthusian doctrine of limiting the population by curtailing births among the laboring class. This doctrine has been generally accepted by economists during the present century, both in Europe and this country, as the only means of raising wages. Yet in the face of this continuous over-supply of labor, wages have risen seven hundred per cent. It is therefore clear that wages do not necessarily fall when the supply of labor is in excess of the demand, but that they may, and often do, rise in spite of that fact. It is very doubtful if it can be shown that a single step in the rise of wages, from twelve cents to two dollars a day, has taken place in accordance with the doctrine of demand and supply, but almost invariably contrary to it. Obviously, therefore, the first postulate upon which the demand- and supply-theory is based, namely, that the prices of all commodities and labor rise and fall as the relative demand exceeds or falls short of the supply, utterly fails.

SECTION III.—*Economic Prices cannot Possibly be Determined by the Mere Ratio between Demand and Supply.*

We come now to the second postulate upon which this theory rests, namely, that the variation in the price of commodities and labor is caused by the alteration in the rate of demand and supply. Although the variation in price may often be similar to that in the demand and the supply, it can easily be shown that the mere proportion between the quantity demanded and supplied cannot possibly determine economic value. The very idea of value is *quid pro quo.* The conception of economic exchange necessarily implies that each obtains an equivalent for what he gives. Therefore, in seeking the law of value, we are not seeking to explain that process of exchange by which, through ignorance, fraud, and other devices, one can get the advantage of another ; but we are seeking the law by which different quantities of various kinds of wealth and service can be equitably exchanged as the economic equivalents of each other, and according to which a given amount of service can become the equivalent of an increasingly large amount of wealth.

In what sense, then, are ·commodities the equivalents of each other ? It cannot be their similarity in quantity, quality, or form, because it is their very dissimilarity in these respects which makes their exchange desirable and necessary. The only sense in which different quantities of various kinds of commodities and services can be the equivalents of each other is as economic products—*i.e.*, in the sense that they represent the same amount of economic expenditure. An econonomic equivalent is that which will afford as much gratification to the buyer as he could, with due preparation, otherwise have obtained by the wealth and service devoted to procuring that which he gave for it. Can this be in any way affected by the mere presence or absence of quantity ? Is there any thing in the fact that the demand is greater or smaller, or equal to the supply, that can make different quantities of wealth and service,—the procuring of which involves different amounts of expenditure,—the economic equivalents of each other ?[1]

If one gives a day's labor to procure a pair of shoes, and then exchanges the shoes for twenty grains of gold, unless he can obtain as much of other commodities, or service, for the gold as he could for the labor that he put into the shoes, the gold is not the economic equivalent of the shoes. Whether or not the gold will reimburse him for making the shoes—*i.e.*, will be an equivalent for the shoes—cannot possibly be affected by the mere fact that there are many or few grains of gold. The ability to exchange a pair of shoes for twenty grains of gold, as an equivalent, can no more be affected by an increase or a decrease in the number of shoes or the quantity of gold than the weight of a pound of lead can be affected by the presence of a larger or smaller number of pounds of lead. There is absolutely nothing that can enable a man to give his shoes for the gold, without losing, which does not enable him to obtain the shoes with a smaller amount of wealth and service. McCulloch pointedly remarks[2] : " No variation of demand, if it be unaccompanied by a variation in the cost of production, can have any lasting influence in price. If the cost of production be diminished, price will be equally diminished, though the demand should be increased to any conceivable extent. If the cost of production be increased, price will be equally increased, though the demand should sink to the lowest possible limit." As the proportion between the demand and supply cannot enable the producers of either gold or shoes to make their articles one fraction cheaper, it canot affect the ratio in which these articles will exchange as economic equivalents, and consequently cannot determine their economic value.

To recapitulate, then, four important facts are established,— any one of which is sufficient to invalidate the claim of the theory that the ratio between demand and supply is the law of economic prices. They are : (1) That the value of commodities and labor does not always rise and fall as the demand exceeds or falls short of the supply, and so continue until the demand and the supply are equalized. (2) That prices may and do rise when the supply

---

[1] De Quincey's " Logic of Political Economy," p. 8.
[2] " Principles of Political Economy," Part III., sec. iii., p. 137.

is in excess of the demand, and fall when the demand is in excess of the supply. (3) That prices may and do rise or fall without any perceptible change in the ratio between the demand and the supply. (4) That, from the nature of things, it is impossible for the mere scarcity or abundance of quantity to alter the ratio in which different quantities of wealth and service become economic equivalents of each other.

SECTION IV.—*The Economic Relation of Demand to Supply.*

Sometimes the most effective way of showing what a thing is not, is to to explain what it is. The error of the doctrine that economic prices are determined by the ratio between demand and supply will become still more apparent if we examine the economic relation which these phenomena sustain to each other. We shall then see that this quantitative relation is more the consequence than the cause of economic prices.

Attention has already been called to the fact that, while economists have defined value as the ratio in which quantities exchange, they have treated the subject as relating exclusively to wealth. The natural outcome of this position is that even such a careful writer as Cairnes [1] has insisted, that demand and supply are identical phenomena—"Simply different faces of the same fact." The only effectual demand being actual supply, and *vice versa.* Consequently, the only way to increase the demand for one class of commodities is to enlarge the production of other commodities to exchange for them, or, as Cairnes [2] expressly states : " Purchasing power, in the last resort, owes its existence to the production of a commodity and, the conditions of industry being given, can only be increased by increasing the quantity of commodities offered for sale ; that is to say, demand can only be increased by increasing supply." Accordingly, the panacea for a glutted market—" over-production "—is more production,—a delightful tonic for industrial depressions.

The inevitable effect of this view of the subject, which limits economic phenomena to wealth and makes demand and supply identical facts,—each equally dependent upon the other—is to

[1] "Some Leading Principles of Political Economy," ch. ii.
[2] *Ibid.*, p. 31.

reduce economic movement to a vicious circle and make progress impossible. The result of this class of reasoning was recently illustrated in the attitude of a gentleman, who had devoted more than a generation to the study of economics, and had digested the literature of several languages upon the subject. He clearly saw the social necessity of doing something to improve the laborer's condition ; but it was equally clear to him that this must be done by scientific means. He said (and in a protracted correspondence repeated the argument in several ways): "We are all anxious that the laborer should receive more wealth. This he can do in but one of three ways : by theft, charity, or economic exchange. To increase his income through either of the first two would be to injure instead of to help him, and he can only obtain more wealth through exchange by having more to give for it, which is exactly what he lacks. Therefore," exclaimed the gentleman, "unless you can show how the laborer can be put into possession of something to give in exchange for the wealth he desires, there is no feasible way by which society can economically increase his income." Thus, by the logic of his position, my friend was forced into the vicious circle where he finally was compelled to exclaim : "There is no way by which society can increase wages ; that question must be left to settle itself by natural law." Consequently, like most of the leading economists of the present century, he was compelled to assume the negative, pessimistic position of *laissez-faire*, and, in spite of himself, become an ardent free-trader, though very desirous of being a social reformer.

The intellectual quagmire into which this argument leads is due to the mistaken definition of " demand. It is a radical error to regard demand and supply as identical phenomena, and assume " that demand can only be increased by increasing the quantity of commodities offered for sale." As a matter of fact, not one tenth of the world's demand consists in " commodities offered for sale." The great market of the modern world is made by the daily wants of the people who have practically no commodities to offer for sale. All they have to offer for sale is service, and it is with that they purchase. When we once recognize the fact that all exchanges are ultimately the exchange of wealth for service, and not wealth for wealth, this matter assumes

a new aspect and the pessimistic vicious circle disappears. Instead of saying that all demand for commodities is the supply of
commodities offered for sale, we shall then say : *the demand for
commodities is the desire to consume them, coupled with the supply of
service necessary to produce their equivalent.*

From this view there is no difficulty in seeing how the demand
may be increased, and, through it, the supply enlarged. It is
undoubtedly true that demand and supply are closely related
and interdependent, but they are not identical phenomena. The
distinction and economic relation of demand and supply will be
greatly simplified if we keep two obvious facts in mind, namely :
that no matter how complex the relations, or how involved the
phenomena, demand always means want—*consumption*, and supply
means service—*production.*

Although Bastiat's statement of "wants, effort, and satisfaction"
is correct, it should be remembered that the first two only are
active forces. The first represents the active feeling or motive ;
the second, the effort or action. The third is simply the result
of these ; it is the actualization of the first, of which the second
is the means. To-day's wants determine to-morrow's efforts, and
yesterday's actual consumption determines to-day's actual production. Clearly, then, consumption is not only potentially prior
to, but it is actually the cause of production. Since consumption
constitutes the actual demand, and production the actual supply,
it follows that demand is the cause of supply.

There is no more obvious fact in economic experience than
that supply follows the line of, adapts itself to, and finally depends upon, demand. This is why mankind always lives from
hand to mouth, as it were, and society can never be made to permanently produce more than will supply the normal current demand in any state of civilization. Indeed, were it otherwise,
industrial depressions would increase instead of social welfare
being promoted. It is for this reason that nothing can permanently increase the quantity and reduce the cost of wealth
which does not multiply the wants, enlarge the consumption, and
therefore expand the social character of the people.

The way in which demand exercises its controlling influence
over supply is through the instrumentality of value or price.
Upon the same principle that man will not give something for

nothing, he will refuse to supply the wants or demands of others except on the conditions that he obtains an equivalent in return. It is only when the demand is strong enough to induce the giving of full equivalents for the efforts of production,—*i.e.*, a price equal to the cost—that a continuous supply will be forthcoming. Supply, then, not only depends upon demand, but it depends upon demand at a certain price. Demand really creates the price, and the price induces the supply.

In order to more clearly see the economic relation of these phenomena, let us suppose the existence of a community where the division of labor and exchange have not yet made their appearance ; where there is neither buying, selling, nor barter. Here demand and supply, exchange and value, are unknown ; every one supplies his own needs by his own personal efforts. Let us further suppose that some one person in this community, more ingenious than the rest, contrives to make a bow and arrow, by the aid of which he is soon able to procure more game in one day than he previously could in three or four. No sooner has the advantage of this new weapon become known than others want it. How to obtain bows and arrows is now the question, and the price-creating forces at once begin to operate. Since the advantage of the new instrument in getting a living is so great, all who are unable to make it for themselves are willing to give something to obtain one from others. Here the want begins to assume the form of an economic demand, and price emerges. How much will he give? A deer is offered for the bow and arrow. Whether the offer is accepted or not, the bow and arrow now have a price. It is one deer, but this is not enough. The maker of the bow and arrow can obtain more game by hunting with his new weapon than by staying at home and selling it for one deer. Hence he declines to make them and there is no supply. Two deer are offered, but he declines for the same reason, and still there is no supply,—although the price has doubled through the strength of the demand. Two deer and a beaver are offered ; here the bow- and- arrow-maker yields, and the supply commences. At this price those who have the aptitude for making bows and arrows are willing to stay at home and make them, because they can obtain as much, or more, game in exchange for their weapons than by hunting for themselves.

It will thus be seen that bows and arrows not only had a price long before there was any supply, but it was only when the price rose to the economic, or remunerative, point that the supply commenced and the ratio between demand and supply had any existence. Manifestly, the first fact in the movement of these phenomena was the demand for the game. When the bow and arrow was known to be capable of aiding in the gratification of this demand the desire for venison was extended to the bow and arrow also, and the amount that was offered for it was determined entirely by the strength of the desire ; and this price, —when it became large enough to make it more profitable to manufacture bows and arrows than to hunt for a living,—was the sole cause of the weapons being supplied. It is therefore obvious that the price of the bows and arrows was not created by the ratio between the demand and the supply.

This principle obtains with the same force in the most complex business transactions of modern society as in the most primitive stages, although its origin and operations are not so easily observed. It is true that an article sometimes is produced before there is any demand for it, *i.e.*, before its utility is generally known—but this does not alter the case. When a commodity is supplied in advance of the demand for it, the supply is impelled by the same cause as when it is produced in response to a known demand, the only difference being in the certainty of the result. In the former case the supply of the article is based upon confidence in its capacity to serve some purpose to the community sufficiently well to induce willingness to give a remunerating price for it. If the utility of the article and the wants of the people have been correctly estimated, a remunerative price-making demand for it will ensue as soon as its merits are known. But, on the other hand, if the relative degree of these influences has been miscalculated, no effectual demand for it will arise, in which case the production will prove to be an entire mistake, resulting in loss to those who undertake it. This has been painfully illustrated in thousands of instances,—as the almost interminable list of unsuccessful patents clearly shows. Hence, whether the demand and supply commence to operate in their natural order, from the known utility of the article,— as in the case of the bow and arrow,—or in anticipation of it,—

8

as in the case of the patents,—makes no real difference.   In both cases the result is governed by the same law.

Evidently, the more closely we examine the economic relation of demand and supply, the clearer it becomes that demand is the active force, to which supply is but the ultimate response. And that, to the extent supply exists without demand, is it devoid of social utility and economic force.   In other words, products become waste or wealth in proportion as they precede, or are preceded by, wants.   Therefore, instead of economic prices being dependent upon the ratio between the demand and the supply, they have no necessary relation to it.   The order of the economic relation of these phenomena is that *supply immediately depends upon the price, and the price is created by the demand, and the demand depends entirely upon the habitual wants or social life and character of the people.*

CHAPTER IV.

THE LAW OF ECONOMIC PRICES.

SECTION I.—*The Scope and Importance of the Subject.*

THE law of prices may be said to occupy the keystone position in the arch of economic science. It involves the principle upon which the equity of all human relations finally rests. All the advantages of social intercourse, however simple or complex, ultimately depend upon the exchange of equivalents. This is as true in the realm of the affections, ideas, ethics, and politics, as it is in economics. If all could secure the equivalent for what they give, they would receive an absolutely equitable reward for what they do, and injustice would be impossible. All industrial political, moral, or religious endeavor to improve society being efforts to promote justice, it must rest finally upon the principle involved in the law of economic prices, namely, *quid pro quo.* Nothing is truly economic which is not entirely equitable, and equity is the highest form of ethics.

The phenomena that are subject to the law of prices may be grouped under two general heads, as WEALTH and SERVICE. There can be no economic change in society except through the alteration of the ratio in which these exchange for each other. The prices of wealth and service move inversely to each other, promoting social welfare only as the ratio in which wealth will exchange for service increases. Since all economic exchanges are of the same general character and belong to the same class of phenomena, they must be subject to the same general law. Consequently, to explain the law of prices is to furnish a clue to the law of wages, rent, interest, and profit, and really to lay the foundation for a scientific solution of the whole problem of Economic Distribution.

At the outset we must remember that we are not seeking the explanation of some special cases of exchange, but we are seeking the law to which all exchange may be referred, and through which all prices may be adequately accounted for.

The true theory of economic prices must be capable of explaining why the price of agricultural products tends to conform to the ratio of demand and supply, while that of manufactured products does not ; and why the price of labor rises when the supply is in excess of the demand ; why the price of certain agricultural and dairy products constantly tends to rise, while that of manufactured products tends to fall ; and why this disparity in the permanent tendency of prices in these classes of commodities is the greatest in the most highly civilized countries. In short, it must be capable of explaining the variation in the economic prices of all kinds of commodities and service under all conditions.

SECTION II.—*The Meaning of Economic Law.*

It is important, in this connection, clearly to define in what sense the word *law* is to be understood in Economic Science. We frequently hear the expressions natural law and artificial law —as if the phenomena created by art were unnatural,—the implication being that nothing is natural except what results from the unaided forces of nature. This erroneous notion is the basis of much of the unscientific conduct of the *laissez-faire* doctrinaires. Upon the assumption that natural law means the uncontrolled operation of cosmic forces, they conclude that " natural law " can only prevail in commerce and industry under a *laissez-faire* régime. It is difficult to conceive a notion more unscientific. All laws are natural. Unnatural law in the scientific sense is a contradiction in terms.

Law in science simply means the necessary order in which phenomena succeed each other as cause and effect. A law is not more or less natural because its operation results from cosmic or from human influences, nor because its effects are good or bad. Almost every thing that will preserve life under certain conditions, will just as surely destroy it under others, and the law is equally natural in both cases. In seeking a scientific law, therefore, it is not a question of distinguishing the natural law from the artificial law, but solely one of ascertaining the necessary order in which phenomena lead to given results, and the conditions which favor or retard that order of movement. Understanding this, we shall be in a position to act scientifically regarding the influences that aid the recurrence of desirable, and prevent that of undesirable, phenomena.

Since the advancement of social welfare primarily depends upon cheapening wealth, it is one of the chief functions of economic science to explain how a smaller amount of labor can become the equivalent of a larger amount of wealth. In studying the law of prices, therefore, our chief concern is to ascertain the order of economic phenomena which makes given quantities of wealth and service the economic equivalents of each other. When this law is clearly established we shall have a scientific basis for industrial development, and instead of having to take refuge behind the doctrine of *laissez-faire* to protect us from the irrational hit-or-miss policy which has characterized so much of modern statesmanship, we shall be able to increase the influences which promote, and diminish those which retard, industrial and social progress, with the same scientific accuracy that we can now travel by steam and communicate by electricity.

This does not mean that economic science is of the same exact character as mathematics or chemistry. The phenomena with which it deals do not admit of the same exact statement, for two reasons : first, because the change that is constantly taking place in social phenomena is so universal and persistent that in no two succeeding instances are the phenomena exactly the same ; and second, because much of the change in this class of phenomena is due to human desire and human will, neither of which admits of exact quantitative statement. Although economic phenomena are not susceptible of being reduced to exact mathematical statement, they are susceptible of positive explanation. Economic science deals with the social relations of the human race, and the law of their continuous development. Since social progress is an almost imperceptible evolution, it is more necessary that knowledge regarding the tendency of phenomena should be exact than that the precise quantitative relations should be known at any given time.

In economics, then, the term law must be understood as expressing the order in which phenomena necessarily tend to move in any given direction. Hence, in studying the law of economic prices, we must endeavor to ascertain, first of all, the necessary tendency of economic prices, and how that tendency is determined. When the primary law of economic tendency is clearly established, the action of the secondary influences, which tend to modify its operation, can be ascertained with comparative ease and accuracy. We shall then be in a position to distinguish the economic tendency from its uneconomic perturbations. The law of the first will of necessity furnish the key to the second, because to know the one is, by implication, to know the other.

SECTION III.—*The Primary Law of Prices.*

It is a characteristic of all phenomena with which science has yet been able to deal, that their actual movement is governed by a composite law, resulting from a variety of forces which act and react upon and modify each other. This is especially true of economic and social phenomena. These forces may be divided into two classes : as primary and secondary forces. The former determines the constant tendency of the main current ; the latter affects the rate of movement, and hences modifies the quantitative result at any given time. Thus, for example, in gravitation the primary forces attract bodies towards each other directly in proportion to the quantity of matter which they contain ; but this movement is modified by the secondary forces, which diminish the power of attraction as the distance increases. Consequently, until the relative influence of these two classes of forces was accurately ascertained, the actual movement and relative position of bodies under given conditions could not be correctly predicated. Hence, in stating the actual law of gravitation, we express the action of both these forces and say : "All bodies are attracted to each other directly in proportion to their size and inversely to the square of their distance." So it is in the sphere of economic prices. While the order and direction of economic movement is determined by the direct action of the primary forces, the degree is modified by the secondary forces, and the result at any given time cannot be correctly predicated unless the relative power of the secondary to the primary forces is accurately known. Therefore, correctly to understand the scientific law of economic prices, we must first ascertain the primary law of price-determining phenomena, and then consider the modifying influence of secondary forces and the degree to which they operate in determining the actual ratio of exchange.

In order clearly to observe the action of the primary forces upon the tendency of prices we must eliminate all secondary influences from the problem. To do this we must assume that all who participate in a transaction are adequately informed as to the quantity, quality, and other conditions affecting the commodity for which they are negotiating; and also that they are entirely free to act according to their best interest and judgment. Moreover, to be sure that the movement is entirely economic, we must assume commodities whose production is wholly determined by economic forces, such, for instance, as manufactured products, leaving agricultural products, whose quantity and quality are largely influenced by gratuitous forces, to be considered later. How, then, upon the ʼprinciple of self-interest and economic equity, is the price of a commodity determined ?

Since the action of both producer and consumer is governed by the motive to obtain the greatest result for the least effort, it is quite clear that no exchange will take place unless each can obtain more gratification from what he receives than he could have procured from what he gives. Let us examine the economic movement under the simplest known conditions—namely, where man produces for his own personal consumption. The economic movement is as complete here as in transactions where thousands of miles and millions of people intervene between the producer and the consumer, the only difference being in its relative simplicity or complexity. If our isolated producer wants cotton cloth, the first question that arises is how to get it. That being settled, the next point in the problem is, will the gratification derived from the product be sufficient to compensate for the effort necessary to obtain it ? If it will, the cloth will be made ; if not, the enterprise will be abandoned.

In modern society where, through the division and specialization of labor, all produce for others and receive what they actually consume through exchange, the principle is the same, though the process is more complex. When making cotton cloth for a stranger, it is essentially the same question which arises as when making it for one's self, namely : can the producer, in exchange for the cloth, obtain as much utility as it cost in painful effort, or as he could otherwise have obtained by the expenditure of the same amount of energy? If not, the cloth will not be made. Obviously, therefore, the first condition necessary to secure the production of cotton cloth is that the consumer shall be willing to give an economic equivalent for it. Economic equivalents, as already explained, are not necessarily equivalents of utility. The utility of an article may differ with different persons according to temperament, taste, intensity of desire, and other conditions peculiar to the individual, but that does not affect it as an economic quality. The fact that an eastern manufacturer can obtain twice as much gratification from a bushel of wheat as from ten yards of cotton cloth, while a western farmer could only get one tenth more gratification from the cloth than from the wheat, does not prevent the wheat and the cloth from being economic equivalents. Of course the farmer will not give the wheat for the cloth unless it has more utility for *him* than has the wheat, but the fact that it would possess twenty times as much utility for the manufacturer would not affect the economic relation of the producers. The economic equality of commodities does not depend upon the equality of the utility, but upon the equality in the amount of reluctant productive energy expended in procuring them—in other words, the necessary cost of production. Clearly, then, the minimum price at which the cloth can be obtained is determined by the producer, and it is fixed at a point equal to the cost of its production. For the same reason that the minimum price is determined by the producer, the maximum price will be determined by the consumer. What, then, under these conditions, will the maximum price be ? Since the producer will not permit the consumer to obtain the cloth for less than it cost, will the consumer permit the producer to obtain more for it than it cost ?

It must be remembered that the motives which influence the producer to refuse to supply the cloth for less than it cost operate with equal force to make the consumer decline to give more than it cost. Unless there is some ethical or economic reason why the consumer should give more for the cloth than the equivalent of its cost, he certainly will not do so. There is manifestly no good reason for compelling the consumer to give more for an article than its equivalent, since to do so would be to receive less —an obvious violation of the principles of equity. The ethics of economic exchange are : *quid pro quo,*—price, the exact equivalent of the cost.

Nor is there any economic reason why this should be otherwise. If the consumer demands the cloth for less than it cost— *i.e.,* for a smaller amount of wheat, shoes, or other products, than its economic equivalent, the manufacturer has an effective remedy at hand, namely : to refuse to make the cloth and devote his energies to producing the wheat or shoes for himself. On the other hand, the consumer of cotton cloth, who is a producer of other things, has an equally effective means of protecting himself against the encroachments of the producer. If the manufacturer demands more wheat or shoes for his cloth than its economic equivalent, the consumer of cloth can, and unquestionably will, refuse to furnish wheat or shoes and devote his energies to making cloth. And all the power which the producer possesses for preventing the price of cloth from falling below the cost of its production, the consumer has in an equal degree to prevent it from rising above the cost of production. Therefore, upon the principle that two equal opposing forces neutralize each other, the consumer cannot force the price below, and the producer cannot force it above, the cost ; consequently this is the only point at which the exchange can take place. In a word, it is the only point at which all exchanges become economic and mutually advantageous, and at which everybody obtains an increase of utility by giving an economic equivalent.

Moreover, if there were any economic force by which the producer could exact more than he gives, it would be neutralized by the consumer in his capacity as a producer, and again reduce the relation of the producer and the consumer to a purely economic cost basis. It will thus be seen that, in the absence of secondary and modifying influences (hereafter to be considered), the primary law of economic prices is, that commodities exchange in the ratio of the cost of their production.

It may be well to pause here a moment to explain precisely what is meant by the expression, "cost of production." The cost of a commodity is simply what its owner gave for it, or must give to replace it   The aggregate cost of producing cotton cloth may be divided into three items : cost of service, cost of raw material, and cost of tools.   Under existing methods all whose services are found necessary to the manufacture of cotton cloth are included in the cost of service, or labor.   All classes of labor must, for the reasons already stated, receive as much from the enterprise as they put into it, or they will devote their energies in some other direction.   What the laborers put in is their whole working force ; the cost of their working force to them is their living—whatever that may be,—and that they must have in order to be able to continue to supply their productive energy.   This cost of service will vary according to what enters into the living. In one case it may be a dollar a day ; in another, ten or twenty dollars a day.   What determines that difference will be considered under the head of wages.   It is sufficient for our present purpose that each class of service must receive from the product the equivalent of its cost ; none can obtain more, because none will accept less.

The same is true of raw material.   If we follow the history of its cost we shall find that it is again resolved into the same. three classes of cost, and, in the last analysis, they will all prove to be the cost of labor.   We will assume that all previous demands in producing the raw material have been settled, and therefore its cost is represented in what the manufacturer has to give for it. For the same reason that the laborer must receive the equivalent of the cost of his labor, the manufacturer must obtain from the product the equivalent of the cost of the raw material.   And he cannot obtain more than the cost, because to do so would be to take something for nothing, and to this nobody will consent. The same is true of tools and implements.   The wear and tear of tools and machinery must be replaced from what is received for the product, or they would soon disappear.   Less than the equivalent of this the owner will not accept, and more the consumer will not give.   Now, what is true of service, raw material, and tools separately is equally true of them collectively.   For the same reason that each of these must receive the equivalent of what is expended, the producer or owner of the finished product will not accept less, and cannot obtain more than the equivalent of its aggregate cost. In other words, the cost of manufacturing cotton cloth is increased by exactly the amount that each of these three factors impart to it, and the ratio in which it will exchange for other commodities and service—*i. e.*, its value—must, and will be, exactly equal to what will replace them or their equivalents. The question of profits is naturally suggested here, but in order to keep the primary movement of price-regulating phenomena unobscured, the consideration of that subject will be deferred to a subsequent chapter.[1] At the price-determining point of the economic relations which we are now considering there is no profit and can be none. It may be remarked in passing, however, that it is a great mistake to confound the manufacturer or entrepreneur's income with profits. Profit, as we shall hereafter see, is the net surplus which is left after all the factors have received a full economic equivalent for their contribution to the product. Unless such an economic margin can be found, the socialist's claim that profit is robbery must be correct. That such a surplus is possible and does exist we shall subsequently see; and exactly how it takes place, on the basis of the economic equivalents and absolute equity, the law we are considering will adequately explain, if our hypothesis is correct. For the present we are concerned only with the purely price-making point of economic conditions.

Since no factor will contribute something for nothing, the manufacturer must, and will, receive an equivalent for his contribution to the product. His reward takes the form of a salary for superintendence,—which is a necessary part of the cost, just as much as that of the clerk, or the wages of the spinner and weaver.

But what, it may be asked, under these conditions is the return for the use of pure capital. Capital receives exactly the same kind of reward as every other factor, namely, the equivalent of its cost. It gets back all that it gives, or an equivalent for it. If any of the factors are governed by law, they must all be subject to the same law. If one can obtain more than it gives, they all can. This principle becomes quite clear if we once recognize the fact that gratuitous forces of nature charge nothing for their contribution of productive energy. For the same reason that air

[1] Part III., chapter iv.

and sunlight have no price because they cost nothing, do products which possess utility have a price only because they cost something, and the price is commensurate to the cost.   Every improved machine which diminishes the cost of production, to that extent approximates gratuitous natural forces, and nothing can be demanded for that part of the product.

If the improvements should reduce the cost of making cotton cloth by a cent a yard (since 1820 it has reduced the cost more than ten cents a yard) such reduction would be exactly as if one quarter of the cloth had been supplied gratuitously by nature. Capital, whose sole function is to aid and save labor, really sustains the same economic relation to production that natural forces do.   Indeed, it only succeeds in economizing labor when it substitutes the use of natural forces for human energy.   All the wealth that is thus produced is free, and no price can be charged for it.   The difference in the cost resulting from the improvement, through the automatic operation of economic law passes to the consumer by a reduction of the price.   This is why improved methods of production cheapen wealth.

Under conditions of uniform cost of production, therefore, with free economic movement and adequate knowledge of the phenomena, the price and cost of a commodity would be identical.   In other words, the primary law of prices, in the absence of secondary modifying influences, is, that commodities and services exchange in the quantitative ratio of exact economic equivalents ; and, consequently, unimpeded economic law establishes exact industrial equity, or absolute justice.

It will be observed that thus far we have considered the movement of prices only under purely hypothetical conditions, namely, where the product is made at a uniform cost.   As a matter of fact, there is probably no commodity, in the production of which ⹁ capital is employed, which is not produced at a great variety of costs ; hence no hypothesis can adequately explain the law of prices which is not applicable to conditions of varying costs of production.   We will therefore consider the subject in its most complex aspect, where the cost of making the same article varies. In order to do this, we will suppose that there are six (there may be six hundred) manufacturers, or groups of manufacturers, who produce the same grade of cotton cloth and sell it in the same market. And let us further suppose (what actually exists on every hand) that, from various causes, such as different degrees of skill, quantity of capital, quality of machinery, size of plant, location, etc., the actual cost of making the cloth and delivering it to the market is slightly different in each case. For example, suppose that A, who for some reason produces under the greatest disadvantage, can barely make print cloth of 64 x 64 quality at 4 cents a yard ; that B, through some economic advantage derived from larger capital, better location, superior management, etc., can produce the same cloth at 3⅘ a yard ; C, at 3⅗ ; D, at 3⅖ ; E, at 3⅕ ; and F, at 3 cents a yard.

Now, according to the law just stated, what will be the price of the cloth under these conditions? In the case where the cost of production was uniform we saw that the price was equal to the cost, but here we have six lots of the same commodity each produced at a different cost. For reasons already stated, the self-interest of both consumers and producers would make it impossible for the cloth to be sold at six different prices in the same market. The lowest price at which any producer will sell will be the highest at which consumers will buy ; and conversely, the highest price the consumers will give will be the lowest any producer will take. If the minimum price is fixed by the producer at cost, and the producer's minimum is the consumer's maximum, the price must still be fixed at the cost ; and if, as is generally admitted, there cannot be two prices in the same market, then the price of the whole must necessarily be determined by the cost of some one of the six classes of producers. Which of them occupies that price-making position ?

While the producer will not sell below cost, he will sell at any price from that point upwards, and he will only consent to sell at cost when the consumer refuses to buy at a price above it. Through the efforts of consumers to buy at the minimum, and their refusal to buy above the cost, the price will be forced down until it reaches the cost. Since the cost of A's cloth is the highest it will, of course, be the first to be reached. Therefore the downward movement of the price must necessarily be arrested at the cost of A's cloth, if his product is to be sold. Since to make his portion of the product costs 4 cents a yard, so far as he is concerned, that is the equivalent of the cloth, and must be the minimum price.   On the other hand, the consumer will not give more than 4 cents a yard, for the obvious reason that B, who can make it for $3\frac{4}{5}$ cents a yard, though anxious to get more, would willingly take 4 cents and make $\frac{1}{5}$ of a cent profit, rather than not sell.   So long as the consumer can obtain it from B for 4 cents a yard, he certainly will not give more than that for it to A. Therefore, 4 cents a yard is both the lowest A can afford to take, and the highest he can possibly get for his cloth.

It will be observed that A is here in exactly the same position that the producer was in the former case, where all the product was made at a uniform cost, namely : that he can neither accept less nor obtain more than the equivalent of the cost.   Manifestly what A must have for his cloth all the others can have for theirs, and 4 cents a yard will be the selling price of the whole product in that market.   Under these conditions, then, A will sell exactly at cost.   He will give and receive exactly *quid pro quo* and have no surplus or profit whatever.   All the other five being able to sell their product at the same price as A, while producing it at less cost, can give the same equivalent for what they get and still have a surplus equal to the amount by which their cost of production is less than his.   Here profit emerges, and the relative position of the various groups of producers will be as follows :

Manufacturers.	Cost per yard.	Price per yard.	Surplus profit per yard.	Total profit per 1,000 yards.
A	4 cts.	4 cts.	— cts.	—
B	$3\frac{4}{5}$	4	$\frac{1}{5}$	\$2.00
C	$3\frac{3}{5}$	4	$\frac{2}{5}$	4.00
D	$3\frac{2}{5}$	4	$\frac{3}{5}$	6.00
E	$3\frac{1}{5}$	4	$\frac{4}{5}$	8.00
F	3	4	1	10.00

It will be observed that two movements are here indicated : one of price, the other of cost.   Under conditions where different portions of the general supply are produced at a different cost per unit (as in all civilized communities), one of two things must occur : either the selling price must vary with the variation of cost, or a surplus equal to the difference must arise.   Since the self-interest of both consumers and producers operates to make prices tend to a uniformity in the same market, a surplus equal to the difference in the cost is inevitable. Nor is there any violation of ethics in either case. The uniformity of prices is strictly equitable, because each producer gives to the consumer the full equivalent of what he receives. The only reason that the producer of other commodities will give 4 cents, or its equivalent, to A for his cloth is, because they could not produce it for less if they devoted their energies and capital to the business. Therefore a yard of cloth to them is the exact equivalent of 4 cents. If, then, a yard of A's cloth is an equivalent for 4 cents, that of B, and all the others, must be equally so, because it is just like it.

Manifestly B, C, D, E, and F give just as complete an equivalent for what they get as does A. Hence the surplus is not obtained at the expense of equity. They pay the same wages and fulfil all the other economic requirements just as completely as does A, or as do the shoemakers or farmers with whom they trade. Their profits are due entirely to influences peculiar to them, and come from nature through them, and not from the consumer or laborer through injustice. Just as soon as the peculiar skill, or other means, by which B makes nature give him $\frac{1}{3}$ of a cent a yard surplus, becomes accessible to the shoemaker or farmer, so that by the application of the same amount of capital and labor they can produce the cloth at $3\frac{2}{3}$, it will cease to be an equivalent to them for 4 cents. They will then refuse to give 4 cents for it,—for the same reason that they previously refused to give $4\frac{1}{3}$. When that point is reached, rather than give 4 cents to A, they will withdraw their capital from shoemaking or farming and make cotton cloth, and A will have to leave the business unless he can adopt the superior methods employed by B, because he will have ceased to give an equivalent for 4 cents. The price of the cloth will then be $3\frac{2}{3}$ cents a yard, consequently B will have no profit, and the profit of all the others will be reduced by $\frac{1}{3}$ of a cent a yard. That is exactly the way the price of cotton cloth has been reduced from 30 to 4 cents during the present century.

What is true of cotton cloth and other manufactured articles, the production of which is entirely subject to economic and social forces, *i.e.*, the conscious effort of man—is equally true of agricultural products—whose production is largely influenced by unconscious cosmic forces. The reason the economic price of manufactured products does not necessarily follow supply and demand is because, in their case, an increase or diminution of the quantity does not necessarily affect the cost of production, or, if at all, but slightly. Conversely, the economic price of agricultural products does follow demand and supply because, in their case, an increase or diminution of the quantity—being chiefly due to the condition of the seasons—implies a similar change in the cost per unit.

We are now in a position to affirm four important postulates from which the primary law of prices can be definitely stated. (1) That under conditions of economic freedom, the general price for any given article in the same market tends to uniformity. (2) That, when the general supply of a commodity in any market is produced at a uniform expense per unit, the selling price will be the exact equivalent of the cost, and no surplus will exist. (3) That, wherever the aggregate supply of a given commodity is produced at different rates of cost per unit, the price will tend to a uniformity on the basis of the cost of those units which are produced at the greatest expense. (4) That a surplus, or profit, arises inversely to the cost of producing the different parts of the necessary supply, increasing as the cost diminishes below that of the most expensive, or price-making, portion.

SECTION IV.—*Influences which Modify the Operation of the Primary Law of Prices.*

In the preceding section we considered the movement of prices under purely economic conditions, namely : where cosmic forces did not influence production, except as consciously manipulated by man, and where both buyer and seller had the right and power to act in accordance with their own interests and best judgment, with adequate knowledge of the conditions affecting the commodity. We have seen that, under these conditions, there can be but one price for the same article in the same market,—which price will be the exact equivalent of the cost of producing the most expensive portion of the necessary supply in that market.

In actual experience, however, we find that these conditions do not literally fit the facts. We know that there frequently is more than one price for the same article in the same market, and also that commodities are sometimes sold below the cost of producing the dearest portion, and also below that of any portion of the supply. Consequently, if the primary law formulated in the previous section is correct, we must be able to explain in accordance therewith why and how this variation takes place, and whether it is an uneconomic perturbation which should be eliminated, or an economic variation which should be accepted and counted upon. Whenever there are two prices for the same article in the same market, it is manifest that either some consumers are giving more, or some producers are selling at less, than the cost. The exchange, under these conditions, is against the interest of one or the other of the contracting parties. Another fact, which is equally self-evident, is that neither the producer nor the consumer will do that which is inimical to his interest if he knows it and is free to prevent it. Therefore, whenever there is more than one price for the same article in the same market, it must be because the party giving more or taking less than the cost is either ignorant of the facts or is not free to act in accordance with his knowledge and interest. For example, to recur to our previous illustration, suppose the supply of cotton cloth, the dearest portion of which cost 4 cents a yard, is sold by one producer at 4 cents a yard, and by another at 5 cents. It is very clear that the purchaser who gives 5 cents a yard would not do so if he knew that he could just as easily obtain it for 4 cents. Therefore when he gives 5 cents it must of necessity be either because he does not know that it can be obtained for 4 cents, or that he is induced to believe that it is of a better quality than that which is sold at 4 cents, or else because his right, to purchase from the 4-cent dealer is restricted. On the other hand, if the prices vary in the same market through the producer selling at less than cost, as is not infrequently the case, that too must be the result of similar causes. To sell for less than cost is to lose ; and to continuously do that willingly is to voluntarily become bankrupt,—a course too absurd for sane people to pursue. Whenever a dealer sells at a loss, it must be because ; (1) that he either does not know at the time what his

9

goods cost him, or what it would cost him to replace them ; (2) that he did not know when he purchased them at what price he would have to sell them ; (3) that he miscalculated his own necessary cost in handling them ; (4) that he offers them for less than cost in order to attract customers to his place of business in the hope of selling them other commodities at an overcharge equal to or greater than his undercharge ; (5) that he is compelled to sell at a loss in order to meet urgent demands of previous indebtedness ; (6) that he is uneconomically handicapped by arbitrary authority.

It will readily be seen that, in the absence of all these conditions, the consumer would not give more nor the producer take less than the cost, and the price would be governed by the primary law formulated in the last section. It will also be observed that the changes of price from these causes are not economic variations, but that they are all uneconomic perturbations. That is to say, they are fluctuations from the economic price, and are always exchanges in which one gets more, or the other less, than an equivalent. That these perturbations are due to the causes here indicated is clearly shown by the fact that they are greater in the retail than in the wholesale market, and greatest of all in those sections of the retail market where poverty and ignorance are most prevalent. The obvious reason for this is that in such localities the average consumer is more ignorant, and therefore more easily imposed upon, both as to the price and the quality of the commodities. He is also often under pecuniary obligations to the merchant, and therefore less free to trade elsewhere. It will also be found that in these sections of the community the greatest amount of misrepresentation as to the quality of goods prevails. Among retailers who sell to the more intelligent and characterful customers this variation diminishes, and the same articles are sold at a more uniform price. This is inevitable for two reasons. First, because the fraudulent element is largely eliminated through the impossibility of imposing upon the consumers as to the quality ; and second, because the prevailing prices at the various stores are more generally known to the consumer. If we go to the wholesale markets, where the prices, quality, and cost are still more correctly known by the purchaser, we find almost no variation in the price for the same article in the same market at the same time, the only difference being in the discount to purchasers of larger quantities, which is a purely economic transaction, it being possible to handle large quantities at a lower cost per unit than small quantities. It will thus be seen that, just in proportion as the causes of these uneconomic perturbations are eliminated, the price tends to conform to the primary law.

Since all these perturbations from the economic price involve loss to the producer or the consumer, according as it is above or below the cost, it follows that all the motives for human action will tend to influence both the consumer and the producer to avoid disadvantageous exchanges just as fast as they become informed of the fact. As soon as the consumer discovers that he is buying roasted peas for coffee, cotton for wool, or paper for leather, he will endeavor to trade where this fraud is not practised upon him. Accordingly, we find to-day that, in the best houses on Broadway, the reputation for integrity is an important feature of business success, while on Canal Street and the extreme east side, ethics in business is of no commercial importance. On the other hand, as soon as the producer discovers that he is selling at a loss—whether through a miscalculation of the market, a wrong estimate of his own expenses, a misrepresentation of the quality of the goods, or other cause,—he will retrace his steps and endeavor to correct the error for the future ; and every correction of the error arising from any of these causes tends to bring him back to the position which he thought he occupied, namely : purchasing the genuine article at the minimum price. It is thus evident that the same influences which, under conditions of economic freedom, make prices equal the cost of production, will, under conditions of uneconomic perturbations, constantly force prices to tend towards that point.

Therefore, the actual law of prices—the law to which the price of commodities and service constantly *tends* to conform —may be stated thus : *the price of commodities and service tends to adjust itself to the cost of producing the most expensive portion of the supply consumable in any given market, this tendency increasing in uniformity and persistence directly as the knowledge of economic phenomena and the freedom of the economic action are increased.*

SECTION V.—*Verification of the Economic Law of Prices.*

If this hypothesis is correct it will enable us to explain the price-movement of all classes of commodities and service with equal correctness. Will it stand the test ?

For the purposes of verification price phenomena may be conveniently grouped as follows ; (1) manufactured articles whose production is entirely subject to economic influences : (2) agricultural produce, which includes all classes of farm and garden products, fruits, etc., whose quantity and quality are largely effected by non-economic influences—*i. e.*, uncontrollable cosmic forces : (3) labor, or human service, which is chiefly affected by social influences.

1. First, then, will this hypothesis account for the price-movement of manufactured commodities ? The history of the price of manufactured products in the wholesale market shows two characteristic facts. One is the constant tendency of prices to permanently fall with no disadvantage to the producer, and without any perceptible variation in the ratio of demand and supply. The other is a tendency to periodic " over-production," which, instead of permanently lowering prices proportionately to the relative over-supply, results in the closing of factories and of workshops, discharging labor, loss, bankruptcy, and other uneconomic conditions. Both of these facts are adequately accounted for by our hypothesis.

The reason that the price of manufactured products tends to permanently fall—with mutual advantage—is that the cost of producing the most expensive portion of the supply is gradually diminished through the concentration of capital and the use of improved methods of production, giving a larger aggregate product per unit of productive force. This theory affords an equally clear explanation of why loss and bankruptcy follow so-called over-production. It is because the increased supply involves a corresponding increase in the cost of productive force that no reduction in the price can be made without loss. Consequently one of two losing alternatives is inevitable, namely : either to sell at less than cost, or to suspend business. When, after disposing of the surplus through one or the other of these losing avenues, the normal process of production is again resumed, it must be at the prices which previously prevailed ; that is to say, the price of commodities must sustain the same ratio to that of labor as before, for the reason that no diminution in the cost, per unit of productive force, has taken place. Thus prices under both conditions obey the same law, namely : of *constantly tending towards the cost of producing the most expensive portion of the supply.* Any variation of prices contrary to this law involves economic loss and social disadvantage.

2. The price-movement of agricultural products is quite different from that of manufactured articles, but, if examined in the light of this hypothesis, it will be found to follow exactly the same law. In manufactured commodities we have seen that the general tendency has been towards lower prices without loss ; and that periodic increase of production (over-production) fails to lower prices, except by loss and bankruptcy. In agriculture, these two facts are reversed. The general tendency of agricultural prices is to rise without increasing the profits, and the periodic increase of production (exceptionally large crops) lowers prices without loss. In other words, the general tendency of agricultural prices is to rise without any perceptible variation in the ratio of demand and supply, but in the yearly product prices rise and fall with the demand and supply ; nor is the reason for this hitherto unexplained phenomenon difficult to understand.

The price of agricultural produce—especially meat, butter, poultry, and garden products—tends to rise for the reason that the cost of their production tends to increase. This is due to the obvious fact that the use of labor-saving methods has not reduced the cost of productive energy per unit as much as the general rise of wages has increased it, and consequently the net cost of producing the most expensive portion of the supply in agriculture has, in many instances, increased during the present century. Nor is the fact that agricultural prices tend, from year to year, to rise and fall with the variation in the demand and supply, less easy to explain. The reason for this is that the sudden increase in the supply is not accompanied, as in the case of manufactured products, with a corresponding increase in the cost. Hence, every unit of product added to the crop diminishes the cost of every other unit. For example, if the normal wheat crop in 1889 were 20 bushels per acre, and, through the influence of a favorable season, the crop in 1890 should be 30 bushels per acre, each bushel in 1890—with the exception of the items of harvesting, threshing, and transportation—would cost about one third less than in 1889.   Therefore the price per bushel of that crop might fall about 25 per cent. without any injury to the farmer, because, with the exception of the items referred to, the 30 bushels in 1890 did not cost any more than did the 20 bushels the previous year. The increased supply being chiefly gratuitous, it reduced the cost per bushel of the whole crop to that extent.   This explains the fact, so common in the history of agriculture, that farmers often get as much for a small crop as for a large one.

The increased or diminished quantity only affects the price through operating upon the cost.   And the only reason why the price of shoes does not fall with the increased supply—without loss to the producer—and the price of wheat does, is because the increase in the supply of shoes does not diminish the cost of producing the shoes, while with every increase in the supply of the wheat the cost of its production is proportionately reduced. Therefore, while the price of agricultural products follows the variations of supply and demand, it is really governed by the same economic force as that of manufactured products, namely : the cost of producing the most expensive portion of the supply.

Moreover, this hypothesis not only accounts for the disparity between the general movement of the prices of agricultural and manufactured products in civilized countries, but it also affords a rational explanation of why they practically move together in uncivilized countries.   When we recognize the fact that the price of agricultural produce in civilized countries tends to rise, because the general rise of wages has increased the cost of production more than the use of labor-saving methods has reduced it; and that the price of manufactured products tends to fall, because the use of labor-saving methods in their production has reduced the cost more than the general rise of wages has increased it, we have no difficulty in understanding why this disparity of movement does not exist in less civilized countries, where machinery is but slightly employed in either manufacture or agriculture.

3. In the light of this theory the infinite variation in the price of labor, which has hitherto been an economic enigma, at once assumes a rational aspect and obeys the orderly operation of

economic law. The price of labor, like that of every thing else, constantly tends to follow the line of the cost of producing the most expensive portion of any given commodity in the same market. The price of the Asiatic is lower than that of the European, ·and the price of the European is lower than that of the American, because his cost is less. The price of the farm-laborer is lower than that of the mechanic, and the price of the mechanic is lower in the country than in the city ; the price of the mechanic in the city is lower than that of the professional classes, and the price of the labor of women is lower than that of men in the same grade, for the simple reason that the cost of living, and consequently the cost of their labor, is less.

What we have seen to be true in the case of manufactured products is also true of labor. The mere increase in the quantity, if of the same social quality, cannot permanently reduce the price, and *vice versa.* It may create enforced idleness which, as in the case of over-production, will inflict serious loss, but those who are employed must still receive the equivalent of their cost. If, however, the increased supply of labor is due to the introduction of a lower social quality—*i.e.,* less expensive grade of laborers,—this will tend to reduce the price. But the fall of the price in this case, as in that of agriculture, is due to the fact that the increased quantity was accompanied by reduced cost. It is the failure to recognize this distinction in the movement of price-making phenomena that has given such a general acceptance to the doctrine of demand and supply. The presence of the quantity is more easily observed than is the influence of the social quality, or cost. Hence the former has been assumed to be the determining cause, when it was only the accompanying incident, and the real cause has been generally overlooked. In order to illustrate this movement in the case of wages, let us suppose that there were 10,000 men employed in a given industry—the minimum cost of the most expensive 1,000 of them being $2.00 a day —if the laborers in that industry were increased to 15,000, and the least expensive of the new-comers required $2.00 a day, and the remainder of them required more, this increase of laborers seeking employment would not reduce wages. The result would be that the new-comers would fail to obtain employment. If, on the other hand, the 5,000 new-comers were from a lower civilization, and their cost of living were only $1.00 or $1.50 a day, their influx would cause a reduction in the rate of wages. This would not be brought about by reducing the pay of the most expensive that had been previously employed, but by substituting the new-comers for the old, in which case the dear men would be supplanted by the cheap men. The $2.00-a-day men would not be working for $1.00, but they would be discharged and the $1.00-a-day men would take their places. Thus, while the rate of wages would have fallen, it would not have fallen for the same laborers, but it would have fallen to the level of the new laborers because their cost was lower. This is what investigation has shown to be the case in hundreds of instances where non-union men have taken the places of strikers at a lower rate of wages. The non-union men do not take lower, but in such cases often receive higher, wages than they have previously obtained, which increase is made possible for them by the union men, and the union men who struck for the rise, and were superseded by the non-union men, seldom go to work elsewhere at lower wages, but, as a rule, find employment at their trade or in some other occupation at rates approximating those which they struck to secure.[1]

If the market for labor were increased with the advent of the new laborers so that the whole 15,000 could be employed, then no reduction of wages would take place ; because, in that case, the original $2.00-a-day laborers being necessary, they still would form the most expensive portion of the supply, and their cost would consequently determine the rate of wages, and $2.00 a day would continue to be paid. It will be seen that, while the fall in the wages accompanies and seems to be fixed by the increased supply, it is really governed by the cost of the most expensive portion of the necessary supply. The fact that the $2.00-a-day laborers were no longer needed destroyed their price-regulating influence.

Suppose, for example, that 10,000 $3.00-a-day American mechanics should emigrate to a given locality in China where 10,000 laborers were working, at the same trade, at from 10 to 20 cents

[1] The exception to this is where the strike has been inaugurated through the undue influence of a few individuals, and in advance of the demand of the most advanced 20 per cent. of the class or trade.

a day ; it is very clear that the competition of the $3.00-a-day Americans against the 10- or 20-cent-a-day Chinamen could not reduce their wages,—although the supply was increased over the demand by 100 per cent. The result in such a case would be exactly the reverse of the one just referred to, namely : that the new-comers, instead of supplanting the old, and thereby establishing a lower rate of wages, if employed at all, would necessarily establish a much higher rate of wages, because their cost would be higher. Other things remaining the same, the fact would be that the new-comers would not be employed,—because their cost would be so much greater than the old laborers, and therefore the rate of wages would remain unchanged, and the new-comers would remain unemployed ; whereas, in the other case, the old workers became the unemployed, because the new-comers were less expensive. It is clear then that the increased supply affects wages only when the new-comers introduce a variation in the cost. If they are cheaper a lower price will be established, because the cost-level is lower ; if they are dearer the price will be raised (if they are employed), because the cost-level will be higher. But the latter case seldom occurs, because the dearer man will seldom be employed in preference to the cheaper. This is why all emigration is from countries with a lower wage-level towards those with a higher wage-level ; why there is no emigration of European laborers to Asia, nor of American laborers to Europe. Here, then, we have a universal, scientific law of prices which explains both the permanent economic tendency and the uneconomic perturbations of all classes of price-receiving phenomena.

CHAPTER V.

THE LAW OF THE COST OF PRODUCTION.

Section I.—*Popular Errors Regarding the Cost of Production.*

Having seen that the cost of production is the controlling factor in the law of prices, we are now led to the consideration of what determines the cost of production. The popular theory upon this subject, though suggested by Adam Smith, was formulated and most ably stated by Ricardo—who insists that the "natural price of commodities," and the cost of their production, are determined by the quantity of labor involved.

Assuming the existence of primitive hunters and fishermen, Ricardo says : "The comparative value of the fish and the game would be entirely regulated by the quantity of labor realized in each ; whatever might be the quantity of production, or however high or low general wages or profits might be." [1] What is true under these simple conditions, he asserts, will always be equally true in the most complex society.

It may be readily admitted that the same principle which governed the cost of production in the earliest state of society would obtain under the most complex conditions, but before we can consent to interpret the complex phenomena of modern society by a hypothesis based upon the simple conditions of the most primitive social state, we must at least be sure that it affords the true explanation of the phenomena from which it was constructed. It frequently happens in the more simple stages of phenomena that two facts occur simultaneously, either of which appears to be the cause of the succeeding phenomena ; and, from direct sense

---

[1] " Political Economy and Taxation," p. 18.

impression, that which is most easily observed is most likely to be regarded as the cause. When the phenomena become more complex, however, and the variations more numerous and subtle, the effects of the two facts are separated, and it becomes of vital importance to learn which of the two enters the hypothesis.

For example, when only the simpler astronomical phenomena were known, the geocentric hypothesis was sufficient to account for them ; but as the observations increased, and more complex phenomena appeared, the theory that the earth was the centre of the solar system became wholly inadequate, and the heliocentric hypothesis was necessary. So, too, when only the simpler geological phenomena were observed, the theory of a special creation appeared all-sufficient, but as the knowledge of geological phenomena increased, this theory became inadequate to explain the age of the earth, and had to be abandoned. The same plausible error is also apparent in the law of supply and demand. At first glance, the statement that the quantity of labor devoted to procuring the game and the fish determines their cost seems quite plausible, but if we examine the case of the primitive man a little closer we shall find that an oversight similar to those just mentioned has been committed. We will assume, as Ricardo evidently does, that the habits and customs of the hunter and the fisherman are identical. If so, and the hunter can average one deer a day, and the fisherman can catch two salmon a day, the quantity of labor devoted to procuring one deer and that devoted to procuring two salmon would be exactly alike. It would then be perfectly correct to say that the cost of two salmon would be exactly equal to that of one deer. In other words, the cost of producing either salmon or deer would always be identical with the *quantity* of labor devoted to procuring either of them. It will be observed, however, that it would be equally correct to say that the cost of producing either the deer or the salmon was always identical with the *cost* of the labor devoted to procuring them, because, under these conditions, the cost of a given quantity of labor is exactly the same in either case. Therefore, the variation of the quantity of labor is a variation of the cost of labor. Hence, so far as explaining this simple class of phenomena is concerned, it would make no difference whether we assume that the cost of the deer or the beaver is determined by the *quantity* or by the *cost* of the labor which is devoted to their production, because in this case the two facts are identical.

If we push the inquiry a little further, and ask why the quantity of labor devoted to procuring deer or salmon determines the cost, the true answer is because a given quantity of effort involves a given amount of cost to the laborer ; hence, the more labor he puts into a thing the greater is its cost. And if we ask why the cost of labor should affect the cost of the product, the obvious answer is because the laborer must obtain as much for his labor as it cost him, or he could not continue to furnish it.

It thus appears that the mere quantity of labor devoted to catching the deer or salmon affects their cost only as it represents the cost of the effort to the laborers, and hence the amount which they must obtain for it. In other words, the same quantity of labor involves the same cost to the hunter and the fisherman only because the cost of a unit of labor is the same to each man. Therefore, while it is true in this case that the cost of producing the deer or the salmon varies exactly with the change in the quantity of labor devoted to obtaining them ; in the other cases the cost of the product varies with the *quantity* of labor, because every variation in the quantity carries with it a variation in the *cost* of that labor. To show this more clearly, let us take the same two men and suppose that the cost of living of the hunter is double that of the fisherman ; that he either consumes more expensive things, or that a greater number of things enter into his life. In this case, if he can only kill a deer a day, and the fisherman can catch two salmon a day, one deer will cost twice as much as two salmon, although no more labor is devoted to catching it. The reason that the deer costs more is because the labor devoted to catching it is more expensive. Since the labor of the hunter costs twice the labor of the fisherman, an hour's labor devoted to hunting costs twice as much as an hour's labor devoted to fishing ; consequently the cost of the product of the hunter will be double that of the fisherman. Thus we see that in the last analysis—even in the case of the primitive man—it is not merely the quantity, but the cost, of the labor that really determines the cost of the product. Therefore, the statement, that the same amount of labor always involves the same cost in production, is only true when it is accompanied by the other fact, namely, that the labor in both cases *costs* the same.

If we follow Ricardo from his primitive hunter and fisherman to his modern " stocking maker " we shall see how completely the error resulting from the failure to recognize this distinction permeates his whole doctrine and vitiates his conclusions regarding the cost of production. He says : " If we look to a state of society in which greater improvements have been made, and in which the arts and commerce flourish, we shall still find that commodities vary in value conformably with this principle. . . . To convince ourselves that this is the real foundation of exchangeable value, let us suppose any improvement to be made in the means of abridging labor in any one of the various processes through which the raw cotton must pass, before the manufactured stockings come to the market, to be exchanged for other things, and observe the effect which will follow. If fewer men were required to cultivate the raw cotton, or if fewer sailors were employed in navigating, or shipwrights in constructing, the ship in which it was conveyed to us ; if fewer hands were employed in raising the buildings and machinery, or if these, when raised, were rendered more efficient, the stockings would inevitably fall in value, and consequently command less of other things. They would fall because a less quantity of labor was necessary to their production. . . . No alteration in the wages of labor produces any alteration in the relative value of these commodities." [1] It will be observed that Ricardo's conclusions in regard to the stockings are true only on the condition that something else is true— namely, that the price of labor has remained the same. Although reducing the quantity of labor in the manufacture of stockings may, it does not follow that it necessarily will, produce the effect here stated.

As, for example, suppose that, through the use of improved machinery, the stockings could be made with one tenth fewer men, and, at the same time, that the price of the laborers still employed in making them were increased ten per cent., the cost of producing the stockings would remain absolutely unchanged, although ten per cent. less labor was devoted to their production. And, consequently, if the price of labor were advanced ten per cent., and the quantity of labor required to make the stockings remained the same (a fact of common occurrence), the cost of

[1] " Principles of Political Economy and Taxation," pp. 17-19.—McCulloch's edition, 1881.

producing the stockings would then rise ten per cent. without any change whatever in the quantity of labor required to produce them. It is thus very clear that the cost of producing the stockings may change without any alteration in the quantity of labor expended upon them, or the quantity of labor may change without any variation in the cost of making the stockings. Whether or not a change in the quantity of labor required to make the stockings will change the cost of their production, depends entirely upon whether it makes any change in the total amount paid for the labor employed in producing them.

The experience of Mr. Thomas Brassey, who probably employed a greater number of laborers in more countries than any other man in the world, fully establishes this position. Some of Mr. Brassey's experiences while employing labor in the construction of railroads in England, France, Spain, Italy, Saxony, Austria, Hungary, Belgium, Moldavia, Austria, Canada, the Argentine Republic, Syria, Persia, and India, when, according to Sir Arthur Helps, he sometimes had over eighty thousand persons in his employ at one time, are given by his son in his book called "Work and Wages."

In the construction of the Grand Trunk Railroad, so far as French Canadians were employed, he shows that about two fifths more labor was required to do the same work than in England.[1] Still the total cost was about the same. In the construction of the Paris and Rouen railroad in France a similar result is shown. Five days of a Frenchman's labor was only equal to three of an Englishman's; still a mile of road built by the French laborers cost no more than the road built by the English laborers, simply because two fifths less wages were paid to the French than to the English laborers.[2] So, in the quarry at Bonnieres, four Frenchmen, or three Irishmen, were found to be equal to two Englishmen.[3]

In contrasting the quantity of work and wages in England and Ireland, Mr. Brassey shows that, although about twice as many laborers were required in Ireland as in England to build a mile of railroad, "sub-contracts in the Irish railroad were let at the prices which had been previously paid in Staffordshire."[4] And

[1] "Work and Wages," pp. 86, 87.
[2] *Ibid.*, pp. 79–82.
[3] *Ibid.*, p. 82.
[4] *Ibid.*, p. 69.

in India, where the "sweat and sacrifice" of twelve or more native laborers was bestowed on making as much road as would be accomplished by one Englishman, Mr. Brassey declares that, "mile for mile, the cost of railway work is about the same as in England."[1] The same is true of other industries. The toil of fifty-two laborers is required in smelting the same amount of pig-iron in France as is done by twenty-five laborers on the Tees[2]; and the cost of producing the iron in the two countries is about the same. Statistics show that the same variation in the quantity of labor required to produce the same commodities in different countries prevails in different branches in the same countries, and consequently that *it is invariably the total amount paid, and not the quantity of labor employed, which determines the cost of production.*

SECTION II.—*High-Priced Labor Makes Low Cost of Production and Cheap Products.*

After what has been said, to affirm that a rise in the wages of labor will lessen the cost of production and diminish prices, may have a paradoxical seeming. If the value of commodities is determined by the cost of production, and the cost of production is determined by the price—and not by the quantity,—of labor it would, at first, seem to follow, that a rise of wages involves an increase of cost and a consequent rise in the price of products. But this is one of the many instances in economics where things are not as they appear from direct observation. Ricardo could see that, other things being the same, any variation in the quantity of labor expended causes a corresponding variation in the cost of production ; but he could not see that any change in the price of labor has the same effect. To him, the only result of a rise in wages is a fall in profits. Indeed, he explicitly declares : " No alteration in the wages of labor could produce any alteration in the relative value of these commodities "[3]; but he adds : " Not so with the other great cause of the variation in the value of commodities, namely : the increase or diminution of the quan-

---

[1] " Work and Wages," pp. 79–82.

[2] F. A. Walker, " Wages Question," p. 44. See also Brassey's " Work and Wages," p. 165, 2d edition.

[3] " Principles of Political Economy and Taxation," p. 19.

tity of labor necessary to produce them. . . . Every improvement in machinery, in tools, in buildings, in raising the raw material, saves labor and enables us to produce the commodity to which the improvement is applied with more facility, and consequently its value alters." [1]

In saying that improved machinery is the potent means of reducing the cost of production, Ricardo recognized a fundamental truth, but by failing to see the connection between machinery and wages, he entirely overlooked the influences which promote the use of the labor-saving methods. If he had seen the logical necessity of explaining the causes that promote the use of machinery as clearly as he did see the fact that machinery reduces the cost of production, his investigations would have forced him into recognizing the absurdity of his cheap-labor doctrine. All writers on economics have shown a due appreciation of the fact that the extensive use of capital and improved methods is indispensable to the large and cheap production of wealth. Nor have they had any difficulty in seeing that, by the increased concentration of capital, the cost of production and the price of commodities have been lowered ; but they have made practically no effort to explain how the successful use of capital and machinery becomes possible. Adam Smith did go far enough to see that the division of labor and the use of capital was "limited by the extent of the market," but it did not occur to him to consider the economic relation that wages sustain to the extent of the market, and that relation has been largely overlooked since his time.

American writers have recently attempted to approach this subject on independent lines. The most creditable efforts in this direction are those of Stuart Wood and John B. Clark.[2] Both of these writers fully recognize auxiliary capital as the means of lessening the cost of production and of cheapening commodities. Indeed, they go one step further and recognize the fact that capital, or machinery, can only be employed in production when it is cheaper as a productive force than labor. " Machinery is preferred," says Stuart Wood,[3] " simply because

---

[1] Principles of Political Economy and Taxation, p. 24.
[2] " Publications of American Economic Association," vol. iv., No. 1.
[3] *Quarterly Journal of Economics*, pp. 67, 68.

the cost of production is lessened by its use. Also, in many processes now executed by hand, machinery would be equally efficient, but it is not used because it would involve a greater cost
of production, . . . but there are other cases in which the
cost is equal, or very nearly equal, whether labor is employed, or
auxiliary capital. In such cases, the slightest change in the price
of labor immediately affects the demand for it . . . Where
the cost is just equal, labor and capital will be used indifferently.
On either side of this point that one of the two will be employed
which is relatively the cheapest."

Stuart Wood manifestly sees that something in addition to the
mere existence of capital is necessary to make its economic use
possible. It is also clear to him that nothing can do this which does
not make capital cheaper than labor, as a means of production.
The important question that arises here is the same as that which
confronted Ricardo, namely : how, or under what conditions,
will the use of capital become cheaper than labor ? To this
question Wood, like Ricardo, is silent. The nearest that he
comes to dealing with it is to suggest that the one will be employed which will accept the least return for its effort.

According to this theory, capital can only be employed by discharging labor. If this doctrine is correct, the anti-power-loom
rioters in England were right, and the ignorant laborers—who to-
day oppose the introduction of improved machinery—are acting
upon sound economic principles. In short, the factory methods of
production would simply mean the degradation of labor, and the
charge so commonly made by the socialists, that capitalists are
the natural enemy of the laborer, would be fully sustained, because the effect of capital would constantly be to compel the
laborer to choose between low wages and enforced idleness.

Again, if capital could only be employed by discharging labor
it would destroy its own success. By discharging the laborer it
would destroy his power to consume, and thereby reduce the
markets for its own products. The enforced idleness thus created reduces the market in exactly the same proportion that the
use of capital saves labor, and consequently all that is gained by
the cheap product is lost by the increased idleness.

This theory is clearly contrary to experience. It is one of the
most obvious facts in the history of machine-made products

10

that the use of capital and machinery in production does not permanently increase enforced idleness among the laborers. There are three important facts always connected with the use of machinery. (1) It can only be employed when it can do the work cheaper than labor. (2) It can only do the work cheaper than labor when it produces the same amount with less labor. (3) It can only successfully save labor when it is accompanied by new employment creating conditions. Displaced labor can only be saved when it is re-employed. How to create new employments to absorb the discharged laborers must be explained before the question—how capital can become a cheaper productive force than labor—can be answered.

The great fact underlying all successful production is consumption. The first condition to the success of any method in production is a market for the products ; therefore nothing can make the use of capital successful which does not supply a market for the products. The mistake of Wood's theory is that it fails to reckon with this fact. It assumes that which Clark more explicitly states,[1] namely : " As capital outgrows labor in quantity . . . it pushes outward the independent margin of its own field." This is an entire mistake. Capital can only become an active, productive force under certain social and economic conditions, and it is wholly powerless to create these conditions for itself. Capital is a tool, or instrument, and its function is to supply markets, but not to make them,—a fact that these economists have overlooked. If their doctrine were correct, every increased supply of a commodity at a reduced price would be certain to find a market ; and yet the patent-offices of the world supply evidence to the contrary. Thousands upon thousands of examples of improved contrivances, that can produce commodities at less than current price, cannot be used because their products cannot be sold.

It is true, within certain limits, that to reduce the price of a commodity will increase the sales, because that will put it within the reach of those who previously desired it, but whose desire was not sufficiently strong to induce them to give the larger price. It is only because the desire already exists, however, that the product can be sold, even at the reduced price.[2] The most that

---

[1] Publications of Economic Association, vol. iv., No. 1, p. 57.

[2] This much was clear even to Ricardo, for he says : " If the natural price of

can ever occur in this line is that the price can descend to meet the weakest effectual demand.

It is entirely outside the province and power of capital to create the conditions for its own successful employment. Were this otherwise, capital would never be idle, and failure, bankruptcy, and industrial depressions could never occur, because it could always make investments profitable by creating markets for its own products ; whereas we know that hundreds of millions of dollars are constantly waiting for an opportunity to be profitably employed, and failure, bankruptcy, and industrial depressions are among the most painful industrial experiences.

Since capital can only be profitably employed when it can work cheaper than labor, and since neither the formation of new industries nor the extension of old ones is possible without an increase in the consumption, it follows that the employment of capital in production finally depends upon the extension of the market for commodities. No theory, therefore, can explain the employment of capital which does not explain the creation of new or larger markets. This neither Ricardo, Wood, nor Clark has done, and consequently they have failed to explain how capital can become cheaper than labor, and machinery be economically substituted for muscle.

It should be remembered that it is a characteristic feature of the use of machinery that its superiority over labor does not consist in its capacity to produce a small amount of wealth at a less cost than labor, but chiefly in its power to produce a much larger quantity at a relatively less cost, *i.e.* a smaller cost per unit of product. And, as the cost of the whole product must be defrayed by the income from that portion which is sold, the economic success of the machine depends upon the possibility of selling all the increased quantity which it produces.

There is no fact in modern history more easily demonstrated than that the products of steam-driven machinery are mainly consumed by the common people—the masses. While the mid-

labor should fall 50 per cent. from some great discovery in the science of agriculture, the demand would not greatly increase, for no man would desire more than would satisfy his wants ; and as the demand would not increase, neither would the supply, for a commodity is not supplied merely because it can be produced, but because there is a demand for it."—" Principles of Political Economy and Taxation," chapter xxx., p. 234, McCulloch's edition, 1881.

dle and, to some extent, the upper classes consume machine-made products, their consumption constitutes such a small proportion of the market that probably no modern factory or railroad could be sustained by their demand, at present prices. It is therefore the consumption of the laboring classes which determines the success or failure of factory methods of production. This explains why the railroads and the factory system cannot be employed in Asia, Africa, and the more backward countries in continental Europe, where the wages are low and the masses consume but slightly of manufactured products.

Therefore, as wages must measure the extent of consumption by the masses, we are inevitably driven to the conclusion that instead of the advance of wages being dependent upon the more extensive use of capital and machinery,—as Wood and Clark[1] and the wage-fund economists would have us believe, the fact is exactly the reverse, and the successful use of capital depends upon the general and permanent rise of wages. Clearly, then, it is to the influences that promote the rise of wages that we must look for the extension of the use of capital, and the consequent lessening of the cost of production and lowering of prices. Although the consideration of the law of wages, and the influences that promote their increase, will be deferred to a subsequent chapter, it is not difficult to see at present how, through the normal operation of economic law, a rise of wages necessarily tends to promote the use of capital and machinery.

Wages, being the price of labor, are chiefly influenced by the social forces that determine the life and character of the laborer. Although their upward movement is always subtle and composite, moving in almost insensible gradations, it is none the less positive and aggressive. The first economic effect of the laborer's demand for high wages is an increase of pressure upon the employer's profit, who will endeavor to avoid it by passing it on to the consumer in the form of higher prices. The consumer, acting upon the same principle, endeavors to resist the higher prices by refus-

[1] " By this twofold action only can wages rise with greater rapidity. But that movement of the margins is possible only by means of a considerable excess in the supply of capital unbalanced by labor."—" Possibility of a Scientific Law of Wages," in Publications of American Economic Association, vol. iv., No. 1, p. 59.

ing to purchase, or by buying a smaller quantity of the products, thus forcing the manufacturer to lose by smaller sales what he gains by increased prices. On the other hand, if the employer attempts to resist the upward tendency of wages, he is met by the stoppage of his works, and this involves an economic loss which will only be encountered as a last resort. Ultimately, therefore, the employer is compelled to choose between the use of the improved methods by which his commodities can be made cheaper, or the loss of his profits, and perhaps of his capital. Thus, while unconsciously avoiding the dangers that beset him, he becomes able to produce a larger amount at the same cost, and by this means he can comply with the demand of his laborers for higher wages without diminishing his profits—and often reduce the price of the commodity as well. A reduction in the price puts commodities within the reach of another large class who were previously unable to consume them, and the market is thereby extended, thus enlarging the income without raising the rate of profit ; all of which tends to further increase the demand for labor, and to improve the general well-being of the community.

We are now in a position to present a complete formula of the law of prices, thus : (1) The price of commodities constantly tends towards the cost of producing the most expensive portion of the necessary supply in any given market—the movement toward that equilibrium increasing directly as economic knowledge and freedom are extended, and inversely as they are restricted. (2) The cost of production is ultimately determined by the price of labor and moves inversely with wages. (3) Prices are finally governed by wages—rising as wages fall, and falling as wages rise.

If we regard the fact that high wages make low prices as a principle in economic law, it will become clear that a low paid man is the dearest thing on earth ; and that, through the democracy of natural law, the wealth and civilization now enjoyed by the most advanced people can be made cheaper for all, than the poverty and barbarism which now prevail among the great mass of mankind.

CHAPTER VI.

MONEY AND ITS ECONOMIC FUNCTION.

Section I.—*What is Money?*

Money is generally defined as the medium of exchange. The chief objection to this definition is its indefiniteness. In order to receive any clear idea from the expression, "medium of exchange," it is necessary to know in what way money facilitates exchange. Is it wealth, or is it only a representative of wealth? If a representative of wealth, how does it represent it,—as property, or as credit?

Francis A. Walker has endeavored to solve this difficulty by defining money [1] as "that which passes freely from hand to hand throughout the community in final discharge of debts and full payment for commodities." This has been accepted by Sidgwick and others as the best and most complete definition of money yet given, and as such it is used in the last edition of the " Encyclopedia Britannica." [2]

If this definition be correct, money must be wealth. A debt, being simply wealth due from another, can only be finally discharged by the payment of the wealth due, or its equivalent in some other form of wealth. Obviously, nothing but wealth can economically cancel an obligation to deliver wealth. If money is wealth, then every increase of money must be just so much actual addition to the aggregate wealth of the community,—a notion which is too absurd to need refuting. Yet it is exactly because, in one way or another, money has been regarded as wealth, or capital, that so many schemes have been invented for enriching society by increasing the value of money.

[1] " Money, Trade, and Industry," p. iv.
[2] Vol. xiv., p. 720.

150

In considering the question whether or not money is wealth, we must be careful not to confound the idea of money with the material of which it is made. If money is wealth, it must necessarily contain the equivalent in wealth of that for which it will exchange. This we know is frequently not the case. When sheep, or cattle, or corn were used as money, or when money is made of gold or silver of full weight and standard fineness, this may be true, but when it is made from almost any other substance this is not true. When a gold dollar of full weight and fineness is exchanged for a given amount of cloth, furniture, or other commodities, property in the dollar is the economic equivalent of the commodity. But when a hundred bronze pennies are exchanged for the same amount of commodities, an equivalent in property is not given because the value of the wealth in the pennies is not as great as that in the commodities. And when a dollar bank-note is given for a gold dollar or its equivalent in any other commodity, the receiver of the note does not get the equivalent in wealth of one per cent. of what he gave. But, as money, he received as much in the paper bank-note, or in the bronze pennies, as in the gold or silver dollar. Indeed, if the pennies, or bank-notes, were regarded simply as wealth, they never would be accepted in exchange for the commodities, or for the gold. It is only as money that they are ever so accepted. The reason for this is that, as money, the notes and pennies were the equivalent of the gold, silver, or commodities, but, as wealth, they were not. Obviously, therefore, money and wealth are not identical. Wealth may be made into money, but money *per se* is not wealth.

If we examine a few transactions in which money is employed, the difference between wealth and money, and the functions that they fill, will be more easily discerned. For example, take a transaction between the producers of apples and shoes. The shoemaker desires a barrel of apples and the farmer desires a pair of shoes. When the farmer delivers the apples to the shoemaker the latter is in the farmer's debt, say $2.00. When the shoemaker delivers the shoes, the debt is finally cancelled. But suppose the shoemaker wants two barrels of apples, and the farmer wants only one pair of shoes ; when the apples and the shoes are both delivered, a balance, equivalent to one barrel of apples, will remain to the credit of the farmer. The shoemaker offers him a second pair of shoes, but these he declines, having no use for them, or having a stronger desire for something else. Since the shoemaker wants the apples and has no other commodity to offer in exchange that is acceptable to the farmer, in order to balance the transaction, he gives him $2.00 in money. For our purpose it does not matter what the money is made of, so long as the farmer will accept it. This transaction represents myriads that take place every day. Here the farmer delivered two barrels of apples, for one of which he received an equivalent in a pair of shoes, for the other he received $2.00 in money. Now what position did the money occupy in this transaction? Did it figure as wealth? Was it accepted by the farmer as an equivalent for the second barrel of apples in the same sense that the shoes were accepted for the first? Nothing of the kind. There is no way in which the farmer can consume the $2.00 in the gratification of any of his wants or desires, physical or social. It is absolutely of no use to him except as he can exchange it for wealth or service. It was only on the assumption that others would receive it from him in exchange for an amount of wealth equivalent to what he gave the shoemaker for it, that he ever consented to take it at all.

It is very clear then that the farmer received the money in lieu of wealth. In the case of the first barrel of apples, where an exchange of wealth actually took place, no money was required. It was only when the shoemaker did not give wealth for the apples that he had to give money. In short, the money was simply a substitute for wealth ; an evidence that an equivalent had not been delivered. Therefore, instead of the $2.00 having been the final settlement of the debt to the farmer, it was exactly the reverse. It was simply the evidence that the debt had not been finally settled.

The same is true of labor. When the laborer works a day and receives $2.00 for it, he has not received the equivalent of his service in wealth ; but only that by which he can obtain wealth,—the evidence that he has rendered the services for which he has not yet received an equivalent.

It may be said that if the money given to the farmer for his apples, or to the laborer for his day's service had been gold, the debt would have been finally cancelled. That would be correct, but the debt in that case would not be cancelled by the money, but by the gold of which the money was .made—which is quite different. Gold is property, or wealth, just as much as shoes, wheat, or any other product, and therefore it cancels debt. A given quantity of silver, iron, tin,. copper, leather, or any other product of the same value, would equally cancel debt. The only difference between receiving gold, and other property for which one has no immediate use, is in its convenience for being handled, the general knowledge of its value, and the uniform willingness of others to accept it. An ounce of gold in bullion will cancel a debt just as effectively as an ounce of gold in coin. But when gold is used for money, so far as the money function is concerned, it is accepted solely with the view to being subsequently exchanged for other commodities. It is only because it will be so accepted that people will give their commodities for it. Were this otherwise, the farmer would have taken another pair of shoes in preference to two gold dollars for his second barrel of apples, for, while he did not need the shoes, he could probably have utilized them sooner than he could the gold in any other way than exchanging it for other things.

So long as wealth can be directly exchanged in convenient quantities, no medium is required. It is only when we desire a commodity and have not an acceptable article in convenient quantities to give in exchange for it, that money is of any service. Thus, by introducing the element of credit—of which money became the circulating evidence—the farmer and the shoemaker were greatly assisted in obtaining what they most desired. In other words, it made an *indirect complex process of exchange* possible by substituting an accepted token of obligation for present payment of debt.

Money, then, may really be defined as : a title to wealth not delivered ; as the medium through which the most indirect and economic exchanges are facilitated by giving currency to credit and substituting obligation for present payment in economic transactions.

SECTION II.—*The Economic Functions of Money.*

In order to constitute an efficient instrument for facilitating economic exchange, through a series of incomplete transactions giving currency to credit, money must be capable of filling at least two functions. It must supply : (1) A standard or denominator of value ; (2) A convenient medium for circulating obligations which will be uniformly accepted.

Since value is the ratio in which specific quantities of wealth and service will exchange for each other as economic equivalents ; for money to be a measure of value, it must have relation to a specific quantity of a special kind of some particular commodity. Upon the same principle that things which are equal to the same thing are equal to each other, the value of any given commodity will constitute the measure of value for all commodities. Whatever therefore will correctly indicate the value of a definite quantity of a given commodity of specific quality, and will be uniformly accepted at par in exchange for commodities and service, will fulfil all the functions of money.

Money, *per se*, is not a physical quantity, but only a mental measure of the exchange relation of quantities. Its economic function is to furnish a standard by which the value of different quantities of wealth and service can be measured and compared ; thus facilitating exchange and the mobility of wealth, by enabling credit to be substituted for barter without violating equity in the final fulfilment of obligation.

Nor has the community any interest in money being cheap as is commonly assumed. The principal object in all economic transactions is to obtain wealth, and the process whether simple or complex, always involves the giving of service. Service being the human, and wealth the nature, side of all economic movement, it follows that the community is wholly interested in the value of wealth falling and that of service rising ; and were money wealth, the public would be equally interested in having its value diminished, but it is not. No class in the community, except mere money speculators, can have any interest in promoting either a rise or fall in the value of money.

Since wealth is cheap or dear only as it will exchange for a large or small quantity of service, nothing can cheapen wealth which does not reduce its value as compared with that of labor. Now this is precisely what a change in the value of money cannot accomplish. Money being merely the general denominator of value, to which the value of all other things is referred, any change in its value would affect every thing else equally. To assume that the relative value of one article could be altered by a change which equally affects all, is to assume that things which are equal to the same thing are not equal to each other. For example, if there should be a fall of ten per cent. in the value of money, the effect would be a rise in the value of commodities and all who own commodities would receive ten per cent. more money for the same quantity, but this would be equally true of labor. For the same reason that ten per cent. more money would be received for a bushel of wheat, or a suit of clothes, ten per cent. more money would have to be given for a day's work. The necessary consequence of such a change would be that, while the employer received more for his goods, he would have to give more for his labor and raw material ; and conversely, all the laborer received as increased wages he would have to pay in higher prices, and the amount of wealth obtained for a day's service would remain absolutely unchanged. The relative value of wealth and service thus remaining the same, the only result of the change would be that more money would be used in each transaction,—for which nobody would be the gainer.

If, however, this change should occur suddenly, it would cause a temporary disturbance in economic relations. All who had contracted debts would gain ten per cent., because money would be worth ten per cent. less than when their obligations were contracted. But this gain by the debtor class means just ten per cent. loss by the creditor class ; and this would only apply to previously existing contracts ; all future transactions would be entirely unaffected by the change, because the new obligations would be assumed on the basis of the new value. Thus, whatever gain would result from such a change in the value of money would be of the most uneconomic character : like robbery, it would simply enable one to gain by the loss of another. Moreover, such uneconomic changes in the value of money involve serious disturbances in business relations, and consequently an economic loss to the whole community.

It thus appears that society has nothing to gain, but much to lose, by fluctuations in the value of money.

Clearly, then, while it is of vital interest to the industrial and social welfare of the community that the value of wealth should fall, and the value of service should rise as rapidly as possible, it is scarcely less important that the value of money should change as little as possible.   The efficiency of money in economics, like that of weights and measures in business, depends upon the stability of its character and the convenience of its form.   Therefore the important question to settle is not how to make money cheap or abundant, but, how to minimize the variations in its value and maximize its circulating convenience.

Section III.—*The Value of Money.*

In considering the value of money two things should ever be borne in mind, namely, that value is simply the ratio of exchange, and that money is the accepted standard for measuring this ratio. No matter, therefore, of what money is made, or even if it were never reduced to material form, but simply consisted of verbal expression passed from person to person, it must necessarily relate to some definite quantity of one or more of the commodities subject to exchange.   Otherwise the expression, penny, shilling, pound, cent, dollar, etc., would convey no definite idea to either buyer or seller.

Two questions here arise : (1) Is it essential that money be made of the commodity it represents ?   (2) Would a multiple unit form a more invariable basis for the value of money than a unit of a single commodity whose value is least variable ?

(1) Whether or not money shall be made of the commodity it represents and contain property to the full amount of its face value depends upon the state of civilization.   In a state of society where commercial and social integrity are so high that a promise will never be violated, money can be purely representative ; it only needs to have sufficient material in it to convey the evidence of an expressed promise, but in a state of society where the moral character is not sufficiently developed to make the written word the highest bond, it becomes necessary to have the promise secured by property in the money.   In other words, just in proportion as the security of the fulfilment of obligation is lacking in the moral character of the community, it has to be furnished in the material, or property-character, of its money.   And conversely, as the moral character of the community rises, the property-character of the money departs.   Accordingly in the

lowest stages of civilization we find money entirely composed of property, and, as civilization advances, of token-money and purely representative-money (written or printed obligation). Furthermore, so long as property-money is needed in the transactions of any portion of the community, it must be the basis of the transactions of all, because, unless the money used by the highest is such as to command the confidence of the lowest, commercial intercourse would be impossible. Since no country has yet risen above the necessity of using property money in some portion of its exchanges, and many countries still need it for the greater part of their transactions, some portion of the money of every country must continue to be made of the commodity which it represents. And conversely, the commodity of which the property-money is made must be that upon which all the pure, or representative, money is based—that is to say, the value of a given unit of that product must be the standard by which the value of all other commodities is measured when referred to in terms of money.

Therefore, in selecting the commodity, or commodities, which would best serve as property- or barter-money, several questions should be considered in addition to the stability of its value. (1) It must possess utility—that is, it must be a commodity in itself, generally desirable for the purposes of consumption, entirely apart from its use as money. (2) In order to be a generally acceptable instrument of exchange it must be easily transferred, in which case it must possess the maximum value in the minimum quantity. (3) It must be a commodity whose form and qualities have the maximum durability, so that its value will not deteriorate. (4) It should be of uniform quality, so that every unit of it will be equal to every other unit. (5) It should be a commodity whose value is subject to the minimum variation.

While almost any commodity would serve as a unit of measurement and a basis of value which pure money could represent, very few commodities possess the above qualities in the degree necessary to constitute them a good circulating medium as property-money. Almost every commodity has been employed for this purpose, in some stage of civilization, but experience has shown that if barter- or property-money must be employed, the precious metals, particularly gold and silver, are best suited to fill that function.

It is commonly held that, in addition to its other advantageous qualities, the value of gold is less liable to variation than that of any other commodity. Whether this claim can be fully sustained or not, it is well known that the value of gold is subject to considerable fluctuation. Even if the value of gold were less firm than that of some other commodities, its superiority for the purposes of money in so many other respects would still make it preferable to any other commodity. The question arises, therefore, would not the aggregate value of a large number of units of products form a more invariable standard of value than the unit of a single commodity like gold ?

(2) It has been frequently contended by able writers that the double standard of silver and gold tends to form a less variable value than could be obtained by the use of either one alone. It is claimed that the two exercise what Wolowski calls compensatory action. This is brought about, they say, by the fact that if either silver or gold falls in value there at once arises a tendency to transport the cheaper metal to the point where it is most needed, and *vice versa*, thus tending to establish an approximate equilibrium between the two metals, and a less net variation in the value of both. There may be some strength to this claim, but it has not yet been established by any extensive experience.

It has been suggested by some writers that a more invariable standard of value could be obtained by taking a given quantity of a large number of staple commodities, and making their aggregate value the standard upon which the unit of money should be based. This idea was first presented in England by Joseph Lowe, in a work, " The Present State of England in Regard to Agriculture, Trade, and Finance " (1822) ; and again in 1833 by Mr. G. Poulett Scrope, and in 1875 by Stanley Jevons, in his work on "Money and the Mechanism of Exchange." The idea in this proposition is that while the value of each of a hundred different articles might vary more than gold, their variation would frequently be in different directions and offset each other ; and, in the general movement of the value of the whole body, much of the fluctuation of any particular article would be eliminated.

This is seen in the movement of, prices during the present

century. While some commodities have fallen 60 and 70 per cent. in value, and others have increased considerably, the mean level of prices, compared with gold, has only fallen about 14 per cent., so that the general price-level has probably varied less than that of any one commodity. If one commodity is used as the unit of value, and in the production of that article improved machinery should be introduced to any considerable extent, its value would be greatly reduced, as that of all machine-made products has been. On the other hand, if it is an article in whose production hand-labor is chiefly employed, then its value will rise just as fast as wages increase and civilization advances, as in the case of farm and garden products. But if the price-level of a hundred or more principal commodities, including both manufactured and agricultural products, and the aggregate value of a definite quantity of each were taken as the standard unit of value, it is quite certain that their value would be far more steady than if based upon any particular one. The movement of the variation in value would not only be more permanent and gradual, thereby avoiding sudden perturbations, but the change in value would represent the influence of civilization upon the cost of producing wealth in general, and not that of some abnormal force, like speculation, upon any particular article which may produce a temporary change in value out of all proportion to the general movement. Even this method would not dispose of the use of the precious metals as money so long as property-money is necessary, but it would obviate much of the business disturbance and loss to the debtor and creditor class consequent upon a sudden change in the value of gold or silver, because, while gold might remain the nominal denominator of value, its value would be measured by the aggregate value, at any given time, of the hundred or more articles of which the multiple standard is composed.

For example, if the stipulated quantity of the hundred articles composing the tabular standard of value will exchange for $1,000 in gold on the first of January, 1890, and on the first of January, 1891, they will only command $900 in gold, it would be evident that the gold had risen in value 10 per cent., as compared with the articles in the tabular standard. Therefore, all obligations, whether in the form of mortgages, borrowed money, or general purchases contracted on the first of January, 1890, could be cancelled on the first of January, 1891, with 10 per cent. less gold than at the time of the agreement. But, by receiving 10 per cent. less gold, the creditor would receive the equivalent of exactly the same amount of the various commodities as if they had been paid in gold when the contract was made. By this means the debtor would avoid the loss consequent upon the rise in the value of gold during the year. Thus whether a debt was paid by the same amount of gold or not, it would always be cancelled by an amount of gold equivalent in value to the same quantity of general commodities that the debt originally represented. Therefore, whatever effect the variation in the value of gold had upon the quantity of money received, it would have practically none upon the quantity of wealth received. By thus making the value of money depend upon that of the general body of staple commodities, it would, at least, remove it further from the influence of mere capricious speculation and confine its fluctuations to the normal movement in the general value of wealth.

The principle involved in a tabular standard is unquestionably sound. That it would tend to minimize the fluctuations in the value of money is as certain as that the movement of large bodies is more steady than that of small ones. It is simply the application of the law of averages to the unit of value, which has been so completely demonstrated in the sphere of insurance. Like all instruments of increased complexity, however, it presents some difficulties in application, on its first introduction. In the first place, it would necessitate the extensive collection of exact data regarding the prices of commodities, particularly those included in the tabular standard. It would require a well-defined system of computing the purchasing capacity of gold as compared with a given unit of these commodities ; and it would also be necessary that the results, thus scientifically established, should be authoritatively published every week, or oftener. Perhaps the most difficult feature connected with the scientific application of this principle to the value of money, is the method by which the actual price-level of a given unit of these commodities shall be arrived at. This subject has already occupied the attention of statisticians for a considerable time, entirely independent of the idea of its use in the construction of a tabular standard for the value of money. Soetbeer, Jevons, Laspeyre, Newmarch, and Mulhall have all endeavored, with varying success, to construct a scientific system for ascertaining the general price-level of all commodities. All but Mulhall have adopted the index-number method; he has adopted the "volume-of-trade" method, which, though more laborious, is doubtless the more accurate system. That a scientific method will be established for ascertaining the exact price-level of any given number of commodities can hardly be doubted; and that it should be established is of the utmost importance to economic science. Indeed, what the science most lacks to-day is exact knowledge of economic data. Therefore the idea of the tabular-standard theory should not be rejected merely because of the difficulties of its practical application. On the contrary, if it is sound in principle, it should serve as an additional incentive for establishing a scientific system of ascertaining the actual general price-level of commodities, without which the knowledge of economic data will become less exact as industrial phenomena increases in volume and complexity.

It will be observed, however, that the only object in adopting a single, double, or tabular, monetary standard, is simply to obtain the most invariable basis for the value of money. Consequently the only question of economic importance connected with the whole subject of money is, how to maximize the convenience of its form, and minimize the variation in its value.

SECTION IV.—*The Depreciation of Money.*

The depreciation of money and a fall in its value are distinct phenomena, and produced by very different causes, although they have the same effect upon its purchasing capacity. The difference may be stated thus : A fall in the value of money means that the value of a particular class of property—gold, silver, or the like,—upon which it is based, has undergone a change. The depreciation of money means that it does not represent the amount of property which it professes to. The former is an economic variation ; the latter an uneconomic diminution. For instance, if gold and silver are both used equally as money, and their value as bullion is as 1 to 15, they will circulate as money in just that ratio, and every gold coin, of whatever denomination, will be equal in value to a silver coin of fifteen times its own weight.

11

If, however, by lessening the cost of production, the value of silver bullion should fall, so that seventeen grains were only equal to one of gold, then the relative purchasing capacity of the two coins would be as 17 to 1. This would constitute a fall of $\frac{2}{15}$ in the value of the silver money. But, on the other hand, if the quantity of pure silver in the coin were diminished $\frac{2}{15}$, the purchasing capacity of the money would fall to the ratio of 17 to 1 as compared with gold, exactly as before, but this would be a depreciation of the silver money. Although the alteration in the purchasing capacity of the silver money would be the same in both cases, the cause and effect of that alteration would be very different. In the former case the silver dollar, though diminished in purchasing power as compared with gold and all other commodities, would still exchange for the same amount of the property it claimed to represent (silver bullion), showing that its reduced purchasing power was due to the fall in the economic value of silver, as property. But, in the latter case, the 17 grains of silver coin would not only have fallen in value as compared with gold and all other commodities, but also as compared with silver bullion, showing that the change is not due to an alteration in the economic value of any commodity whatever, but solely to the fact that it pretends to contain more property than it really does.

Nor is there any difficulty in determining which of these two movements has occurred when a fluctuation in the purchasing power of money takes place. If it is a change in the economic value of money, then the money will continue to exchange at par with the specific quantity of the particular commodity which it represents. If it is made of gold or silver, the mint price will be approximately the same as the bullion price; and if it is paper currency, whether private or governmental, it will exchange for the amount of coin or bullion, or whatever specific property its represents, at its face value. The rise of the bullion price above the mint price, or of the property price above the paper price, is infallible evidence of the depreciation of the money; and the extent of that difference correctly indicates the degree in which the depreciation has taken place.

It should be observed that the depreciation of metallic money is produced by a different cause from that of paper money. The reason for this is, that the former is barter-, or property-money, while the latter is credit-, or representative-money. Metallic currency is wealth, and paper currency is the promise to deliver wealth ; consequently the appreciation of the former depends upon the amount of property it contains, and the appreciation of the latter upon the amount of confidence it can command. There can never be a depreciation of metallic money unless there is an actual diminution in the quantity of property put into it ; it may fall in value, but it can never be depreciated so long as there is the quantity of material in it which it professes to contain—*i.e.*, if it is not fraudulently manufactured. There is therefore no more difficulty in preventing, than there is excuse for promoting, the depreciation of metallic or property-money.

If coin were the only money used, the question of depreciation might be dismissed as being too simple to need discussion ; but this is far from being the case. Experience has shown that, under the complex conditions of modern industry, a purely metallic, or property-currency, is wholly inadequate to meet the needs of the community. There are two reasons for this : (1) There is probably not enough gold and silver coin in the whole world to do the business of one or two of the most advanced countries. (2) If there were, its cumbersome inconvenience would render its use impossible in the greater portion of modern, commercial transactions.

To be forced to actually transfer "thirty-six cart loads of silver," or its equivalent in gold, in order to transact a business of £400,000—as in the case of the amount paid for the delivery of Charles I. to the parliamentary party—would annihilate the major part of the commerce of Christendom. The utter inadequacy of metallic, or property-money, for the requirements of modern industry, is demonstrated by the fact that only about .81 of one per cent. of the business in this country is now done with coin,—99.19 of the payments being made in paper money, —95.13 per cent. of which is in personal checks, drafts, etc.

Many writers on this subject appear to regard coin as the only form of real money. Hence, when distinguishing between metallic and paper money they generally speak of the former as money and the latter as currency. Even Jevons and MacLeod do not entirely escape this notion. In discussing this point the latter says : " It would therefore be *currency*, but it would not be *money*, because it has no intrinsic value," [1]—the evident idea being that currency is only money in proportion as it contains wealth.

The simple fact is that all money is currency. Its currency or circulation may, under some conditions, depend upon the material of which it is made, but it is money by virtue of its being currency and not because of the property which it contains. The difference between a metallic and a paper currency is that the former is both property and money, and the latter is simply money. Ricardo has well said : " A currency is in its most perfect state when it consists wholly of paper." [2]   Indeed, the more perfect a currency is as property, the less perfect it is as money. Coin of full weight and fineness, instead of being the only real money, is the only kind of currency which does not fill all the functions of money,—because it is not an instrument of credit and does not give currency to transferable obligation, which is the most important of all features of money. To the extent that money does not transfer credit, it fails to promote indirect exchanges, and reduces all transaction to literal barter. Paper money, being simply the evidence of credit and not property *per se*, instead of finally cancelling debts, as coin does, only transfers obligation. Its acceptance and circulation therefore depend upon the degree of confidence it inspires in the actual fulfilment of the obligation it represents. Whatever impairs the confidence and destroys the credit, necessarily depreciates the money representing it. Clearly then the only way to prevent the depreciation of paper money is to sustain the confidence in the promise it conveys. Nothing can sustain the confidence in a promise but fulfilling the obligation whenever it is required. To the extent that this is inconveniently deferred is the confidence in the promise impaired.

In order that confidence in this promise may be complete and unshaken, it is necessary that those who accept the money know that a specific amount of wealth will be delivered on demand, and also exactly of what this wealth shall consist. Otherwise, the debtor would frequently offer what the creditor did not want, and the creditor demand what the debtor could not deliver, and the

[1] " Elements of Political Economy," p. 35.
[2] " Principles of Political Economy and Taxation," p. 218.

confidence would constantly fluctuate according to the desirability of the things offered and received.

What shall this wealth be, is the next question. Whatever may be the commodity selected for this purpose, it must be that which already circulates as property-money among that portion of the community which will not accept paper or credit-money. The reason for this is very simple. Whoever accepts money in a transaction does so because the commodities at the disposal of the debtor are such as he does not desire. So long as the money will be accepted by those who possess the commodities, it is unimportant what commodity it represents; but when the purchaser desires an article which those who have confidence in his money do not possess, and those who do possess it will not accept his money, it is necessary that he should be able to demand from those who issue the promise a specific kind of property, which those who declined to receive his credit-money will accept. Otherwise his commercial dealings will be restricted to the limited area in which his money freely circulates. This would necessarily impair his confidence in it as an instrument of exchange. So long, therefore, as we have commercial intercourse with any people who continue to insist upon property-money, all paper, or credit-money, must be a promise to deliver upon demand a specific quantity of the commodity of which their property-money is made—be that whatever it may. In no other way can the depreciation of paper money be prevented.

Wherever property-money prevails to-day—and it is used more or less in all commercial countries,—it is made of gold or silver. Hence these are the commodities upon which all credit, or paper-money, must be based. There are those who think that any other commodity would answer the purpose just as well,—and some, indeed, who even insist that the aggregate property of the community would be still better.. Those who urge these views, however, overlook the fact that but a very small portion of the race have entirely dispensed with the use of property-money; and unless credit-money is redeemable in some specific commodity which is uniformly acceptable to those who insist upon property-money, commercial intercourse, with by far the greater portion of the human race, would be practically cut off. This would not only involve the destruction of commerce, but the arrest of civilization.

It should always be remembered that the fundamental principle underlying economic and social law is, that all institutions
are based upon and adapted to the character of the people, becoming less arbitrary and restrictive as the characters of the social
units rise in moral strength and social integrity, and also that the
barbaric element in institutions and laws is always retained for
the least advanced.   Thus, all criminal and restrictive laws are
not made to govern the most orderly but the most unruly element
in the community.   This is why the most moral and advanced
portion of a community has to be subject to the despotism necessary to control the most disorderly classes.   The same principle
operates with equal force in the sphere of money.   Property-
money represents the barbaric element in commercial intercourse,
only the most advanced being capable of using pure credit-money,
and since property-money is only used by the higher classes because it is essential to their dealing with the lower, the commodity
which is the most acceptable to those who insist upon barter-
money must be used by those who employ credit-money.

It is undoubtedly true that any other commodity would serve
as a basis for credit-money just as well as gold or silver, provided
it would be as readily accepted among those who insist upon
property-money.   The only reason these metals are necessary is
that they are the only commodities that will currently pass in
payment for debt where credit-money is rejected ; and this fact
makes them indispensable, because, for the very reason that a
redemption of the promise conveyed by credit-money is necessary to give it confidence, its redemption in any other commodity would be useless.   All money, of whatever it is made, is
received in trade only on the assumption that other people will
take it on the same conditions.   Since nothing can fill the functions of money which will not be accepted as currency, and since
nothing can sustain a paper money from depreciation except the
assurance that it will be redeemed in a commodity acceptable as
currency to those who insist upon property-money, and since
gold and silver are the only commodities that will be so received,
it is clear that these metals must necessarily constitute the basis
of all paper money.

SECTION V.—*Who Should Furnish the Money ?*

The only interest the community has in the supply of money is
that it should be furnished by those who can most completely

adjust it to the necessities of the people. Can this duty be performed better by the government than by private enterprise? As explained in another chapter,[1] it is a principle in society that the efficiency of governmental action diminishes as the enterprise becomes involved and complex, requiring quick decisions, expert judgment, and frequent changes. Consequently, with the development of society, all forms of industrial and commercial enterprises have gradually passed into the sphere of individual control and responsibility. The same is true of money. In the earlier stages of society the government supplied all the money. But with the development of industry and commerce, the financial requirements became too intricate for the government to adequately supply, and public or legal tender-money had to be supplemented by private money. This has increased with the advance of society until only about one per cent. of the debts in this country are now paid with property-money, and less than five · per cent. are paid with legal tender-money, about ninety-five per cent. of the business being transacted with private money—notes, checks, drafts, etc.

Since personal-money has no legal backing except to the extent of the property of those who make it, its utility rests mainly upon the confidence that it can be exchanged for any form of property desirable or be converted into property-money at the pleasure of the holder. Therefore, so long as any property-money is necessary in the domestic or foreign transactions of a nation, the stability of the whole currency rests largely upon its supply, however small the amount may be. If the supply of this relatively small quantity of property-money were as completely adapted to the needs of the community as the amount of personal-money is to-day, financial panics would be of very rare occurrence; indeed with proper financial statistics they might be practically avoided.

To supply this small but indispensable increment of property-money to suit the varying requirements of modern society, is a duty the government is manifestly incapable of performing. The reason for this is easy to understand. Being a representative institution, the government must act either upon a general rule or according to specific legislation. And the more democratic the government, the more its action is limited by the

[1] Part IV., chapter ii.

popular will as expressed in legislation.   Consequently it cannot vary its action with sufficient promptness and wisdom to meet the requirements of special emergencies.   When circumstances arise making an increase of money necessary, there is no means of supplying the demand until Congress can be called together to legislate upon it.   Before this can be accomplished a stringency or even a panic may arise disturbing the industrial relations of the whole country—a fact of frequent occurrence.   Moreover, when Congress is called upon to readjust the currency to the commercial needs of the community, the question is liable to be decided by political rather than economic considerations.[1]   On the other hand, if the amount of money thus authorized is larger than is needed, it is uselessly stacked away in the government vaults and is a mere waste of public revenue.   Financial disturbances from these causes would be far more frequent than they are, but for the large proportion of the money that is furnished by individuals.

Manifestly the remedy for the evils inevitably connected with such an inadequate system must be sought in some method of transferring the money-supplying function from the State to private enterprise.   Nor is there any thing revolutionary in this proposition.   It is simply obeying the law of evolution and transferring the duty of making the remaining five per cent. of the money to those who, by virtue of superior fitness, already furnish about ninety-five per cent. of it.

It must not be assumed, however, that in taking this position I accept the reasoning of Herbert Spencer in his claim for a "complete free trade in currency."[2]   He assumes that under free competition good money will always drive bad money out of use, for the same reason* that, *cæteris paribus*, a superior article will always be preferred to an inferior one.   The objection to this assumption is that it does not agree with the facts.   The experience of centuries shows that, instead of superior money driving

---

[1] Witness the recent action of Congress on the silver question.   The representatives from the silver-mining States demanded the free coinage of silver, and for fear of losing the political support of those States a silver bill was passed, which on economic grounds would not have received the support of either party.

[2] "Social Statics," chap. xxix.

inferior money from circulation, it is always inferior money that drives out the superior.[1] The reason for this is very simple.

Suppose for illustration that the money is made of gold, and that there are in circulation three kinds of dollars containing 24, 22, and 20 grains of gold respectively. Since the 20-grain dollar will do the same service as the 24-grain dollar, every one would gain sixteen per cent. by melting down the 24-grain dollar, it being worth one sixth more as property than as money. So long as a profit can be made by converting the superior money into property, nothing but the most absolute despotism can keep it in circulation as money. Thus free competition in money (if more than one kind is used) would produce the opposite effect from what Mr. Spencer's *laissez-faire* hypothesis pre-supposes. Moreover, if competition would do all that Mr. Spencer assumes, it would still be uneconomic and hence undesirable for two reasons : (1) Because competition necessitates a plurality of competitors which implies two or more kinds of money in circulation at the same time. (2) Because competition between two or more kinds of money necessarily disturbs the confidence in some portion of the currency, and this is precisely what a sound monetary system should not do. As pointed out in the last section, the community has nothing to gain but much to lose by fluctuations in the value of money.

There are three important things to be accomplished by a correct monetary system : (1) to secure the greatest stability and uniformity of value to the money ; (2) to supply it in the most convenient form ; (3) to adjust the quantity to the needs of the community. Before we are justified in putting the entire control of the legal-tender money in the hands of private enterprise we must be reasonably certain that all the above objects can be accomplished better by the individual than by the State.

(1) Since the value of money is governed by the value of the commodity of which it is made, and that in turn depends upon the cost of production, it is clear that the individual has no more

---

[1] The principle that bad money drives good money out of circulation and that good money never drives out bad, was discovered in the sixteenth century by Sir Thomas Gresham, and is known as the " Gresham Law." This theorem has been so completely verified by experience that it is now accepted by economists and financiers as scientifically established.

power to increase its stability than has the government. Nor could its uniformity either of value or style be increased if made by private concerns. On the contrary, the maximum uniformity can best be obtained by having all the money made under one management.

(2) Neither is there any reason for assuming that a more convenient form of money could be furnished by private enterprise than by the government. The government will make the money of whatever material and issue it in such form as the people desire ; and the reasons for a change in these respects occur so seldom, and develop so gradually, that no inconvenience can result from having these points determined by law. Since private enterprise could do nothing to increase stability of value in money or its uniformity and convenience, there is obviously no reason for taking from the government the duty of determining the material of which it should be made and the form in which it should be issued.

(3) To adjust the quantity of money to the needs of the community is a much more difficult task. The quantity of legal-tender money required in a highly complex industrial community is liable to great and sudden variation. A change in the ratio of exports to imports, an increase or decrease in the opening up of new territory, or a change in other industrial relations with people who insist upon barter-money, all affect the quantity of legal-tender money required. For the reasons already explained, the government cannot act with sufficient alertness to adapt the currency to these ever increasing variations. The quick decision, expert judgment, and rapid changes required are precisely what individual enterprise can supply. The question is how to transfer to private enterprise and retain in the hands of the government that portion of the duty of supplying money which each can perform better than the other.

This is not so difficult a task as may at first appear. All that is necessary is to have the money furnished by private enterprise in the same way that food, clothing, and other commodities now are, with the exception that the form and quality of the money be determined by law. This would involve government control or supervision of the mint and the printing of coin certificates as at present, the business and risk of buying bullion, the cost of minting and distribution being left to private enterprise. Thus the business part of the monetary system would pass over to the individual, and the duty of protecting the public interest still be reserved to the government. Under such conditions the monetary system would be greatly simplified and far more adjustable to the needs of the people. The money would then be furnished purely as a matter of business, and the banker would sustain the same economic relation to the community as any other merchant. And his success, likewise, would depend entirely upon the efficiency with which he supplied the wants of the people.

Should there be an increased demand for money, it would not be necessary to petition Congress to pass a law on the subject as at present. It would only be necessary for the banker to purchase more bullion and have it coined or the certificates printed, just as the shoe merchant would increase his stock of shoes if the demand should rise. To get this bullion would be easy, as soon as the terms of commerce in bullion were established between bullion producers and bankers. The bankers would then be in the habit of ordering bullion from the miners on their established credit, just as a man orders clothes from his tailor. Money being especially needed, he would telegraph an order to send, say one thousand pounds of bullion. This would come on usual terms, say sixty days, and could be coined at once and put into circulation, thereby promptly supplying the demand for money. In other words, sound credit would be turned into real money to suit the emergency and the evils of a financial panic avoided. The self-interest of the banker would inspire prompt action in this regard, since those who could supply their customers in times of emergency would be sure to obtain the greatest amount of normal business. No business man would care to deal with the banker who was liable to fail him at the time of greatest need. More money than is needed would not be made, because nobody would have any interest in making it any more than a hatter has in making hats for which there is no market.

One important advantage of this over the present system is, that when more money is needed in business, it can be directly placed in the hands of those requiring it. If the government makes an increased amount of money, it can be put into circulation only through its expenditures in salaries, pensions, and the purchase of bullion and bonds.   Hence the banks and the merchants can only obtain the money through the indirect route of business circulation.   Whereas, if the money was made for the banks instead of the government, it could pass directly from the mint or printing-press to the bank, and thence to the manufacturer or merchant who most needed it.   Under this system the supply of money would be governed by economic law instead of political influence.

The transfer of the money question from the domain of politics to that of economics would be beneficial in many ways.   In the first place, it would remove the banker's excuse for exacting exorbitant interest, on the plea that the government is responsible for a scarcity of money.   The banker being responsible for the supply, would lose his business by failing to keep up his stock just as would any other merchant.   In the next place, this change would take the gold and silver industries out of politics.   Instead of lobbying in Congress to increase the market and fix the price of their product, the gold and silver men would have to go into the open market on the same terms as other producers.   Thus the success of legitimate public business would not depend upon trading for the political influence of the producers of the precious metals as at present.[1]   To adopt the proposition here suggested would be to transfer to the individual that portion of the money-supplying function which he can perform better than the government, and would retain in the hands of the government that portion of the duty which it can perform better than the individual.   We would then have in our monetary system all the advantage of competition, together with the energy and business skill of private enterprise—without the risk of adulteration and other "tricks of trade."   We should also have all the protective power of the state, without the monopoly and bungling incompetency inseparable from the public administration of business affairs.

[1] The recent silver bill was passed chiefly through the fear of losing the political support of the silver-producing States.

PART III.

THE PRINCIPLES OF ECONOMIC DISTRIBUTION.

CHAPTER I.

THE DISTRIBUTION OF WEALTH.

SECTION I.—*Distribution Inseparable from Production.*

DISTRIBUTION is frequently regarded as if it were separate from production. In the opening paragraph of his recent work, "The Wages Question," Francis A. Walker makes a formal division of political economy into the following four distinct departments : " The production, the distribution, the exchange, and the consumption of wealth." This naturally encourages the popular idea that distribution can be dealt with independently of production.

Although the socializing influence of wealth penetrates all phases of society, there are but two economically distinct states in which wealth ever exists—namely, that of production and that of consumption. Production properly includes every thing that directly or indirectly increases the utility of consumable wealth.

The fact that the manufacturer divides his products between a number of wholesale merchants, and these in turn further divide them among retail dealers, does not constitute distribution in any economic sense. Such division of products into small quantities facilitates their delivery to the consumer, and is production. It is as incorrect to call a dry-goods dealer, or merchant-tailor, a distributer of clothing, as it would be to call the planter of wheat a distributer of food. As already explained,[1] every thing which aids in compassing the satisfaction of any human want is properly production.

Consumption is every thing which gratifies human wants and desires, whether put to immediate use or reserved solely for that

[1] Part II., chap. i., p. 72.

175

purpose by the owners.   In economic science therefore, consumption only applies to the ultimate use of the finished product, and never to the use of raw material or tools.   We frequently hear such expressions as the consumption of pig-iron in the manufacture of rails, and the consumption of wool in the manufacture of cloth.   The wool used in the manufacture of cloth is not consumed ; it has simply changed its form in order to assume a higher degree of utility.   It ceases to exist as fleece only to become broadcloth.

The wool does not enter a state of consumption until it is in the possession of the wearer of the cloth ; all its previous uses have served no economic or social purpose except as they have been a means to that end.

There is production, distribution, and consumption of wealth ; there are producers and consumers ; but there are no economic distributers of wealth.   There is no class of persons in the community whose distinctive function is to distribute wealth except the keepers of charitable institutions and jails.   Distribution is that automatic phase of economic movement by which wealth passes from the sphere of production to that of consumption ; that is to say, from those who use it as a means to those who use it as an end.   The means through which this takes place are wages, rent, interest, and profit.   The consumable wealth which finds its way to the various classes in the community through these channels, does so, not as the result of any effort to distribute wealth, but solely as a necessary and inseparable part of the process of production.   Wages in the hands of the laborer are distributed wealth, but in the hands of the employer they are capital devoted to production.   What the employer pays out in wages is invested in production, exactly the same as is that which he expends for tools and raw material, but when it reaches the laborer it is transferred from the sphere of production to that of consumption.

Economic distribution is neither more nor less than investment in production.   Production and distribution are inseparable phenomena ; the one involves the other, and neither can take place without the other ; therefore to talk of production without distribution, or of increasing distribution except by promoting production, is to ignore economic law ; and any attempt to permanently improve the social condition of any class in the community by such means is chimerical.

The only interest the community can have in either class of wealth is that it shall fill its function most effectively, and thereby make the greatest possible contribution to social welfare. Since it is only in the sphere of consumption that wealth ministers to human well-being, consumable wealth can only successfully fill its function by being in the possession of the individual consumer, as it cannot yield the maximum social benefit for one person while under the control of another.

On the contrary, productive wealth can and frequently does render its maximum service to one class while in the possession of another. The only concern the community can possibly have in the distribution or ownership of productive wealth is that it shall be most effectually employed in making consumable wealth cheap and abundant. Therefore the idea, so persistently propagated by Karl Marx and sacredly cherished by socialists everywhere, that it is necessary for the laboring classes to own the instruments of production in order to secure the social advantage of the product, is an unmixed delusion. Whether or not productive wealth should be concentrated in a few hands, or evenly distributed throughout the community, or owned by the government, is absolutely of no importance to the general welfare *except* as it may affect the efficiency of its use as a productive factor.

Productive wealth, whether in the form of land, machinery, buildings, raw material, or unfinished products, is of no advantage to its owner except as it passes into consumable wealth, and the possession of consumable wealth does not in any sense depend upon the ownership of productive wealth.

More than eighty per cent. of the consumable wealth daily produced in this country is consumed by those who possess no productive wealth. Since production is impossible without consumption, and productive wealth can only confer benefit upon its owner as it increases consumable wealth, it follows that the concentration and increased efficiency of productive wealth tends to promote the general distribution of consumable wealth.[1]

There is no fact in the history of civilization which is more conclusively established than that every departure from handlabor to factory methods of production, and therefore from dear

---

[1] *Cf.* "Wealth and Progress," pp. 7–9.

to cheap consumable wealth, has been accomplished by the concentration of productive wealth. Nor could this be otherwise, because all the motives that make the concentration of productive wealth desirable tend to make the distribution of consumable wealth indispensable.[1]

It will thus be seen that, in considering the subject of economic distribution, we are concerned only with the movement of consumable wealth, in regard to which four facts should be recognized. (1) That wealth never contributes to social welfare except when in the sphere of consumption. (2) That no movement of wealth is distribution which does not transfer it from the producer to the consumer. (3) That this distributive movement is not separate from production, but is an inseparable part ·of it. (4) That the forms in which wealth passes to the community are wages, rent, interest, and profit.

SECTION II.—*The Order of Economic Distribution.*

The order of economic distribution generally held by English economists is rent, wages, and profit, thus making the amount the laborer receives depend upon what is left after rent is paid. Consistently with this classification, Henry George declares that rent is the great social "robber," and demands, as the remedy for social ills, the confiscation of rent by the abolition of private ownership in land. Had he not placed rent first in the order of distribution, his reckless misstatement of facts regarding wages [2] would have availed him little ; but having made rent the first claimant he found little difficulty in declaring that the remaining shares would be lessened by that amount, and consequently that the wealth of the landowner caused the poverty of the laborer.[3]

During the last twenty years a departure has been made from the orthodox position. Jevons, the most prominent representative of the "new school" in England, says : "The view which I accept concerning the rate of wages is not more difficult to comprehend than the current one. It is *that the wages of a working man are ultimately coincident with what he produces, after the de-*

---

[1] *Cf.* article in *Political Science Quarterly*, vol. iii., pp. 405, 406.

[2] "Wealth and Progress," Part II., chapter i., section iii.

[3] "Progress and Poverty," pp. 162, 163.

duction of rent, taxes, and the interest of capital." [1] Francis A. Walker, with an astonishing amount of inconsistency, adopts the same classification. After several times alternately affirming opposite positions, he says : " I hold, with Professor Stanley Jevons, that wages equal the whole product minus rent, interest, and profits." [2] It will be seen that this classification not only places · rent before wages, as George does, but it places interest and profits there also, making wages the contingent amount after all else is paid, and thus completely verifying the socialists' charge that under the capitalistic system of production, wages are merely the leavings after rent, interest, and profit are paid. These statements of George, Jevons, and Walker involve two errors : one regarding the nature of economic distribution, the other the order in which the distribution takes place.

(1) They all discuss the question of distribution as if it were the disbursement of a fixed amount of existing wealth ; hence they constantly speak of the " division of the product between landlords, capitalists, and laborers " as the " shares of the different claimants," etc. The idea of dividing a fixed quantity of wealth involves the assumption that if the amount obtained by any one class increases, that of the other classes must necessarily diminish in the same ratio. This popular error pervades the writings of all the schools. Among the English writers it is expressed in that familiar statement of Ricardo and Mill, that " profits depend upon wages, rising as wages fall and falling as wages rise." [3] It is no less frankly expressed by Perry in his " Rule of Three " discussion of wages," [4] and by Henry George

[1] " Theory of Political Economy," p. 292.

[2] " Political Economy," p. 284, 1st edition. Compare, *ibid.*, pp. 197, 198 with 203, 1st edition ; also 254 with 264 1st edition. See also, 262, 263, 1st edition.

[3] Ricardo's Works, pp. 63, 74, 75, 93. Mill's " Principles of Political Economy," vol. i., p. 512.

[4] " There is no use arguing against any one of the four fundamental rules of arithmetic. The question of wages is a question of division. It is complained that the quotient is too small. Well, then, how many ways are there to make a quotient larger?· Two ways. Enlarge your dividend, the divisor remaining the same, and the quotient will be larger ; lessen your divisor, the dividend remaining the same, and the quotient will be larger."—" Political Economy," p. 123, 1st edition.

in his " Tom, Dick, and Harry " partnership illustration. [1] Were this view correct, the employing and laboring classes would indeed be the natural enemies of each other, and revolution would be the only means of assuring progress, as many ill-informed enthusiasts would have us believe.

The whole idea of regarding distribution as mere division is erroneous. Economic distribution through wages, rent, and interest is not the division of wealth that exists, but an investment to bring wealth into existence ; hence *wages are not related to production as the residual share of a division, but solely as an antecedent cost of production ;* and since that which each productive factor receives is determined by its own cost, the amount it obtains can in no way increase or diminish that which any other factor shall receive.

(2) The position of these writers in discussing the order of distribution is no less unsatisfactory. Mr. Walker appears to think that in being " the residual claimant of the product of industry," the laborer has a superior command over the increased quantity of wealth which he produces, and says : " In this view the laboring class receive all they help to produce " [2] ; and adds : " So far as by their energy in work, their economy in the use of materials, or their care in dealing with the finished product, the value of that product is increased, that increase goes to them by purely natural laws, provided only competition be full and free." [3]

By what natural law this increased product " inures directly and immediately to their (the laborers') benefit," he does not explain. In his " web-of-cloth " illustration, Walker assures us that the laborer is never paid before the manufacturer. [4] And, in his chapter on profits, he says : " The fact that these wages are so high is

---

[1] " To fix Tom's share at 40 per cent., is to leave but 60 per cent. to be divided between Dick and Harry. To fix Dick's share at 40 per cent. and Harry's share at 35 per cent. is to fix Tom's share at 25 per cent."—" Progress and Poverty," p. 118.

[2] " Political Economy," p. 263, 1st edition.

[3] *Ibid.*, p. 266.

[4] " There remain but two parties as claimants . . . on the one side stands a crowd composed of persons engaged in the mill . . . on the other side stands the manufacturer. All that these do not take will *be his ;* and as piece after piece is rapidly cut off, he seems to fear that not enough will remain for him. . . . At last the manufacturer is left with his share."—" Political Economy," p. 188.

the reason why the employers are unable (other things being the same) to realize any profits for themselves." [1] If it is true that "wages are an essential part of the cost to the employer" and must be paid before he can have any profit, they cannot possibly be a contingent surplus after profit is made. Either Walker is wrong in his "web-of-cloth" and entrepreneur discussion, or his doctrine that wages are the "residual claimant" is wholly fallacious. That factor which receives the contingent surplus must of necessity also bear the contingent losses ; and this, it is needless to say, the wage-receiver never does.

If Walker can point to any "natural law" by which the increased production "inures directly and immediately" to the laborer as wages, he will have discovered an economic force the existence of which was never before heard of. The fact is that no such thing ever occurs, nor can it possibly do so under the wages and entrepreneur régime. That an absurdity so obvious to Walker when discussing the theory of the "entrepreneur's profits," should, within a dozen pages, be dogmatically affirmed as natural law, is not a little astonishing. Fortunately for the stability of social institutions it can easily be shown that the George, Jevons, and Walker classification is radically erroneous. All economic and social forces conspire to make wages the first and profit the last, in the order of distribution.

The economic order in which wealth is distributed—as wages, rent, interest, and profit—must necessarily follow that in which the classes to whom they are paid came into existence. That this was the laborer, the landowner, the capitalist, and the entrepreneur is an historic fact too obvious to need discussing.

The economic reason for this is not difficult to understand. There are two facts co-extensive with the human race : (1) that no class will permanently aid in production unless it receives the equivalent of the cost of its contribution. (2) That the community will not continuously pay for a contribution to production which does not yield them as much as it costs. Every change of method or policy, whether economic, ethical, or political, has simply been an effort to improve existing conditions. Established methods and institutions never were, never will be, and never should be abandoned for any other reason. Indeed, were this

[1] "Political Economy," p. 241.

otherwise, there would be no certainty in progress and no safety to civilization.

Obviously, then, the only condition upon which primitive man would devote his efforts to production is that it would afford him a living. It is equally clear that he would not give a portion of the product for the use of any new factor unless he could obtain a still better living by so doing. For the same reason that no-rent land will only be cultivated when it will yield more than can be obtained from the chase, rent will be paid for land only when it will yield as much, or more, plus the rent, than could be obtained from no-rent land. In other words, nothing can make rent possible that does not make land yield more than the labor-cost of its use.

As society advances, with the division of labor and the production of manufactured commodities, capital, the third factor, begins to be employed in production. The capitalist, like the landowner, wants pay for his contribution—tools, machinery, buildings, etc. There is no economic force by which he can obtain any thing by excluding either of the other two factors, namely, wages and rent. If he prevents the laborer from receiving a living, his tools and capital cannot be employed. If he demands all that remains after paying the laborer, the landowner will refuse him the use of the land ; and this also would prevent his capital from being used. Clearly, the capitalist cannot prevent the other factors from being employed in production ; but either of the others can ; and unless he pays their cost they will surely prevent him. He is the last comer, and the only way he can be employed and receive any thing for his service is, to so increase the aggregate product that a surplus will remain after paying the other two. It is only on condition that the capitalist contributes more to the product than he takes from it that he can become a permanent factor in production, and this is precisely what he has always done.

Finally, in the most complex state of society the fourth factor—the entrepreneur class—appears. Under this régime, the division of labor and the complexity of productive methods are such that the laborer, and, to a large extent, the capitalist, has no ownership in the product, but the whole enterprise is conducted by the entrepreneur. He hires all the factors, and takes all the risks and all the results. Instead of the laborer obtaining the product and paying the landowner, the entrepreneur pays the laborer his wages, the landowner his rent, and the capitalist his interest. Then the whole product is his. If he sells it for more than the aggregate cost of these three factors and his own living (which is his wages), the remainder is his as profit. If he sells it for less than cost the loss is his. Wages, rent, and interest are all indispensable to the entrepreneur régime of production. None of these can be eliminated without destroying the entrepreneur, but he can be eliminated and the others remain intact. And so on all the way down. The subsequent factors can never produce without the preceding ones, but by returning to simpler methods the preceding ones can always produce without the subsequent ones.

It is thus evident that, in the progress of society, the factors have entered production in the order stated, and therefore economic distribution must necessarily be first wages, then rent, interest, and profit. In this order they will be considered in the succeeding chapters.

In the natural order of distribution, the laborer being necessarily the first to be supplied, the most utopian scheme ever contemplated could not put him nearer the product than natural law has placed him. In studying how to improve his economic condition the question is not how to change his position in the order of distribution, but how to increase the amount which he receives. This involves a consideration of the law of wages and will next occupy our attention.

CHAPTER II.

SOME RECENT THEORIES OF WAGES CONSIDERED.

Section I.—*Dr. Stuart Wood's Theory.*

In a previous work[1] the merits of the three most prominent theories of wages then current were considered, namely, the Wages-fund theory, and the theories of Francis A. Walker and Henry George. Since that time another theory has been presented by Dr. Stuart Wood.[2] This theory being presented by a scholar and a close student of economic science, and propagated through the journal of Harvard University, is entitled to consideration.

He begins by affirming that: "The market price of labor is that price which prevails at any given time in virtue of the existing supply and demand. . . . But price can only be in equilibrium on the condition that supply and demand are equal."[3] Then he proceeds to argue that both commodities and labor are used inversely to their price ; increasing as the price falls and decreasing as it rises, until the equilibrium between demand and supply is reached. He formally presents the law of wages as follows :

"We may state this law of wages in the following terms : *The price of a given amount of labor is the same as the price paid for the use of such amount of capital as would replace that labor in those employments where labor and capital are interchangeable and where either can be used to equal advantage.*"[4]

[1] "Wealth and Progress," 1887.

[2] *Quarterly Journal of Economics* for October, 1888 and July, 1889 ; also "Publications American Economic Association," vol. iv., No. 1.

[3] "Publications American Economic Association," vol. iv., No. 1, p. 7 ; also *Quarterly Journal of Economics*, vol. iii., No. 1, p. 61.

[4] *Ibid.*, p. 15 ; *cf. Journal of Economics*, vol. iii., No. 1, pp. 68, 71.

After nine pages of elaboration he repeats the above formula and says : " The same prices, which are paid for such amounts of labor and capital as are interchangeable in those occupations where they are indifferently employed, are also paid for equal amounts of labor and capital in whatever other employment they may be engaged in." [1]

It will be seen from the above that this doctrine affirms : (1) That wages are governed by supply and demand rising or falling until the " supply and demand are equal." (2) That the general rate of wages thus determined is fixed by the final (minimum) utility of that portion of the supply of laborers " which come into use last." [2] (3) That at the wage-determining point, the price of labor and the price of capital are identical—*i.e.*, the amount paid in wages and that paid in interest for the same amount of productive energy are exactly equal to each other. (4) That the same rate of wages and interest that prevails at that point are paid in all other employments where capital and labor are jointly used.

The first proposition is simply a reaffirmation of the wages-fund theory. The fallacy of that doctrine has already been so completely shown, that comment here is entirely unnecessary.[3]

The second point in this theory is that the rate of wages which supply and demand determines, is fixed at the point of the final utility of those laborers who are employed last. " The price of labor," says Mr. Wood, " is regulated as are the prices of all commodities by its final utility ; by the utility, that is, of that portion which comes into use last." Here again he affirms a proposition without attempting to prove it. Why we should believe that the prices of all commodities are regulated by their final utility, he does not attempt to show.

By final utility is meant, that portion of the general supply of a commodity which possesses the minimum utility for the purchaser. For example, suppose in a given community a thousand pairs of shoes a week could be consumed, there would doubtless be a few who would give $10 a pair rather than go barefooted, but there is a certain portion who would go without shoes rather than give more than $2 a pair. The point at which they would

[1] " Publications American Economic Association," vol. iv., No. 1, p. 29.
[2] *Ibid.*, p. 9.
[3] " Wealth and Progress," pp. 35–52. See also present work, pp. 105–107.

go without shoes rather than pay a higher price, is called the final utility of the shoes. The price at which those can obtain the shoes, for whom they possess the least utility, will of course be that at which all can buy them. The uniform price will thus always *represent* the point of final utility, but it does not follow from this that the price is "*regulated by* the final utility." All that this proves is that the price-determining point and that of final utility are identical.

A very little examination will show that instead of the final utility determining the price, it is more frequently the price that determines the point of final utility. If, for instance, the cost of producing the shoes should be increased so that they could not be made for less than $3 a pair, all those who would buy at $2 but would not give $3, would have to go without shoes. The point of final utility would thus be changed from $2 to $3 a pair, and the shoes would only be sold to those who would rather give $3 than go without. On the other hand, if by any improved methods of production the shoes could be made for $1 a pair, all those who would not give $2, but would give $1 a pair, could have shoes, then the point of final utility would at once move from $2 to $1 a pair. It is obvious that in this case the price would not be fixed by the final utility, but the final utility would be fixed by the price, and this is precisely what occurs in every-day experience. Clearly then, while the final utility will always be at the same point as the price, it is an error to say that the final utility *determines* the price. This is another of the numerous instances of trying to elevate a mere truism into a general law. Like the wage-fund theory, the final-utility doctrine at most only states a quantitative fact—not a dynamic principle.

Nor does Mr. Wood make any effort to explain why the point of final utility is necessarily fixed by the "portion which comes into use last." It is a well-known fact that, in the evolution of industry, the accessions to every working group are always on the outer edge of the industrial field. The movement of labor, whether slow or rapid, is constantly from barbarism to civilization, from pastoral to agricultural life, from agriculture to manufacture, and from inferior to superior manufacturing countries and localities. Thus we see in England the accessions to the manufacturing districts generally consist of the cheaper laborers from the agricultural districts, and in America the accession is from the cheaper labor of other countries. In fact the mobility of labor is universally towards more remunerative fields of employment, and therefore the last increment is always the cheapest —*i.e.*, the poorest.

Thus if prices determined by the final utility, and the point of final utility were fixed by the " portion which comes into use last," then wages would necessarily be determined by the poorest laborers. Moreover, since, according to Mr. Wood's theory, the same price which is paid for a given amount of labor at the price-fixing point, will determine the price that is paid for a similar amount of labor in any other employment, it follows not only that the rate of wages in any industry is governed by the cheapest laborers in that industry, but that the general rate of wages in all industries is determined by the poorest laborers in the least remunerative industry. Now this is precisely Henry George's doctrine of the " Margin of Cultivation " which we have already shown to be contrary to the commonest facts of experience.[1]

If there were any truth in this proposition, wages in all industries would be either uniform or constantly tending towards uniformity on the level of the poorest. The wages of the carpenters, plumbers, painters, bricklayers, printers, and highest-paid mechanics of New York City would constantly be tending towards the level of the lowest continental and Asiatic immigrant and the poorest agricultural laborer, which is too obviously absurd to need discussing. Instead of wages tending towards a general uniformity at the lowest point, they are constantly tending towards a greater diversity as the differentiation of productive groups or industries advances. And, as we shall see in the next chapter, whatever tendency there is towards uniformity, it is towards uniformity with the dearest and not with the cheapest labor in each industrial group.

The third postulate in this theory is, that at the price-fixing point the amount paid in wages and that paid in interest are exactly equal to each other, and that the same prices are paid for the same amounts of either labor or capital in all other employments.[2] In other words, that the amount of capital which will produce as

---

[1] " Wealth and Progress," Part II., chap. i,, sec. iii.

[2] " The same price, whether it is called wages or interest, is paid for that amount of labor and for that amount of capital which can supplant each other

much as a given amount of labor, will everywhere receive the same in interest as the labor does in wages.

Mr. Wood evidently regards this point as the most important in his whole argument, repeating it several times in italics, as a formula of the new law of wages.[1] This is essentially the position taken by Marx.[2] The only difference is that Marx claims that all the product rightfully belongs to the laborer and treats that which goes to the capitalist as unjust " exploitation,"[3] while Mr. Wood regards the equal division of the product between the laborer and the capitalist as the result of natural law.

Now assuming this postulate to be entirely correct, what does it establish ? what explanation does it afford of the law of wages ? If all it affirms is true, it only shows that wages equal interest. Wages may equal interest and still be very high or very low.   It affords no explanation of why wages are 10 cents a day in China, 40 cents in Russia, 60 cents in Germany, $1.25 in England, or $2 in America, to say they equal the amount paid in interest. Nor is it any advantage to the laborer who is receiving low wages to tell him that the income of his employer is at zero.   The laborer's social welfare depends upon his actual, not his relative, income.   It is the absolute amount of opportunity, comfort, and luxury he enjoys which determines the extent of his social well-being, and not whether or not the employer has more or less of these things.

Nor does this theory appear to any better advantage when tested by the facts.   It should be remembered that by the expression, " price of using capital," Dr. Wood means the net gain to the capitalist from its use, and not the cost of keeping the capital (machinery, etc.) intact, as his language would sometimes

and render the same services in those industries where their relative superiorities merge, or which can in different industries render services equally esteemed by effective desire. And the same prices as are paid in these cases for labor and for the use of capital are also paid for them in all their other employments."—*Quarterly Journal of Economics*, vol. iii., No. 1, p. 86.

[1] *Quarterly Journal of Economics*, vol. iii., No. 1, pp. 68, 71, 72, 84, 86 ; *ibid.*, No. 4, p. 478 ; also " Publications American Economic Association," vol. iv., No. 1, pp. 15, 19.

[2] " Capital," chap vii., sec. ii., pp. 166–176.

[3] Karl Marx's Doctrine of Exploitation and Surplus Value is considered in chapter iv. of this Part.

seem to imply.[1] The statement, that "the price of a given amount of labor is equal to the price which is paid for the use of such amounts of auxiliary capital as can replace it in those occupations where the two things may be indifferently employed with equal pecuniary advantage,"[2] and that "the same prices as are paid in these cases for labor and for the use of capital are also paid for them in all their other employments,"[3] affirms : (1) that all capital receives interest, the rate of which is the same in all employments ; (2) that "the rate of wages or the price of using labor" is determined by "the rate of interest or the price of using capital."

The first of these affirmations is so manifestly at variance with all industrial experience that it almost seems trifling to discuss it. Instead of interest or profits being uniform—*i.e.*, the same "in all other employments," the reverse is everywhere the case. In all fairly well established industries where any appreciable amount of capital is employed, interest or profit varies from zero up. In farming and every branch of manufacture there are to be found some who are barely holding their own and keeping their capital intact. There are many who for years together receive no interest for the use of their capital, and frequently some who continue to employ it at a net loss, while others in the same business and often in the some locality receive five, ten, and sometimes twenty per cent. profit. It is exactly at this no-interest point that the price of the product is determined[4] ; and every time this price-fixing point is lowered by the use of improved methods of production, these no-interest producers are compelled to produce at a loss or leave the business. This is the only means by which the price of commodities is permanently reduced. It is in this process of pushing the price below the plane of the no-interest producer that

[1] This point he makes clear by saying : " But the charges for insurance and for renewals, or wear and tear, are not strictly charges for the use of capital, but simply a provision to preserve its amount unimpaired. . . . Disregarding, therefore, all items of cost of employing auxiliary capital except interest, the law of wages assumes this form : *The interest on capital and the price of labor, in all employments, are fixed by the rates paid for their use in those of their actual employments in which they are used indifferently,*" etc.—*Quarterly Journal of Economics*, vol. iii., No. 1, pp. 71, 72.

[2] *Quarterly Journal of Economics*, vol. iii., No. 1, p. 68.

[3] *Ibid.*, p. 86.   [4] Part II., chapter iv., section iii.

small concerns are constantly being "crowded out of business by large ones'; and this tendency increases as the use of capital and specialization of industry develops and civilization advances. Since, in all well established industries subject to free competition, there is capital employed which receives a liberal return as interest or profits, and in the same industries capital is employed for the use of which no interest whatever is paid, it is manifestly incorrect to say : "The same prices . . . are also paid for equal amounts of labor and capital in whatever other employments they may be engaged in."

Nor is the second affirmation any more consistent with the facts. If it were true that the rate of wages is determined by, or only equal to, the rate of interest, the rate of wages could never exceed the amount paid for the use of the capital representing an equal amount of productive force. According to this hypothesis, wherever the capital is employed without interest the laborer must also work without wages. It is unnecessary to say that such a state of things is nowhere to be found in the industrial world, not even under slavery. In every industry we can find capital employed without interest, but in no industry can we find labor working without wages.

Since capital is frequently used without interest, and labor never used without wages, it is manifestly incorrect to say the rate of wages is determined by or equal to the rate of interest ; and since both the rate of wages and interest vary in different industries, and vary in different localities in the same industry, it cannot possibly be true that "*the same prices as are paid in these cases for labor and for the use of capital are also paid for them in all their other employments.*"

The only really important point in Mr. Wood's argument is the recognition of the fact that capital can only be successfully employed when it is cheaper than labor as a means of production, a fact hitherto generally overlooked.

Since social progress chiefly depends upon increasing the quantity and reducing the cost of wealth, and this in turn depends upon the use of capital in production, a correct understanding of the law governing the economic use of capital is of the utmost

[1] *Cf.* chapter iv. ; also author's article, *Political Science Quarterly*, vol. iii., No. 3, pp. 385–408.

importance to economic science. As already explained,[1] that which *undersells always succeeds, and that which succeeds establishes the methods by which its success is accomplished ;* consequently, the principle upon which capital can be successfully employed in production is its relative cheapness as a productive factor.

The fact that " as between two methods of obtaining the same result, cheapness is the sole guide," is clear to Mr. Wood, but its economic significance he has evidently failed to recognize. Like the orthodox economists, he sees that the use of capital is the only means of permanently cheapening wealth. And he further sees what they did not, namely : that capital can only be employed when it furnishes productive force cheaper than labor ; but the principle upon which capital becomes cheaper than labor he appears to be no nearer understanding than was Adam Smith, Gregory King, or Thomas Munn. The chief difficulty with Dr. Wood is that he fails to distinguish between the economic character of labor and capital and consequently confounds the price of labor with interest or profit which are fundamentally different.

The price of labor, like that of all necessary factors in production, is determined by its own cost and not by interest, nor any thing relating to capital. The use of capital depends upon the cost of labor in two ways—its cost as a factor in production, and its expensiveness as an element in consumption. While capital can never be employed unless it can work cheaper than labor, it can only do so when it is accompanied by new employment creating conditions which nothing but an enlarged general consumption and higher wages can supply. Moreover, a general rate of wages and profits in all industries, such as Wood struggles to explain, is nowhere to be found. The rate of wages tends to uniformity only within specific industrial groups. In such countries as India and China and to some extent in Russia and Austria, among purely agricultural producers, there is the nearest approximation to a general rate of wages, because there industrial differentiation is at the minimum. But in proportion as the division of labor and the complexity of industrial and social relations increase, a general rate of wages becomes impossible, because distinctive industrial groups bring different rates of wages into existence.

[1] Part II., chapter i.

For example, the wages of spinners, weavers, carpenters, masons, tailors, etc., will tend to a uniform rate for each industry in the same market or locality, but that uniformity does not extend throughout the country. Accordingly, we find that the wages for the same occupation in New York City are very much higher than in rural districts and country villages, for the obvious reason that the cost of supplying the labor-power is greater in the former than in the latter places.

Therefore while wages and prices always tend to a uniformity, it is a uniformity for the same quality in the same market. But even this is in no sense true of profits ; on the contrary, all the force of self-interest and economic law tend to make profits move in the opposite direction. The reason for this is very simple. Profits being the net surplus after all costs are paid, it is because prices tend to a uniformity that a variation in the cost makes profits possible, and therefore the greater the variation in the cost of production per unit of product, the greater the variation in the profits. And conversely the more uniform the cost of production per unit, the more uniform and the smaller the maximum amount of profit. Instead of profits tending towards a uniformity, they tend towards diversity, varying from zero up, in proportion as the complexity in productive methods and variety in the cost per unit increases.

SECTION II.—*Professor Clark's Theory.*

In a recent monograph [1] Professor Clark presents a theory of wages which, if not new, has some new features in it. The fundamental point in this theory is, that the price of all factors in production is determined by what the last and no-rent increment can produce, which when applied to labor is, that the general rate of wages is determined by what the laborer could produce " empty-handed " or with such land and tools as can be had for nothing.

As a theory of wages this is essentially the doctrine of Henry

[1] A paper on the " Possibility of a Scientific Law of Wages," read before the Third Annual Meeting of the American Economic Association, in Philadelphia, December 27, 1888. " Publications American Economic Association," vol. iv., No. 1.

George, which we have shown to be contrary to all experience.[1] Mr. Clark, however, seems to think the fallacies which we exposed in the theory of Mr. George are not due to the principle of the doctrine, but result from a too restricted application of it.

Instead of limiting the theory to no-rent land, as George does, he extends it to no-rent instruments in all departments of the social working-field.[2] This theory affirms : (1) that there is a no-rent point at which every productive factor is employed ; (2) that this marginal or no-rent place is where the price of using all productive instruments is determined ; (3) that this price-fixing portion of the supply is always the last increment that is brought into use—hence, "the men who fix the standard of wages are in the rear rank, not in the front " ; (4) that the wages of the last or price-fixing increment depend upon the proportion between the number of laborers and the amount of capital employed ; and consequently, that wages can only be advanced in proportion as capital increases faster than labor.

1.   Is it correct to say that there is a no-rent point in the use of all productive factors ?   Something depends here upon what is meant by the phrase " no-rent."   If by rent he means the cost of maintaining the instrument unimpaired, then the statement is manifestly incorrect.   In this sense a permanent no-rent use of any productive factor is impossible, since its wear and tear would soon cause its total destruction.   If, however, by rent he means that which the owner obtains in addition to maintaining its productive efficiency unimpaired, the statement is unexceptionable. Regarding rent in the sense of net surplus, there is unquestionably a no-rent point at which every productive factor, including labor, is employed.[3]

2.   Whether or not it is correct to say that the price of using the productive instruments is determined at the no-rent (no-surplus) point, depends upon the sense in which the word "price" is used.   If by the *price of using productive instruments* is meant the expense of maintaining their productive efficiency, which

---

[1] " Wealth and Progress," Part II., chap. i., sec. iii.

[2] " The true margin of cultivation—more accurately that of utilization— is not wholly nor chiefly an agricultural thing ; it extends throughout the industrial system. . . . There is a margin of utilization in cotton spinning, in iron-smelting, in shop-keeping."—Pp. 44, 45.

[3] Part III., chapter iii.

constitutes a necessary part of the cost of production, and is paid by the consumer in the price of the product, there can be no exception to the statement.   But if by the price of using productive instruments is meant the rent of land, and the profit or interest of capital, or the savings of labor, in short, surplus incomes none of which enters the cost of production, then the statement would be manifestly incorrect.   Instead of these being determined at the price of no-rent use, they are always determined by variations from it.[1]   It would indeed be a contradiction in terms to say surplus incomes are determined by no-surplus uses.

3. The third proposition will be found to be much less satisfactory.   In affirming that the last increment added to the supply is the price-determining increment, Prof. Clark has made a questionable application of his argument.   He here confounds the *last* with the *dearest* increment as if they were quite equivalent expressions.   In doing this he has committed precisely the same mistake that Marx made in following Ricardo and confounding the quantity with the cost of labor as the determining factor in value.   When Ricardo said "the value of commodities is determined by the quantity of labor devoted to their production," he really meant the cost of that labor.   But he erroneously assumed that a given quantity of labor always represents the same cost[2] ; hence, the cost and quantity at any given time are equivalent expressions.   Marx literally accepted Ricardo's expression, "the quantity of labor" without regard to its cost, the logical application of which led directly to the colossal error of declaring that profits are exploitation of labor, an error which the adoption of the other form of expression, "cost of labor," would have entirely obviated.[3]

The position of Prof. Clark is another instance of the same kind.   Ricardo's theory of rent, which is the evident basis of his doctrine, affirms that the last increment of land brought into cultivation is always the no-rent and hence the price-determining portion.   The idea he endeavors to apply to the whole sphere of

---

[1] See Part III., chap. iv.

[2] See " Political Economy and Taxation," ch. i., sec. ii. and iii.

[3] See article on " Economic Basis of Socialism," *Political Science Quarterly* for December, 1889.

price phenomena. He assumes that the price of all productive instruments is determined by the no-rent increment, and that this is always the increment which is *brought into use last.* It is here that the element of error enters the doctrine and invalidates it as a scientific theory of prices, either of labor or of commodities. In making the last increment of land the rent-fixing increment, Ricardo confounded the last with the dearest increment, exactly as in the previous case he confounded the quantity with the cost of labor. The real reason Ricardo held that the rent of all land was fixed by the last increment brought under cultivation was, because he erroneously assumed that the last increment was always the poorest and therefore the dearest. Here as in the former case he assumed that the two were equivalent expressions but always spoke of the "last." Prof. Clark like Marx accepts the literal form rather than the interior meaning of Ricardo's expressions and with similarly fatal consequences.

It can easily be shown that this "last-increment" theory is inconsistent with the facts, alike in regard to land, capital, and labor. It is well known that Ricardo's assumed order of cultivation is entirely unhistoric. Instead of the best land always being used first and the poorest last, the reverse order more frequently occurs. For instance, when the land brought into cultivation last will yield more for the same investment than that already cultivated, as is often the case, the price of the product will not fall to the cost of production on this last land, because in that case all the previously cultivated land would be thrown out of use by making the price so low as to render its cultivation impossible. If the product of all the land under cultivation is needed, the price must be high enough at least to enable the poorest portion to be cultivated without paying rent. Thus while the poorest portion will be the price-fixing and no-rent increment, it will not be the last, but the last increment, being the best or better than the poorest, will be a rent-paying and not the price-fixing increment.

Having confused the last with the dearest increment, Prof. Clark's argument from this point on, like that of Marx, leads directly to error in proportion to the consistency with which it is pursued.

He says "it is a familiar commercial principle that the last increment of the supply of any commodity fixes the general price of that article." Instead of that principle being familiar in commerce and manufacture, it is even less true there than in the case of land. There is no fact better established in the history of manufacture than that it is the oldest, poorest, and hence the dearest machinery and methods which yield no profits. It is the water-wheel factory, the small mules and slow looms that occupy the no-profit or minimum profit position. The new factories with the most modern improvements are those which yield the greatest profits, because they can sell at the same price while producing at a less cost than their price-fixing competitor. In manufacture and commerce, therefore, instead of being the last it is usually the first or oldest instruments 'in use which fix the price ; but whether the oldest or newest, it is *always* *the dearest.*

According to the last-increment theory, wages will always be determined by " the last laborers added to the social working force." [1] If we observe the history of the mobility of the laborer whether it be from industry to industry, from locality to locality, or from nation to nation, we shall find, except in a few rare instances, that those who enter any given working field last are the most inexperienced, incompetent, and poor. It is the effort to improve their condition that induces people to change their country, locality, or occupation. That is why emigration is always from lower to higher wage-paying countries, why mechanics seldom become farmers, but agricultural laborers are constantly entering the factory and farmers' sons deserting the farms for the cities. The laborer who leaves his country or industry may be and probably often is one of the dearest of the class he leaves, but he is usually among the cheapest in the class he enters. If the poorest laborer fixed the wages when a new man entered any class, the wages of all in that class would fall to his level.

The statement that the standard of wages is fixed by " the actual product created by . . . the men who run no-rent machinery " [2] introduces a new element of confusion. The men who run the no-rent machinery are not necessarily the last comers in that industry. This is really confounding the price of the laborer with that of the product. Other things being the same, the use of the poorest instruments will determine the no-profit and price-fixing

[1] " Possibility of a Scientific Law of Wages," p. 49.   [2] *Ibid.*, p. 49.

point of commodities, because in that case the quality of the in-struments affects the cost of production. But this is not true of labor; since the instruments are not used in producing labor-power, its cost, and hence its price, cannot be affected by their quality. As productive instruments are only used in creating commodities, it is the price of commodities alone that can be affected by the quality of such instruments. The price of the instruments may have been affected by that of the previous labor which was employed in their production, but when used as in-struments in production in conjunction with labor they are both simply items in the cost of producing a future product, whose price is fixed by them and not theirs by it. For the same reason that the price of raw material is not determined by the finished product into which it enters, but by the price of what enters into it, the price of labor power does not depend upon the price of what it produces, but upon the price of what it consumes—*i.e.*, the cost of its own production. Upon no other principle would the product made by the poorest tools be the dearest, and hence the no-profit portion.

Therefore, instead of the price of labor being determined by the quality of the instrument it uses, it is the price of the result-ant product only that is so affected. The fact that the entrepre-neur who uses the poorest tools has to pay wages as high as those who use the best, prevents him from having any profit. As a matter of fact the laborer's wages do not grade up and down according to the superiority and inferiority of the instruments he uses. It is only profits which thus vary, and the reason they do so is because wages do not.

Another source of confusion is the mistake of regarding wages as sustaining the same relation to labor that rent does to land and that profit does to capital. This it will be remembered was one of the chief errors in Dr. Wood's argument, and Prof. Clark seems not entirely to have escaped it. Although for a time he seems to treat wages as identical with prices, in his grand formula he treats wages as governed by the same law as profits and rent,[1]

---

[1] " The earnings of capital (profits and rent) are subject to identically the same law as those of labor ; they are fixed by the product of the last increment that is brought into the field."—" Possibility of a Scientific Law of Wages," p. 53.

which is entirely erroneous. In the use of both capital and land, that which is necessary to replace the wear and tear is not profit or rent but necessary cost. It does not go to the owner of the land or capital, but is all consumed in maintaining its productive efficiency. Wherever land or capital is employed, and the product is only equal to this necessary cost, there will be no profits or rent. In the case of labor all this is different. All the laborer receives is wages, whether it is cost or surplus. Whether the laborer receives what will barely maintain his economic efficiency or a third more than that amount it is all wages because it is all in the price of his labor.

In every class of labor under wage conditions there are some laborers who work at the bare cost point, and others who have a surplus. There is also land that is used at cost point and yields no rent or surplus, and land that yields a rent.[1] So too of capital; there is some that is used without profit and some that yields a profit. Now those laborers who have no surplus above their cost of living receive wages, and as high wages too as those of their class who have a surplus. But the owners of land and capital which only yields the cost of their use do not receive a surplus as rent or profit. To say profit and rent are governed by the same law as labor is to confound the law of prices with the law of surplus. Wages are the price of labor and are governed by the same law as the price of land, gold, or shoes. Profit and rent, like the laborer's savings, are all surpluses and are governed by the law of surplus. The correct statement therefore is this : the surplus or savings from wages, rent of land, and profit of capital, are all governed by the same law—the law of economic surplusage ; and the wages of labor, the price of land, and of commodities are governed by the same law, namely, the law of economic prices.

4. The fourth proposition is the natural outcome of the third.

---

[1] In using the expression " no-rent," the existence of no-rent land and no-profit instruments, is assumed. If however a state of society should be reached where no-rent land does not exist, that would not in the least militate against the law. It would then be the *minimum*-rent land or tools that occupy the price-fixing position. Indeed the prefix " no " should always be taken to mean " minimum." Then where no-rent land or capital exists the statement is correct, and where they do not exist it is the minimum-rent land or capital that is referred to.

25

The doctrine which makes the laborer's income depend upon the quality of his tools naturally leads to the conclusion that wages depend upon capital. Hence it is not surprising that Mr. Clark falls back into the fold of pure wage-fundism which makes the progress of the laborer subsequent to and dependent upon that of the capitalist. He says : " The sole hope of this multitude (the working class) lies in an advance of the margin of the field of capital, and in the retirement of the margin of the field of labor. By this twofold action only can wages rise with great rapidity, but the movement of its margins is possible only by means of a considerable excess of the supply of capital unbalanced by labor." [1] This contains the essence of about all the heresy of orthodox economics. It makes man depend upon wealth instead of making wealth depend upon man.

Whatever the merits of this theory may be, it has three serious defects : (1) in assuming that prices are determined by the last instead of by the dearest increment of the supply ; (2) in treating wages as a share of the division of the product instead of a necessary item in the cost of its production ; (3) in putting wages in the same economic category with rent and profit instead of in the category of prices. The natural result is to confound wages with profits, misplace the price-determining factor, and finally invert the economic relation of capital and labor.

[1] " Possibility of a Scientific Law of Wages," p. 59.

CHAPTER III.

THE LAW OF WAGES.

SECTION I.—*The Test of a Scientific Law of Wages.*

A SCIENTIFIC law of wages must afford a rational explanation of all normal wage phenomena. It must explain what wages are, why they are paid, and how their amount is determined. It must explain why the rate of wages varies in the same industries in different countries and localities, and why it differs in different industries in the same localities ; why the wages in agriculture are always lower than those of manufacturing industries in the same country ; why in the same industries and localities the wages of women are lower than those of men ; and why in all industries a portion of the laborers can save money while others of their class can scarcely make both ends meet. In proportion as any theory fails to account for these constantly recurring facts, it must be deemed insufficient to explain the economic law of wages.

In considering the theories of others I have applied this test, and to the extent that they fail to fulfil its requirements, I have not hesitated to pronounce them incomplete or unsound.[1] All that I ask is that the theory presented in this chapter shall be judged by the same standard ; and if it fails to fulfil the requirements exacted from others, it must share the same fate, and *vice versa.* In order to avoid confusion it is important at the outset that we definitely understand what the term wages is intended to mean.

[1] The criticism of the wages-fund theory, Professor Walker's theory, and Henry George's theory will be found in "Wealth and Progress," Part II., chap. i. ; and that of Dr. Wood and Professor Clark in the preceding chapter.

SECTION II.—*Definition of Wages.*

In the first place, the phrase wages has no economic meaning except under wage conditions ; that is to say, under conditions where the laborer's income consists of a specific amount paid by another for his service as such.   Strictly speaking, wages are economically the *price* of labor.   For instance, if a man works for himself, and either sells or consumes the product of his labor, what he receives will not be wages ; it will be the result of his labor, but that will consist of the product he created, whether little or much, good or bad, or indifferent, but it will not be the *price* of his labor.   Nothing can properly be regarded as having a price which is not subject to the conditions of exchange—*i.e.*, is not bought and sold.   When a man owns and sells the products of his labor, the product has a price but his labor has not, because as labor it has not entered the sphere of exchange, and hence is not subject to the law of prices.

So too in slavery, where the laborer owns neither his labor nor his product.   Here the product is bought and sold, and hence has a price, but the labor-power as such is not exchanged ; it is the laborer himself that is bought and sold.   We do not buy the labor of the horse or the engine.   It is true that the motive for buying the horse or engine is to obtain their productive power, but in order to obtain that power we have to buy that in which it is produced.   Under slavery the laborer is economically identical with the horse or the engine.   It is he and not his labor-power that is bought and sold.   The difference in the two systems, then, may be stated thus : under slavery the *laborer is* a commodity ; under the wages-system it is only his labor-power or service that is a commodity.   With this change came a marked social distinction ; under wage conditions, the capitalist, instead of buying and selling laborers as under slavery, buys service and sells products, and the laborer sells service and buys products.   Thus the laborer ceases to be a commodity and becomes a distinct social unit who buys and sells, and economic price is transferred from his personality to his labor-power.   It is only under conditions where the laborer is personally, socially, and politically free and sells his service as such, that wages can properly be said to exist.   The price at which service under such conditions is sold by the laborer is wages.

It is therefore not the amount received, but the way in which it is received that constitutes it wages. Whether the amount be a hundred dollars a year or a hundred dollars a week makes no economic difference. . There is nothing in the nature of wages as such to prevent them from being increased to any amount. The essential characteristic of wages is that they constitute a definite as distinguished from a contingent income. It will be observed that this definition of wages includes the incomes of all, without regard to sex or social status, who sell their service for a stipulated amount. The term wages, then, as it will be used throughout this book, means neither more nor less than the *price of labor*.

In the text-books there is usually considerable discussion about nominal and real wages. This, however, need detain us but a moment. Nominal wages simply mean the price that is paid for a given amount of service expressed in the currency or money of the community. Real wages mean the actual amount of wealth or social well-being obtainable for a day's labor. Nominal wages are of no special account except as a mode of expressing real wages.[1] In considering the law of wages, therefore, the question is not how is the laborer's income determined when he works for himself, nor how it is determined when he is personally the property of another, but how his income is determined when he voluntarily sells his service as service. What the employer pays to the laborer is not in any sense a division of the product, but it is wholly an expenditure in purchasing the means of production. Thus labor (not the laborer) is in exactly the same economic category as raw material, machinery, or any other productive factor. For instance, when the manufacturer has produced a thousand yards of cotton cloth he does not divide it with his laborers either practically or theoretically ; on the contrary, all the wages for producing that cloth, including those involved in producing the raw material and machinery, have already been paid. They constitute a part of the cost, and hence the value of the cloth. Whether or not the manufacturer will gain or lose by the transaction is a subsequent matter, and entirely depends upon whether he can produce the cloth at as small a cost as his most incompetent competitor.

The economic claim of the laborer therefore is to a definite price for his labor, and not to a proportional share of the prod-

· [1] " Wealth and Progress," pp. 75, 76, 96, 97, 98.

uct. This really constitutes the economic difference between wages and rent, interest and profit, and is the distinction already pointed out between price and surplus. If the laborer were a claimant to a given proportional share of the product, the size of his income would depend upon the quantity produced, and would thus become a contingent instead of a stipulated amount. In short he would be working in partnership and not working for wages. As before stated, the essential characteristic of the wages system is that the laborer is not a commercial partner ; he has no ownership in the finished product. His economic position is to *sell labor and buy products*, and that of the entrepreneur is to *buy labor and sell products*. Obviously then the laborer sells his productive power to the employer at a stipulated price ; he has no more claim to a proportional share of the product than have those who sell raw material or machinery. The law of wages, then, is the law of the *economic price of labor*.

Therefore, in considering the law of wages the question is not what proportion of the product belongs to the laborer, but how the price of his labor is economically determined. When we have discovered the law by which the price of labor is governed, we shall be in a position to consider how that price (wages) can be increased.

SECTION III.—*The Law of Wages.*

One of the essential conditions of a scientific law of prices is that it must be applicable to all price phenomena. Wages being simply the price of labor, must be governed by the same law as the price of commodities. Consequently if the formula of the law of prices presented in a previous chapter [1] is correct, we have only to apply that theory to labor in order to find the economic law of wages. If it does not explain the movement of wages as completely as it accounts for the price of commodities, we may safely conclude that it fails to fulfil the requirements of a scientific law.

This law it will be remembered is : *That economic prices constantly tend toward the cost of furnishing the most expensive portion of the necessary supply in any given market ; and that this tendency increases directly as the impediments to free economic movement are diminished.*

[1] Part II., chap. iv.

'Applied to labor then, this law is : *That wages tend to move towards the cost of furnishing the most expensive portion of the neces-sary supply of labor-power in any given market ;* and *that this ten-dency increases directly as the individual freedom and mobility of the laborer advances.*

By the cost of a thing is meant not what it may have cost somebody else or would cost under any other conditions, but what its owner actually gave for it or would have to pay to re-place it. The cost of labor-power then, is what it cost the laborer to furnish it. Obviously the cost of labor-power to the laborer is the cost of his maintenance or living. The cost of the laborer's living, however, is not limited to the simple maintenance of the individual laborer, but it includes all that enters into the neces-sary expenses of his social life. Since the maintenance of the family of the married man is as much a part of his necessary cost of living as his individual food and shelter, it is an indispensable item in the cost of supplying his labor power. Therefore the fam-ily and not the individual is the economic unit in the labor market.

The law of wages then, may be more correctly stated thus : *The rate of wages in any country, class, or industry constantly tends towards the cost of living of the most expensive families* [1] *who furnish a necessary part of the supply of labor in that country, class, or in-dustry,* as shown in the following diagram :

NO. I.

SAVINGS.	WAGES.	ACTUAL COST.	COST REDUCED BY CHEAP LIVING.	
0 c.	$2	Maximum cost $2		A
5 c.	$2	. . . . $1.95		B
10 c.	$2	. . . . $1.90		C
15 c.	$2	. . . . $1.85	Source	D
20 c.	$2	. . . . $1.80	of	E
25 c.	$2	Minimum cost . $1.75	Savings.	F.

The reason wages in any class or industry are thus adjusted to the standard of living of the most expensive families is exactly the same as that which we saw caused the price of commodities

[1] By the most expensive families is not meant the most expensive single family, but the most expensive ten or twenty per cent. of the class whose labor is required.

to be adjusted to the cost of producing the most expensive portion of the supply. We saw that the price of commodities tends
to a uniformity, because the lowest price at which one producer
would sell was the highest at which the consumer would buy.
This uniformity, through the pressure of the consumer to buy at
the minimum, tends to be adjusted at the lowest point the producer can afford to sell, which is at cost. And since the price
tends to uniformity at cost, wherever the cost varies, the uniformity necessarily takes place at the cost of the dearest increment.

This is equally true of labor, and for precisely the same reason. Upon the same principle that the producer cannot or
will not consent to continuously sell a commodity for less than
it cost him to produce it, or than it will cost him to replace it,
the laborer cannot or will not long consent to sell his service for
less than it costs him (and his family) to live. He will, as experience shows, often work for less than would supply him with
exceptional comforts and luxuries, but he will not continuously
work for less than will furnish him with those things which by
constant repetition and the force of habit have become necessities. Rather than forego these he will refuse to work, and will
inaugurate strikes, riots, and other means of endangering the
peace and prosperity of the community.

If two dollars per day is the minimum amount upon which a certain portion of a given class of laborers can or will consent peace-
fully to live, then that amount must be paid them in order to obtain their labor. What the most expensive portion of a given class
must receive, the others may and will receive. We know that the
general rate of wages in the same industry and locality is nearly
uniform. We know, for instance that weavers, spinners, shoemakers, carpenters, bricklayers, etc., working in the same shop
or factory or on the same job, get the same rate of pay for work
at their respective trades whether they are single or married, have
large or small families, or live more or less expensively than their
fellow-laborers. We also know, for reasons already given, that
the most expensive among them must obtain for his service what
will supply his family with what they regard as necessities. What
will be sufficient to supply the urgent necessities of the most expensive portion of any class of laborers, to induce them to continue to work, will furnish all those whose cost of living is less,

with a margin proportionate to the difference which may be saved or spent in what to them are luxuries.

Thus through the law of price uniformity, by which the cost of producing the most expensive portion determines the general price of the commodity in that market, the minimum amount upon which the most expensive laborers in any class or industry will consent to live and continue at work, determines the rate of wages in that class.

There is one important distinction, however, between these two classes of price phenomena which should not be overlooked. Although all prices are governed by the same general law, the price of commodities and of labor move in opposite directions. While the dearest capitalist and the dearest laborer both fix the prices for their class, they occupy relatively opposite positions. The manufacturers who furnish the most expensive portion of the supply of commodities are the poorest and lowest in their class, while the laborers who furnish the most expensive portion of labor-power are the best and highest in their class, as shown in the accompanying diagram :

NO. 2.

PROFIT.	PRICE.	ACTUAL COST.	COST SAVED BY CAPITAL.	
1 c.	4 c.	Minimum cost . . . 3c.	Source	F
$\frac{4}{5}$ c.	4 c.	. . . . 3⅕c.	of	E
$\frac{3}{5}$ c.	4 c.	. . . . 3⅖c.	Profits.	D
$\frac{2}{5}$ c.	4 c.	. . . . 3⅗c.		C
$\frac{1}{5}$ c.	4 c.	. . . . 3⅘c.		B
0 c.	4 c.	Maximum cost . . . . 4c.		A
0 c.	$2	Maximum cost $2		A
5 c.	$2	. . . . $1.95		B
10 c.	$2	. . . . $1.90		C
15 c.	$2	. . . . $1.85	Source	D
20 c.	$2	. . . . $1.80	of	E
25 c.	$1	Minimum cost . . $1.75	Savings.	F
SAVINGS.	WAGES.	ACTUAL COST.	COST REDUCED BY CHEAP LIVING.	

Here it will be observed the movements are all exactly the same as in the case of commodities (diagram No. 1), but the relative positions of all are reversed. Laborer A, like capitalist A, is the dearest. His labor-power cost him $2 a day, and he sells it for $2 a day, and has no surplus ; but instead of being at the bottom of his class, he is at the top. The wages of laborer A, like the price of manufacturer A, are the same as, and fix, those of all the others. Just as the cost of living of the laborers A, B, C, D, E, and F recedes from the cost line of A on the right, does their net-surplus (or the possibility of it) increase in the savings column on the left. That is to say, in proportion as any of the other laborers live upon less than A they are enabled to sell their labor for more than it actually cost them. And the difference, which in the case of the entrepreneur was profit, constitutes a net-surplus for the laborer either to be saved, expended upon luxuries, or for any purpose whatsoever. Thus the lowest laborers are enabled to obtain wages higher than the cost of their own labor, because the dearest laborers are compelled to demand a higher price for their labor-power in order to obtain the equivalent of its cost.

The relative positions of the laborer and capitalist being the inverse of each other, it will be seen that it is the most advanced laborer and the poorest capitalist who have no surplus. The reason for this is that in the progress of society the movement of the price of commodities is downwards, while that in the price of labor is upwards. That is to say, the dearest laborer occupies the top and progressive position, while the dearest capitalist occupies the bottom and receding position. The surplus of the less expensive laborers is the advantage they receive from the struggles of their most expensive brethren. We have thus a law of wages which is not limited to any special industry, country, or period, but whose application is as universal as the existence of wage conditions.[1]

If wages are governed by the cost or standard of living, it will of course follow that wages will always be the highest where the socially established standard of living among the laborers is the most complex and expensive ; and, conversely, they will be the

---

[1] See chapter on the Universality of the Law of Wages. " Wealth and Progress," p. 162.

lowest where the standard of living is the most simple and inexpensive,—and this is precisely what we find the world over.[1]
We no sooner recognize this than the reason why the wages of
the Asiatic are lower than those of the European becomes obvious. The same difference, and for the same reason, exists
between wages paid in similar industries in Continental countries
and in England, and between those in England and America.
The testimony of history is, that in all countries wages in the
same industries have always been higher in large cities than in
small ones, and so has the cost of living, which generally implies
greater social advancement and general intelligence.

This view is further emphasized by the fact that the industrial
centres of the world have, from the dawn of human history, been
the birthplaces of freedom and the nurseries of civilization.[2]
Upon this principle we have no difficulty in understanding why
the wages of agricultural laborers are always lower than those of
mechanics, and why, as is universally the case, agricultural wages
are higher in the vicinity of large cities and towns than in out-
lying districts.[3]   It is because the wants of the agricultural class
are fewer, their social life simpler, and their standard of living
lower.   As a necessary part of this same fact, we find that agricultural laborers are always in the rear ranks of social advancement, and are the last to acquire industrial and political rights.

The difference between the wages of women and those of men
in the same industry is due to the same cause ; it is an entire
mistake to assume, as some do, that the lower wages received by
women are due to their inferior ability.   If wages were determined
by the skill and competency of the laborer, then the carpenter,
mason, painter, or compositor in the country town with equal
skill would get the same wages as those in the large cities.   And
laborers of equal skill in different industries in Pekin, Tokio, St.
Petersburg, and Constantinople would obtain the same wages as
those in New York City, whereas we know that the common
laborer of New York obtains higher wages than the most skilled
mechanics in most of the former places.

Nor are the lower wages of women caused by difference in sex,

[1] " Wealth and Progress," Part II., chapters iii. and vii.
[2] Part I., chapter v.   Also, " Wealth and Progress," pp. 116-119.
[3] "Wealth and Progress," pp. 163-166.

since in that case the wages of men everywhere would be higher than those of women anywhere, which is by no means the case. The wages of women in America are as high as those of men in the same industry in any other country, and, with the exception of England, and perhaps Paris, are actually higher. Obviously, then, the wages of women, like those of men, do not conform to the fact of personal skill nor to that of sex, but they do everywhere conform to cost of living. As elsewhere shown,[1] the average woman's cost of living is very much smaller than that of the average man, and her wages are correspondingly lower. The wages of women are lower than those of men for the same reason that the wages of agricultural laborers are lower than those of mechanics in the large cities, and wages for the same kinds of labor in Moscow or Constantinople are lower than in Paris, London, or New York. In short, the wages of women are governed by the same law as those of men, namely, the cost of living, and the only reason the wages of women are lower than those of men is because women cost less.

Another fact, of which no theory of wages hitherto presented affords any satisfactory explanation, is the savings-bank deposits of wage-earners. Since these deposits—to the extent that they are saved from wages—represent a net-surplus above the necessary cost of living, they are usually taken as conclusive evidence of high wages. They are frequently treated as a kind of wage thermometer, the rate of wages or social condition of the laborers being regarded high or low as savings-bank deposits are large or small. The correctness of this conclusion is commonly accepted as self-evident, and it is frequently cited as a conclusive proof of the wisdom of an existing or proposed industrial or political policy.

The last presidential election in this country (1888) may be cited as an example of this. In order to show the striking contrast between the wages and social conditions of the laborers in this country and England, one of our most popular statesmen cited the fact that the savings-bank deposits in Massachusetts, with 2,000,000 population, are nearly two thirds as much as those of

---

[1] For the further discussion of this point and the facts relating to the wages and the cost of living of women, the reader is referred to " Wealth and Progress," pp. 172-178.

Great Britain with a population of 38,000,000, or over eleven times as much per capita of the population.   This statement was accepted as showing the difference in the wages and material prosperity of the laborers in the two countries.   A more misleading statement it would be difficult to imagine, as a little examination of the subject will conclusively show.

Although the economic and social conditions of the American laborer are decidedly superior to those of his English brother, this fact cannot be established by savings-bank statistics.   Nor is the difference between the wages in the two countries anywhere near so great as the difference in the amount of savings-bank deposits would indicate.   If we compare the savings-bank deposits of the different States in this country the utter worthlessness of such data, for showing the difference in the rate of wages, will at once be apparent.

According to the official savings-bank statistics in 1887, the deposits per capita of the population were : in Rhode Island, $169.41 ; in Massachusetts, $147.30 ; in Connecticut, $147.18 ; in New Hampshire, $125.52 ; in New York, $89.05 ; while in Pennsylvania they were only $10.81 per capita.   In Ohio they were $4.32, in Minnesota $2.17, and in Wisconsin only .02 cents, and in a large number of the Western States there are no savings-banks at all.   Now, if there is any virtue in savings-bank statistics as indicating the rate of wages and the industrial condition of the community, the laborers in New York State are only a little over half as well off as those in Rhode Island, and less than two thirds as well off as those in Massachusetts, Connecticut, or New Hampshire, while in Pennsylvania the condition of the laborer would only be about one sixteenth as good as it is in Rhode Island.

According to this notion the laborers of Italy are as well off as those in Pennsylvania, and vastly better than those of Ohio, Illinois, Minnesota, Wisconsin, or any of the Middle and Western States, except California.   A theory by which $4.32 per capita in Ohio, $2.17 in Minnesota, .02 cents in Wisconsin, and other Western States, as compared with $169.41 per capita in Rhode Island, are taken to represent the wages and social condition of the laboring classes in those States, bears upon its face the evidence of its own absurdity.   Why the laborers of Rhode Island,

Massachusetts, Connecticut, and New Hampshire should be able to save a third more per capita than those in New York,[1] fourteen times as much as those of Pennsylvania, thirty-four times as much as those of Ohio, sixty-eight times as much as those in Minnesota, and several hundred times as much as those in Wisconsin and other States, is a complete enigma from the standpoint of any of the popular theories of wages, yet they are phenomena which a scientific law of wages is bound to explain.

In the light of the theory here presented, however, these facts assume an entirely normal rôle and become perfectly explainable. In the first place, the laborers' savings-bank deposits, like the accumulations of any other class, are entirely of the nature of a surplus,[2] and therefore, like rents and profits, are governed by the law of surplusage. It will be observed that the surplus, which alone makes savings-bank deposits possible, is simply the difference between the cost of living of the most expensive families of any given class or industry and those who, for whatever reason, live upon less. Thus wages may be very high, and still the possible surplus be very small, and *vice versa.*

For example, if wages in a given class or industry were $3.00 a day, and the established standard of living in that class was substantially uniform, the possibility of saving would be very slight, because the cost of living of each family would be practically equal to, and hence consume, the entire wages. Under those conditions savings would be impossible, except to unmarried persons or those whose families were smaller than the largest, which at best would afford but a small amount of surplus for the class in general. Moreover, the possibility of savings from that cause would exist in any class, whatever the rate of wages. On the other hand, suppose that in a given industry the general rate of wages fixed by the dearest laborers is $1.50 a day, but instead of the standard of living being uniform throughout the class, it greatly varies through the difference in the social habits, as is actually the case in this country where American, English, Irish, French-Canadian, and Continental laborers are all employed in

---

[1] Savings-bank deposits in Italy amount to $9.00 per capita of the population. *Cf. Political Science Quarterly*, vol. iv., pp. 483, 493.

[2] See diagram No. 2., p. 206.

the same industry. Many of these foreign laborers, through their simpler habits of life, will be able to live on one half or two thirds as much as the American or English laborer, and hence will be able to save the difference. With this variation in the cost of living to different persons at the same rate of wages, a much larger proportion of savings per capita will be possible than in the former case, where wages were one hundred per cent. higher.

That is precisely what exists in this country, and particularly in the New England States and manufacturing centres. From this point of view there is no difficulty in understanding why savings-bank deposits per capita are much smaller in the Western than in the Eastern States. In the Western States agriculture is the chief occupation. It is well known that agricultural life is more nearly uniform than that of any other occupation. Being isolating in its influence, it affords the minimum incentive for new wants and a variety of social demands. Consequently, whatever rate of wages prevails, savings will necessarily be very slight in agricultural communities, while they might be relatively large in manufacturing centres, even with the same rate of wages. Indeed the savings-bank deposits in Italy are derived from wages much smaller than those in our Western States, where no savings-banks exist.

The same is true of the different States in this country. Wisconsin, where the savings are but two cents per capita, is more exclusively agricultural than Minnesota, where they are $2 ; and Ohio is more agricultural than Pennsylvania,[1] and Pennsylvania than New York. In New England however the reverse is true. In Rhode Island, Massachusetts, and Connecticut there is the minimum amount of agriculture and the maximum amount of manufacture. Consequently they have a greater concentration of population and variety of social life among their wage classes. In addition to this, they have the greatest number of different nationalities engaged in the same occupation, thus greatly increasing the differences in the standard of living while the same wage level prevails.

If we turn to England we find a very different state of affairs.

---

[1] For social purposes, mining and raw-material-producing industries may be regarded as agriculture, because they are similarly isolating and non-socializing occupations.

There the population is highly homogeneous ; hence, in each class there is a greater uniformity of social habits and cost of living, and therefore less surplus from the same aggregate income —that is to say, there are none of those arbitrary differences in the style of living in the same class occasioned by an influx of foreigners as in this country. The differences in the standard of living there, in the main, are only such as arise from the difference in the size of families and the passing from one social grade to another. From the causes already explained,[1] whenever laborers migrate from one industry or social grade to another, while they frequently represent the top or most expensive portion of the class they leave, they usually represent the bottom, or least expensive, of that into which they enter. Just as fast as they are transferred from a position where they are the dearest to one where they are the cheapest, they are changed from a wage-fixing to a surplus-receiving position. The savings-bank deposits will naturally therefore, be much smaller per capita in a homogeneous country like England than in a heterogeneous country like America, even though the wages were the same in both countries. Savings are not due to the amount of the wages, but to differences in the cost of living in the class where the same rate of wages prevails.

This explains why such a large proportion of the laborers in this country who have bank accounts which is so commonly regarded as conclusive evidence of superior character, are foreigners. If the possession of a bank account, or the ownership of what is so patronizingly styled "a little home "—often a mere shanty,— is evidence of superior character, why did they not have them in their own country, where that "superior character" was developed ? It may be replied that it is because wages there were too low to leave a margin above what would give them a bare living. Precisely so ; but why was there no margin in their own country ? Why is there no margin for the best class of Chinamen in China, of Germans in Germany, Englishmen in England, and Americans in America, while there is a margin in almost any country in Continental Europe for the Asiatic, in England for the Continental laborer, and in the United States for the laborers of every other country in the world ? The answer is obvious. There

---

[1] Section ii., preceding chapter.

is no margin from which the best class of laborers can save in their own country, simply because there the general rate of wages is determined by their own standard of living. They can get wages which will leave them a margin over the cost of living, only by going where the price of labor is determined by a social character and standard of living higher than their own, or, if in their own country, by adopting a standard of living lower than the highest of the class to which they socially belong.

The fact that the lower thus always obtain the advantage acquired by the higher is the economic incentive for all industrial mobility. It is only because the laborer can obtain the higher wages previously established in the new country or industry, that he will ever undertake to face the disadvantages of emigrating to a foreign land or endure the inconvenience of entering into a new occupation. This law also explains why, throughout the history of industrial progress, the most intelligent and socially advanced laborers always constitute the discontented element in their class, and are usually the leaders in labor organizations, strikes, and other forms of industrial agitation. It is because being the most expensive of their class they have no margins and therefore experience the greatest pressure from the non-satisfaction of new wants and desires.

The effect of the earnings of women and children upon the wages of men is another fact which the prevailing theories of wages have entirely failed to explain. Extensive investigations have shown that in those industries where women and children contribute to the families' maintenance, the wages of the men tend to fall directly as the amount contributed by the women and children increases.[1] If it is simply a question of supply and demand, as is generally assumed, the competition of women and children for employment would tend to reduce the wages of all laborers ; because as laborers increase in one industry they would migrate to others, and thus the effect would be the general reduction of the rate of wages. Such, however, is not the case. The effect is mainly upon the wages of the man in the class where the women who work are a part of the same household. Thus we find that in the same social grade and locality, in the trades where the man supports the whole family, his wages are fully as

---

[1] For the facts upon this point see '' Wealth and Progress,'' pp. 167 and 172.

high as those of the whole family where the wife and one or two children contribute to the family's support.

A table will elsewhere be found [1] constructed from the individual statements of wages and cost of living of three hundred and ninety-seven families employed in ten different industries in Massachusetts. These facts show that the total yearly income of the family in the highest class was $821.40, and cost of living $772.21, and in the lowest the total income was $682.05 and cost of living was $650.81. In the highest class where the women and children who work were only as one fourth of one to a family, the wages of the man were $752.36. In the lowest class where the women and children who work were as one and one third to a family, the man's wages were only $424.12. In other words, in those industries where the women and children contribute only $69 a year, the wages of the man were only $19 less than the total cost of the family's living, whereas in the industries where the earnings of the women and children were $257 a year, the wages of the man were $226 less than the total cost of the family's living. It will thus be seen that while the difference between the total income of the family in the highest and lowest class was almost exactly the same as that in the total cost of the family's living, the difference in the highest and lowest yearly wages of the man was greater than that in the cost of living by almost exactly the amount of the difference in the earnings of the women and children. That is to say, while the total income of the family varied with the total cost of the family's living, the ratio of the man's wages to the cost of the family's living diminished directly as the total earnings of the women and children increased. [2] Thus whether the income of the family is all derived from one source or from several sources, its total amount tends to equal the total cost of the family's living.

Therefore, from whatever standpoint we study the movement of wage phenomena, we find that the general rate of wages in any country, class or industry, constantly tends to equal the

[1] "Wealth and Progress," 171.

[2] "Thus, it is seen that in neither of the cases where the head of the family is assisted by his wife or children, does he earn as much as other laborers. Also, that in the case where he is assisted by both wife and children, he earns the least."—Report of the Bureau of the Statistics of Labor, Massachusetts, 1876, p. 71.

cost of living of the most expensive families furnishing the necessary supply of labor.

The cost of living may be affected in two ways, either by a change in the price of the commodities which the laborer consumes or by a change in the quantities of those commodities which enter into his habitual consumption. An increase in the price of commodities would be a rise in the money cost of living, but not a rise in the standard of living ; hence, while it would increase the money wages, it would not increase the amount of wealth the laborer receives for a day's labor. It would therefore be a rise in nominal wages, but not a rise of real wages.[1] An increase in the cost of living, arising from an increase in the commodities habitually consumed by the laborer, would constitute a rise in the standard of living. It would increase the actual amount of wealth daily received by the laborer, and hence would be a rise of real wages. Thus a rise in the cost of living and nominal wages is of no social advantage to the laborer except when accompanied by a rise in the standard of living and of real wages.[2]

It is therefore a rise in the actual social standard and not in the nominal money cost of living, which is of importance in considering the question of wages. Indeed it is in the minimizing of the money cost and the maximizing of the social standard of living that industrial and social progress really consists. In other words, the condition of the laborer improves only as the price of commodities falls and the price of labor rises. The standard of living in any class or country depends upon the social character of the people. Social character is chiefly determined by the number and variety of established social wants, and the consequent simplicity or complexity of social relations.[3] It may therefore be said that wages finally depend upon the social character of the laboring classes, the restriction or development of which is mainly determined by the extent and permanence of their social opportunities. When we learn to regard

---

[1] " Wealth and Progress," pp. 96–98.

[2] This law is just as true in " piece-work " as it is in " day-work." See chapter on " Piece-Work," " Wealth and Progress," p. 179.

[3] For an extended discussion of the relation of social wants and character to the standard of living, see " Wealth and Progress," Part II., chap. ix., pp. 187–203.

wages simply as the price of labor which is governed by the laborer's standard of living, we shall see that the laborer is not poor because the capitalist is rich, but that wages are low because the laborer is socially cheap. The true remedy for low wages therefore is not to be sought in profit-sharing, nationalization of land and productive instruments, or in any other schemes for *restricting the economic opportunities of the capitalist*, but solely in conditions for *extending the social opportunities of the laborer*.

CHAPTER IV.

RENT, ITS LAW AND CAUSE.

SECTION I.—*The Definition of Rent.*

THE definition of rent generally accepted by economists is that given by Ricardo,[1] namely, "that rent is that portion of the produce.of the earth which is paid to the landlord for the use of the original and indestructible powers of the soil."[2]

It is manifest that if rent is limited to what is paid for "the powers of the soil," or the *fertility* of the land, then what is paid for land used for building, manufacturing, and commercial purposes is not rent at all, since the price paid for such land is entirely independent of the quality of its soil. Moreover, the rent paid for some of the most sterile land for building purposes is greater than that paid for the most fertile land in the world. A definition of rent that does not apply to land which pays the highest rent of all, and which is increasing as civilization advances, must surely be regarded as defective. Nor is this definition materially improved by Mr. Walker's qualification that the expression "original and indestructible powers of the soil " includes "not only arable land, but pasture and timber land, mineral deposits, water privileges, and building sites."[3] While in this case it includes all that is paid for the "original and indestructible powers " of any kind of land, it fails as a definition of rent, because as we shall see rent is never paid for "the original and indestructible powers " of any land.

It is true that some agricultural land has a high degree of original fertility, but there is no land whose fertility is inde-

[1] " Political Economy and Taxation," pp. 34–36.

[2] Walker's " Political Economy," p. 193. Also, McCulloch's " Political Economy," p. 142.

[3] " Political Economy," p. 193.

structible. Every intelligent farmer knows that continuous cultivation without fertilization will impoverish or destroy the fertility of the most productive land ever known. The fertility of land is not only always destructible, as in the case of mines, but it is frequently not original; indeed much of the most productive agricultural land in the world to-day owes its fertility not to its "original powers," but almost entirely to improvements created by the application of labor and capital. And the greater part of the land whose fertility is thus created commands a higher rent than much of that which possesses the greatest amount of "original fertility." [1]

In the case of land for building purposes alone, the so-called "powers of the soil," or qualities of the land for which rent is paid, are neither original nor indestructible. Indeed it does not depend upon any quality whatever peculiar to land. On the contrary, rent is entirely due to the presence of a highly civilized industrial community. If New York City were removed a hundred miles from Manhattan Island, the rent of the greater part of the land, some of which is the highest paid for any land in the world, would entirely disappear. Clearly therefore, if rent is limited to that "which is paid to the landlord for the use of the original and indestructible powers of the soil," almost none of the income from land is rent, since a very small portion of such income is paid for its "original" and none at all for its "indestructible powers."

The chief difficulty with this definition is that it fails to distinguish between price and surplus. Rent is not the price of land; it is only the economic surplus arising from its use. In order to avoid confusion I define rent as *the net surplus resulting from the productive use of land under all economic conditions for any purpose whatsoever.* To explain how this surplus arises is to furnish the law of rent.

SECTION II.—*The Law of Rent.*

Rent being an economic surplus, in seeking the law of rent we are simply seeking the law of surplus in relation to the produc-

---

[1] Witness the high rents paid for the land used for market-gardening and the highly cultivated farms in such countries as Belgium and England, whose fertility is largely artificial, and the low rent paid for the most fertile land in our Western States, whose productiveness is largely original.

tive use of land. And as surplus is included in and received with the price, it being the difference between price and cost, it follows that the law of surplus is a necessary corollary of the law of price. In order, therefore, to ascertain the law of rent, we have only to apply to land the general law of prices presented in a previous chapter [1]—namely, that in a given market prices tend towards uniformity on the basis of the cost of producing the most expensive portion. It is objected by some that since land is the " free bounty of nature " it can have no cost of production. This is a mistake. It should be remembered that economic production does not mean physical creation but only economic and social adaptation. This may involve a great deal of physical modification both in form and location, or it may involve little or none of either.

The production of broadcloth or a gold watch involves a great deal of physical change in the wool and in the gold, steel, and other metals of which the cloth and watch are made, whereas the production of nuts and bananas involves very little. The more nearly complete is an object furnished by nature the less will be the cost involved in appropriating it to human uses, and *vice versa*. The cost of producing a power-loom includes all the expenditure necessary to complete it as an instrument for weaving. This of course does not mean the creation of the iron or wood of which the loom is made, but only their adaptation to productive purposes. It is in this sense that we speak of the cost of producing land, the term *production* having not a physical but only an economic signification. For economic purposes therefore, the cost of producing land, like that of any other productive instrument, includes all the expenditure necessary to utilize it as a means of production.

The law of price in relation to land, therefore, may be stated thus : That under conditions of economic freedom, the price of land in any given community tends to equal the cost of its production—*i.e.*, the cost of actualizing its economic and social utility. Hence when the cost per unit of using all the land is the same, the price and the cost of production (economic use) will be identical, and no surplus or rent will remain. And whenever the cost per unit of using different portions of land varies, the price per

unit will tend to a uniformity on the basis of the cost of actualizing the utility of the most expensive portion of the land· used
for that purpose in that community. Thus while the price per
unit of the whole land in that community tends to a uniformity,
that of the portion whose utility costs the most to actualize it
will consist entirely of cost, and that of the others will consist of
cost and rent (surplus), the rent increasing as the cost of utilization diminishes below that of the most expensive portion used.

Having found the law of prices in relation to land, we have as
a necessary corollary the law of surplus—*i.e.*, the law of rent. It
may be stated as follows : *That under conditions of economic
freedom, the rent of land used for any purpose tends to equal the
difference between its productive utility and that of the poorest
land used for the same purpose in that community, or which contributes to the necessary supply of the same market.*

It will be observed that the conclusion here reached is substantially the same as that of Ricardo, stripped of many misleading assumptions by which the Ricardian theory has ever been
accompanied.

In the first place, by treating rent as the net surplus resulting
from the productive use of land, we entirely avoid the error involved in the Ricardian definition of rent as the price paid for
" the original and indestructible powers of the soil." And by regarding land simply as a productive instrument, thereby putting
it in the same economic category with other forms of capital, we
remove all grounds for the perplexing controversy as to whether
the income from improvements in land is properly rent or profits.
Since rent and profits are both economic surpluses, whether or
not they are designated by the same term is a matter of entire
indifference. We also avoid the confusing consequences of that
erroneous assumption of Ricardo, that land is always utilized in
the order of its fertility, the best being taken first and the
poorest last, an assumption which Carey devoted tedious space
to exposing, and which Walker and other Ricardians are still
laboring to defend.

From the point of view here presented, it is absolutely of no
importance whether the land is cultivated in the order claimed
by Ricardo or that claimed by Carey, the law will operate the
same in either case. If the inferior land were used before the

superior, as is frequently the case, the only difference would be this :. instead of the land employed last being used at cost, and that employed first yielding rent, as Ricardo assumed, the order would be reversed and the land employed first would be used at cost, and that employed last would yield a rent. Neither the amount of land used nor the amount of rent paid would be affected by that change. The difference in the productive utility of the land will be rent just the same, whether the inferior or superior is brought first into use. It is not the historical order of their use, but the difference in the degree of their productive utility, that determines the amount of the rent. The difference in the fertility of two pieces of land yielding twenty and twenty-five bushels of wheat respectively will obviously be just as great whichever is brought into use first.

If the subject had been treated from the point of view here presented, these errors would have been avoided. It would then have been obvious that the order of use of superior and inferior land has no necessary relation whatever to the price-fixing or surplus-producing influence of either labor, land, or machinery. For in all cases and under all conditions where economic freedom prevails, the price is determined by the cost of using the least effective, and therefore the most expensive increment, and whether that be first or last makes absolutely no difference. By this treatment of the subject, we not only avoid the error and retain what is true in the popular theory, but we have a consistent classification of economic phenomena, by which the price of land commodities and labor is governed by the law of price, and on the other hand, the rent of land, the profit of capital, and the savings of labor are governed by the law of surplus.

Section. III.—*The Cause of Rent.*

No theory can be regarded as furnishing an adequate explanation of rent phenomena which does not explain the cause of rent. When we know how rent comes into existence, and by what social force it becomes economically possible, we shall be able to determine whether it arises from an economic necessity and is a social advantage, or whether it is due to economic despotism and is a social burden,—as is commonly believed. Upon this point the popular doctrine is perhaps least of all satisfactory. Francis

Walker, who has probably taken more pains than any other writer to make good the deficiencies in the Ricardian theory of rent, endeavors to show that the difference in the productiveness of land is not only the measure and regulator of rent, but that it is also the cause or source of rent. He has endeavored to illustrate exactly how, under the influence of self-interest, rent arises.[1] Like Ricardo, he begins by assuming the existence of a new country with four grades of land, which will yield, with the same expenditure of labor and capital, 24, 22, 20, and 18 bushels of wheat per acre respectively. He also, like Ricardo, assumes that the best land, or 24-bushel tract, will be cultivated first, and the others in the order of their fertility, and says : " Cultivation then descending to the 22-bushel tract, rent emerges. Under what impulse ? Why, by the simple operation of the principle of self-interest ; inasmuch as some of the would-be cultivators must go upon the 22-bushel tract, every person now in the occupation of a lot on the 24-bushel tract may just as well—may he not ?—pay something for the privilege of remaining where he is, as take up a lot of the new land for nothing ? If not, why not ? How much shall he pay ? Why, clearly, 2 bushels per acre, the difference between the yield of the two tracts under the same application of labor and capital."[2] This continues until the whole four tracts are brought under cultivation, rent rising 2 bushels per acre on each tract under cultivation, when the next is brought into use, and the rent on the different tracts is 2, 4, and 6 bushels per acre respectively. Then further "to illustrate the operation of this cause" he assumes the existence of a distant tract of land that will yield with the same labor and capital 30 bushels per acre. But through its greater distance from the market 12 bushels are consumed in transportation, reducing the amount delivered to the market to 18 bushels, or the same as the product of the poorest home tract. He then, by a series of improvements in the methods of transportation, reduces the cost of bringing the crop of the distant tract to market from 12 to 9 bushels per acre, and says : " The net produce of the distant tract (30—9) has now risen to 21 bushels. The 20-bushel tract must be abandoned. . . . The highest grade of land now yields a rent of but 3 bushels an acre (24—21), the second of but 1 bushel. The aggre-

---

[1] " Land and its Rent," pp. 10, 57.   [2] *Ibid.*, p. 18.

gate amount received by the owners of land in rents sinks from 9 to 4." [1]

It will be observed that at the commencement of Mr. Walker's community we found the best land producing 24 bushels per acre and paying no rent ; then the same land, without any increase in its productiveness, pays a rent first of 2 bushels, then of 4 bushels, and finally of 6 bushels an acre. And then after the discovery of the 30-bushel tract, without any diminution in its productiveness, the rent of the same tract falls from 6 to 3 bushels per acre. That of the 22-bushel tract falls to 1 bushel and that of the 20-bushel tract disappears altogether.

The question here is "under what impulse" does the rent of this land rise and fall without any change in its productiveness? What new force came into operation to make the tract of land, which formerly could be had for nothing, yield a rent of 6 bushels and subsequently fall to 3 bushels per acre? "Why," replies Mr. Walker, "by the simple operation of the principle of self-interest." By what course of reasoning can it be shown that the principle of self-interest in the land owner will always prevail against the self-interest of the tenant?

Again, if rent is caused by the fertility of the land or the self-interest of the land owner, or both, why did it not emerge when cultivation first began on the 24-bushel tract? This was impossible, Mr. Walker would reply, because it was not until "cultivation descended to the 22-bushel tract" that "rent emerges." If rent was impossible on the 24-bushel tract until the 22-bushel tract was cultivated, whatever power forced the 22-bushel tract into use, or made its cultivation possible, is manifestly the real cause of rent on the 24-bushel tract. This could not possibly be the fertility of the land or the principle of self-interest in the landowner, as these were just the same before as after rent was paid.

Nor does Mr. Walker's distant-tract illustration throw any real light upon this question. It is true that rent on the home tracts falls when the distant tract is cultivated, but from what cause? Mr. Walker replies, because "the net produce of the distant tract has now risen to 21 bushels." Nothing of the kind. So far as Mr. Walker, has shown, no change whatever has taken place in the

[1] " Land and its Rent," p. 25.

productiveness of the land. When we first saw the distant tract it produced 30 bushels per acre ; it does the same now. The only change that has occurred is a reduction of 3 bushels per acre in the cost of transporting the crop. Manifestly that is not due to any quality or condition of the land nor to the degree of self-interest in the landowner. These are entirely unchanged. It may with truth be said that cheapening transportation reduces the cost of producing the wheat; but it in no way changes the influences of this land upon the cost of the wheat. The cost of the wheat has been reduced by the use of capital, but it is by a class of capital quite distinct from land.

Mr. Walker has shown that rent began on the 24-bushel tract when " cultivation descended to the 22-bushel tract," and also that rent on all the home tracts fell when the cost of transporting the crop of the distant tract was reduced. But this does not explain the cause which brought all this about. To say that rent rises when inferior lands are cultivated and falls when transportation is cheapened, is only like saying the train moves when the engine starts. But what starts the engine remains to be ascertained before the cause of this movement is explained. In stopping at this point Mr. Walker repeats one of the chief mistakes of orthodox economists—namely, the failure to connect economic phenomena with the social influences from which they arise.[1]

What is the cause of rent is therefore still the question. Nor will the answer be very difficult to find if we pursue the inquiry along the lines already travelled and bear in mind the conclusions reached in the preceding section ; namely, that land like all other forms of capital is simply a productive instrument, and that rent is a net surplus resulting from its economic use. Since an economic surplus is the difference between the price of products and the cost of their production, rent can only be obtained from the price of the commodities in the production of which it is used as an instrument. Clearly therefore, it is to the influences which govern the price of the products that we must look for the cause of rent. Let us return to Mr. Walker's community and see if we can ascertain the cause that made the existence of rent possible, which he failed to explain.

---

[1] This limitation in regard to the use of improved machinery has already been pointed out. See pp. 143–149.

15

In the first place why did not the 24-bushel tract pay a rent when first cultivated ? It was not because of its inferiority, since it was the best land in the community ; nor was it from any lack of self-interest in the landowner, for there never was a time when he would not exact rent if he could. The reason no rent could be obtained for it was that, there being only one grade of land in use, the cost of production, so far as it affected land, was uniform. Hence according to the law of price already stated, the value of every part of the product was only equal to the cost of its production. Since the price of the wheat equalled the cost of production on the 24-bushel tract, in order to cultivate the 22-bushel tract without loss one of two things must necessarily occur—either the price of the product must rise, or the cost of production must be reduced.

We will consider first, how a rise in the price of the produce would affect the situation, since the expounders of the popular doctrine always assume that this takes place. It is insisted upon by these writers that rent does not increase the price of commodities to the consumer, because the rent is the effect of the price and not the price the effect of the rent.[1] But if it is true that rent can only be paid or, if already paid, can only be increased by a rise in the price of the produce, and that the rise in price is

[1] " It is because its (the produce) price is high or low, a great deal more, or very little more, or no more than what is sufficient to pay these wages and profits, that it affords a high rent, a low rent, or no rent at all." Adam Smith, " Wealth of Nations," book i., chapter i., p. 115. " Corn is not high because a rent is paid, but a rent is paid because corn is high." Ricardo, " Political Economy and Taxation," p. 39. See also *ibid.*, pp. 40, 61, 62. " The inhabitants must consent to pay such an additional price for raw produce as will enable the second quality of land to be cultivated. No advance *short of this* will procure them another bushel of corn. . . . If they choose to pay a price sufficient to cover the expense of cultivating the land of the second quality they will obtain additional supplies, if they do not, they must want them." McCulloch, " Principles Political Economy," p. 142. " Rent is the effect of high price. . . . It is not from the produce, but from the price at which the produce is sold, that rent is derived." Buchannan, note, p. 40, Ricardo's works. " It is not the diversity of soils nor the law of diminishing returns, that causes rents, since these continue as before when rent ceases to be paid, but it *is* the price of produce under demand and supply that causes rent." Perry, " Political Economy," p. 292. " The rent of land is determined by the value of its produce." Wade, " Political Economy," p. 101.

paid to the landowner in rent, it is little more than a quibble to say that the payment of rent does not increase the price of commodities. Whether rent is the cause or effect of rise in price, is of very little importance to the community if every rise in rent is accompanied by a rise in the price. If for example, it cost a dollar a bushel to raise wheat on the 24-bushel tract, it would, under the same conditions, cost a dollar and ten cents a bushel to produce it on the 22-bushel tract. If the wheat could all be sold at that price, it would of course yield a surplus of ten cents a bushel, or two bushels an acre on the 24 bushel tract. Were this the only effect it would be a simple matter, but there are other influences to be reckoned with. A rise in prices would be a practical fall in wages ; hence every extension of cultivation to poorer soils which increased the rent of the landowner would increase the poverty of the laborer. Were such the case, the con- dition of the masses would indeed be hopeless. Henry George's pessimistic declaration that "rent swallows up the whole gain and pauperism accompanies progress " would be literally true. Fortunately for civilization however, the testimony of history is all against such a notion. Rents have never increased so much as during the present century, and the general fall in prices was never so great as during the same period.

Nor is it possible that it should be otherwise, except in a state of political despotism or industrial piracy. Under conditions of economic freedom, it is as impossible for rent to rise through increasing prices and reducing real wages, as it is for civilization to advance by increasing poverty. Economic law presents an ab- solute barrier to any such parasitic movement by which a surplus- receiving class can be permanently enriched by the impoverish- ment of the community. For the same reason that the landowner cannot obtain rent except when the land yields a margin above the cost of production, the cultivator cannot sell his produce at a price higher than the consumers can afford to pay. Clearly therefore, the product cannot be sold at a higher price unless the purchasing power of the masses is commensurately increased. A general increase of prices without a rise of wages would not only defeat itself by destroying the market for the products, but it would necessarily lower the standard of living and actually put back civilization. If a rise of prices is accompanied by a commensurate rise of wages, as it admittedly must be,[1] it would increase the cost of cultivating the land as much as it increased the price of the crop, making the cultivation of the 22-bushel tract as impracticable as ever.

Nor would a mere increase of population change the result. If population should increase and the consumption or effectual demand per capita of the community (real wages) remain stationary, prices could not advance except with the same consequences as before. The mere fact presented by Mr. Walker, that the 24-bushel tract is "inadequate to the needs of subsistence," is not sufficient to insure the cultivation of the inferior tract. The community may lack subsistence, people may die of starvation, as they often have ; but nobody will cultivate the 22-bushel tract unless its products can be sold at a price at least equal to the cost.

It may be said that if the population increases, the aggregate income and purchasing power of the community would be increased, though wages were stationary. This is true, but since in that case the number among whom the purchasing power is divided would be increased in the same ratio, no one would be richer than before, and consequently, the purchasing power of the individual members of the community would not be increased. A mere increase of the population, other things remaining the same, would enable a larger amount to be consumed at the same price, but it would not increase the capacity of anybody to pay a higher price.

If an article of food, clothing, or the like, cannot be produced for less than 25 cents, and at the prevailing rate of wages the laborer can only pay 20 cents, it is clearly out of his power to

---

[1] " As the wages of labor are everywhere regulated partly by the demand for it, and partly by the average price of the necessary articles of subsistence, whatever raises this average price must necessarily raise those wages." Adam Smith, "Wealth of Nations," book v., chapter ii., p. 691. *Ibid.*, p. 693. " With a rise in the price of food and necessaries the natural price of labor will rise." Ricardo, " Political Economy and Taxation," p. 50. " There can be no permanent fall of wages, but in consequence of a fall (in the price) of the necessaries on which wages are expended." *Ibid.*, p. 75. " If they (the laborers) had to pay 8s. per quarter in addition for wheat . . . wages would inevitably and necessarily rise." *Ibid.*, p. 93. *Cf.* Mill's " Political Economy," vol. ii., pp. 423, 424, 425.

consume it. Nor would any conceivable addition to the number of 20-cent purchasers add one whit to their capacity for purchasing 25-cent articles. The consumption and production of 25-cent articles can never be promoted by increasing the number of 20-cent consumers. Nothing can make the production of 25-cent articles possible but the creation of 25-cent purchasers. Manifestly, therefore, other things remaining the same, it is impossible in any general sense to extend cultivation to inferior land by merely increasing the price of commodities.

Since the use of the 22-bushel tract cannot be made feasible by advancing prices, the only means by which it can be made feasible is by reducing the cost of production. There are only two ways by which the cost of production can be lessened, either by a reduction of wages or the use of improved methods.[1] The former is impossible for the same reason that prices could not be advanced. The latter, therefore, is the only alternative consistent with a progressive state of society. What form improved methods will take depends upon the state of civilization. In a very early stage of society it might consist of substituting a spade for a crooked stick, or at a later period a plough for a spade, or mowing and threshing machines for the scythe and flail. At whatever period it occurs or whatever form it takes, since it cannot *cheapen*, it must *save* labor. This does not mean that it must merely discharge labor for, as already explained, labor is only economically saved when it is re-employed. Thus in the case of land, as in every other phase of economic movement, the successful use of improved methods of production must necessarily be accompanied by new employment-creating conditions. Nothing can create new employments except new demands, or an increase in the consumption of wealth per capita of the population, which of course means an increase in real wages. When by this means inferior land can be cultivated

---

[1] Improved methods include every thing that makes the same land yield more or yield the same amount at a less cost. This may result from superior skill, better division of labor, more capital in the form of fertilization, better drainage, the substitution of animals for men, or steam for animals, improved implements for either, or any other labor-saving or cost-reducing appliances.

without loss, the superior land can be cultivated at a profit ; that is to say, when the price of 22 bushels of wheat will defray the cost of cultivating an acre of the 22-bushel tract, the 24-bushel tract will yield a surplus or rent equal to ten cents a bushel or two bushels per acre, without either increasing the price of the product or reducing wages.   In the last analysis therefore, the determining cause of the use of inferior land and the payment of rent on the superior land is the increased consumption of wealth by the masses.

If we examine the cultivation of Mr. Walker's 30-bushel tract we shall find that its use finally depends upon the same cause. He explains how what he calls its " net productiveness " rose from 18 to 22 bushels per acre, by improved methods of transportation.   The moment we ask what made improved methods of transportation possible, the answer is simple and obvious.   The railroads and steamships which enabled the lands of Dakota to contribute to the wheat supply of Liverpool and London were clearly due to the increased consumption of wealth per capita of the population, which made the construction and use of railroads economically feasible.   Nor could this result from a mere increased consumption of wheat, but it required a vast increase in the demand for numerous manufactured articles whose production and consumption involved a large amount of travel and transportation.   An increased demand for commodities and a higher social standard of living, which makes steamships and railroads possible, are simply the economic embodiments of higher wages.   Thus whether land is cultivated in the order of the best first, and the poorest last, as represented by Mr. Walker's four tracts, or the reverse, as claimed by Carey, the result is the same, namely, that rent or a surplus from the use of land, like that of all other productive instruments, finally depends upon the increasing consumption of wealth per capita of the community. In other words, the cause from which economic rent arises is the advancing standard of living and the rise of real wages among the masses.

SECTION IV.—*Is Rent a Social Tax ?*

Were it not commonly believed that rent is an unjust burden upon the community, the abolition of which warrants the subversion of existing institutions, the consideration of this question might properly seem superfluous. The claim that rent is a tax by which the land-owning class are enabled to live at the expense of the industrious community, legitimately arises from the Ricardian postulate that " rent is that portion of the produce of the earth which is paid to the landowner for the use of the original and indestructible powers of the soil." No more fallacious notion was ever taught than that rent, or any other economic surplus, is a price paid for the free contribution of nature. There is no economic law by which a charge can ever be exacted for the use of gratuitous natural forces.[1] This view is further supported by the no less popular doctrine that, in the economic order of distribution, rent is paid before wages, and that consequently the laborer can only receive as his share of the product what is left after rent and profits are taken out.[2]

The utter untenableness of both these positions having been already pointed out, the answer to the question "is rent a social tax ?" need not detain us long.

Like all other forms of surplus, rent arises from the sure operation of the law of economic prices ; being simply the difference between the maximum and the minimum cost of production per unit of product.

If this difference in the cost is due to the difference in the methods, such as a better division of labor, higher skill, more capital, better machinery, etc., the surplus created will go to the entrepreneur and in common phrase will be called profits. And if the difference in the cost of production is due to the different degrees of productive utility of the land, the surplus created will go to the landowner as rent. If the poorest instruments and the poorest lands are used together no surplus can arise for either the landowner or entrepreneur. But if superior instruments are used with inferior land, the entrepreneur may have a surplus without the landowner having rent, and conversely, if the superior land is operated with inferior instruments, the landowner may obtain a rent, while the entrepreneur can have no profit. Thus there can

---

[1] Part II., chap. iv., pp. 21, 22.

[2] Jevons' " Theory of Political Economy," p. 292. Walker's " Political Economy," pp. 248, 249. Sidgwick's " Principles of Political Economy," p. 322. Henry George's " Progress and Poverty," pp. 162, 163.

neither be rents nor profits unless the joint use of the land and implements produce at less than maximum cost, and the surplus if any, will be divided between the owners of these two classes of productive instruments or all accrue to either one, just in proportion as it is due to the superiority of the land or of the instruments.

There is this difference, however, between land and other productive instruments : the different qualities of machinery always come into use in the order of the poorest first and the best last, whereas in the case of land, sometimes the best comes into use first. The reason for this is that, machinery being a human invention, each new device is the result of an effort to improve upon the last ; its superiority over existing methods being the only reason for using it, and the only motive for making it. On the other hand, land being a natural product whose quantity and locality are unchangeable, the use of the poorer or less productive land can only be made feasible by the employment of superior appliances. Thus, while it is always the best land and the best machinery which yields a surplus, in the case of land when the best is used first (as in the Ricardo-Walker assumption) it does not yield a surplus until the second grade comes into use, whereas in the case of machinery the surplus always commences on the best which is last when its own use becomes possible. But whether the use of land-descends from the superior to the inferior through the use of capital in better drainage, improved tools, machinery, etc., or whether it ascends from the inferior to the superior through improved methods of transportation (as in the case of Walker's distant tract), makes no difference either in the amount of rent paid or the effect of rent upon wages and the welfare of the community.

In whatever order improvements are applied to the use of land and a surplus is created, the rent will always depend upon the difference between the cost per unit of the product due to using the best land and that of using the poorest land employed for that purpose within the same competing group or community. Since rent can only be obtained from a surplus that remains after all costs of production are paid, and since wages are governed by social causes independent of the quality of land or machinery, and prices are determined by the cost of producing the most expensive portion of the supply which always includes wages, it follows that rent can only be obtained when a surplus remains after wages and prices have been determined. The economic relation of rent to wages and prices is illustrated in the following diagram, which represents Mr. Walker's four tracts producing 24, 22, 20, and 18 bushels per acre respectively, the assumption being that with wages at $1.50 per day the cost of production on the 18-bushel tract is a dollar a bushel.

No. 3.

RENT PER ACRE.	SURPLUS PER BUSHEL.	PRICE PER BUSHEL.	WAGES PER DAY.	COST PER BUSHEL.	BUSHELS PER ACRE.	
$6.00	25 c.	$1.00	$1.50	Minimum cost, 75 c.	24	D
$4.00	18 c.	$1.00	$1.50	. . . . . . 82 c.	22	C
$2.00	10 c.	$1.00	$1.50	. . . . 90 c.	20	B
$0.00	00 c.	$1.00	$1.50	Maximum cost . . $1.00	18	A

From the above, four things will be seen : (1) That A, who uses the poorest land and pays no rent, sells at cost and has no surplus. (2) That, the price of wheat being the same with all, B, C, and D, whose land yields 2, 4, and 6 bushels per acre respectively more than that of A, have a surplus of $2, $4, and $6 per acre. (3) That the surplus in the rent column on the left only begins and increases as the cost line per bushel on the right recedes from (falls below) that of A. (4) That the increase of the amount in the rent column in no way affects the price or wages column ; D, whose rent is the highest, sells at the same price and pays the same wages[1] as A, who pays no rent at all.[2] Since the consumer's price and the laborer's wages are both determined at the point where no rent is paid, it is manifest that

[1] As a matter of fact the large concerns in both manufacture and farming represented by D, where the largest capital and best methods are used, are constantly tending to pay higher wages and sell at lower prices than small farmers or manufacturers represented by A.

[2] If we assumed the four tracts of land to be of uniform quality and suppose the difference in the product to arise from superior skill, larger capital, better implements, etc., the result would be exactly the same, only the surplus column instead of representing rent would represent profits as shown in diagram No. 1, p. 204.

the surplus paid to the landlord is in no sense a burden upon either the consumer or the laborer ; that is to say, prices are not higher nor wages lower because rent is paid. Indeed, if rent were obtained at the expense of the consumer or the laborer, we should find that prices rise and wages fall as rents increase, whereas the reverse is universally true.

The highest rents are paid in the most civilized countries, and in such countries rent is higher in the city than in the small town or rural district. And it is precisely in these countries and cities where rents are the largest, that wages are the highest, and general prices are the lowest.[1] Consequently we find the migratory movement of the laborers (which is always towards higher wages and better living) is constantly from low-rent countries to high-rent countries, from the rural districts where the rent is low to the cities where rent is high. This also explains why commodities can often be obtained more cheaply in large cities than in small towns, as shown by the fact that thousands of people travel from fifty to a hundred miles to a city to make their purchases. This does not mean that things are cheaper or wages higher because a rent is paid, but that things are cheaper and rents are larger because wages are higher there than elsewhere.

Nor is there any means, except charity or theft, by which the amount in the rent column can possibly be made to find its way to the laborer or consumer. The only economic way it can be given to the consumer is to compel B, C, and D to reduce the price of their product the full amount of their surplus—10, 18, and 25 cents per bushel respectively. Should D sell his wheat at 75 cents a bushel, nobody would continue to buy from C, B, and A, unless they sold theirs at the same price, which they could not do, since it cost them more than that amount. If the product of C is needed, 82 cents a bushel is the lowest price at which it can be supplied ; and if that of B is required, the price cannot fall below 90 cents a bushel ; and so long as that of A is needed, the price must be a dollar a bushel, because less than that will not repay the cost of producing it. No matter how the price is fixed or who fixes it, it cannot possibly be less than equal to the cost of producing the most expensive portion.

---

[1] That is to say, the price of a day's labor will purchase the largest amount of wealth.

If the surplus is to be given to the laborer in any other way than by reducing the price, it must go in the form of increased wages. In order to do this wages must rise directly as the surplus increases. The same difficulty arises here as in the case of prices ; indeed, wages are simply the price of labor. If D pays higher wages, then the laborers of C, B, and A will refuse to work unless they can have the same. If A is compelled to raise wages equal to 25 cents a bushel, the cost and hence the minimum price of his product will necessarily rise to $1.25 a bushel, which will then be the price of the whole product. Thus, all that D, C, and B are by this means forced to give to the laborer in higher wages, A is forced to demand back again from the consumer in higher prices, and the difference or surplus will be exactly as before, the only change being that both wages and prices have risen 25 cents. In short, there are no economic means by which A can obtain an equivalent of the cost of his product which will not give B, C, and D a surplus ; and conversely, there are no means by which D can sell at cost which will not bankrupt C, B, and A.

There are two conditions which, under economic freedom, all competing producers must fulfil or leave the business : other things being the same, they must pay the same wages and sell their products at the same price as their competitors in the same market. For the same reason that D's price cannot be reduced without lowering that of C, B, and A, the wages paid by A cannot be reduced without lowering those paid by all the others, since whatever will enable A to either raise the price or reduce wages will enable B, C, and D to do the same. Manifestly therefore, if the landowner were prohibited from taking the surplus of B, C, and D in the form of rent, it would simply remain in the hands of the farmer or entrepreneur as profits. Since the surplus is not increased by virtue of its being divided between the landowner and entrepreneur, it could not be diminished by giving it all to either one of them. In other words, as the surplus arising from the difference in the cost of producing with the poorest and the best land would be the same whether rent is paid or not, the abolition of rent would simply be an increase of profits. Rent, in short, is entirely a question between the landowner and the entrepreneur and does not enter into the problem either of prices

or of wages.   It being impossible for the surplus of B, C, and D
to go to the consumer either in higher wages or lower prices,
whether it shall all remain in the hands of the entrepreneur or be
shared between him and the landowner is of no economic or
social importance to the laborer or to the community.

The social welfare of the people can advance only as prices
fall and wages rise, results which cannot be promoted by any
manipulation of rent.   It is by lessening the cost of production
and not by appropriating the surplus that prices must be reduced.
The cost of production can be lessened only by using improved
methods.   The successful use of improved methods depends
upon increasing consumption and higher wages.   Therefore the
improvement of the social condition of the masses and the general
advancement of society must be sought in the influences which
promote the advance of real wages and not in any schemes for
abolishing rents.

The question of economic rent then, may be summarized thus :
(1) That rent is a net surplus arising from the use of land as an
economic instrument ; (2) That rent tends to equal the difference in the productive utility of the different portions of land
used for the same purpose in the same community or competing
group ; (3) That the economic use of inferior land simultaneously with superior, and hence the payment of rent, finally depends upon the employment of improved methods of production
(use of capital) ;   (4) That the successful use of improved methods depends upon the increased consumption of wealth per capita
of the community or a higher social standard of living among
the masses and, that rent is not the cause of low wages, but
the economic consequence of high wages ; (5) That since rent is
an economic surplus the existence and increase of which depends
upon the social progress and increasing wages of the laboring
classes, it is in the broadest sense the interest of the landowning
class to promote in every way possible the economic and social
advancement of the laboring classes.

CHAPTER V.

THE LAW OF INTEREST.

SECTION I.—*Popular Theories of Interest.*

INTEREST is economically analogous to rent; it sustains precisely the same relation to capital that rent does to land. In considering the question of interest, therefore, we have to deal with essentially the same economic problem we considered in the last chapter. All the popular objections urged against the payment of rent as a burden to the community, an exaction from the laborer, etc., are presented with equal force against the payment of interest. And conversely, the same reasons that justify the payment of rent apply equally to that of interest. Scientifically therefore, all that is necessary in dealing with the question of interest is to apply to capital the law already stated in regard to land.

Unfortunately however, in this instance, as in almost every other question in economics, a simple direct statement of the subject is practically impossible without first clearing away some of the confusion in which it has been involved. The utter lack of logical consistency which characterizes the body of economic doctrines authoritatively taught is such that there is practically no mutual relation between the different departments of the subject. There being no recognized common centre of movement, no order of relation and mutual dependence of phenomena, and hence no accepted general law which they shall obey, each phase of the subject is discussed for the most part as if it had no necessary relation to the whole but were governed by laws peculiar to itself. Thus we find Ricardo and other English economists teaching that profits are governed by a law entirely different from that which regulates rent. And now more than half a century later we have Mr. Walker declaring the same thing with regard to interest.

This is the more astonishing in Mr. Walker's case, because he makes special claim to having presented a logical order of distribution.[1] When dealing with the question of rent, which he puts first, he never tires of proclaiming the doctrine that rent does not affect the price of the product, since that is determined by the use of no-rent land ; yet he fails to recognize this principle in the case of interest, and emphatically declares that "there is not any no-interest capital," and says :

"We have seen that the whole theory of rent rests on the assumption that there is a body of no-rent lands. . . . In the theory of capital there is nothing to correspond to this. The economist does not find any no-interest capital. In theory, all capital bears an interest, and all portions of capital bear equal interest. . . . But what has been stated shows how fundamentally the theory of interest differs from that of rent."[2]

Why should we assume that "there *is* a body of no-rent lands" and that "there is not any no-rent capital"? Upon what ground should we assume that "all portions of capital bear equal interest"? Surely we have a right to demand some explanation, some pertinent facts in experience, or a well-established principle before we can be expected to accept such sweeping affirmations. If, as Mr. Walker says, "interest forms a part of the price of all products,"[3] then all interest is a tax upon the consumer, and the wealth of the rich, so far as interest is concerned, is obtained at the expense of the poor. It will not be difficult to show that Mr. Walker's position on interest, which is essentially the same as that of Marx on profits, and George on rent, rests like theirs on pure assumption unsupported by established facts or verified principle. When discussing profits he insists that there is no-profit capital and says :

"The employers of the lowest grade—the no-profit employers, as we have called them—must pay wages sufficient to hire laborers to work under their direction. These wages constitute an essential part of the cost to the employer of the production of the goods. The fact that these wages are so high is the reason why

[1] "Political Economy," pp. 193, 248.
[2] *Ibid.*, pp. 222, 223.
[3] *Ibid.*, pp. 235, 236.

these employers are unable (their skill, etc. being the same) to realize any profit for themselves." [1]

If we ask Mr. Walker why there are " no-profit employers," which of course means no-profit capital, he will reply, as he has at length, that it is because, under free and active competition, prices tend to equal the cost of production under the greatest disadvantage.[2] If there is any economic power by which prices can be forced down to the no-profit point and to the no-rent point, why can they not, by the same power, be forced down to the no-interest point ? If the owner of the poorest tools in use is powerless to demand a price sufficiently high to yield a profit upon the capital invested in those tools, by what force in economics can he demand a price high enough to yield interest for that capital ? Obviously the same power that will enable him to insist upon the one will enable him to obtain the other.

When considering the law of prices,[3] we saw that, at the price-determining point (producing at the greatest disadvantage), each factor in production obtained only the exact equivalent of the cost of its contribution to the product ; that is to say, that no factor in production can add more value to the product than it loses in the process. Consequently the price of the product cannot be greater than the equivalent of the aggregate cost of the factors jointly employed in its production. Clearly if there is any power by which more can be demanded from the product for capital than the equivalent of what it gives (the cost of maintaining its productive efficiency), the same power will enable the consumer and the laborer to do likewise. It is only upon the principle that capital employed under the greatest disadvantage will barely yield the cost of maintaining its productive efficiency, that no-rent land and no-profit employers are possible. It is solely because their product sells at cost that they occupy the datum-line or price-fixing position. Manifestly any social conditions or economic law which will make no-rent land and no-profit factories possible, will also make no-interest capital possible.

[1] " Political Economy," pp. **240, 241**.
[2] *Ibid.*, pp. 236-242.
[3] Chapter iv., pp. **20-22**.

Moreover, facts everywhere sustain this theorem.   There is probably no well-established industry, either in agriculture, manufacture, or commerce, in which there is not permanently a certain amount of no-interest capital employed.   There are hundreds and perhaps thousands of small farmers, merchants, and manufacturers in this and every other commercially advanced country, who remain in business for years and barely obtain a living and keep their capital intact.   Nor do I refer to those results of bad judgment and inexperience which Mr. Walker calls "accidents," [1] but only to capital which is so employed as the necessary result of economic law.

Mr. Walker may reply that no one will accumulate wealth and invest it in production unless he can obtain a reward at least to the extent of interest.   Even if this were literally correct and without an exception, it would not prevent the use of no-interest capital.   Indeed if capital were never invested for less than the maximum profit the use of the no-interest capital would be not only possible but inevitable.   Through the concentration of capital and the use of improved methods, maximum-profit yielding capital is constantly being reduced to the no-interest point.

Suppose for example, that in the manufacture of cotton cloth half a million dollars are invested in the plant which at the time is of the most modern type, and that the capital not only yields interest but a profit.   In the course of a few years a great improvement in machinery is discovered by the use of which the cost of cotton cloth is greatly reduced.   Through the fall in price resulting from the use of this new machinery, the profits of those who still produce by the previous methods are entirely destroyed.   The capital which at first yielded a high profit ceases to yield any thing above the bare cost of production—wages, raw material, and actual wear and tear.   Consequently, if this capital continues to be employed it must be used without profit or interest.   Moreover, when through still further improvements the price falls too low for this now inferior machinery to be used without loss, the capital invested in the tools of the next grade above will fall to the no-interest point, and so on.   Thus, while it may be true that no capital is originally invested without interest or even high

[1] "Political Economy," p. 235.

profit, it constantly tends towards the no-interest point through the use of improved methods. This does not mean, however, that the same capital, or the capital of the same persons, continues to be employed at the no-interest point ; on the contrary, such capital is constantly struggling to move from no-interest to high-profit uses. This however, is often difficult to do without loss. If the capital is invested in machinery which is reduced to the no-interest point by the competition of larger concerns using superior methods, then it can only be transferred to high-profit uses by being invested in the superior methods and producing on a larger scale, and this usually involves a larger amount of capital, the lack of which often makes such transfer impossible. Capital is often thus retained in the same business for a considerable time after it ceases to yield interest, partly in the hope of doing better and partly from fear of a loss of the principal in any sudden transfer to new fields. From these and many other causes which are constantly in operation, especially among small producers, capital is often continued in a business, not merely until it reaches the no-interest point, but in many cases until it is forced by competition to the losing point. Thus, while capital is constantly struggling to move from no-interest to high-profit uses, that portion of it which is used under the poorest conditions is always no-interest capital.

If prices could never fall below the interest-paying point for the capital invested in the poorest tools, then the use of improved machinery would not cheapen commodities, but would simply increase profits. Nothing but working at a loss or the failure to obtain interest will enforce the disuse of the most inferior instruments, and permit prices to fall to the cost of producing with superior methods, and thus compel the advantages of improved machinery and concentrated capital to pass to the community in lower prices instead of remaining in the hands of capitalists as higher profits.

This is what is constantly taking place in every progressive community. There is scarcely a machine-using industry in which capital has not been reduced from the high-profit to the no-interest point several times over during the present century. Take, for example, the cotton industry. In the first quarter of this century, capital invested in machinery that could produce

16

calico at 30 cents a yard would yield a high profit. And before 1830 the capital invested in the same machinery could not yield interest, nor even be used without loss, the price of calico having fallen to 17 cents a yard. And the high-profit capital of 1830 reached the no-interest or losing point by 1843, when the price had fallen to 12 cents a yard. And the high-profit capital of 1843 again reached the no-interest point by 1850, when the price had fallen to 9¼ cents a yard ; and so on, until to-day the capital cannot receive interest which is unable to produce the same commodity at less than 5 cents a yard. Thus the whole circle from high-profit to no-interest has been traversed several times over during the present century. In fact, every dollar's worth of capital invested in the print-cloth business since the invention of the power-loom, that could not produce print-cloth at 4 cents a yard, has been reduced to the no-interest point.[1] Since Mr. Walker admits that this takes place in the sphere of both profits and rents, why he should fail to see that through the same law it must also take place in the sphere of interest, is not a little surprising. He appears to have fallen into the same error that the English economists committed in regard to rent and profits. They saw that rent is paid from a surplus above the cost, and hence is not an addition to the price of the product ; while they regard profits as the reward for the abstinence of the capitalist, and hence a necessary addition to the price.[2] Mr. Walker saw their error in not regarding profits as a surplus similar to rent, yet he has repeated the same oversight regarding interest. Indeed, he has taken their formula for profits and used it as a definition of interest, and says : " Capital, as we have seen, is the result of saving. Interest, then, is the reward for abstinence."[3]

---

[1] In the iron industries there are many large properties that are barely up to the level of no-interest use without loss to-day which a few years ago yielded high profits. The introduction of successful inventions has in many instances reduced millions of dollars' worth of machinery not merely to the no-interest point, but forced it out of use altogether.

[2] " Wealth of Nations," book i., chapter vi., p. 39 ; chapter vii., p. 42 ; book v., chapter ii., p. 691. Ricardo's " Works," pp. 39, 63. McCulloch's " Principles of Political Economy," p. 42. Mill's " Principles of Political Economy," vol. i., pp. 569-72.

[3] " Political Economy," p. 224 ; also p. 66 ; cf. Mill's " Principles of Political Economy," vol. i., p. 495.

This definition is as unfortunate for interest as it was for profit, and for the same reason. If all capital is the result of abstinence, and all abstinence is necessarily rewarded by interest, then not only would all capital receive interest, but the interest would be in proportion to the degree of sacrifice or abstinence involved in its accumulation. The difficulty with this view is that it is inconsistent with the facts. In the first place, there is no inductive warrant for the broad assumption that all capital is the result of abstinence. As we have already shown, much the larger portion of capital in use to-day has been accumulated without any conscious abstinence whatever. It is undoubtedly true that in all countries accumulations at first represent abstemiousness and sometimes painful sacrifice. The amount thus accumulated, however, represents a small fraction of the productive capital of to-day. Take, for example, the Rothschilds, Goulds, Vanderbilts, Sages, and Astors. While it may be true that the first few thousands of their accumulations represent abstinence, it is doubtful if one per cent. of the capital accumulated after the first half million represents abstinence in the remotest sense. From what do these gentlemen abstain ? what gratification that wealth can give do they forego ? It is because the greater part of their capital is not due to abstinence, but to the surplus earnings of the capital already in use, that it increases much faster after they cease to practise abstinence than it ever could before.

If interest were only the reward for abstinence, then all the capital which is accumulated without abstinence would receive no interest ; whereas that is just the capital which most uniformly receives the highest interest, while the capital of the small farmers, manufacturers, and merchants, which is the result of the most painful abstinence, is that which is most generally used without interest. In fact, the whole idea of a reward for abstinence is fallacious. Nature does not reward abstinence ; she only rewards effort. Capital does not receive a reward because it represents parsimony, but solely because it aids in production ; and its reward depends entirely upon the degree of its exceptional productive efficiency. And from the causes above enumerated it tends towards the no-interest point directly as improved methods are introduced, without regard to whether it was painfully or unconsciously accumulated.

SECTION II.—*The True Theory of Interest.*

If we bear in mind the conclusions already reached regarding prices, and the nature and function of capital, there need be no difficulty in understanding the question of interest. That interest and rent are of the same economic species is apparent from their every characteristic. They are both paid in the same way and for the same reason—namely, to obtain the use of capital belonging to another. Had land and other forms of capital always been used by those who owned them, no distinction between rent, interest, and profits would ever have been made. It was not until the different productive factors began to be used by those who did not own them that any such distinction became necessary. Manifestly, when the producer owned all the land and other instruments he used, all the surplus product resulting from their use was his, and it might be designated either as rent, interest, or profits ; but there could be no reason for calling different portions of it by different names. But when the productive instruments began to be owned in varying degrees by different persons, that portion of the surplus product resulting from the use of each instrument naturally belonged to the owner of that instrument. In order to distinguish between that portion which goes to the owners of the different instruments, it was necessary to designate them by different terms. Instead, therefore, of rent, interest, and profit being economically different from each other and governed by different laws, it will be seen that they are simply different portions of the same aggregate surplus and are governed by the same general principle.

Let it be assumed for illustration that A, B, and C represent three classes of producers contributing to the supply of the same market, A owning all the land and other instruments he uses, B owning his implements but hiring his land, and C hiring both land and instruments. And for the sake of simplicity let it be further assumed that, through the superior quality of their land and tools, they produce 15 per cent. more than their most inferior competitor (he using the most inferior methods), and consequently have a surplus of 15 per cent. Under these conditions it is quite clear that A, owning all the means of production, will have the whole surplus ; he will obtain 15 per cent. more for his product than it cost him in wages, raw material, and wear and tear of implements. B, not owning the land, has to give 5 per cent. of his product to the landowner as rent. Consequently his production being the same, his surplus will equal that of A, minus the amount paid for rent (15—5 per cent.). The case of C is like that of B, only more so. Owning neither the land nor the instruments, he has to hire both ; hence, for the same reason that he must pay 5 per cent. of his product to the landowner for the use of the land, he must pay 5 per cent. of it to the capitalist for the use of the capital in tools and stock ; while the selling price and all other costs being the same, his surplus will equal that of B, minus the rent, and that of A, minus rent and interest (15 — 10 per cent.). They all produce at 15 per cent. more with the same investment than those who use the poorest tools, and hence create a surplus of 15 per cent. But A, who owns all the means of production, receives all the surplus ; while B, who does not own the land, has to give one third of the surplus to the landowner ; and C, who owns neither land nor capital, has to give one third to the landowner and one third to the capitalist, leaving only one third for himself.

Clearly therefore, rent, interest, and profits all come from the same source—the economic surplus,—the only difference being that rent and interest are stipulated portions of the general surplus, while profit is the contingent remainder. In the case of A the whole surplus is contingent profit. In the case of B rent is stipulated and the surplus, minus rent, is contingent profit. And in the case of C, both rent and interest being stipulated, only the contingent remainder after these are paid is profit. There is manifestly no economic force by which C can add his interest to the price of the product or abstract it from the wages of the laborer, which will not enable B to do the same with rent. For the same reason that prices tend to equal the cost of producing with the poorest land in use without the payment of rent, they will equal the cost of producing with the poorest tools in use without the payment of interest.

If the poorest land and the poorest tools and most inferior management were all used together, we should find the no-rent landowner, no-interest capitalist, and no-profit entrepreneur all represented in the same farm, factory, or other enterprise. It is because the best instruments and skill are sometimes applied to the poorest land, and the best land is sometimes used with the poorest skill and management, that we often find those who pay high rents failing to obtain interest or profits, while those paying less rents can pay interest and make profit. In other words the surplus, being the result of the superiority of the land, instruments, or skill over the poorest in use, is (through the natural equity of economic law) distributed among the owners of those factors which produce it. If it is all due to the land, it all goes to rent ; if it is all due to the instruments, it all goes to interest ; if it is all due to management of the entrepreneur, it all goes to profits ; if it is equally due to them all, it will be evenly divided in rent, interest and profits. Thus whichever way we consider the subject, interest is economically identical with rent, it being to capital precisely what rent is to land. In other words, rent and interest are simply differentiated portions of profit—stipulated disbursements of the aggregate economic surplus,—while the entrepreneur's profit is the undivided contingent remainder.[1]

It may be said that the rent of B and the rent and interest of C are indispensable items in the cost of production. This is correct, but they are not indispensable items in the cost of A, with whom B and C have to compete. Since B and C can make no charge to the community for any cost which A is willing to do without, the only economic means by which B and C can be reimbursed for their rent and interest is by enlarging their surplus through increased production. Indeed that is the only reason rent or interest is ever paid. No one will pay rent for the productive use of land unless he can obtain an advantage by so doing. The only reason a person will pay a dollar a foot for land in one place when he can get it for a dollar an acre in another is, that by paying the higher rent he saves a greater expense in some other way. For example, there is plenty of land admirably suited for market.garden-

---

[1] The producer who uses his own capital never receives interest ; if he has any surplus over the necessary cost of production, which includes the remuneration for his own services—it is profit. Because the interest paid for the use of capital is a definite percentage, it has become more or less habitual in business circles to speak of profits as interest up to a certain amount. Hence, we sometimes hear it said that a concern has not made the interest on its capital. All this expression means is that the profit or surplus has not been equal to what they would have had to pay as interest if they had borrowed the capital.

ing which can be had for nearly nothing. But it is so far from the city market that the cost in transportation and waste in product would be much greater than the high rent paid for land by the market gardener in the suburbs of the large city. Instead of the high rent increasing the cost, it simply obviates the necessity of the still greater cost that would be involved in using land that could be obtained without rent or at a lower rent.

The same is true of interest. The only motive for borrowing capital is to increase the contingent surplus by more than the amount to be paid as interest. Whether or not this will be achieved will largely depend upon the correctness with which the possible surplus is calculated. If the surplus is overestimated, rent and interest may absorb it all, or they may even be greater than the total surplus, in which case the entrepreneur will suffer a net loss. This is what occurs when the profits of small farmers are all absorbed by the interest on their mortgages, and those of small manufacturers and merchants by the interest on their borrowed capital, of which we hear so much.[1] The only means, therefore, by which rent, interest, and profits can be obtained is the creation of a surplus by producing at less than the maximum cost. The non-landowning capitalist can only have a profit by creating a surplus more than equal to the rent. The entrepreneur can only have a profit by creating a surplus more than equal to both rent and interest. Interest then is not the necessary reward for abstinence, nor is it a part of the price-fixing cost of production, but it is simply that portion of the economic surplus which is paid for the use of capital (tools) owned by another ; and since it can neither be added to the price of commodities nor subtracted from the wages of labor, it cannot be a tax upon the community.

Interest is not only not injurious to the community, it is a positive advantage. It is one of the most effective means of concentrating capital and bringing improved methods of production into successful operation. There are thousands of millions of dollars invested in railroads, steamships, and other modern enterprises, which could not have been utilized for such purposes

---

[1] Over sixty per cent. of the capital invested in railroads in this country in 1888 failed to yield a profit, because the surplus was all absorbed in paying the interest on the bonds.

without the payment of interest.   It is doubtful if there is a railroad in existence that could have been built with the capital owned by its actual projectors.   The payment of interest was the only means of obtaining the capital from those who had neither the wisdom, energy, nor capacity to put it to such use.   Indeed such enterprises as the Suez Canal, the great railroad and steamship lines, Atlantic cables, petroleum pipe-lines, and the modern telegraph, would have been utterly impossible but for the concentration of capital which the payment of interest made possible.   Interest, instead of being a burden to the community, is thus one of the great wealth-cheapening agencies of civilization.

CHAPTER VI.

THE LAW OF PROFIT.

SECTION I.—*Orthodox Economics Responsible for Socialistic Theories.*

Since the time of Adam Smith and Ricardo economists have generally taught : (1) that profit is a necessary part of the price of the commodity to the consumer ; (2) that profit can rise only as wages fall. In supporting the first proposition Mill devotes several pages to showing that, in proportion as the capital expended in production is invested in machinery, buildings, etc., profit becomes an increasing item in the cost of production, and consequently an increasing addition to the price of the commodity.[1]

According to this view, when any commodity goes through a considerable number of hands during the process of manufacture, the price paid by the consumer largely consists of profits. For example, if iron goes through ten different stages before it is converted into steel, and the rate of profit is five per cent., about two

[1] " The flax-spinner, part of whose expenses consists of the purchase of flax and of machinery, has had to pay, in their price, not only the wages of the labor by which the flax was grown and the machinery made, but the profits of the grower, the flax-dresser, the miner, the iron-founder, and the machine-maker. All these profits, together with those of the spinner himself, were again advanced by the weaver in the price of his material, linen yarn ; and along with them the profits of a fresh set of machine-makers, and of the miners and iron-workers who supplied them with their metallic material. All these advances form part of the cost of production of linen. Profits, therefore, as well as wages, enter into the cost of production, which determines the value of the produce."—" Principles of Political Economy," vol. 1., p. 568. *Cf.* " Wealth of Nations," book v., ch. ii., pp. 691, 692.

thirds of the price of the finished product would consist of profits. It will be seen that this theory supports the popular notion that all so-called middle-men are parasites upon the product of the community. If this were true, heroic measures for their elimination would certainly be in order.

The second postulate—that profit can rise only as wages fall [1] —implies that the wealth of the capitalist simply represents the poverty of the laborers. The employing classes are thus taught that their interest invariably lies in keeping wages low, and the laboring classes are just as effectually taught that the only way to increase wages is to reduce profit. The natural effect of this doctrine is seen in the antagonistic attitude which these two classes assume towards each other.

As a legitimate outcome of the English doctrine—that profits can only increase as wages diminish,—we have the theory, first of Rodbertus, that the laborer receives "a smaller fraction of the product in proportion as his productiveness increases," and hence becomes more dependent as society advances [2]; and next, the

[1] " There can be no rise in the value of labor without a fall of profits."—Ricardo's " Works," p. 23. " Can any point be more clearly established than that profits must fall, with a rise of wages?"—*Ibid.*, p. 63, "It has been my endeavor to show throughout this work, that the rate of profits can never be increased but by a fall in wages."—*Ibid.*, pp. 74, 75. "Whatever raises the wages of labor lowers the profits of stock."—*Ibid.*, p. 122. See also *ibid.*, pp. 60, 65, 93, 136. " The *whole produce of industry* under deduction of rent is divided between laborers and capitalists. . . . . The proportion falling to the capitalist is increased when that falling to the laborers is diminished, and diminished when it is increased. . . . . Mr. Ricardo has endeavored to show . . . . that a rise of profits can never be brought about, except by a fall of proportional wages, nor a fall of profits, except by a corresponding rise of proportional wages." —McCulloch's " Principles of Political Economy," pp. 192, 193. "We thus arrive at the conclusion of Ricardo and others, that the rate of profits depends upon wages ; rising as wages fall and falling as wages rise."—Mill's " Principles of Political Economy," vol. i., p. 512. "Wages *equal* the product of industry *minus* the three parts (rent, interest, and profits) already determined in their nature and amount."—Walker's " Political Economy," p. 248. "What remains after subtracting the aggregate price paid for the use of capital . . . . is obviously the share of labor."—Sidgwick : " Principles of Political Economy," p. 322.

[2] " Rent and wages are thus shares into which the product is divided so far as it is income. Whence it follows that the larger one share is the smaller must be the other. If the rent takes a larger share of the product, a smaller share must remain for wages. As one share varies in size so must the other in inverse

doctrine of Karl Marx, that all forms of rent, interest, and profit are robbery.[1] These two formulæ have become the accepted basis of the whole socialistic movement, so rapidly increasing in all civilized countries. By a critical examination of the process of economic production, Marx endeavors to scientifically demonstrate how, in the nature of the capitalist system, unpaid wages constitute the source of all rent, interest, and profit. It must be admitted that if this proposition can be scientifically sustained, the theory of socialism—which demands the public ownership of all the means of production—cannot be successfully disputed. And on the contrary, if this proposition can be shown to be erroneous, the whole economic fabric of socialism falls. It is of the utmost importance, therefore, in discussing the question of profit, that the claim of this theory should be fully considered.

SECTION II.—*Marx's Theory of Exploitation.*

After an elaborate explanation of his theory of value which is substantially that of Ricardo ; namely, that commodities and labor exchange on the basis of the quantity of labor expended in their production,[2] Marx illustrates the process of exploiting the

ratio. . . . . The share of the working class, that is of the great majority of society, does not remain a fixed unchangeable fraction of the product in precisely the same proportion as the productiveness increases." . . . . (Therefore, " There must be produced that fatal contradiction in society, that the more equal and the more free all its members become before the law and politically, the more unequal and dependent are the majority of the working classes economically. . . . . The conclusion follows that the existing form of division of the national product cannot continue."—Views of Rodbertus translated from the work of Dr. Rudolf Myer ; Appendix to Hyndman's " Historical Basis of Socialism."

[1] " The capitalist mode of production and accumulation, and therefore capitalist private property, have for their fundamental condition the annihilation of self-earned private property ; in other words, the expropriation of the laborer." —"Capital," p. 800.

[2] " Commodities, therefore, in which equal quantities of labor are embodied, or which can be produced in the same time, have the same value. . . . . As values, all commodities are only definite masses of congealed labor time." —"Capital," p. 6. "So far as it (labor-power) has value, it represents no more than a definite quantity of the average labor of society incorporated in it. . . . Given the individual the production of labor-power consists in his reproduction of himself or his maintenance."—*Ibid.*, p. 149.

laborer by the manufacture of cotton yarn, which he states with great precision, and says :

"We assumed on the occasion of its sale that the value of a day's labor power is three shillings, and that six hours' labor are incorporated in that sum. . . . . The same quantity of labor is also embodied in a piece of gold of the value of three shillings. Consequently by the mere labor of spinning, a value of three shillings is added to the cotton. Let us now consider the total value of the product, the ten pounds of yarn. Two and a half days' labor have been embodied in it, of which two days were contained in the cotton and in the substance of the spindle worn away, and half a day was absorbed during the process of spinning. This two and a half days' labor is also represented by a piece of gold of the value of fifteen shillings. Hence, fifteen shillings is an adequate price for the ten pounds of yarn, or the price of one pound is eighteen pence. Our capitalist stares in astonishment. The value of the product is exactly equal to the value of the capital advanced. The value so advanced has not expanded, no surplus value has been created, and, consequently, money has not been converted into capital." [1]

The capitalist is then described as being in any thing but a tranquil state of mind at the result ; and after giving some weak but truly othodox reasons why he should have had a profit, he is represented as leaving "all such like subterfuges and juggling tricks to the professors of political economy who are paid for it," and as turning his attention to concocting a new scheme for the creation of surplus value—in which he succeeds. The capitalist then analyzes the factors in production and finds that no surplus can be squeezed out of the raw material or the machinery ; hence it must be exploited from the labor-power. This he decides can be done by making the laborer work twice as many hours for the same wages. He then resumes business on his twelve-hour plan with complete success, the process of which Marx states thus :

"The laborer therefore finds in the workshop the means of production necessary for working not only during six but during twelve hours. Just as during the six hours' process our ten pounds of cotton absorbed six hours' labor and became ten pounds of yarn, so now twenty pounds of cotton will absorb twelve hours'

[1] "Capital," p. 171.

labor and be changed into twenty pounds of yarn. Let us now examine the product of this prolonged process. There is now materialized in this twenty pounds of yarn the labor of five days, of which four days are due to the cotton and the lost steel of the spindle, the remaining day having been absorbed by the cotton during the spinning process. Expressed in gold the labor of five days is thirty shillings. This is therefore the price of the twenty pounds of yarn, giving as before eighteen pence as the price of a pound. But the sum of the values of the commodities that entered into the process amounts to twenty-seven shillings. The value of the yarn is thirty shillings. Therefore the value of the product is one ninth greater than the value advanced for its production ; twenty-seven shillings have been transformed into thirty shillings ; a surplus-value of three shillings has been created. The trick has at last succeeded ; money has been converted into capital." [1]

Thus, according to Marx, in the spinning process six shillings of value have been added to the twenty pounds of yarn by the use of labor, for which the laborer has received only three shillings, and the laborer has been exploited of half he produced. Throughout the whole discussion in the remaining 625 pages of his book, Marx never tires of reminding the reader of this fact. [2] It must be admitted that "the trick has at last succeeded," and it almost looks as if the capitalist had performed it ; but let us examine the process a little closer.

In the first instance the case stood : 15s. value of yarn = 10s. raw cotton + 2s. machinery + 3s. labor power. If we ask why the value of the yarn was just 15 shillings, Marx promptly explains that it is because only "fifteen shillings were spent in the open market upon the constituent elements of the product, or what amounts to the same thing, upon the factors of the labor process." [3]

Let us examine the twenty pounds of yarn produced under the "prolonged process" in the light of the law Marx has applied to the production of the ten pounds. Here the different items of cost were as follows :

[1] " Capital," pp. 175, 176.

[2] *Ibid.*, pp. 176, 198, 200, 201, 203, 211, 219, 220, 222, 289, 533, 541, 542, 543, 544, 550, 592.   [3] *Ibid.*, p. 171.

Raw material, ...	20s.
Wear and tear of machinery, ...	4s.
Twelve hours' labor power, ...	3s.
Total cost, ...	27s.

Thus, according to the above law, the total value of the product is twenty-seven shillings. " Oh no," exclaims Marx, that would give no surplus value. He admits that the cost of the yarn in this case is only twenty-seven shillings, but he insists that *its value* is thirty shillings.[1] According to Marx then, his economic law of value works thus : 10s. + 2s. + 3s. cost = 15s. value ; while 20s. + 4s. + 3s. cost = 30s. value. That is to say, 15s. *equals* 15s., but 27s. *equals* 30s. Now by what application of his own law of value, according to which fifteen shillings' cost can only produce fifteen shillings' value, can he make twenty-seven shillings' cost produce thirty shillings' value ? Clearly if the twenty pounds of yarn, the production of which only cost twenty-seven shillings, can have a value of thirty shillings, then by the same law the ten pounds of yarn whose production cost fifteen shillings can be sixteen shillings and six pence. To assume that, while a cost of fifteen shillings cannot yield a value of more than fifteen shillings, a cost of twenty-seven shillings can yield a value of thirty shillings, is to violate alike the laws of logic and the rules of arithmetic. Manifestly, surplus value was no more created in the production of the twenty pounds of yarn than in that of the ten pounds. The three shillings here paraded as surplus value is a pure invention of Marx. True, " the trick has at last succeeded " ; but it was performed by Marx and not by the capitalist. It is obviously a trick of metaphysics and not of economics. The only exploitation here revealed is the exploitation of socialistic credulity, and not of economic labor power. A theory according to which 15s. value = 15s. cost, while 30s. value = 27s. cost, needs only to be stripped of its metaphysical garment in order to be rejected.

The fallacy here so boldly flaunted—and made to do service as the scientific basis for a radical reconstruction of society—can be

---

[1] " The sum of the values of the commodities that entered into the process amounts to twenty-seven shillings. The value of the yarn is thirty shillings. . . . A surplus value of three shillings has been created."—" Capital," pp. 175, 176.

exposed in many ways. It is true that in Marx's second case the laborer is made to produce twenty pounds of yarn for the same wages which he previously received for producing ten pounds. But this change of labor cost, according to Marx's own theory, would not create a surplus value of three shillings for the capitalist ; on the contrary, it would reduce the price of the product three shillings to the consumer. It is a well-established law in economics that the value of commodities tends to diminish as the ratio of product to cost of labor increases. That Marx recognizes this principle, when discussing other phases of the subject, is clear from the following statement :

"Let us assume that some invention enables the spinner to spin as much cotton in six hours as he was able to spin before in thirty-six hours. His labor is now six times as effective as it was for the purposes of useful production. The product of six hours' work has increased sixfold, from six pounds to thirty-six pounds. But now the thirty-six pounds of cotton absorb only the same amount of labor as formerly did the six pounds. One-sixth as much new labor is absorbed by each pound of cotton, and conquently, the value added by the labor to each pound is only one-sixth of what it formerly was." [1]

This is exactly what occurred in the hypothetical case just considered. When the laborer, in Marx's second case, produced twice as much yarn for three shillings as he produced in the first, he only added half as much value to each pound of yarn he produced. Hence, for the same reason that he added three shillings to the value of the ten pounds of yarn, he only adds three shillings to the value of the twenty pounds ; and, consequently, its value can only be twenty-seven shillings; and no surplus value is created.

Suppose for illustration, that, instead of doubling the length of the laborer's working day, the price of raw cotton should fall fifteen per cent. The cost of the different factors in the production of twenty pounds of yarn would then be as follows :

Raw material, ...	17s.
Cost of wear and tear of machinery, . .	4s.
Twelve hours' labor, ...	6s.
Total cost, ...	27s.

[1] "Capital," p. 183. See also pp. 151, 171, 172, 175, 176, 194, 195, 196.

The laborer in this instance receives twice as much as when working for Marx, but the result is exactly as before, the only difference being that the three shillings is saved on the cost of raw material, instead of the cost of labor power. Would Marx claim that the value of the yarn is now thirty shillings? Certainly not. On the contrary, he would insist that it could not possibly be more than twenty-seven shillings since, as he repeatedly declares, auxiliary capital and raw material can only add to the value of the product the value which they lose in the process—*i. e.* the cost of replacing them,[1]—and every fall in the cost of raw material shows itself in a fall in the price of the product. Indeed, were this otherwise, cheap raw material and improved machinery would have no influence in reducing the price of commodities. If then, the twenty-seven shillings' cost in this instance could only yield twenty-seven shillings' value, by what rule of logic or experience can it be assumed that, by transferring three shillings of the cost from the labor power to the raw material, the twenty-seven shillings' cost would yield thirty shillings' value? As a matter of economic law, it can make absolutely no difference to the value of the product whether the twenty-seven shillings' cost is all in one item, or is spread over a hundred items ; if it will yield a value of thirty shillings when it is all spent in labor power, it will do the same when it is all spent in raw material and machinery, and nothing is paid for labor. Clearly therefore, the attempt of Marx to show that fifteen shillings' cost can yield only fifteen shillings' value, and that by a mere change in the distribution of the items of expenditure, a cost of twenty-seven shillings will yield a value of thirty shillings, is a complete failure, and consequently his theory of surplus value, and that of the "exploitation of the laborer," entirely breaks down.

SECTION III.—*The Cause of Marx's Error.*

The cardinal mistake in the argument of Marx arises from a too literal acceptance of the Ricardian theory that the value of

---

[1] "The value of a commodity therefore varies directly as the quantity and inversely as the productiveness of the labor incorporated in it."—"Capital," p. 7. " It (machinery) never adds more value than it loses on an average by wear and tear."—*Ibid.*, p. 383. " The less labor it (machinery) contains the less value it imparts to the product. The less value it gives up so much the more productive it is, and so much the more its services approximate to those of natural forces." —*Ibid.*, p. 386.

commodities is determined by the quantity of labor expended in their production.   If he had been more of an economist and less of a revolutionist, he might have seen that this is one of the many instances where Ricardo came very near the truth but just missed it.   The error of this postulate, as already pointed out,[1] consists in making the value of the product depend upon the quantity instead of the cost of the labor power expended in its production.

In considering the relation of the cost of labor to the value of the product, it should always be remembered that it is the total cost of the aggregate labor consumed in a given unit of product which affects its value, and not necessarily the cost per unit of labor.   If the *cost of labor per unit of time is diminished, the quantity of labor consumed in a unit of product may be increased without increasing its value.*   And conversely, *if the cost of a unit of labor is increased, the quantity of labor consumed in a unit of product may be diminished without reducing its value.*

Thus it is that the value of a commodity varies with a variation in the quantity of labor devoted to its production only when the cost of the labor per unit of time remains the same.   If Marx, instead of unqualifiedly accepting Ricardo's crude formula, had recognized this fact, he would have seen that when the laborer's working day was doubled without any change in his daily wages, although the quantity of labor expended was double, the total cost of labor power was the same ; hence, as double the amount was produced, the cost of labor power per unit of product was reduced one-half.   It would then have been clear to him that the value of the twenty pounds of yarn could have been increased only three shillings by the twelve hours' labor, because three shillings was all that the twelve hours' labor cost.   The product of the three shillings' worth of labor being twenty instead of ten pounds of yarn, the labor cost of each pound was of course fifty per cent. less, and therefore the value of the twenty pounds of yarn was only twenty-seven shillings instead of thirty shillings, as Marx assumed.

The first condition of scientific law is that it must explain existing and constantly recurring phenomena.   This is precisely what Marx and the English economists have not attempted to make their theory of profit do.   They have assumed that from the general principle of self-interest in human nature no one will

---

[1] Part II., chapter v., section ii.

use capital in production except he can obtain a profit. From this they concluded that all capitalists must of necessity obtain profit, and that the rate of profit tends to approximate uniformity in all industries. Since all capitalists are assumed to be governed by the same principle of self-interest, each one is regarded simply as a duplicate of the rest, instead of being treated as one of the ever varying units of a highly complex aggregate. Consequently, in treating the question of profit, while assuming free competition, Marx deals only with a single producer, or if with more than one, he assumes that they all produce at the same cost per unit and have substantially the same rate of profit.

This is precisely what does not occur. Neither uniform cost of production nor a uniform rate of profit exists in any civilized country, nor have they ever existed under the capitalistic system of production. On the contrary, the characteristic feature of that productive system is free competition among numerous producers, who produce at an ever increasing variety of costs per unit of product and an equally varying rate of profit. It is precisely because profits are not uniform, but that in the same industry some can secure large profits while others can obtain none, that the profit system is so fiercely assailed as unjust. The chief charge against trusts and syndicates is that they undersell the smaller producers, and through obtaining a monopoly secure to themselves large profits. It is not surprising that Marx, like the English economists, should fail to find equitable profit when he ignored the only conditions under which profit always exists.

SECTION IV.—*How Economic Profit is Equitably Evolved.*

If profit is necessarily inequitable, it is uneconomic ; if it cannot be obtained without injustice, it should be prohibited. Profit has already been defined as the undivided surplus remaining after all costs are paid. It has also been explained that the law of surplus is a necessary corollary of the law of price, which also has been presented in a previous chapter.[1]

The movement of both price and surplus, according to this law, was shown in diagram 2 (p. 206), which for convenience is here reproduced and may be assumed to represent six manufacturers of cotton cloth of the same quality.

[1] Part III., chapter iv.

NO. 4.

PROFIT.	PRICE.	ACTUAL COST.	COST SAVED BY CAPITAL.	
1 c.	4 c.	Minimum cost . . . . . 3 c.	Source	F
$\frac{4}{5}$ c.	4 c.	. . . . 3$\frac{1}{5}$ c.	of	E
$\frac{3}{5}$ c.	4 c.	. . . . 3$\frac{2}{5}$ c.	Profits.	D
$\frac{2}{5}$ c.	4 c.	. . . . 3$\frac{3}{5}$ c.		C
$\frac{1}{5}$ c.	4 c.	. . . . 3$\frac{4}{5}$c.		B
0 c.	4 c.	Maximum cost . . . . 4 c.		A

It will be seen that A, who represents maximum cost, produces his cloth at four cents a yard and sells it at four cents. He occupies the same position that Marx's capitalist did—he sells at cost and has no profit. If the case of A was considered alone, or if he was an exact duplicate of all other manufacturers, then the result would be exactly what Marx found, and there could be no profit without either raising the price to the consumer or reducing wages. But it is precisely because A is not a duplicate of the others that to consider him alone leads to an erroneous conclusion. It is only because the others produce under conditions different from A, while being able to sell at the same price, that they obtain any profit, which is what everywhere takes place.

It will be observed that the only point of uniformity among the six manufacturers is the selling price. They all obtain the same price for their cloth, but each one has a different amount of profit, because he produces at a different rate of cost. Just to the extent that the amount in each case on the cost side is diminished, does that on the surplus or profit side increase— that is to say, directly as the cost line of B, C, D, E, and F recedes from that of A on the right does the amount increase in the profit column on the left. It will also be observed that the increase in the profit column in no way affects the price column.

Thus it appears, when we study production as it actually occurs, that profits can arise without injustice. In the case of the six competing manufacturers, who correctly represent modern industry under free competition, all the conditions of economics and ethics are fulfilled ; equivalent is given for equivalent, price equals cost, and profit is produced. If it is asked why B, C, D,

E, and F should receive the same price for their cloth as A, when they can make it at a less cost, the answer is that they furnish the same equivalent for what they receive that he furnishes. To give A more than four cents a yard would be both inequitable and uneconomic ; inequitable because it would be giving more than an equivalent for the cloth ; uneconomic because it would be adding a burden to the consumer in order to give a premium to the most incompetent producer, thereby destroying the incentive for developing improved methods of production. All that the consumer can in equity demand or by economic law exact from the producer is that he shall obtain the full equivalent of his four cents. This he obtains from B and from all the others as completely as from A. The only difference between the producers is that, from causes peculiar to themselves, some of them make nature do more than others. Nature does one fourth more for F than for A, but they all do precisely the same for the consumer ; they all give him a yard of exactly the same quality of cloth for four cents. The consumer has no claims upon B which A is not equally bound to satisfy. And if B should consent to sell at three and four fifths cents a yard, nobody would continue to buy from A at four cents. There is no principle in equity which demands that B or C or D or E or F shall give more cloth for four cents than A gives ; nor is there any law in economics by which they can be made to do so.

Moreover, profit thus evolved is not merely economic and equitable, but it is actually beneficial to the community. So far from being obtained by exploiting the laborer, it is the premium offered by economic law for the invention of superior methods of production, by the use of which the community, including the laborer, obtains a larger amount of wealth for the same service. It is the community that ultimately reaps the greatest advantage, for the great profits of F constitute an incentive to increase production, and the only way F can insure the sale of his larger product is by reducing the price so as to undersell his competitors. Just as frequently as this occurs, the profit of the last profit-man is handed over to the community in lower prices. This is what is constantly taking place as fast as the concentration of capital is increased and improved methods of production are employed.

It is clear, therefore, that the profits of B, C, D, E, and F are not obtained at the expense of equity. They pay the same wages and fulfil all the other economic requirements just as completely as does A, or as do the shoemaker and the farmer, with whom they exchange their product. Just as fast as the dearest man is undersold these profits are passed to the public ; and the only means by which the consequent diminution of profits can be checked is by capital making another draught upon nature. Thus capital, through the incentive of profit, becomes the constant means of exploiting nature for the benefit of society—instead of exploiting the laborer and consumer for the benefit of the capitalist, as Marx and his disciples so persistently claim.

If we pass to the sphere of labor we find that the Ricardian-Marx theory is as inadequate to explain the facts there as it is in the case of commodities. Marx admits that the value of labor power is determined by the cost of its production, just as is the value of commodities. According to this hypothesis, the value of every pound of yarn must be equal to the sum of values that enter into its production, the value of every day's labor must be equal to the sum of values that enters into its production—*i.e.*, the wages of every laborer must be equal to the cost of his own living. Now we know that in every industry the wages of the same class of laborers tend to a uniformity. while the cost of living of the individual laborers varies greatly. For example, we know that in New York City painters, carpenters, bricklayers, cigarmakers, tailors, etc., who work on the same grade of work or in the same shop get the same wages, but individually the cost of their living varies in some cases several dollars a week. On the Marxian hypothesis, that the capitalist who sells his yarn for more than it costs him exploits some of the factors of production, the laborer who obtains more for his labor than it cost him must also have exploited some other factor. Marx would object to charging the laborer with robbery ; his purpose is to prove the other man the thief. Yet, if it is a law in economics that the possession of a surplus proves exploitation, then a surplus in the hands of the laborer who has sold his labor power for more than it cost him is as conclusive evidence of exploitation as is a surplus in the hands of the capitalist who has sold his commodity for more than it cost him. Scientific law does not discriminate between individuals ; there is no operation of natural law under which the laborer is an honest man and the capitalist a thief, when both are doing the same thing. A theory which thus puts vice at a premium and virtue at a discount by showing that none but thieves succeed and that the only reward for honesty is failure and poverty, should only need stating to be rejected.

SECTION V.—*The Ratio of Profit to Product and to Wages.*

One of the most prevalent assumptions regarding profit is, that it takes an inordinately large proportion of the product. The point upon which Marx lays exceptional stress is that profit practically equals wages. Although few careful writers would now venture to contend that wages are actually diminishing, the idea of Rodbertus, that the laborer's share of the product diminishes as his productiveness increases, is very commonly accepted. How much of the product goes to profit and the ratio of profit to wages are mainly questions of fact ; it is therefore to facts that we must turn for any satisfactory explanation of the subject.

If the law of prices and wages presented in these pages is sound, and its corollary of the law of surplus (rent, interest, and profit) is correct, we may expect, under modern productive conditions, to find three important facts : (1) *that real wages (wealth obtainable for a day's service) tend to increase both actually and relatively to the quantity of consumable wealth produced ;* (2) *that, while the surplus or profit increases in its actual amount, it diminishes relatively to the aggregate net product ; that is to say, profit absorbs a diminishing proportion of the consumable wealth produced ;* (3) *that the ratio of wages to profits tends to increase, and that both the actual amount of consumable wealth and the relative proportion of the net product which goes to labor are greater than the amount which goes to capital, and that this tendency increases as the concentration of capital and the use of improved methods advance.*

1. Is the proposition that real wages tend to increase both actually and relatively to the quantity of consumable wealth produced, sustained by the facts ? Fortunately, the industrial history of the present century affords ample data for a conclusive answer to this question. Let us take the cotton industry, which by this

time the reader has become quite familiar with. Moreover, this industry affords an excellent illustration of the principles under consideration, because it is a very extensive industry. It is also completely representative of the factory system, and as such has been in existence longer than almost any other industry. At the commencement of the present century the weaver could only buy ten yards of cloth with a week's wages. To-day (1890) he can obtain a hundred and fifty yards of his own product for a week's wages, while working about thirty hours less per week. That is to say, through a rise in his wages and a fall in the price of the product, he is able to obtain fifteen times as much of his own product for a day's work in 1890 as he could obtain in 1800. The factory period in this country really dates from about 1830. From that time to 1880 the investment of capital, the number of establishments, the amount and price of product, and the wages paid in that industry were as follows :

	1830.	1880.
Number of establishments	801	756
Aggregate capital invested	$40,612,984	$208,280,346
Number of lbs. cloth produced	59,514,926	607,264,241
" persons employed	62,208	172,544
" spindles "	1,246,703	10,653,435
Amount of capital to establish	$50,702	$275,503
Ratio of lbs. produced to capital	1.4 to $1.00	2.4 to $1.00
" capital to persons employed	$652.85 to 1	$1,207.17 to 1
" spindles to persons "	22 to 1	62 to 1
" capital to spindles "	$32.58 to 1	$19.55 to 1
" lbs. produced to persons employed	950.7 to 1	3,519.5 to 1
" " " " spindles	47.6 to 1.	57.0 to 1
Annual consumption of lbs. of cotton cloth per capita	5.90	13.81
Price of cotton cloth per yard	17 cents	7 cents
Operative's wages per week	$2.55	$5.40

It will be seen that in the 756 large establishments in 1880 in which the aggregate capital invested was five times as great as that in the 801 small establishments in 1830, the capital invested per spindle was one third less, the number of spindles operated by each laborer nearly three times as large, the product per spindle one fourth greater, the product per dollar invested twice as large, the price of the cotton cloth nearly sixty per cent. less, the consumption per capita of the population over one hundred per cent. greater, and wages more than double.

If we take the New England States, which comprise the leading cotton-manufacturing district in the country, and also that where the greatest concentration of capital and machinery in this industry has taken place, the results in this direction are still more striking. According to the statistics on Wages and prices from 1752, gathered by the Massachusetts Labor Bureau,[1] in 1831 the ratio of spindles to operatives was $24\frac{2}{100}$ to 1. In 1880 they were $71\frac{8}{100}$ to 1. And the ratio of pounds of product to operatives employed in 1831 was 1,484 to 1, and in 1880 it was 3,633 to 1. That is to say, during fifty years the ratio of spindles to operatives increased 184 per cent., and the ratio of product to operatives 145 per cent. During the same period the aggregate wages of men, women, and children rose 115 per cent., and the hours of labor were reduced 12 per cent., while the price of calico print fell from 17 to 7[2] cents a yard. Thus, while the wages in this industry rose 115 per cent., the purchasing power of those wages in the finished product increased 241 per cent. ; that is to say, through a rise of wages and fall in prices accompanying the concentration of capital and use of improved methods, the laborer was enabled to obtain over five times as much of his own product for a day's labor in 1880 as he did in 1830—the increase is still greater now (1890).

If we consider the matter from the standpoint of value instead of quantity of product, a similar result is apparent. In 1850[3] the value of the product per operative in New England was $707 ; in 1880 it was $1,139 per operative, an increase of $61\frac{24}{100}$ per cent. The wages in this industry for 1850 for New England are not obtainable, but if we assume that the proportion of the 115 per cent. increase from 1830 to 1880 was as great after as before 1850, a perfectly safe assumption, the rise in wages from 1850 to 1880 would be 69 per cent. Measured in money, therefore, the value of labor (wages) of cotton operatives rose 8 per cent. more than the value of their product. If we extend this generalization to the whole United States the result is very similar. The value of product per operative in the cotton industry in 1850 was $709, and in 1880 it was $1,112, being an

---

[1] Report for 1885, pp. 185-189.

[2] *Ibid.*, p. 455.

[3] I have taken 1850 because the value for 1830 is not obtainable.

increase of $56\frac{59}{100}$[1] per cent., or 12 per cent. less than the rise of wages. Therefore, whether we view the question from the standpoint of quantity of wealth, purchasing power of wages, or the ratio of wages to product, it is equally clear that wages have increased both actually and relatively to the quantity of consumable wealth produced, as capital has been concentrated and as improved methods of production have been employed.

Notwithstanding this rise of wages and fall of prices, it is insisted that the laborer is despoiled of a large part of the wealth he produces. As evidence of this we are pointed to the fact that in many industries the product per laborer has increased more than a thousand per cent. during the last fifty years, while their wages have not much more than doubled. This claim has been virtually conceded by Mr. Giffen, President of the British Statistical Society. He says : " On this head it may be admitted, to begin with, that there is apparent foundation for some of the complaints. Workmen in particular employments do not get a reward at all in proportion to the increase of production in those employments. The illustration of a cotton-mill is familiar. A single attendant on a number of machines will ' produce' as much in an hour as formerly in a year or two, but his wages are only double—or perhaps not quite double—what they were when the production was so much less.[2] . . . But the increased severity of toil, without proportionate remuneration, might be admitted in those special employments without altering the fact that remuneration has increased generally. What seems to have happened in these cases is that the development of society imposes a heavy burden on a special class." [3] While he tries to break the force of this complaint by showing that remuneration has increased generally, he practically admits the injustice, and treats it as an inherent element in the present industrial constitution of society. This is all that socialistic reconstructionists claim ; it is because they believe that equity is impossible under the present industrial system that they demand its abolition. Nor can their claim be reasonably resisted unless these phenomena can be explained without assuming either that society

---

[1] See U. S. Census (1880), volume on Manufactures, pp. 541–547.

[2] " Gross and Net Gain of Rising Wages," *Contemporary Review*, December, 1889, p. 835.   [3] *Ibid.*, p. 838.

has developed in the wrong direction or that natural law is inherently unjust.

Here is another instance of the error of treating wages as a *share* in the *division* of the product, instead of an item in the cost of production. If this view were correct, and wages in each industry should rise directly as the product per laborer increases, as Mr. Giffen's argument implies, the result, instead of being more equitable, would be unjust to the laborers and more inimical to society. It would be unjust to the laborers because it would give all the increased product resulting from improved machinery to the particular laborers who happen to use the improved implements, thus depriving the laborers in non-machine-using industries of any advantage arising from superior methods of production. Upon what principle of equity should a weaver or shoemaker who happens, without any virtue on his part, to use improved instruments, receive fifty or a hundred times as much wages as the bricklayer, painter, compositor, and other hand-workers whose industries do not admit of the use of steam-driven machinery? Manifestly any industrial system which would increase the wages of the factory-worker fifty or a hundred-fold, while it would only advance those of hand-workers ten or twenty per cent., simply because, in the nature of the occupations, the former could and the latter could not use labor-saving machinery, would be the very embodiment of injustice.

It would be inimical to society, because it would make any general reduction in the price of commodities impossible, as the increased wealth would all go to the particular laborer who used improved machinery, thus depriving the community in general of any participation in the advantages of industrial development. It is hardly necessary to say that the use of steam-driven machinery is no more due to the particular operatives who use it than it is to the millions of compositors, bricklayers, farmers, and other laborers who do not use them. In the first place, it is the consumption not of the machine workers merely, but of the whole community that supplies the market which makes the use of the factory methods possible. And in the second place, it is the inventive genius developed by an advancing civilization, together with the capital invested in the production of machinery to supply the need thus created, that furnishes the increased product. Clearly therefore, if only the wages of those laborers were increased who used the improved instruments the market for the machine-made products would be too small to enable factory methods to be profitably employed. Thus a system which would give all the increased product resulting from improved instruments to the particular laborers who use those instruments would not only be highly unjust, but would defeat itself and arrest the industrial progress of society.

If we examine the case of machine-using and non-machine using laborers in the light of the law of wages and prices heretofore presented, it will be apparent that the mere fact that the laborer produces more, has practically nothing to do with what he shall receive, because it has nothing to do with the cost of his living. The amount he produces by a day's work depends far more upon the kind of tools he uses than upon his personal quality. A twelve-year-old child in a New England factory can spin more yarn than a hundred of the most expert spinners that ever lived could produce with a spinning wheel. It is the price of the product, and not the price of the labor, that is determined by the quantity the laborer produces in a day. The cost of his living being the same if he produces twice as much, the cost of production and hence the price will be proportionately reduced. Thus any improvement of productive instruments which enables the laborer to produce more, his cost of living being the same, will show itself not in a rise of his wages, but in a fall of the price of the commodities he produces.

On the other hand, the price of hand-made commodities rises in proportion as the laborers' wages increase. It thus appears that wages are determined by conditions which affect the character and cost of the laborer, and not by those which influence the quantity and cost of the product. When the standard and cost of living of the compositor, bricklayer, painter, etc., increase, the community has to pay more for the products of their labor, because there is not much improvement in the tools they use ; whereas the product of the factory worker is so much increased that, although his wages rise as much as those of other laborers, the cost of production is greatly diminished. That is why the price of all hand-made products tends to rise while that of machine or factory-made products constantly tends to fall. It is because the wages of the hand-workers have increased in a greater proportion than their product that those of machine workers have increased less proportionately to their product. By this means the disadvantage of inferior and the advantage of superior instruments is distributed uniformly to each person in the community to the extent that he is a consumer. Thus the two prime movements of industrial progress, the rise of wages and the fall of prices, benefit laborers in all occupations and conditions directly as their wealth-consuming capacity increases and social character rises.

It will be observed that, from this point of view, the case of the workman to whom Mr. Giffen referred as not getting "a reward at all in proportion to the increase of production," appears entirely different. What to him appeared to be a necessary injustice is in reality the évidence of the supreme equity of economic law. The increased product being mainly due to the use of capital and improved tools, which has been made possible through the use of increased consumption and higher social life of the general community, it is to the community in general, and not to particular laborers who happen to use those tools, that the increased product in equity *should* go, and by economic law *does* go. The important fact that cannot be too much emphasized here is, that wages are paid for the economic cost, and hence for the social quality of the laborer. It is therefore what the laborer *is* rather than what he *does* that determines his wages, and this is true without regard to the nature of his occupation or the quality of his tools.

2. This brings us to the second proposition, that profits tend to absorb a diminishing proportion of the consumable wealth produced. In view of what has already been said, a discussion of this proposition might be properly deemed unnecessary. And were it not that one of our most trusted statistical authorities has apparently affirmed the opposite, I should so regard it. In the report of the Massachusetts Bureau of Statistics of Labor for 1885 the data for nine industries are given, which show that the percentage of the net product paid as wages fell from $59\frac{6}{10}$ per cent. in 1850 to $48\frac{2}{10}$ per cent. in 1880, and, after commenting upon the peculiarities of each industry, the report (p. 191) says :

"An examination of these two tables would, we think, lead to the conclusion that, although in every case money wages have considerably increased, yet in certain industries in which the principles of the factory system (*i.e.*, the subdivision of labor, co-ordination of processes, and the application of a series of mutually dependent and practically automatic machines) have been most effective, such, for instance, as in the cotton and woollen industries, the relative share of net product gained by the workmen tends to decrease. That is to say, in these industries perfection of machines and processes constantly tend to create a larger product with less capital, and the ratio of increase in productive capacity tends to outrun the ratio of increase in wages, so that of this larger product labor obtains a less relative share."

They then take from the United States Census the same data for all industries in the country, and find that 51 per cent. of this net product was paid in wages in 1850 and only $48\frac{1}{10}$ per cent. in 1880, and say : " It appears that when the field is broadened so as to include the entire manufacturing industries of the country, labor's share of the net product has declined from 51 per cent. to $48\frac{1}{10}$ per cent."

In view of such emphatic statements apparently sustained by facts from such a reliable source, it can hardly be a matter of surprise that it is generally believed that wages obtain a constantly diminishing and profit gains an increasing proportion of the wealth produced. It is important, therefore, even at the risk of being a little tedious, to examine the process by which this conclusion is reached. Nor will this be very difficult, since both the data and the method of treatment are amply stated. The method of procedure is to divide the product into gross and net value, the former being the value of the aggregate product, and the latter that of the product less the cost of the raw material. This is regarded as representing the net value created by the joint operation of the labor and capital employed in the enterprise.[1] If a diminishing proportion of this net product is paid as wages, it is concluded that an increasing proportion of it must go to

---

[1] "Net product, or value of product remaining after deducting value of raw materials of manufacture, represents the direct result of the productive forces in the given industry ; or, in other words, it represents the value created over and above the value of raw materials by the effective operation of labor and capital united."—Report of Bureau of Statistics of Labor, p. 190.

profits.[1] This method of treating the subject is defective in two
respects : (1) in regarding the ratio of the total wages to the
net product (product less raw material) as indicating the economic
condition of the laborer ; (2) in assuming that a diminution in
the ratio of the total wages to this net product necessarily implies
a proportional increase of profit.

(1) That it is a mistake to treat the ratio of the aggregate
wages to the value of product as indicating the economic condition of the laborer, is shown by the fact that this ratio may
increase and the laborer grow poorer, and it may diminish while
the laborer's condition improves. Take, for example, the hand-
loom weaver and the factory laborer. After deducting the raw
material, nearly all the value of the product of the hand-loom
weaver went to wages ; while, according to the bureau's figures,
only about 48 per cent. of the product now goes to wages, yet no
one would pretend that the hand-loom weavers were in a better
economic condition than are the factory operatives to-day.
Whether the amount paid for labor is one million or one thousand millions of dollars in no way affects the laborer's condition,
except as it gives a larger amount to each laborer. The same is
true of the proportion. Whether the 80 or 90 per cent. of the
product received by the hand-weaver gave him more actually or
relatively to the product than 50 per cent. will to-day, depends
entirely upon whether it is paid to a relatively larger or smaller
number of laborers. If the aggregate amount paid in wages
relatively to the product were doubled, and either the number of
laborers to whom it was paid or the time expended in producing
it with the same laborers was more than doubled, instead of indicating an improvement in the laborer's condition, it would show
a deterioration.

Suppose for example, that under hand labor, 80 cents out of
each dollar's worth of product go to labor, and are paid to 20
laborers, the ratio of wages per laborer to the value of the
product will be as 4 cents to the dollar ; whereas, if, under the
factory system, only 50 cents out of every dollar's worth of
product goes to labor, if it is all paid to five laborers, the ratio
of wages per laborer to the value of the product would be as 10
cents to the dollar. Thus every laborer would receive relatively

[1] *Ibid.*, p. 90.

to the product created two and a half times as much with the 50 per cent. under factory production as with the 80 per cent. under hand labor. Now this is precisely what has occurred in the development of factory methods of production. Clearly therefore, it is not the proportion between the aggregate wages and the product, but the proportion between the amount paid to each laborer and the product that indicates his economic condition. In other words, it is the rate and not the aggregate amount of wages that is the true basis of comparison, because it is the rate of wages only that affects the laborer's economic status, either actually or relatively.

(2) The assumption that a diminution in the ratio of aggregate wages to the so-called net product necessarily implies a proportional increase of profits is also a mistake. The fact that 51 per cent. of the net product was paid in wages in 1850 and only $48\frac{1}{10}$ was so paid in 1880, does not prove that the percentage of the product going to profit has increased ; on the contrary, this might occur and profit be greatly reduced or annihilated altogether. All this fact reveals is that in 1880 the total amount paid in wages represented $2\frac{9}{10}$ per cent. less of the value of the product, after deducting value of raw material, than it did in 1850 ; but this does not show that more of the remaining $51\frac{9}{10}$ per cent. of the product went to profit. Until that remaining portion is accounted for, there can be no more warrant for saying that it went to profit than that it went to the moon. The only condition under which the amount of one item can be properly inferred from that of another is when the two represent the whole, or when the amount they do not represent is a known fixed quantity. Since all the product, less raw material, is not divided between wages and profit, the inference that the ratio of profit to net product increases because that of wages is diminished can only be valid when all the other items are definitely ascertained. That this has not been done in the present instance is shown by the following statement : " The value of net product forms, as we have said, a fund divisible into interest on capital, interest on loans, insurance, freights, rents, commissions, wages, and profits. Now if the relative share paid in labor in the form of wages is decreased, it is, of course, obvious that the share remaining for the other purposes mentioned is increased. If capital is also

relatively decreased, then it is fair to suppose that the share chargeable to interest is also diminished. It is well known that the relative cost of freights and insurance has decreased." [1]

It will be observed that the above not only fails to definitely explain the relative amount of the other items in the cost of production and thereby obtain the proportion going to profit, but it omits some items altogether. In the first place, it only accounts for a portion of the amount which is paid for service, no account being taken of salaries of managers and other overseers, and agents, which are a part of the payment to labor, and are included in the cost of production as much as the day-wages of the laborers in the shop. In the next place it omits entirely the depreciation of capital, which is also a necessary item in the cost of production. The items thus unaccounted for necessarily go to swell the undivided surplus which is put down as profit. By this means it may be made to appear that a large profit exists, when in truth there has been a dead loss, and when a profit does actually exist this method of investigation will invariably make it appear very much larger, sometimes more than double what it really is. [2] Both these items of cost affect the result in two ways. In the first place, other things being the same, they both reduce the undivided surplus going to profit to the full extent of their amount. In the next place, they both absorb an increasing proportion of the net product in proportion as factory methods of production are increased.

It is impossible to state the exact proportion of the net product paid in salaries in the different periods, because that item has been entirely omitted by all industrial statistics until the Massachusetts Census for 1885. According to this report, the total amount paid in salaries in that State in 1885 was $10,846,367, which was equal to $3\frac{80}{100}$ per cent. of the value of the net product. In order correctly to understand this data, however, it must be observed that this amount was all paid by less than 10 per cent. of the establishments. That is to say, out of the 23,431 manufacturing establishments only 2,144 paid salaries, and of these 949 were corporations. The 949 corporations own an aggregate capital of $300,649,758, or an average of $316,806 each, while the

[1] Report of the Bureau of Statistics of Labor, Mass. (1885), pp. 190, 191.

[2] A case of this kind appears in the 20th vol. of the Census, 1880, pp. 111, 112.

22,482 private concerns have an aggregate capital of only $199,-944,619, or an average of $8,893. In other words, the 949 corporations, which only represent $4\frac{5}{100}$ per cent. of the establishments, own $60\frac{6}{100}$ per cent. of the capital, use $36\frac{47}{100}$ per cent. of raw material, produce $35\frac{20}{100}$ per cent. of the finished product, employ $40\frac{54}{100}$ per cent. of the laborers, and pay $36\frac{68}{100}$ per cent. of the total wages. Thus it is quite clear that the salaries are nearly all paid by the large concerns, over 90 per cent. of the smaller ones not paying any salaries at all.

In 1850 the average amount of capital invested per manufacturing establishment for the whole country was $4,334, or only about half the amount that is invested in the average establishments in Massachusetts to-day which pay no salaries. In 1880 the capital invested in the average establishment was $10,991. Thus, while it is impossible from these data to ascertain the exact ratio of increase, it is obvious that the amount paid in salaries becomes an increasing proportion as the concentration of capital into large establishments increases. Since the $3\frac{80}{100}$ per cent. of the net product paid in salaries in Massachusetts (which may be taken as representative of the whole country, though it is probably a fraction higher) is practically all paid by concerns having a capital of $250,000 or upwards, it is quite safe to assume that not more than one fourth as much was paid in 1850, when the average amount of capital per establishment was only $4,334. To estimate this item as representing one per cent. of the net product in 1850, will therefore be quite liberal. Of the remaining $2\frac{80}{100}$ per cent. which this item has increased since 1850, $1\frac{1}{2}$ per cent. may safely be assigned to the period from 1850 to 1880, which alone accounts for more than one half of the apparent relative decrease in wages.

The other omitted item, the depreciation of capital, affects the result in a still greater degree. This also has hitherto been entirely overlooked in all our industrial statistics, but taking twenty corporations together in four different industries for eight years successively, I find the general depreciation of plant, machinery, buildings, etc., together with transient repairs, equals about six per cent. on the capital invested. Nor does this represent all the depreciation of capital. Every improvement in machinery which makes a considerable saving in the cost of

18

production, and reduces the selling price of the commodity, throws out of use a large amount of machinery that was previously producing under conditions which barely repaid the cost. It is a common thing for millions of dollars' worth of capital to be almost annihilated at a single stroke in this way. In the iron industry it is a frequent experience that the machinery of whole factories, which, so far as its normal productive capacity is concerned, is in excellent condition, is reduced to the value of old iron by the introduction of superior machinery in a competing factory. The percentage of depreciation from this cause increases just in proportion as new methods of production are introduced. While there are no accurate statistics of this kind of depreciation, it may safely be assumed to equal one sixth of the normal depreciation, making the depreciation of capital from all sources fully 7 per cent. Since the ratio of capital invested to the value of the net product in 1850 was as $1.15 to $1, the depreciation of capital would represent 8 per cent. of the net product. In 1880 the ratio of capital invested to the value of the net product had reached .41 to $1. Consequently, the depreciation represented $9\frac{8}{100}$ per cent. of the net product, an increase of $1\frac{8}{100}$ per cent. Thus, on a very moderate estimate, the relative increase of the two items omitted in the Census returns more than offsets the seeming proportional decrease in wages. Consequently, assuming other items of cost to have remained the same, instead of wages having decreased $2\frac{9}{100}$ per cent. relatively to the net product from 1850 to 1880, they have actually increased $\frac{4}{100}$ of 1 per cent.

If we take the data down to 1885, which the ample statistics for Massachusetts now enable us to do, the evidence that an increasing percentage of the net product goes for service becomes more conclusive. According to these, in 23,431 establishments, with a capital of $500,594,377, producing $574,634,269 worth of product, the amount paid in wages equalled about $51\frac{16}{100}$ per cent. of the value of the product, less the value of raw material. The ratio of capital invested per dollar of net product was $1.75 to $1. The depreciation of capital represented $12\frac{28}{100}$ per cent. and salaries $3\frac{8}{100}$ per cent. Taking the period from 1850 to 1885, and putting salaries with wages—where they properly belong, for they are the payment for service precisely the same as wages, the only difference being that one is estimated by the year and the other by the day or week,—the case stands as follows :

	Per cent. of net product paid for service.			Ratio of capital to $1 net product.	Per cent. of depreciation in net product.
	Wages.	Salaries.	Total.		
1850..........	51.	1.	52.	$1.15 to $1	8.
1880..........	48.1	2.5	50.6	$1.41 to $1	9.8
1885..........	51.7	3.8	55.5	$1.75 to $1	12.2

Since the whole amount taken in depreciation is consumed in maintaining the working efficiency of the plant, it not only does not go to the capitalist, but it reduces the amount of net product divisible among all classes. Thus it will be seen that, in 1850, after deducting the proportion paid in wages and salaries, 40 per cent. remained for all the other costs and profit. After making similar deductions in 1880, only $39\frac{6}{10}$ per cent. remained for the other items of cost and profit, and in 1885 only $32\frac{3}{10}$ per cent. remained for profits and other costs. It is obvious, therefore, that if the proportion of the net product paid in rent, taxes, insurance, commissions, freights, etc., remained the same, the proportion going to profits must necessarily have decreased, though its aggregate amount may have increased. ·

A close examination of the facts would undoubtedly show, as the bureau suggests, that the relative costs of freights and perhaps insurance have slightly diminished. It must be remembered, however, that all freight charges are made on the basis of quantity, as so much per ton. If estimated on the value of the product the result would be very different. For example, the product per operative in the cotton industry measured in pounds increased 145 per cent. from 1830 to 1880, but measured in value it only increased a little over 60 per cent. Thus a reduction of 50 per cent. in the cost of transportation per quantity would not show any reduction per dollar of value. Assuming that profits in 1850 were equal to 10 per cent. of the net product, and that the proportion of the net product paid for transportation has since decreased 2 per cent., and that paid in taxes, rents, commissions, etc., has remained the same—though Carroll D. Wright thinks they have actually increased,—the aliquot parts of the

net product going to service and profit in 1850 and 1885 would
be as follows :

	Service.	Other costs.	Depreciation.	Profit.	Total.
1850...........	52.	30	8.	10.	100
1885...........	55.5	28	12.2	4.3	100

It thus appears that, although the proportion of the net product
paid for service has only increased about 4 per cent. and that
paid in wages less than 1 per cent., the proportion going to profit
has diminished $5\frac{7}{10}$ per cent.   It should also be observed in this
connection that the value of raw material, which represents 57
per cent. of the total value of the product, and also that nearly
all the other costs, representing 28 per cent. of the net product,
are very largely made up of wages.   Indeed, if we take the
finished product and trace the various items of its costs back to
the crude raw material, we shall find that its value is nearly all
finally resolved into the amount paid for service.   The reason
the proportion paid for labor in the last stages of manufacture
appears to represent so small a percentage of the total value is
(1) because, in the prior stages of its development, so much of
the value has been previously paid for in wages ; (2) because, in
the last stages, the greatest amount of capital per dollar of product is employed, and consequently a greater proportion of the
product created in that stage goes to depreciation of plant, all of
which must of necessity be eliminated before any scientific comparison of the proportional shares going to wages and profit in
any given industry can be made.

Clearly therefore, in order to ascertain whether or not the
laborer is obtaining an increasing or a diminishing proportion of
the consumable wealth produced, we must compare the value of
what goes to labor, *not in the aggregate but per laborer*, with the
value of the product after deducting the cost of raw material,
depreciation of plant, and all other fixed costs incident to the
increased production.   From this method of examining the case
it will appear that, in each given stage of the productive process,
as the concentration of capital and the use of im roved methods
of production are employed, the laborer receives a constantly
increasing proportion of an increasing product.

3. We now come to the question of the actual ratio of wages to

profits in modern industry. It is assumed by socialistic writers, as already shown in the case of Marx, that under the present industrial system profits are not only increasing actually and relatively to the product, but that they approximately equal wages.[1] Since this is wholly a question of fact and is one of the chief reasons urged for revolutionizing the existing industrial system, it may be well to compare this claim with the facts in the case. The question of profits and wages is one which cannot always be settled by public statistics because they are seldom taken in such a way as to furnish the correct data upon both these points. As already intimated the service item is nearly always incomplete and profits are seldom given. The Massachusetts Labor Bureau, which has ever been the best source of reliable industrial data in this country, made an extensive investigation of the subject of profits and earnings for 1875[2] and 1880, the result of which was published in their report for 1883. The results of this investigation, which covered 14,352 establishments in 80 industries, show that the ratio of wages[3] to profits in 1875 was as $2\frac{45}{100}$ to 1, and as $3\frac{11}{100}$ to 1 in 1880.

In 1889 I made extensive investigations on the same points, but instead of taking a large number of industries for a given year I took a limited number of large industries for a number of years together. It will readily be seen that the normal ratio of wages to profits will be much more accurately indicated by taking a few

[1] "There is left the sum of £3 10s. 0d., which is the variable capital advanced; and we see that a new value of £3 10s. 0d + £3 11s. 0d. has been produced in its place. Therefore $\frac{s.}{v.}$, $\frac{£3\ 11s.\ 0d.}{£3\ 10s.\ 0d.}$, giving a rate of surplus value of more than one hundred per cent. The laborer employs more than one half of his working day in producing the surplus value."—Marx, "Capital," p. 203. "Now, gentlemen, if you compare the working time you pay for, you will find that they are to one another, as half a day is to half a day; this gives a rate of one hundred per cent., and a very pretty percentage it is."—*Ibid.*, p. 211. "But the fact is —and on that we lay stress—that the workers receive only about half of what they produce."—Gronlund, "Modern Socialism," p. 23.

[2] These are exclusive of Boston. I have omitted Boston because for some unexplained reason the net product in Boston fell about 75 per cent. Such a change must be the result of some abnormal occurrence perhaps in a few industries. Although it would greatly reduce the ratio of profits to wages in 1880, rather than use doubtful results, I prefer to exclude the whole of Boston data.

[3] Exclusive of salaries.

representative concerns for a considerable number of years together, than by a very much larger number of concerns for a single year. For instance, the complete facts for ten large corporations for ten years together will much more accurately show the normal ratio of wages to profits in that industry than would the facts, equally complete, for all the concerns in the country for any given date. This investigation shows that the ratio of wages to profits in thirteen leading industries for a number of years together,[1] to be as 4.20 to 1. Taking the basis adopted by the Massachusetts Bureau for 1880, the relative movement of profit and wages from 1850 to 1885 has been as follows :

ALL MANUFACTURING INDUSTRIES FOR THE UNITED STATES.

Value of aggregate product.	Percentage of raw material and fixed costs in total product.	Percentage of wages in total product.	Percentage of profits in total product.	Average[2] yearly wages.	Ratio of wages to profits.
1850—$1,019,106,616 . .	67.61	23.23	9.16	$247.37	2.53[3] to 1
1860— 1,885,861,676 . .	67.92	20.09	11.99	288.94	1.67 to 1
1870— 4,232,325,442 . .	71.79	18.34	9.87	376.59	1.85 to 1
1880— 5,369,579,191 . .	76.37	17.67	5.96	346.91	2.96 to 1

ALL MANUFACTURED INDUSTRIES FOR MASSACHUSETTS.[4]

1875—$456,400,458 . . .	62.57	27.06	10.37	$445.00	2.60[5] to 1
1880— 631,135,284 . . .	72.79	21.75	5.46	364.00	3.98 to 1
1885— 674,634,269 . . .	70.88	23.45	5.67	388.62	4.13 to 1
1888—				402.45	

THIRTEEN LEADING INDUSTRIES FOR 8 YEARS TOGETHER TO 1889.

1889—$112,393,804.98 .	67.98	25.93	6.09	——	4.20 to 1

[1] Ten of these were for eight years in succession, two for ten years, and one only for four years.

[2] It should be remembered that these figures do not represent the wages of men, but the average wages of men, women, and children all taken together. Since in manufacturing industries there is generally one worker besides the head of the family, and sometimes more, these wages only represent about half the income of the average family in these industries.

[3] This column is exclusive of salaries.

[4] Exclusive of Boston. I have omitted Boston because for some unexplained reason profits fell from an aggregate of $27,640,680 in 1875 to $7,162,768 in 1880. Such a change must be the result of some abnormal occurrence perhaps in a few industries. Although it would greatly reduce the ratio of profits to wages in 1880, rather than risk doubtful results I prefer to exclude the whole of Boston data for 1885.   [5] This includes salaries.

It will be seen from these facts, which represent the greatest body of statistical data ever collected upon the subject,[1] that the industrial tendency during the last thirty years has been steadily towards a greater concentration of capital and economy in productive power, resulting in an actual increase in wages both relatively to the product and per laborer employed, and also a relative proportional decrease of profit as compared with wages.

[1] The figures for the United States are taken from the Census of 1880 and those for Massachusetts are taken from the industrial census of that State, representing for 1880 14,352 establishments in 80 industries with an aggregate capital of $271,056,051 ; for 1885, 23,431 establishments in 83 industries, with an aggregate capital of $500,594,377.

PART IV.

THE PRINCIPLES OF PRACTICAL STATESMAN-
SHIP; OR, APPLIED SOCIAL ECONOMICS.

CHAPTER I.

LAISSEZ FAIRE AS A GUIDING PRINCIPLE IN PUBLIC POLICY.

SECTION I.—*A Protest Against Paternalism.*

ALTHOUGH *laissez faire* has never been the accepted rule of public policy in any country, the fact that for more than a century it has been taught by leading economists as the guiding principle of industrial statesmanship entitles it to prominent consideration. It should be remembered in the first place that the idea of *laissez faire* as applied to industrial statesmanship does not represent an inductively established principle in society; that is to say, it is not a logical conclusion drawn from an extensive study of industrial phenomena. On the contrary it came into existence as a watchword to express a protest against the high-handed paternalism of the feudal and mercantile systems; and by the force of habitual. repetition, sustained by a pardonable bias against a land-owning class, it was subsequently elevated to the position of an economic principle.

During the Middle Ages government was not only essentially paternal, but it was exclusively in the hands of the land-owning class. The interest class being chiefly local, industrial policy was naturally restrictive in character. Accordingly, in the earliest stages of manufacture and the growth of the free towns, industry was hemmed in by innumerable arbitrary regulations. Scarcely any occupation could be engaged in without paying tallage or tribute to the baron. And with the growth of the Free Cities and the decline of baronial power this privilege of exacting tribute for the right to engage in an industry was assumed by the guilds, and finally took the form of charters, by which the government became the exactor of booty. In proportion as manufacture and commerce increased, the evil effects of this policy became more and more inimical to public welfare, and made a new industrial policy necessary. Nor is it surprising that the new policy should be the very opposite of the old one. The remedy for the evil effects of too much government interference was naturally sought in a policy of no government interference.

By the last half of the seventeenth century this anti-paternal feeling had become very strong, and was finally voiced by a prominent French merchant, who, when asked by Colbert, "What can we do to aid you?" promptly answered, "*Laissez faire*"—Let us alone. This expression so completely represented the feelings of the mercantile class that it became the watchword for a new policy, and by the middle of the next century was made the basis of an economic theory by Quesnay and the Physiocrats, whose policy was concisely expressed as "Laissez faire et laissez passer"—Let us alone and keep the ways free. In the last quarter of the eighteenth century this doctrine was revised and recast in England by Adam Smith. In many important respects the great Scotchman improved upon the doctrines of the French Physiocrats, especially in bringing out the economic importance of manufacture and commerce. But in view of the fact that the public policy of England was still largely determined by the landed aristocracy, who were traditionally hostile to the interests of the manufacturing and trading classes, Adam Smith naturally adhered to the doctrine of *no government interference*. Since his time the idea of *laissez faire* has been generally presented as representing a fundamental principle upon which the industrial policy of all nations should be based, any departure from this rule being justified only in special emergencies.

In the next place it should be observed that the doctrine of *laissez faire* has not been verified by subsequent experience; consequently, instead of being more implicitly accepted, its economic validity is denied just in proportion as the scientific treatment of the subject increases. As an axiom in public policy *laissez faire* is rejected by the inductive economists of the present generation with almost as much uniformity as it was accepted by the deductive economists of the previous half century. Therefore, the claim that the theory of *laissez faire* represents a universal principle in nature and society, and is entitled to the same unquestioning acceptance in economics that is accorded to the principle of gravitation in physics, is wholly unwarranted.

SECTION II.—*Laissez Faire Essentially Unscientific.*

Considered as a fundamental principle in statesmanship, *laissez faire* is essentially unscientific. It is necessarily negative, while statesmanship is positive. All government, order, and progress imply affirmative action, and therefore are the opposite of *laissez faire*. Science is essentially aggressive; it implies the active policy of investigating, knowing, and controlling things. Every improvement in the arts and sciences, every labor-saving appliance, is the result of man's interference with nature, of subjecting natural forces to human purposes. By studying the laws of chemistry, electricity, and mechanics, we know that under certain conditions heat, light, and force are developed. And instead of adopting the rule of *laissez faire*, and waiting till nature produces the desired result, we have learned to bring the particular forces together in just such relations as will produce that result much quicker. Consequently, we make steam produce our wealth, electricity do our errands, and natural forces serve us in every phase of life.

The same is true in the animal and vegetable world. Our choicest flowers and vegetables are not the result of unaided natural selection, but of artificial cultivation ; that is to say, of the scientific application of the law of development. We have studied the conditions under which certain kinds of fruit, flowers, and vegetables develop their best specimens, and where nature fails to supply these conditions they are substituted by man. Our fast horses and finest breeds of cattle and sheep have all been produced in the same way. What is true in chemistry, mechanics, botany, and biology is equally true in sociology.

Since affirmative statesmanship is necessary to government, and government is necessary to civilization, it is a contradiction in terms to speak of *laissez faire* as the basis of statesmanship. The science of government is not the knowledge of what not to do, but it is the knowledge of what to do and how and when to do it. To know *what to do* implies the knowledge of what *not to do*, but to know what *not* to do does not imply the knowledge of

what to do. So long as government exists it must have a function
—a sphere of action. Scientific statesmanship implies a knowledge of the principle by which that action should be directed.
Because the history of state interference with industry is the
history of mistakes, it is commonly assumed that the only way to
avoid mistakes of the past is to do nothing in the present. It
would be just as correct to say that because all mistakes are the
result of affirmative action, inaction is the only means of avoiding
error, the logic of which would involve the destruction of the
human race. We cannot choose between doing and not doing,
but only between doing wisely and unwisely. The doctrine of
laissez faire, therefore, has no place in the science of statesmanship or the art of government.

This theory derives its chief plausibility from a seeming universality in its postulates, which are : (1) That self-interest is a
universal principle in human nature. (2) That each individual
knows his own interest best, and in the absence of arbitrary restrictions is sure to follow it. (3) That free competition always
develops the highest possibilities by enabling each to do that for
which he is best fitted, and thereby most surely advances the
welfare of all.

The proposition that self-interest is a universal principle in
human nature is undoubtedly correct ; but there is nothing in
experience or logic to warrant the assumption that the other
two follow from it. That whatever is for the best interest of
each promotes the welfare of all is indisputable, but that each
individual always knows what is best for his own interest, and in
the absence of arbitrary restrictions is sure to follow it, is by no
means certain.

Before each can know how to promote his own best interest he
must know what his best interest is, which is precisely what the
great bulk of the human race do not know. This knowledge can
only be acquired by a more or less intelligent generalization from
experience. Whatever tends to improve man's condition materially,
socially, and morally, and increase the advantages of social life,
promotes his best interests. To assume that every one knows
what is best for himself is as unphilosophic as to assume that the
child knows best what will promote its own welfare. Although
many parents are ignorant, and often injure when they think to

help the child, the fact remains that the successful rearing of children chiefly depends upon the number of instances in which the wisdom of the parent, developed by experience, prevails over the ignorance of the child. Indeed the race would die out if the experience of parents were not transformed into authority over the child.

What is true of the child in this respect is still true to a very great extent, of a vast majority of the human race. Take for instance the people of Central Africa. The principle of self-interest is as universal there as in any part of the world. But no one would seriously claim that the average individual in that dark continent knows what is best for his own interest. On the contrary, the most advanced scientists, philanthropists, philosophers, and statesmen agree that the best interests of the inhabitants of Africa can only be promoted by the interference of more advanced and civilized nations. This same lack of knowledge of what is best for one's own interest, which is simply ignorance of the laws of social development, is still painfully apparent, not merely in every country, but, more or less in every class in the most advanced countries. Those familiar with the laws of sanitation and hygiene know that cleanliness, fresh air, good drainage, and wholesome food are of vital importance to physical health, and therefore are of the highest interest to the laborer. But the experience of health authorities shows that only with the utmost difficulty can the laboring classes, and particularly the poorer and more ignorant portion, be induced to pay any attention to these conditions.

So too the employing classes, while more enlightened upon questions of science, literature, and art, exhibit scarcely less ignorance in regard to their economic interests. Take, for instance, their attitude towards the social condition of the laborer. They have assumed and have acted almost uniformly upon the assumption that high wages are inimical to their own interests, and consequently that to resist the rise of wages and social improvement of the laboring classes is to promote their own prosperity ; whereas, had they known their true economic relation to the laborer, they would have seen that every limitation of his social and material progress reacts injuriously upon the permanence and extent of their own prosperity. The reason for their mistaken attitude is precisely the same as that which governs the laborer when he endeavors to improve his condition by using dynamite, and when he resists the introduction of improved machinery, or evades the instructions of the Board of Health, —namely, ignorance of what is for his own best interest. It is therefore fallacious to assume that every individual knows his own interest best, and in the absence of arbitrary restrictions is sure to follow it.

The idea that free competition always develops the highest possibilities by enabling each to do that for which he is best fitted, is equally misleading. The popular idea of free competition is that it means an unconditional struggle for existence among individual units, and that is the sense in which the term is usually employed by economists. This view is commonly regarded as the application of the doctrine of natural selection to society ; and hence the policy of *laissez faire* is claimed to be based upon the doctrine of evolution. This is a mistaken conception both of the doctrine of evolution and of the nature and function of competition, as will appear from the following considerations.

The doctrine ·of evolution is simply a theory of growth as distinguished from that of special providence. It teaches that whatever may have been the origin of things, progress towards higher forms of existence in all classes of phenomena takes place in accordance with a law of cause and effect, and that higher and more complex types of formation and the existence of new functions, appear only under conditions favorable to their development. In other words, *opportunity* for actualizing the potential qualities of higher types is indispensable to progress. There is nothing in this doctrine to warrant the assumption that such opportunity can always, or even generally be best secured by the new type for itself, through a mere unrestrained struggle for existence. On the contrary, the whole implication is that existing types must prepare the way and therefore create a favorable opportunity for the birth and growth of the higher type. Much of the error in this connection is due to a mistaken use of the phrases "nature" and "natural law." We commonly employ the term nature as if it represented only unconscious cosmic forces as distinguished from conscious human forces. And thus we speak of the products of cosmic forces as natural and the products of human device as artificial, just as if human arrangements were necessarily unnatural.

The term "natural" applies no more to cosmic than to human forces. The consciousness and intelligence of man are as natural as the unconsciousness of gravitation or of inorganic substances. The term "natural" simply means that which is necessary to or inherent in the constitution of things. It is natural that man should have blood, nerves, and brain, because without these he would not be man, but it is equally natural that stones should not have them, because in that case they would not be stones. So with natural law ; a law is not natural or unnatural because it relates to conscious or unconscious objects, but solely because it relates to the nature and inherent constitution of things. It is just as much in accordance with natural law that under certain conditions electricity destroys our house, as it is that under other conditions it should light our streets. Natural law is simply the order in which phenomena necessarily occur under given conditions. Man cannot impose artificial laws ; he can only artificially change the relations of objects so that through the operation of cause and effect desired phenomena may occur sooner, more frequently and more continuously than they otherwise would. It is in this way, and in this way only, that man is ever able to aid progress.

Therefore, in considering whether *laissez faire* or human intervention is to be preferred, the question is not whether one is more natural than the other, because in any case the result will be natural, but it is whether the desired end can be more surely obtained by intervention than by the unaided operation of unconscious forces. And this will depend entirely upon whether those who manipulate the conditions understand the laws of the phenomena with which they are endeavoring to deal, and therefore can correctly predicate the result. Ignorant or unscientific interference may be worse than *laissez faire.* But this by no means implies that *laissez faire* is superior to scientific regulation.

Another expression which is misleadingly employed is " natural selection." Here again the term natural is used as if all selection were unnatural that is not blind and unconscious. There are no natural and unnatural selections ; there are wise and unwise

19

selections, and there are conscious and unconscious selections. It is as natural that ignorance will make poor selections as that intelligence will make good ones. Because progress in the physical world has taken place mainly by unconscious selection, it is assumed that progress in society will necessarily be more rapid and continuous under a régime of *laissez faire*.

If it were true that in physical phenomena an unconditioned struggle of units always produces the highest types and the greatest progress, it would not follow that the same should be true in society. But it is by no means clear that this is true even in the physical world. It is of course true that in the development of the earth and other physical formations where surviving forms were determined by the action and reaction of unconscious physical forces, those forms only were able to survive which could withstand the struggle. But it is scarcely less certain that many higher forms may have been destroyed during early stages of their development, which, had they been able to reach maturity, would have been better able to withstand opposing forces than those which did survive.

It is highly probable that by this means millions of potentially higher forms were destroyed in their infancy by mature and lower types of formation. Thus under a régime of pure *laissez faire*—the action and reaction of blind physical forces—progress *may have been* greatly retarded, while inferior types for ages perpetuated their existence by preventing the development of superior types. Indeed, this is what we see taking place in every domain where *laissez faire* prevails, and development is left to an unconditioned struggle for existence among individual units.

In the sphere of vegetation for instance, it is now a matter of scientific knowledge that the choicest trees and most highly developed plants of any species may be stunted and even destroyed by the presence of weeds and brush that had prior existence. This is a fact that every scientific farmer and horticulturist understands. As an illustration of the law of natural selection and the survival of the fittest, we are pointed to wild animals, say a drove of wild horses. It is assumed that those which survive are always best and that those which were killed off were inferior, from the mere fact that the former lived and the latter died. This conclusion, however, does not necessarily follow from these facts. Suppose, for example, a foal, which possessed all the possibilities of being a faster or tougher horse than any in the herd, was kicked in the ribs by one of the inferior though mature horses and fatally injured. It is quite clear that in that case the inferior type would prevent the development of the superior. And this is what is constantly taking place wherever an unrestrained struggle for existence prevails, as all experienced horse-breeders know. By the study of appropriate mating and the protection of the superior young against the violence of the inferior old, speed, strength, and other desired qualities of the horse have been developed to a degree never before known. Thus under scientific selection, the higher possibilities of the horse have been developed incomparably faster than they ever were under natural selection. This is true in every sphere of phenomena to which human knowledge can be applied. In fact, progress everywhere increases directly, as scientific selection can supersede natural selection—in proportion as knowledge of relations can be substituted for blind experimentation. Were this otherwise, science and civilization would be no better than ignorance and barbarism. Clearly therefore *laissez faire* is not the surest way to promote the survival of the fittest even in the physical world.

In society this is still more uniformly true by virtue of a different character in the phenomena. One of the most marked distinctions between physical and social phenomena is the manner in which existing units influence the environment of future units. In the lower forms of life the opposition of the inferior mature to the superior immature (the established old to the unestablished new) is limited to a direct struggle between contending units. Consequently, the potentially superior has always a limited chance (say one in a million) of surviving, if only by evading the deadly opposition of an established type. In society this is different, and the chance of the new to escape the repressive power of the old is more difficult. Man, having acquired the power of consciously adapting means to an end, can not only resist the undeveloped new with the advantage of prior possession and mature development, but he also has the power of manipulating the environment of the subsequent generation so as to make the development of the superior impossible.

One of the prime conditions of human society is consciously regulated order, and this implies government. Government necessarily dominates the social environment of the individual. Through social and political institutions, therefore, the opportunities for enabling the fittest to survive will necessarily be aided or repressed according to the notions entertained by those who determine the policy of government. By this means, through mere accident of priority, the inferior man can so regulate the conditions of existence for subsequent generations that the development of the potentially superior shall be impossible, and thus secure the survival of the unfittest instead of the fittest.

The history of society is replete with evidences of this fact. Indeed every arrest of social progress is due to the fact that the inferior who obtained possession of authority have so dominated the environment as to cut off opportunity for the development of others, who with favorable opportunities would have been superior to themselves. Under such conditions not only does the unfit survive, but its influence tends to perpetuate the reign of the less fit in two ways. 1. By stifling the germs of superiority in humble classes, and thus cutting off the possibility of its development and actualization. 2. By stereotyping the character of the successful in giving it a monopoly of power and position. This is what took place in ancient Egypt, Greece, and Rome, and in mediæval Europe, where both religious and civil authority was exercised to cut off all opportunity for the development of character in those classes of the community not recognized as noble or royal. The masses, who have ever constituted the laboring classes, have been regarded as an inferior portion of society. Their social inferiority has not only been made a reason for their exclusion from social power and authority, but by destroying the opportunity for actualizing their best possibilities it has been made the means of preventing their development and thus keeping them inferior. *Laissez faire*, therefore, is literally impossible in society. There can be no choice between natural selection and human selection, but only a choice between scientific human selection and ignorant human selection ; not between government and no government, but only between wise or unwise government interference.

The chief fallacy underlying the doctrine of *laissez faire* is a mistaken notion regarding the nature of competition. Because competition is rivalry between contending units it is assumed that all rivalry is competition, and hence that free competition is simply an unrestrained struggle for existence. As we have already seen, unrestrained struggle may and often does mean repression and despotism instead of development and freedom. It is entirely true that competition is indispensable to development, but in order to have competition that develops instead of a struggle that destroys, rivalry must take place under conditions which make the object sought reasonably possible to either contestant. There can be no advantageous competition where the prize is impossible to one and certain to the other. Such an unequal struggle instead of developing the highest possibilities of both competitors, inspires neither contestant to do his best. To have effective competition the contest must be of such a character as to compel the winner and inspire the loser to the maximum degree of effort. This can only occur when the contest takes place between approximately equal competing units. Competition between unequals necessarily tends to crush rather than develop the weaker, although he possesses all the potential possibilities of superiority.

Take, for instance the child of the poor laborer and that of the wealthy merchant. The former is sent to the factory or mine without any education or opportunity for social development ; it is reared in an atmosphere of ignorance, brutality and vice, while the latter receives all the education and incentives for culture that wealth and leisure can supply. When these two children grow up, can there be any inspiring competition between them as citizens for social position, public confidence, or even in the sphere of business, where education and mental training are necessary, indeed anywhere outside the sphere of manual labor? The difference between them in this respect, which nothing but a difference in their opportunities creates, instead of inspiring both to do their best, will naturally create a feeling of shrinking inferiority in the one and an undue feeling of superiority in the other. These two opposite feelings necessarily tend to give the power of authority to the latter and the submissive position to the former.

Clearly therefore instead of *laissez faire* necessarily securing free competition and "the survival of the most fit," it is the policy which in society is most likely to prevent free competition and to promote the survival of the less fit. It is an indispensable condition to free competition and the maximum development of the competitors, that the contest should be between approximately equal competing units. To secure approximate equality among competitors and hence the success of the superior, we must secure to each the opportunity for developing his best possibilities. In other words, to obtain the inspiring influence of free competition and to develop instead of crushing the potential capacity of the individual we must substitute scientific statesmanship for ignorant authority. The question of statesmanship then is not whether or not the state shall interfere in the affairs of society,—this it is sure to do so long as society exists,—but upon what principle it shall act in order to promote maximum prosperity and freedom in the community. This involves a consideration of the economic and social functions of government, which will be the subject of the next chapter.

CHAPTER II.

THE STATE; OR, THE NATURE AND FUNCTION OF GOVERNMENT.

Section I.—*What is the State?*

It is very common to use the term state as if it were synonymous with society. That such a use of the term is too indefinite for scientific purposes becomes apparent the moment we attempt to consider the functions of the state. It is essential to the idea of society that there be more or less social intercourse and interdependence among the individual units having some recognized common centre of interest and action. This is not true of all mankind. The human race is divided into groups or nations composed of individuals who have more or less social and industrial affinity. There is a great diversity of feeling, interest, and action within these groups, but each group has a common interest and will take common action as distinguished from any other group or nation. The maintenance of this common interest we call patriotism. Society therefore may be defined as an aggregate of individuals in any group, nation, or tribe. We cannot speak of the functions of this aggregate, because in its entirety society never acts. Even under pure communism, where the greatest uniformity of the units prevails, children, minors, and usually though not necessarily, women are excluded from active participation. Thus society as an aggregate never acts except through a more or less extended representation by which a portion acts for the whole. This representative portion, large or small, constitutes the state as distinguished from society ; it is the largest acting aggregate, and the individual is the smallest acting unit.

The state then may be defined as the conscious authoritative expression of society. Since the aggregate is greater than, and includes the individual, the authority of the state necessarily includes and is superior to that of the individual. The state then not only represents the authoritative action of the aggregate (society) as distinguished from that of the individual, but its authority is necessarily absolute over both the individual unit and social aggregate.

We often hear such expressions as "absolute rights," "inalienable rights," etc. Strictly speaking, there are no such rights in society; not only the right to "liberty and the pursuit of happiness," but even the right to life in society is necessarily subject to the will of the aggregate, as authoritatively expressed in the state or government. This is indispensable to the existence of society. Society being an association of individuals whose immediate interests are not always identical and whose conceptions of the equity of their relations are frequently very different, the existence of a power superior to both, whose authority shall be absolute, is indispensable to social order. All rights of the individual in society therefore, must in the very nature of the case, be conditional. Absolute individual rights are a social impossibility.

It is equally indispensable that these conditions should be determined and enforced by the collective authority, the state, since nothing short of that would command the confidence, support, and obedience of the individual units. While the authority of the state is always absolute over both individual units and the social aggregate, it always represents a consensus of both. Although the state is always representative, it does not always represent in the same manner, nor derive its authority in the same way. In some stages of society collective authority is all invested in one person, as in the chief of primitive tribes, and forms an absolute despotism. This is sometimes due to superior physical force, and sometimes to a fiction of divine appointment. In other stages of society authority is invested in a number of individuals by hereditary descent, forming an aristocracy or constitutional monarchy, and in others it is vested in a still larger number, chosen by popular vote, forming a democratic republic. But in every case the state represents the authority of the aggregate. The Czar's proclamation is not the act of a mere individual, but the recognized authoritative expression of Russia. The Pope's edict is not the voice of an individual Italian, but that of the Church.

It may be said that one-man-power, as represented by a shah, a sultan, a czar, or a pope, is not representative but despotic. It is indeed despotic, but it is also representative. Representation is to speak and act for others authoritatively. In this sense, despotism is no less representative than is democracy, but its authority to act for others is acquired in a different way. The essence of all collective or state authority is that the government derives its "powers from the consent of the governed." The absolute authority of the despots who rule Persia, Russia, and Turkey rests upon the consent of the governed as completely as does that of the President or Congress in democratic America. If the Czar of Russia had not the consent and confidence of the Russians, his proclamations would have no more authority in Russia than would those of any other individual. It is because they recognize his fitness to rule (to act for them) that they obey and support him. Their confidence may be misplaced, or may be due to a superstitious belief in his divine appointment as the head of the church and ruler of the nation ; but whatever the reasons, their confidence and consent are none the less complete, as is shown by the fact that they will not only work for him and worship him, but will by the millions fight and die for him. The only difference between despotic and democratic representation is that through poverty, ignorance, and superstition, the consent of the governed under despotism is given by silent acceptance of their rulers as inherently fitted and divinely appointed to govern, while under democracy this consent can only be obtained through the volitional action of the individuals. Thus the essential distinction between despotism and democracy is not that the latter is more representative than the former, but that it is more elective. Poverty, ignorance, and superstition make political and social incapacity inevitable, which in turn make elective representation impossible.

Just in proportion as the individual units of a community become more intelligent and positive in character, does their consent to the authority of the state become less dependent upon traditional usage and supernatural injunction, and more dependent upon individual judgment. Hence it changes from silent acquiescence to conscious choice, and then the representative function of the state becomes less hereditary and more elective in character. In such countries as Persia, Turkey, and Russia the consent of the governed to the authority of government consists entirely in silent acquiescence, while in such countries as Austria, Italy, and Germany, where material conditions and the intelligence of the people are more advanced, there is a limited amount of elective representation. In England the elective principle is still more general, and in America it is most general of all, being directly or indirectly applied to every branch of government. But there is no country in which the representation is all elective. Even in democratic America women are still excluded from elective representation. The state, or collective governing authority, sustains exactly the same representative relation to women in the United States as does that of the Czar of Russia or the Shah of Persia to the whole people of those countries. Hence the state, whether despotic or democratic, is always the authoritative expression of the aggregate.

This is only another form of stating the principle so frequently emphasized in these pages—namely, that all social institutions rest upon the habits and social character of the people. Society, therefore, differs from the individual, in that it represents a literal aggregate of which individuals are the units. The state differs from society and from the individual, in that it is the representative collective action of both, and its authority is absolute over both. In short, the state expresses authoritative social policy.

SECTION II.—*The Relation of the State to the Individual in Progressive Society.*

In order to ascertain the true relation of the state to the individual, it is necessary, first of all, to examine the structural constitution of society. This brings us directly to the question, is society a higher organism, for whose preservation and development the individual units are the tributary means, or is it an association created by and utilized for the preservation and development of the individual units composing it? Upon the answer to this question depends the character of statesmanship and the governing principle by which public policy should be shaped and directed. If society is an organic entity, to whose development the individual is subordinate and simply tributary, then the true public policy would be to increase the functions of the state and limit the sphere of individual action and authority. And conversely, if the development of the individual is the end to promote which society is only a means, the true public policy would be to so mould and direct public institutions as to increase the functions, responsibility, and authoritative sphere of the individual, and to diminish those of the state. It will be observed that these two conceptions of the relation of the state to the individual logically lead to opposite theories of statesmanship, the one towards socialism and the other towards individualism.

It is a peculiar feature of sociological literature that both socialist and individualist writers assume that society is an organic entity, and that it sustains the same relation to individuals that the individual organism does to the parts of which it is composed. This was the controlling idea of the Greeks and Romans, who regarded the state as every thing and the individual as nothing, except as he served the state. In his ideal republic, Plato makes the state stand for a great personality, in whom the different social classes are simply the functions. The ruling class, the military class, and the industrial class are presented as corresponding to the faculties of reason, will, and passion or force in the human organism. Upon this point at least, it may be truly said that all that has been written during the last two thousand years has been simply Platonizing. Hobbes endeavored to establish literally by minute detail what Plato only introduced in general outline, by making society a colossal artificial man. He not only made certain classes of the community correspond to the reason, will, and passion of the human organism, but he went so far as to divide society into limbs, joints, nerves, memory, conscience, and even ascribed to it a soul.[1]

This idea, with some qualifications eliminating the minutiæ of detail introduced by Hobbes, is reaffirmed and extensively elaborated on the basis of modern science, by Herbert Spencer.

[1] See preface to his " Leviathan ; or, The Matter, Form, and Power of a Commonwealth, Ecclesiastical and Civil."

Therefore Rodbertus had the full warrant of the continuous teachings of philosophy from Plato to Spencer for his basic-socialistic postulate that "*the community is the end in itself.* Individuals are only the means for the promotion of social well-being ; they are in no sense ends in themselves."[1] From this point of view he logically held that public policy should constantly be directed towards putting the ownership of property, especially the means of production into the hands of government. This idea has been more thoroughly developed by Karl Marx, who endeavors to show that from the nature of economic phenomena the ownership of the means of production can only reside in the community, which theory is made the basis for public policy by all shades of socialists. That socialists should readily accept the traditional theory is not surprising, because it sustains their *a priori* assumption that the state should do every thing. But with Mr. Spencer the case is quite different, as he is the most extreme representative of the individualist school. He regards socialism as slavery,[2] and state ownership and control of industrial enterprises as inimical to progress. Now the supremacy of industrial individualism is incompatible with the existence of a social organism. The question, however, is not whether Mr. Spencer's position on the organic structure of society is consistent with his theory of individualism, but whether it is scientifically and philosophically sound. This is the more important, because Mr. Spencer stands pre-eminently for the scientific method of investigation. Indeed, his conclusions upon this point are regarded as the sociological embodiment of the doctrine of evolution, and may be taken as representing those of evolutionists generally upon this subject. The fact that Mr. Spencer occupies this leading position in the world of scientific sociology makes a careful consideration of his position on this subject of the utmost importance. In setting forth his reason for concluding that society is an organism, he says :

"So completely, however, is a society organized upon the same system as an individual being, that we may almost say there is something more than analogy between them. . . . A still more remarkable fulfilment of this analogy is to be found in the fact,

---

[1] *Political Science Quarterly*, September, 1889, p. 546.
[2] "The Coming Slavery," *Popular Science Monthly*, April, 1884.

that the different kinds of organization which society takes on, in progressing from its lowest to its highest phase of development, are essentially similar to the different kinds of animal organization."

After a detailed illustration of the similarity between society and an individual organism, he says :

" Thus do we find, not only that the analogy between a society and a living creature is borne out to a degree quite unsuspected by those who commonly draw it, but also that the same definition of life applies to both. Thus the union of many men into one community—this increasing mutual dependence of units which were originally independent—this gradual segregation of citizens into separate bodies, with reciprocally subservient functions—this formation of a whole consisting of numerous essential parts—this growth of an organism, of which one portion cannot be injured without the rest feeling it—may all be generalized under the law of individuation. The development of society, as well as the development of man, and the development of life generally, may be described as a tendency to individuate—*to become a thing.* And rightly interpreted, the manifold forms of progress going on around us are uniformly significant of this tendency." [1]

In a later work,[2] Mr. Spencer discusses the social organism at still greater length and defends his conception from the inconsistencies of the Greeks and also against those of Hobbes. After criticising these writers, he says :

" Notwithstanding errors, however, these speculations have considerable significance. That such analogies, crudely as they are thought out, should have been alleged by Plato and Hobbes and many others, is a reason for suspecting that *some* analogy exists. The untenableness of the particular comparisons above instanced is no ground for denying an essential parallelism ; for early ideas are usually but vague adumbrations of the truth. Lacking the great generalizations of biology, it was, as we have said, impossible to trace out the real relations of social organizations to organizations of another order." [3]

He then discusses the points of general analogy between society and living organisms, which he sums up by saying :

---

[1] " Social Statics," pp. 490, 493, 497. See also " First Principles," pp. 408, 413, 433–437.

[2] " Illustrations of Universal Progress," chap. x.

[3] *Ibid.*, p. 391.

" Thus we find but little to conflict with the all-important analogies. . . . The principles of organization are the same ; and the differences are simply differences of application.   Here ending this general survey of the facts which justify the comparison of a society to a living body ; let us look at them in detail." [1]

After devoting thirty pages to the discussion of details sustaining this analogy he concludes by saying :

" Such, then, is a general outline of the evidence which justifies, in detail, the comparison of societies to living organisms.   That they gradually increase in mass ; that they become little by little more complex ; that at the same time their parts grow more mutually dependent ; and that they continue to live and grow as wholes, while successive generations of their units appear and disappear, are broad peculiarities which bodies politic display, in common with all living bodies, and in which they and living bodies differ from every thing else." [2]

It will be seen from the foregoing that although Mr. Spencer objects to Hobbes' presentation of the analogy between the social and the human organization, he quite as emphatically holds to the conclusion that society is an organism, whose organic structure is fundamentally the same as that of animal organisms.   If this be correct, it of course follows that the relation of the units to the aggregate is the same and that the order of progress in society is the same as in the animal organism.   In short, that a biological hypothesis adequately explains sociological phenomena.

The fact that a theory correctly accounts for one class of phenomena does not warrant its application to another, unless it can be shown to adequately explain the new phenomena independently of its use in any other field of investigation.   If we examine social phenomena independently of biological hypothesis, we shall find : (1) That although there is a general resemblance between society and the animal organism, the difference between

---

[1] " Illustrations of Universal Progress," pp. 397, 398.

[2] *Ibid.*, p. 428.   That this represents Mr. Spencer's views upon the subject is shown by the fact that it is repeated in his latest utterances.   See " Sociology." Also correspondence with Huxley in the *Times*, September, 1889, republished in the *Popular Science Monthly*, February, 1890.

them is sufficiently radical and fundamental to destroy the basis for the conclusion that society is an organism. (2) That such an assumption is not necessary in order to apply the theory of evolution to social phenomena.

It is unquestionably true that there are many points of resemblance between society and individual organisms, and so there are between individual organisms and inorganic bodies. The question, therefore, is not whether there are any points of agreement between society and an organism, but whether the points of agreement are sufficiently numerous and fundamental to make them constitutionally identical. Mr. Spencer presents four characteristics in which society resembles an individual, which he regards as sufficiently fundamental to warrant the classification of society as an organism ; they are :

" 1. That commencing as small aggregations, they insensibly augment in mass : some of them eventually reaching ten thousand times what they originally were.

" 2. That while at first so simple in structure as to be considered structureless, they assume, in the course of their growth, a continually-increasing complexity of structure.

" 3. That though in their early, undeveloped states, there exists in them scarcely any mutual dependence of parts, their parts gradually acquire a mutual dependence, which becomes at last so great that the activity and life of each part is made possible only by the activity and life of the rest.

" 4. That the life and development of a society is independent of, and far more prolonged than, the life and development of any of its component units, who are severally born, grow, work, reproduce, and die, while the body politic composed of them survives generation after generation, increasing in mass, completeness of structure, and functional activity." [1]

There can be little doubt that in these four characteristics society resembles the animal organism ; nor can there be any doubt that the first two apply with equal force to inorganic development. These are as true of the development of inorganic substances as they are of the growth of plants, animals, or society. If, therefore, we are to assume that society is an organism because in these general and important respects it resembles an individual, then may we not say that vegetable and animal bodies are in-

[1] " Illustrations of Universal Progress," pp. 391, 392.

organic, because, in these fundamental characteristics they resemble inorganic bodies ; and *vice versa*. If we should attempt to draw any such conclusion, Mr. Spencer would soon correct us by pointing out that the lower we go in the scale of development the greater is the simplicity and similarity of form. And thus, while in the first two characteristics animal organisms are similar to those of inorganic bodies, in the last two they greatly differ ; for, though mineral substances like organisms, increase in mass and complexity of structure, they do not develop the functional dependence of parts exhibited in the individual organism.[1]

If the fact that the individual organism has functional activities different from those of inorganic bodies, establishes the distinction between their classification as organic and inorganic, it follows that a similar difference between the constitution of society and that of an individual organism equally warrants a distinction in their classification. If we examine the constitution of society and the individual organism, we find the following radical distinctions which are quite as great as those between organic and inorganic bodies as pointed out by Mr. Spencer.

I. In an individual organism progress consists in the differentiation and specialization of functions in which the aggregate tends to gain a more complete control over the action of the parts, such as eyes, ears, teeth, tongues, feet, hands, etc., whereas in society progress consists in a differentiation of functions and definiteness of polity in which the parts constantly tend to acquire an increasing control over the action of the aggregate.

II. In an individual organism the end of the parts is to serve and sustain the aggregate or organism, and when they fail to serve that end they become atrophied and disappear, whereas in society the end of the aggregate is to serve and sustain the individual units.

III. In an organism, where consciousness and intelligence exist, they reside in the aggregate and never in the parts ; whereas in society consciousness and intelligence reside always in the parts and never in the aggregate. Indeed, the social aggregate has none of the attributes of a conscious entity.

---

[1] " Even such inorganic bodies as crystals, which arise by growth, show no such definite relation between growth and existence as organisms."—" Illustrations of Universal Progress," p. 392.

IV. In an organism the existence of the parts is subsequent to, dependent upon, and developed through the unconscious action of the aggregate ; whereas in society the aggregate and its polity or representative action, is subsequent to, dependent upon, and developed through the conscious action of the parts.

V. In an organism the influences which promote differentiation of function must operate upon the aggregate or organism, and through it affect the parts ; whereas in society the influences which promote differentiation must operate upon the parts or individual units, and through them affect the constitution of the aggregate and its active polity.

VI. In society conscious wants, intelligence, and will, are the characteristic attributes of the units through which all the influences affecting the differentiation of the social aggregate must finally act ; whereas in the individual organism the units have no such characteristics ; where these characteristics exist at all they are the attributes of the aggregate and not of the units, and in the lower forms of animal and all vegetable organisms they do not exist at all.

It will thus be seen that, despite the general resemblance between society and an individual organism, the difference in the functional relation of the parts to the aggregate, and the order of their development, is quite as marked and more fundamental than that between organic and inorganic bodies. The difference between the organic and the inorganic consists mainly in the fact that the complexity of structure and interdependence of the parts are greater in the former than in the latter ; whereas the difference between society and an organism consists in the fact that the units sustain an opposite relation to the aggregate, and that progressive differentiation is in an opposite direction : in society the tendency being to increase the conscious control of the parts over the aggregate, and in an organism to increase that of the aggregate over the parts. So far from being an organic entity, society is only the systematized environment of associated individuals by whom and for whom it is created, and upon whose state of industrial, social, and intellectual development its existence, form, and character depend.

Nor is this view inconsistent with the doctrine of evolution. This theory does not involve the assumption that society is an

20

organism. Evolution simply implies a progressive movement from a less to a more definite, coherent, orderly state of existence. But it does not follow that the more complex form must necessarily be organic ; since in that case inorganic development would not be evolution. Although evolution implies a greater definiteness of functional relation, it does not necessarily mean the individualization of the aggregate. It is not strictly correct therefore, to say "the development of society as well as the development of men and the development of life generally may be described as a tendency to individuate—to become a thing." Society does not tend to become a thing, in the sense of an organic entity. Progress in society is not a tendency to individualize the social aggregate, but rather to de-individualize it, making its action more and more the consciously delegated expression of the individual. Indeed, the only individuality which social progress develops is in the units ; institutions are specialized, but man only is individualized as an organic entity. If we regard society as an association of individuals for their common protection and further development, the theory of evolution becomes rationally applicable to social as well as organic and inorganic phenomena. From this point of view the assumption that society is an organism is unnecessary, and the anomaly of creating a colossal social man with increasing despotic power over the individual disappears. Social progress then is seen to be an orderly movement towards greater individual perfection, and personal freedom for man, which accords with universal history.

So far as human knowledge goes, the highest individual organism yet developed is man. In every stage of physical development, from the most incoherent homogeneous form known or inferred, the movement has been towards higher and more complex types of formation, each of which tended to make the existence of the next possible. And the crowning product of the whole series of inorganic and organic evolution is man. With the appearance of man began another phase of development which was neither inorganic nor organic, but SOCIAL. Progress in this sphere does not consist in the unconscious differentiation of an inorganic mass, nor in that of a living organism, but in a systematization of the environment and specialization of the efforts of individuals, which results in a further development of the individuality of the units. It thus appears that man occupies the objective or crowning position in both physical and social evolution ; with this difference however : in the physical world he presents the highest type of an organic aggregate, and in society he occupies the position of a unit. Thus although evolution is fundamentally the same in society as in the physical world, in that it is a movement from the simple to the complex, the order of development is reversed ; in the physical world, it is a subordination of the parts to the perfection of the aggregate, and in society it is a subordination of the aggregate to the perfection of the units. In order therefore, to complete Mr. Spencer's statement, that " the development of society as well as the development of man and the development of life generally, may be described as a tendency to individuate—to become a thing," we must add, that this individuating tendency ends in the greater individualization, not of society, but of man—physically as an organism, and socially as a sovereign personality.

It is evident, therefore, that the Greek and Roman conception that the state is every thing, the individual nothing ; and the socialistic position logically deduced therefrom, that "*the community is the end in itself*, individuals being only the means for the promotion of social well-being, and in no sense ends in themselves " ; and Mr. Spencer's assumption that " society is an organism," are essentially erroneous. In this, as in all other cases of reasoning from mistaken hypotheses, the error only becomes important when the theory is made the basis of action. Like many of the immature postulates of the English economists, already referred to, Mr. Spencer's theory of a social organism unwittingly lays the logical basis for state socialism, a theory which he himself regards as the greatest of modern fallacies.

The difference between Rodbertus and Mr. Spencer is precisely the same as the difference between Marx and Ricardo.[1] Marx arrived at the conclusion that profits are robbery by the logical application of the Ricardian postulate that the quantity instead of the cost of labor determines value. And Ricardo avoided the fallacy of Karl Marx only by failing to consistently apply his own postulate. So the theory of state socialism developed by

[1] Part III., chap. vi.

Rodbertus is logically sustained by the Spencerian postulate that society is an organism, and Spencer avoids the fallacy of socialism only by disregarding his own hypothesis.

We are therefore warranted in concluding that society is not a colossal " artificial man," as affirmed by Hobbes, nor an " organism " as affirmed by Spencer, nor an " end in itself," as affirmed by Rodbertus ; but on the contrary, that it is an association of individuals as a means for the promotion of individual well-being. Indeed the history of government is the history of making and unmaking social institutions in order to render them more subservient to the needs of the social life of the individual.

Nor is this view confined to Spencer and the socialists, but it is beginning to be accepted by liberal economists. Thus in his chapter on " The Basis of Economic Law " Professor Clark says :

" The analogy between society and the human body was familiar to the ancients. It is a discovery of recent times that a society is not merely like an organism ; it is one in literal fact. . . . Political economy treats not merely of the wealth of individuals who sustain complicated relations with each other, but of the wealth of society as an organic unit." [1]

In a subsequent chapter (" Theory of Value ") he makes this social organism into an active contracting personality who buys every thing from the individual and sells every thing to him, and says :

" Exchanges are always made between an individual and society as a whole. In every legitimate bargain the social organism is a party. Under a régime of free competition, whoever sells the thing he has produced, sells it to society. His sign advertises the world to come and buy, and it is the world not the chance customer that is the real purchaser. Yet it is equally true that whoever buys the thing he needs, buys it off society. . . . In the process the social organism is true to its nature as a single being great and complex, indeed, but united and intelligent. It looks at an article as a man would do, and mentally measures the modification in its own condition which the acquisition of it would occasion, or which the loss of it would occasion, if once possessed." [2]

It will thus be seen that according to Professor Clark society is not merely an organic entity, but it is a single intelligent be-

[1] " Philosophy of Wealth," pp. 38, 39.
[2] *Ibid.*, pp. 85, 86.

ing. If the analysis of the economic relation of individuals to society presented by Professor Clark is correct, then economic collectivism is scientifically sound and should be accepted as the basis of industrial statesmanship. But is the analysis correct? Is it true that "exchanges are always made between individuals and society as a whole"? Do such economic relations actually exist? Where, how, and under what conditions does society "as a whole" buy wheat, potatoes, shoes, clothes, furniture, etc., from individuals? When farmers and manufacturers take their products to the market they do not sell them to society, but to individuals, who invariably purchase them either for their own consumption or to resell them to other individuals. Nor does society, as an organism of which individuals "are but atoms," consume any of these products. They are consumed by individuals, and by individuals only. Neither is the statement that "his sign advertises the world to come and buy, and it is the world and not the chance customer that is the real purchaser," any nearer correct, if the term world is used in any other sense than the individuals in the world.

The social market simply expresses the aggregate consumption of individuals constituting any social group. Neither is there any truth, except as a metaphor, in the statement that "the social organism is true to its nature as a single being, great and complex, indeed, but united and intelligent. It looks at an article as a man would do, and mentally measures the modification in its own condition." Society, as an entity, does nothing of the kind. All the "mental measurement," all the "intelligence," all the conscious action, is performed by individuals. A hundred individuals equally intelligent do not constitute a single intelligence a hundred times as great as one. An intellectual giant cannot be made by simply adding mental Liliputians. Intelligence can only be increased by developing it in the individual organism.

Notwithstanding the immense advantage of society over isolation—and it constitutes all the difference between savagery and civilization,—there are no facts to warrant the assumption that society is a new acting entity, much less an individual organism. On the contrary, the advantage of society is entirely to individuals through their association with each other. In short, society is an association of individuals for the better promotion of their own well-being, and therefore, in studying the law of economic movement we must have for our basis the individual ; in no other way can social progress be promoted.

SECTION III.—*The Function of Government ; or, The Control-ling Principle in Statesmanship.*

Having seen what the state is and the relation it sustains to the individual, we are now in a position to consider its function as a factor in civilization.   Nor will this be a difficult task, if we bear in mind the points already established, namely : that the state is but the representative expression of associated individuals, and that progress in society is a tendency towards the greater indi-vidualization of man, both a *physical organism* and as a *sovereign social personality*. As already pointed out, social progress has two fundamental characteristics ; one is economic, the other social. The former is a tendency towards more wealth for the individual ; the latter is towards more freedom for the individual.   How to promote the increase of wealth and freedom for the individual therefore, is the problem of statesmanship and the end to which collective authority, or state action, should ever be directed.

In considering this question it should be remembered that neither wealth nor freedom can be authoritatively given to the individual ; they must be taken by him.   The only way in which the state can give wealth to the individual is by charity.   Wealth so acquired, instead of promoting freedom, is one of the most powerful means of preventing it.   Charity in any form tends to create obligation, stereotypes dependence, and thereby destroys individuality, and makes freedom impossible.   The history of freedom is a history of the increase of the sovereignty of the individual over his own actions and the diminution of that of the state.   It is sometimes said "that government is best which governs least."   It would be more correct, however, to say that people is best governed which *needs* the least government.   We should be careful, however, not to confound freedom with inde-pendence.   The savage is independent of social restrictions, but he has very little freedom.   He is in constant danger of his life from the defencelessness of his position.   He has no friends because he befriends nobody ; he can obtain no assistance or protection because he assists and protects nobody.   Indeed it is because he is the least dependent upon his fellows that he is the most helpless and has the least freedom of any man in the world.

Mutual dependence is the greatest promoter of freedom. Whenever the freedom of each depends upon the freedom of all, no one has any interest in preventing it, but every one has an interest in extending it. Mutual dependence cancels obligation and extends freedom, while dependence creates obligation and restricts freedom. It is only when everybody's safety depends upon protecting the safety of his neighbor that freedom extends along the whole line of human relations. With the dependence upon authority the case is entirely different. There the obligation is all on one side. It is the relation of creditor and debtor, of the giver and receiver, of the master and ward, and not that of mutual helpers and the receivers of equivalents. Dependence upon authority is scarcely less inimical to freedom than nondependence upon society. The one involves savagery and the other despotism. It is only the mutual assistance born of individual interdependence that can make the highest social life and the maximum individual freedom possible. In other words, the highest individualism promotes the most complete co-operation of effort, unity of interest, equity of relations, freedom of action, and complexity of social life. Evidently then, it is the duty of the state to promote in every way possible the development of the individuality of its citizens, increase their mutual dependence upon each other and to decrease their dependence upon the government. Upon what lines should the public policy be directed to accomplish this result? Paternalism fails to promote this end, because it tends to lessen instead of increase the activities and responsibilities of the individual. Nothing develops power but activity, and nothing creates activity but the necessity for it. We never put forth effort to do for ourselves that which others will do for us. Since inaction is fatal to progress, the increase of paternalism is necessarily a great barrier to individual development. Nor is it less erroneous to assume that the sovereignty of the individual can best be promoted by merely restricting the sphere of governmental activities. It would be as correct to say that the withdrawal of parental care and education from children is the best means for developing the highest manhood.

The way to increase the sovereignty of the individual is not to arbitrarily *lessen* the functions of the state, but to make its activities *less necessary*. The necessity of state action can be minimized only by maximizing the capacity of the individual. To break the egg from without is almost certain to injure if not kill the chick, but when it is broken from within by the increasing power of the chick itself, it only breaks when the chick is strong enough to do without it. So in society; the authority of the state over the individual should not disappear by weakening the forces without, but by increasing those within him. In short, the individual is the initial point of social movement.

The more intelligent and highly developed the character of the individual, the more capable he is of doing for himself and more reluctant to have others do for him. Hence, throughout the history of society we see that the greater the ignorance and poverty the more marked is the lack of individuality in the social units ; and the weaker the character of the individual, the more despotic is that of the government. A most significant fact in this movement is, that this transfer of authority from the state to the individual has always been exacted by the individual and reluctantly yielded by the state.[1] Indeed it is a fundamental principle in both nature and society that man can only continuously have that which he can demand and maintain by force of character. Therefore the increase of wealth and the freedom of the individual must come through influences which tend to envelop his character, thereby making paternalism less necessary and despotism less possible.

It may therefore be laid down as a fundamental postulate in scientific statesmanship, *that the controlling principle in public policy should ever be to minimize the necessary sphere of governmental action and authority, and to maximize the possible sphere of individual action and responsibility.* In other words, the function of government in all phases of industrial, social, and political life is to promote the development of the highest possibilities of the individual.

---

[1] Witness the protracted agitation that is always necessary to extend the rights of the individual in any direction, the right of individual judgment in religion, the right to vote, the right for women to own property, the right to hold public office without regard to religious views, the right to democratic government, the right for women to vote, even in a Republic, etc., etc.

In order to understand the lines of action which the application of this principle involves, it is necessary to consider : (1) Why, on general principle, individual effort and responsibility are preferable to state action and authority ; (2) What class of things can be administered better by the state than by the individual ; (3) What line of public policy should be pursued in order to maximize the sphere of individual action and responsibility and thereby minimize the necessity for governmental authority.

1. On general principle, individual action and responsibility are preferable to state action or collective authority, because they possess the maximum possibility of directness, efficiency, economy, and equity. State action, being representative whether elective or not, is necessarily indirect and arbitrary. Arbitrary action always involves the maximum amount of inequity and mistakes, because it is necessarily governed by stipulated rules, and therefore cannot be modified to suit the great variety of individual cases. The universal experience of mankind confirms the assumption that whenever individuals can settle their affairs between themselves, the adjustment is most likely to be equitable and mutually satisfactory, and hence the decision of a third party should always be a matter of last resort.

This does not mean that all courts and other forms of governmental action, or even war, are unmixed evils ; it only means that they are necessarily clumsy, because arbitrary means of accomplishing the desired end. Indispensable as war may have been, and important as armies, navies, and policemen still are, it is universally admitted that the less the necessity for using them the better. It is because of the injustice which always accompanies battle-field decisions that war diminishes as individuality in the average citizen increases and civilization advances. The same arbitrary element runs through all collective action, though it is sometimes indicated in less violent and repulsive forms.

Take, for instance, taxation. How to equitably adjust taxation has been a perplexing problem since human society began. It is because taxes are levied by representative authority, according to some arbitrary rule which is utterly incapable of being adapted to a very great variety of conditions, that injustice is constantly being done to numerous individuals and frequently to whole classes. The same principle shows itself in our best courts of justice, notwithstanding the jury system and the immense learning of advocates and judges. When a case is given to a jury the legal limits to their decision are fixed by the judge in his charge. They may think the defendant morally innocent or actually justified in his act, but by virtue of a legal technicality they are forced to vote him guilty and subject him to a punishment which both individually and collectively they would regard as unjust. And so on through the whole history of legal decisions. It is because of this preponderating probability of legal inequity that in civil cases wherever disputants can adjust the difference themselves they are generally encouraged to do so by the court. State action being necessarily arbitrary, and hence seldom capable of the highest efficiency, economy, and equity, it is important to consider what class of things, if any, can naturally be administered by the state better than by individuals, and *vice versa.*

2. Since association is better than isolation, and since government is necessary to society, it follows that while there are many things which the individual can do better than the state, there are some things which the state can do better than the individual. How shall we determine between the sphere of state and individual action? If we take an extreme case from either class, there is no difficulty in deciding to which sphere it naturally belongs. For instance, if it is a question of determining one's own religious opinions, we have now no difficulty in deciding that it belongs entirely to the individual. And on the other hand, if it is a question of public defence, such as requires an army and navy, we have no difficulty in deciding it to be clearly one of the functions of the state. But when we come to the outer edges of these spheres of action where they merge together, the line of demarcation is not so easily observed. Here a new difficulty arises, because this is not only the point where a wise decision is most important, but also where the material for making a wise decision is most difficult to obtain. Although there is no difference of opinion to-day as to whether or not the individual should choose his own religion or the government should control the army, there is an immense difference of opinion as to whether telegraphs, banks, mines, and railroads should be conducted by private enterprise or under state control. The difference be-

tween the administration of the post-office and that of the tele-graph is so slight that public management of the former is made the basis for demanding state control of the latter. And if we have nothing upon which to base our decision but the facts in the two particular cases, it will be very difficult to decide. And if government control is extended to the telegraph, the question between that and the railroad becomes equally difficult to deter-mine. The steps from the railroad to the mine, from the mine to the farm, from the farm to the factory, are all equally short and, of themselves, difficult to determine. It is necessary there-fore, to have some broader generalization upon which to base our decision than the data which each individual case furnishes. This can only be found by viewing each individual case in the light of the general class to which it belongs. Since in the progress of society there is a constant tendency to transfer functions from one sphere to another, it is in the distinctive characteristics of these functions that we must seek the principle governing the line of demarcation between the proper sphere of state and indi-vidual authority, and thus be able to establish a scientific basis for determining whether or not in any given instance the sphere of state action should be extended or restricted.

If we study the evolution of society from its homogeneous form, in which every thing was done by authority, to its present highly complex state, where most things are done by individual enterprise, we can readily see the leading characteristics of those functions which tend to pass from the state to the individual and those which tend to become recognized as distinctively the func-tion of government. Among the things which have indisputably passed to the sphere of individual authority are the right to per-sonal freedom, the selection of one's partner in life, and the charge of one's own children, the right of free speech, and of making industrial contracts.

The reason why these are relegated to the individual is that in all such cases there are many subtleties in which the individual is more directly interested, and about which he is more com-petent to decide than any third party can possibly be ; and these subtleties increase with the advancing complexity of social rela-tions. Moreover in many of these intricate personal relations the decision must be made at once in order to be effective, and therefore can be made only by the individual himself. The arbitrary, red-tape character of government action necessarily precludes complete knowledge of detail and the prompt action necessary in such cases. Although no individual is yet perfect in this regard, he has infinitely greater possibilities of becoming so than any form of representative authority can possibly have.

This is equally true of economic relations. In the early stages of society, when industry was very simple, being practically limited to agriculture, with crude hand-methods of production, it could be conducted by collective authority. But as wants were multiplied and occupations differentiated, economic relations grew more involved, and a more special knowledge became necessary, which made arbitrary administration very much less efficient. Consequently the ownership of property and the administration of productive enterprise gradually pass from public to private ownership and control, or from the sphere of state to that of individual authority, in proportion as the division of labor, the concentration of productive effort, and the social freedom of the individual increased.

On the other hand, although governments have radically changed their character, certain functions have been relegated to them by common consent. Among these are protection against a common enemy, the maintenance of public order, the protection of individual rights, the enforcement of contracts, the administration of justice, the maintenance of public roads, canals, bridges, parks, museums, libraries and the enforcement of sanitary regulations. Nor is the reason for this difficult to understand. The administration of the army, navy, police, and the like, is preeminently the function of the state, because in such things effectiveness lies in the maximum aggregation of physical force, and this can be best obtained by all acting as one man under a single leader. Indeed the most perfect military force involves the maximum despotism and the minimum individuality, and hence can always be exercised most efficiently by arbitrary authority. The maintenance of public order, the enforcement of contracts, and the administration of law are also functions which can be best performed by the collectivity, for the reason that it acts uniformly for all, and its decisions are backed by the power of all. Nor does the development of individual character tend to transfer the functions of the soldier, the policeman, the judge, and the jailor from the authority of the state to that of the individual. On the contrary, while it tends to make these functions unnecessary, so long as they are needed they can be better performed by the state than by the individual.

The same is true of public highways, such as roads, canals, bridges, sanitary regulations, etc. They are common conveniences which everybody needs, and their management is of the simplest character. To keep such public conveniences in repair calls for no special skill, and changes in method are so slow and infrequent that no inconvenience is experienced by having them under control of routine authority. Although unlike military and police functions, these do not diminish but steadily increase with the advance of civilization, there is no tendency to put them under individual control. The reason for this is that while these can be managed as well by the state as by the individual, the former has the additional advantage of giving greater freedom to travel by obviating the inconvenience of direct payment in the form of tolls, etc. And since these functions relate only to securing the maximum safety and convenience to individual enterprise and mobility, there is no incentive for individuals to undertake them because they have no interest in doing so.

It may therefore be laid down as a general principle, that in proportion as social functions are complex, variable, and personal in their nature and interest, requiring instant decisions and expert skill, individual management is superior to state authority, and conversely, only in proportion as functions are simple, permanent, and arbitrary in their character, and impersonal in their nature and interest, can they be efficiently performed by the state. In other words, the functions of the state are essentially *protective, judiciary, educational, and impersonal in their nature ;* hence, all economic and social functions which are essentially *personal, productive, commercial,* or *experimental* in their nature properly belong to the sphere of individual action and responsibility.

3. This brings us to the consideration of the third proposition, namely, what line of public policy should be pursued in order to maximize the sphere of individual action and responsibility, and

thereby minimize the necessity for governmental authority. The doctrine that the state should do for the individual only such things as he cannot do as well for himself, of course implies that it should continue to do *all* those things which it can, under existing conditions, do better than he. Hence, it does not follow that because the natural functions of the state are protective, judiciary, educational, and impersonal, that it should never perform any others. On the contrary, the state must continue to do whatever the individual is incapable of doing as well. *The state should relinquish no function until it can be performed as well or better by the individual ; otherwise many social duties would be abandoned altogether and progress greatly retarded. Paternalism in government is a necessary substitute for individual capacity, and consequently increases as we descend and diminishes as we ascend the scale of civilization.*

Therefore, whenever it is necessary for the state to perform paternal functions—*doing for* the individual,—it should always be regarded as a temporary duty, to be transferred to the individual as rapidly as he acquires the capacity to perform it. In the last analysis then, while it is the duty of the government to do those things for the individual which he cannot do as well for himself, the governing principle in public policy should ever be to protect and enlarge those *OPPORTUNITIES, and to promote those influences which tend to develop the highest possibilities of the individual to do for himself.*

There is one other point worthy of note before passing to the application of this principle to the various phases of industrial and social life—namely, the importance of distinguishing between *paternal* and *protective* functions. This distinction is indeed indispensable to scientific statesmanship. To confound the paternal with the protective principle in government is to destroy all philosophic basis for a public policy, yet this is commonly done by many of the ablest writers. For instance, such writers as Senior, Spencer, and the leading English economists oppose state regulation of the hours of labor, the sanitary conditions of workshops, employment of women and children in mines and factories, compulsory education of factory children, and free public schools, as being paternal legislation. They thus fail to recognize any difference between the policy of furnishing the child with wholesome sanitary surroundings and an education, and that of furnishing him with food, clothes, and shelter.[1] It is really this unphilosophic opposition to reform which has brought the doctrines of the English school into such disrepute among the more liberal and sympathetic portion of the community, and which in its reaction has given much plausibility to socialism. Indeed it has made individualism the synonym for anti-reform and its antithesis—socialism—the means of reform.

Orthodox economists reason that because paternalism is injurious, protection should be abandoned; while, on the other hand, socialists conclude that because protection has been advantageous individualism should be abandoned and paternalism adopted. By overlooking the distinction •between protection and paternalism, we are logically driven to one of two unscientific theories of statesmanship—*laissez faire* or socialism.

The distinction between paternalism and protection is that a paternal policy implies doing the maximum for the individual, while a protective policy implies providing the individual with the maximum opportunity to do for himself. If this difference were clearly recognized the obvious error in the anti-reform attitude of let-aloneism and the stultifying influence of paternalism would be obviated. The duty of the state as essentially protective and educational in the widest sense of the term would be easily understood. With this as the basis of public policy, the state can always be scientifically used as a means of promoting progress without hindering the growth of individual freedom.

---

[1] This mistake is strikingly illustrated by Buckle in his able arraignment of what he calls the protective spirit in France as contrasted with the non-protective spirit in England. The truth is, however, that what Buckle was denouncing in France as protection, was paternalism. It was a reign of bureaucracy in which the state endeavored to do the maximum for the individual instead of enabling the individual to do the maximum for himself. The contrast was not between protection in France and *laissez faire* in England, but a contrast between paternalism in France and protection in England. See "History of Civilization," vol. i., chapters ix. and x. See also Spencer's "Coming Slavery," *Popular Science Monthly*, April, 1884.

CHAPTER III.

THE PRINCIPLE OF INTERNATIONAL TRADE.

SECTION I. — *Increasing Social Opportunity Necessitates National Development.*

IN the preceding discussion four facts have been established : (1) That social progress is development of the character and sovereignty of the individual, to which end government is but a means. (2) That the let-alone doctrine is theoretically unscientific and practically impossible in society ; a negative government being a contradiction in terms. (3) That since paternalism limits the need of the individual to do for himself, it hinders rather than helps the development of individuality. (4) That freedom can only be increased by the growth of individual capacity, which in turn depends upon the opportunities for developing individual character.

In order to apply these principles to the various phases of social and industrial life it is necessary at the outset to understand what constitutes opportunity. In the first place it should be remembered that we are dealing with man as a social being ; hence it is only with the development of his character as a social individuality that we are concerned. Indeed this constitutes all the difference between savagery and civilization. Opportunity then, is necessarily social, and must be sought in man's social environment—in his intercourse with his fellow-men. And since progress in society as elsewhere, is the movement from a relatively simple to a relatively complex state of existence, the social environment necessary to constitute opportunity must be constantly increasing in complexity. Social opportunity, therefore, may be stated *as necessary contact with an increasing variety of social influences.*[1]

Society then, is a necessary prerequisite to individual advancement. Society does not mean merely an aggregation of human beings, but such an association of individuals as shall make frequent intercourse and mutual dependence between them certain. This implies the segregation of the human race into groups or nations in which the individuals have some industrial, social, and political affinity, without which the contact necessary to individual growth is impossible. Consequently the doctrine of increasing opportunity for individual development includes not only the relation of individuals to each other within a social group or nation, but also the development of the nation as a political entity. Although patriotism and the desire for national autonomy is a prominent feature in the statesmanship of every country, there is no recognized principle by which its policy should be governed. What relation the industrial development of the nation sustains to the civilization and freedom of the people ; why, and under what conditions national and industrial autonomy is necessary to industrial development, and what relation industrial and individual development sustain to each other, are questions to which neither economic nor political science has hitherto furnished any adequate answer. When we recognize the fact however, that a nation is but the social setting of the individual and that government is but a means by which the resources of the nation are utilized for promoting the welfare of the individual, the importance of considering the development of the nation as a necessary means for promoting the progress of society at once becomes apparent.

SECTION II.—*National Development Necessitates the Growth of Manufacturing Industries.*

In considering this question it is important at the outset clearly to understand what we mean by the expression, *national development.* It is commonly assumed that the development of the material resources of a country, as agriculture, mining, or manufacture, is necessarily the development of the nation. This view confounds the physical qualities of soil and climate with the

[1] "Wealth and Progress," pp. 231, 232.

social qualities of the people which are essentially different. Such reasoning logically makes the industrial pursuits, and hence the social life, of the people depend upon the physical characteristics of the country. Thus instead of subordinating nature to man it subordinates man to nature, which is the reverse of all progressive tendencies in social evolution. When we separate physical from social phenomena and recognize the nation as *the people* this difficulty is obviated ; it then becomes evident that the social development of man is an end to which the physical development of nature is but the means.

In considering the development of a nation therefore, the prime question is not development of the natural resources of the country, but development of the character of its people. The mere fact that the soil of a country is prolific is not a sufficient reason why all the people should become agriculturists. The cultivation of the soil or of any material resource of a country should be made subordinate to the cultivation of man. In other words, the development of a nation consists in the development of its civilizing and individualizing influences. To the extent that the people of a nation are isolated in their occupations and daily life, will their social progress be slow ; and the less frequent intercourse between individuals the less socializing will its influences be. In order then, to increase the socializing influences of a nation, it is necessary first of all to promote the concentration of its population. Nor can this be accomplished by mere arbitrary authority. People will not concentrate either in their social life or industrial pursuits merely because they are advised or ordered to do so. The concentration of population means greater complexity of social life, which is what man is apt to avoid except under the pressure of some desire or necessity.

It is proverbial that the savage shrinks from the customs of civilization, and the rural peasant from contact with city life. Indeed, people whose social life is simple, always endeavor to avoid close intercourse with those in highly developed society, because it means new and at first, embarrassing experiences. Nothing will induce people to encounter the difficulties of a new environment but the strong desire for some object not otherwise obtainable. So long as people can gratify their desires without facing the difficulties of new and more complex social relations, they will continue to do so. Nothing will permanently centralize a people which does not make concentration indispensable to getting a living. Thus social concentration depends upon industrial concentration. The possibility of concentrating employments depends upon the nature of the industry. Agricultural occupations cannot possibly be centralized ; they are isolating in their very nature, and hence are essentially non-socializing in their influence. The only industries which tend to centralize and socialize people are manufacturing. Social isolation is as impossible with manufacture as is social concentration with agriculture. The development of manufacturing industries then, is an indispensable condition to national development and social progress.

The development of manufacturing industries is important in many respects. In the first place because it involves socializing occupations. Factory methods of production bring people into close social contact in the ordinary pursuits of industrial life. Whatever compels people to work together, makes their living in close proximity indispensable ; the modern city and all that it implies is chiefly the product of these two facts. From time immemorial the growth of manufacture and trade has been the means of developing towns and cities,[1] and these industrial centres have in turn ever been the nurseries of civilization. It is always in the cities that the most complex social environment arises, and it is always there that the greatest refinement and highest individuality exists, and hence it is there that the successful struggles for social, religious, and political freedom have always taken place.

The difference therefore, between agricultural and manufacturing employments is very marked. Agriculture is essentially isolating and non-socializing as an occupation, and its products relate almost exclusively to physical wants. Hence it does practically nothing either to create or supply the social wants and life of man. Manufacture, on the contrary, relates almost exclusively to the civilizing and refining side of man's character. The supply of clothing, furniture, the development of architecture, music, literature, art, and every thing above the mere

[1] Witness the free cities of the Middle Ages.

physical needs of the savage, is directly or indirectly the result of manufacture and its socializing influence. These things are not only necessitated by man's higher social wants, but are largely consumed as the result of his social relations. Since manufacturing industries tend both to create a socializing environment and to supply the social wants resulting therefrom, they are doubly indispensable to national development.

SECTION III.—*Necessary Conditions to the Development of Manufacture.*

In discussing the economic and social wisdom of any public policy, the two important questions to consider are : (1) What is the end we desire to promote? (2) What means will most surely promote that end ?

1. It may be safely assumed that the desired end, to the promotion of which statesmanship should be devoted and public policy directed, is the material and social progress of the people. We have already seen that this involves the development of the nation as a political entity, and also that national development necessitates social concentration and industrial diversification, which in turn depend upon the growth of manufacturing industries. The immediate question, therefore, for the practical statesman to consider is, what will best promote the development of manufacturing industries. Whatever will promote this end will justify the means necessary to its adoption. The question to ask is *not* what will it cost ? but *will it do it?*

2. It is a universal law in nature and society that growth depends upon opportunity. As already explained, opportunity is not to be interpreted as mere passive possibility, but as actual inducement. In nature opportunity for growth means the existence of conditions and influences which make it easier to grow than not to grow. In society, it is contact with positive social influences which make refinement, knowledge, and general culture easier and more advantageous than ignorance and crudeness ; and in economics it is the existence of conditions which make it more profitable to do than not to do. Opportunity for the development of manufacturing industries therefore, means the existence of conditions which make manufacture not only physically possible but economically profitable.

Obviously the first condition necessary to the growth of any industry is a market for its products. Now an economic market evidently cannot be made by mere fiat of government because it depends on the habits and social life of a people. But it can be preserved by protecting home industry in manufacturers to a certain extent. How far? Why just so far as is necessary to prevent home products from being undersold by the products of lower paid laborers in other countries. This then is the sober rule and principle of protection as ministering to human welfare. *The industries of a country should be protected to the full amount of the difference between the wage-level of that nation and the nations below it in average civilization using similar methods and no further, since thus the maintenance of its place in civilization is secured.* A restrictive policy can be justified only on the ground that it will promote greater social advancement than would otherwise occur. Nothing can justify the restriction of freedom except a demonstration that it will ultimately promote more freedom. Will the protection of the home market increase the opportunities for developing socializing industries? This is the immediate question to consider and it involves a number of most important questions, which will be taken up in their order as follows: (1) The economic and social superiority of the home market over the foreign; (2) the economic basis of international competition; (3) the relation of cost of production to international value; (4) the effect of a tariff upon the price of home products; (5) the relation of tariffs to wages in non-protected industries; (6) the influence of protection in the most advanced countries upon the progress of less civilized countries.

SECTION IV.—*The Economic and Social Superiority of a Home Market over a Foreign.*

There are three important reasons why home markets are superior to foreign markets, and why domestic trade and manufacture should always be encouraged in preference to foreign: (1) Because foreign trade is essentially wasteful; (2) because foreign markets tend to enable employers to permanently profit by low wages; (3) because home markets most surely promote the diversification of industry and social progress.

1. Foreign trade is essentially wasteful because it necessarily tends to maximize instead of minimizing the distance between the raw material and the factory, and between the factory and the market. For instance, before the development of cotton manufacture in this country, our cotton cloth was made in England. The raw cotton was produced in South Carolina, sent to England to be manufactured, then brought back to America. The consumer of cotton cloth in this country had to pay the cost of transporting it twice across the Atlantic, which was so much waste made necessary by uneconomic conditions. To carry a product six thousand miles in order to deliver it to consumers a hundred miles away is to perpetuate the most costly way of doing.

Nothing can justify such waste except absolute inability to avoid it. The mere fact that England could, under existing conditions, do the manufacturing at so much less cost than we, as to be able to pay the transportation both ways, was no economic justification for our continuing to buy cotton cloth of her, instead of developing the methods for making it ourselves. Indeed such a policy would have been as obviously uneconomic as to have persisted in using the hand-loom and stage-coach in preference to the factory and railroad. The question in that case was not, can England, under existing conditions, supply our cotton cloth cheaper than we can make it? but can we, by any change of conditions, develop the means of making it as cheaply for ourselves as she can make it for us, and thus eliminate for all time the unnecessary cost of double transportation? This question was answered in the affirmative, and to-day cotton cloth can be made as cheaply here as in England, and more cheaply than in any other country, notwithstanding our wages are so much higher. Consequently that economic waste is saved not only to us, but to all future generations, to say nothing of the social advantage of developing the industry in our own country.

It may be laid down as a fundamental principle in economic production that all commodities should be manufactured as near as possible to the raw material, or the market for finished products. If a nation possesses the raw material for a given article, it should always develop the facilities for manufacturing the finished product for its own consumption ; and any public policy which does not tend to promote this end is inimical to national development. Therefore, instead of constantly encouraging foreign trade, it should ever be a cardinal principle in statesmanship to develop domestic trade and home manufacture.

2. Another disadvantage of foreign as compared with home markets is, that they divorce the economic interest of the employer and the employed. To the extent that the producers in any community rely upon a foreign market for their wares, the employers cease to have any economic interest in the welfare of their own laborers. Whenever the employer is independent of the laborers of his own country as consumers, he has an apparent interest in keeping down wages, because, under those circumstances, every reduction of wages is an increase of profits. Suppose, for instance, an American shoe manufacturer sells all his product in Europe at a dollar a pair ; it is quite obvious that if he can obtain his labor at 10 per cent. less, it would be so much addition to his net profit, because the reduction of wages would in no way affect the consumption of his shoes, they being sold in another country where wages remain the same.

Under a home-market régime the case is very different, because in domestic trade there are no influences that militate against the material welfare of the laborers which do not react upon that of the employing class. The obvious reason for this is that no market for factory-made products can be permanently sustained without consumption by the laboring classes. Consequently when the employing class in any country have to rely on a home market for the sale of their products, their own prosperity depends directly upon the consuming capacity, and hence the wages, of the laboring classes in their own country. Under such conditions, whatever reduces wages and impairs the purchasing power of the laborer diminishes the market and undermines the prosperity of the employer. Thus, under a home-market régime, the employer's success is dependent upon and commensurate with the prosperity of the laboring classes, because their consumption determines the market basis for his production. But the days of foreign markets, as the chief support of highly developed manufacturing industries in any country, are doomed. Frequency of travel and familiar intercourse between the most civilized nations tend to make exclusive knowledge of productive methods practically impossible. Hence, as fast as nations be-

come consumers of manufactured products, they begin to make
them for themselves, and to use the improved methods developed
by their most advanced neighbors.   Thus the tendency of civilization is to make the industries of all countries depend more and
more upon home consumption.   The economics of the future
must be the economics of large production, home-market, and
high wages, which are the only industrial conditions compatible
with social freedom and political democracy.

3. The third and by no means the least important reason why
home markets are preferable to foreign markets is, that they more
surely promote the diversification of production and the socialization of employments.   One of the popular notions regarding
foreign trade is that the prosperity of a nation is indicated by the
amount of its exports, that it is rich by what it sells.   This is a
great mistake.   Nothing indicates the prosperity and well-being
of a people but what they consume.   A nation may produce extensively and export largely and the mass of its people remain
very poor.   To the extent that more manufactured products are
exported from any country than imported to it, are its products
not consumed by those who produce them.   The prosperity of a
nation therefore, cannot be measured by the wealth it exports to
other countries, nor by the wealth it receives through the profits
of foreign trade, but only by the wealth its own people consume,
since that is all which really enters into their social life.   Thus the
extent of domestic consumption—the home market—is the real
measure of the social status.

Moreover, a home market supplies a double social current,
whereas a foreign market for the same products only supplies a
single current.   In addition to the socializing effect of manufacture upon industry, the home use of manufactured articles tends
to increase and diversify the market for such products by the
social conditions necessarily connected with their consumption.

For instance, the consumption of carpets, pictures, music,
millinery, etc., imply more or less refined social relations, which
stimulate not only the desire for more of the same kind of things,
but also create tastes and desires for fresh varieties of products.
Thus, while manufacturing industries always socialize, their socializing influence is necessarily the greatest where they produce
for a home market.   This must not be interpreted to mean that

foreign markets are a disadvantage under all conditions, but only that wherever the development of a home market is possible it is always preferable to a foreign market.　In other words, foreign trade is ultimately an economic disadvantage to a nation unless it can take place without substituting simpler for relatively complex industries or lowering wages, and should be encouraged under no other conditions.

SECTION V.—*The Economic Basis of International Competition.*

Competition is regarded as essential to industry, because it promotes economy in the production of wealth both by developing the highest capacity in the producers and by reducing prices, thus giving the community the advantage of the highest skill and the best productive methods.　This unexceptionable proposition has the advantage of being one of the most uniformly accepted postulates in economic science.　Here then we have a point of common agreement, namely, *that no competition can promote industrial well-being which does not tend to make wealth cheap.* (Neither a free trade nor a protective policy therefore can be economically justified, except as it squares with this proposition.)

In order to apply this test to public policy, however, it is necessary to understand clearly what constitutes cheap wealth, and how to determine accurately when commodities are cheap or dear.　Commodities are said to be dearer as their value rises, and cheaper as their value falls ; but the terms dearer and cheaper have no meaning except as they indicate that the articles referred to have become more or less difficult for man to obtain. Wheat cannot be either cheap or dear to potatoes or gold, any more than Easter bonnets can be cheap or dear to fishes.　The value of wheat may be high or low as compared *with* that of potatoes or gold, but value cannot be high or low *to* those articles ; it can be high or low only *to* man.　Nor is the value of an article high or low to man because it will exchange for a larger or smaller quantity of gold or other commodities, but solely because it will exchange for a larger or smaller quantity of his labor.　In short, the terms value, price, exchange, dearness, and cheapness have absolutely no meaning, and convey no idea except in relation to man.

From this point of view the importance of economic movement does not turn upon the relation of one kind of wealth to another, but depends upon the relation of all kinds of wealth to man. Wealth is not necessarily cheap or dear according as it will exchange for a large or small amount of gold, but only as it will exchange for a large or small amount of labor. That is to say, no matter what the ratio of exchange between different commodities or between all commodities and gold may be, they are cheap or dear only in proportion as a large or small amount can be obtained for a day's service.

It may be said that the ratio in which commodities exchange for gold always indicates the ratio in which they will exchange for labor; that is to say, the gold-price always indicates the labor-price. This may be true to a limited extent within any given country, but it is almost never true as between different countries. Take, for example, this country and China; suppose shoes of a given quality were two dollars a pair in this country and they were only fifty cents a pair in China, manifestly the amount of gold necessary to obtain a pair of shoes in America would purchase four pairs in China. Thus according to the gold standard of measurement shoes in America would be three hundred per cent. dearer than those in China, which is precisely what the current doctrine teaches us to believe. Consequently it is laid down as a self-evident proposition, that any discrimination which would prevent the shoes of China from entering the market of America at less than two dollars a pair would make the shoes of the American consumer dearer by three hundred per cent.; therefore, the true economic policy is to have free trade between America and China, and thus enable the American citizen to have cheap shoes.

If we examine such a transaction from the standpoint of man instead of gold, the utter fallacy of such a position will at once be apparent. To be sure the shoes in America cost two dollars a pair, but as the American mechanic receives two dollars a day he can obtain a pair of shoes for a day's labor, while in China, although the shoes cost but fifty cents a pair, the laborer receiving less than ten cents a day must work fully five days to obtain a pair of shoes. Thus while measured in gold, the shoes in America cost four times as much as those in China ; measured in labor, the Chinese shoes are four hundred per cent dearer than the American. Manifestly the two-dollar American shoes are cheaper for Americans than the fifty-cent Chinese shoes are for Chinamen. Professors Sumner, and Perry would probably reply yes, but Chinese shoes would be cheaper for Americans than American shoes are, because we could get four pairs of Chinese shoes for the amount of service we now give for one pair. It is, they would add, just because the Chinese can make shoes for Americans cheaper than Americans can make them for themselves, that we want free trade in order that we may obtain our shoes from those who can make them cheapest. Why should we give the shoemakers of Lynn or Marblehead two dollars for what we can buy from those of Pekin or Hong Kong for one dollar ?

This argument has a very satisfactory seeming, but it has the disadvantage of failing to reckon with the facts. Like the Ricardian theory, that "profits can only rise as wages fall," it would be true provided the assumption upon which it is based were correct—namely, that every thing else remains the same. Of course the American consumer would receive a net gain by purchasing his shoes from China at fifty cents a pair, instead of paying two dollars in America, if wages and other conditions remained the same, which would be an impossibility. It would be just as rational to say that ' other things remaining the same,' a brick will not sink to the bottom of a bucket of water. It is precisely because no two particles of the water remain the same that the brick sinks ; the disturbance caused by introducing the brick makes a readjustment of every drop of water necessary.

The same is true in the case before us. The introduction of Chinese shoes into the American market would not merely give the two-dollar American laborer one dollar shoes, but to the extent that it operated, would make it a general industrial disturbance and therefore cause a readjustment of economic relations. As already stated, whatever undersells succeeds, and whatever succeeds becomes permanent, and whatever becomes permanent establishes the methods by which its success is accomplished. Therefore if the shoemakers of China could undersell the shoemakers of America in the American market, they would necessarily succeed in obtaining the custom of American consumers. If this caused no other change than to reduce the price of shoes in this country, the case would be very simple, and the logic of the *laissez-faire* economist would be conclusive ; but this is not the case. On the contrary, it would make an entire rearrangement of industrial conditions necessary, at least so far as the 200,000 of American shoemakers are concerned.

As soon as American consumers begin to buy shoes from China several forces will begin to operate, which will tend to revolutionize and ultimately readjust economic relations. The American manufacturer will endeavor to compete with the Chinaman in the American market, to do which he will be compelled to reduce the cost of producing shoes here at least to the level of the cost of production in China, together with the cost of transportation. This could only be accomplished in one of two ways, either by using superior labor-saving machinery or by reducing wages equal to the difference. The improved machinery could not be adopted for any such reason, because nothing has occurred to increase the market sufficiently to make its profitable employment possible.

A slight increase in the consumption of shoes might result from lowering the price, but that would soon be more than offset by the reduced consumption among the discharged laborers. Hence it is manifest that such a change could do practically nothing to create the better machinery necessary to make a difference in the cost of production. The only other alternative would be to reduce the wages of shoemakers here to substantially the same level as those in China. And this would not be limited to the men who simply manufacture the shoes, it must also apply to all those who produce the raw materials and tools used in making shoes. When this reduction occurs, all the cheapness of the imported shoes disappears, because the capacity of American laborers to purchase shoes is reduced exactly as much as the price of the shoes has fallen. If wages are not reduced, then the Chinaman would produce the shoes and the American shoemaker would be forced into idleness, unless he emigrates to China, in which case he would have to work on the same terms as the Chinaman.

Nor is there any warrant for assuming that the discharged laborer will find another occupation. Nothing will create employments except a market for products. Since nothing has occurred in this instance to create either a demand for new commodities or increase the consumption of existing ones, we have no more right to assume that the discharged laborers could find new occupations than we have to assume that they could live in luxury without employment. Thus in the·last analysis the shoes would either have to be made in China or in America by Chinese methods ; and in either case, American wages would be adjusted to Chinese prices. Consequently, instead of the low-priced products from China giving us *cheap wealth* in America, it would serve only to give us *cheap labor* and a lower civilization.

It may be regarded as an ‘economic axiom that nothing can permanently cheapen wealth which does not reduce the price of commodities relatively to wages, and this can never be accomplished by substituting cheaper for dearer labor, either at home or abroad.

Nor is this all. Not only is it true that the low-priced shoes of China would not be permanently cheaper to anybody than the high-priced shoes of America, but to permit the products of the low-paid laborers of Asia to undersell those of the high-paid laborers of America, would be to prevent the growth of the only influences which can make wealth permanently cheaper in the future. Just in proportion as the high-paid labor of one country is superseded by the low-paid labor of another, is the simpler social life and small consumption of the former substituted for the more complex social life and larger consumption of the latter. This check in the demand for an increasing variety of products necessarily prevents the diversification of industry and the development of manufacture, and consequently lessens the incentive for the concentration of capital, the use of steam-driven machinery, and all wealth-cheapening methods of production ; and thus not only fails to furnish cheap wealth for the present, but prevents the possibility of cheaper wealth in the future. It is manifest, therefore, that from a philosophic view of the case any public policy which aids or permits the products of the low-paid labor of one country to undersell the products of the high-paid labor of another, tends to arrest human progress by stereotyping lower civilization and preventing the growth of a higher.

Whenever a struggle for industrial supremacy takes place between producers in countries of differing degrees of civilization,[1] one of two things must necessarily occur : either the higher must descend to the plane of the lower, or the lower must ascend to the plane of the higher.   If the higher-paid producer descends to the plane of the lower, it will not be *economic* competition, because in that case the low-wage products will be sure to undersell the high-wage products, and thus enable the inferior to succeed against the superior.   In such a struggle there is nothing to develop the best in the higher, but every thing to repress it.   The cheap-labor competitor does not succeed through his economic superiority, but solely because of his social inferiority.   Such a contest, therefore, is contrary to all conditions of economic competition.[2]   Instead of being a contest between approximately equal competing units which tends to develop the best in both, it is an unequal struggle in which the inferior is sure to prevail against the superior.

When competition takes place on the plane of the higher wage-level, the result is very different.   In such a contest, whoever succeeds is compelled to do so by employing superior machinery, and that reduces the cost of wealth by *saving* instead of *cheapening* human labor.   Every effort of the lower to succeed against the higher by such means necessarily tends to develop better methods of production, cheapen wealth and promote social progress in the less advanced country, even if it fails to undersell competitors in a foreign market.   On the other hand, in every such struggle the high-wage producer is compelled to make efforts to still further develop the wealth-cheapening methods in the most advanced countries.   Therefore the contest on the higher plane is supremely economic, because it stimulates the best in both competitors, guarantees that only the superior shall succeed, and in so doing helps rather than injures the inferior.

This is precisely what takes place in every other sphere of development.   Evolution is a constant differentiation and higher integration with an ever increasing complexity of relations.   Social progress constantly tends toward a greater variety of relations,

---

[1] The most infallible test of a relatively high or low state of civilization in any country is the material or social conditions of the masses, which is always indicated by the rate of real wages.

[2] See definition of economic competition, p. 293.

specialization of functions, and integration into larger but more diversified aggregates ; witness the tendency towards larger and larger cities and nations, through which greater freedom and more complex and socializing intercourse is steadily developed. In all this progressive tendency each integration takes place by the lower rising to the plane of the higher, and never by the higher descending to that of the lower. And this progress can only take place by the lower becoming approximately equal to the higher. For instance, if one wants to move in a social class more cultured than the one to which he belongs, he can do so only by becoming more cultured himself. The more refined will neither take on coarser manners nor tolerate then in another for the sake of his society. Indeed, were it otherwise, progress would be impossible ; because if the higher would descend to the lower, there would be no incentive for the lower to rise.

Since nothing can cheapen wealth which does not reduce the cost of production without diminishing real wages, and since no industrial contest can be economically competitive which does not take place between approximately equal competing units, and since there can be no approximate economic equality between contestants except on the plane of the higher, it follows that *the true economic basis for international competition is the wage-level of the dearer-labor country.* In order therefore to apply the doctrine of opportunity laid down in the previous chapter, and to establish international trade upon a strictly economic basis, it is necessary for the higher-wage country to discriminate against the products of the lower-wage producer to the full extent that the lower wages affect the cost of production, as this determines the competitive status of the commodity. Thus we have a truly economic basis for a tariff policy that shall be *protective* without being *paternal.* A tariff policy based upon this principle would protect the superior against injury from the inferior, without affording the slightest monopolistic impediment to economic rivalry. Instead of restricting wholesome competition, this would simply protect the competitive opportunity for the "fittest to survive," the test of fitness always being the ability to furnish low-priced wealth without employing low-priced labor. Under such conditions the products of foreign countries could never undersell those of home industry, except when the lower price of the foreign product is due to the use of superior labor-*saving* and not to labor-*cheapening* methods. Consequently whoever undersells confers a permanent advantage on the whole community.

SECTION VI.—*Some Popular Fallacies Considered.*

It is a standing charge against the protective doctrine that it has no definable scientific basis, that it is grounded upon no general principle in nature, society, or economics. Nor is this charge wholly unwarranted when judged by the accepted reasoning on the subject. It is a peculiar feature of the history of tariff legislation that it has been generally advocated for local or special reasons, and almost never based upon any economic principle susceptible of general application. In this country, where the protective idea has reached its highest development, the tariff advocate rests his claim almost entirely upon the fact that we have made marked industrial progress under a protective *régime.* He compares the wages and social condition of the laborers in high-tariff America with those of the laborers in free-trade England, and confidently exclaims : "Behold the superiority of a high-tariff policy !" And, with equal assurance, he ascribes the poverty and social degradation of Ireland and India to the fact that British rule has prevented them from having a protective tariff. On the other hand, while the free-trader objects to this kind of reasoning by the protectionist as confounding coincidence with cause, he employs it with equal assurance in presenting his own case. Studiously confining his observation to European conditions, he compares the wages and social condition of laborers in England under free trade with those in continental countries under protection, but not with those in America, and triumphantly exclaims : "Behold the superiority of free trade !"

By this mode of reasoning the English free-trader is as unable to explain why wages are higher in America under protection than in England under free trade, as is the American protectionist to explain why they are higher in England with free trade than in continental and Asiatic countries under protection. If the mere fact that prosperity accompanied free trade in England justifies the reasoning of the free-trader, then the fact that prosperity accompanies a high tariff in America equally justifies the reasoning of the protectionist. And when the free-trader declares, as he does, that America is not prosperous by virtue of the tariff, but in spite of it, the protectionist can with equal force reply that England is not prosperous by virtue of her free trade, but in spite of it. This line of reasoning furnishes no scientific means of testing the merits of either doctrine ; it shows that progress is possible under both policies, but it affords no logical basis for the application of either. What these facts show is, that neither free trade in England nor protection in America prevented the growth of industrial prosperity in those countries, but they do nothing to prove that this progress was promoted by either policy.

Free trade being simply the absence of protection, it follows that to discover the law of economic protection is to discover that of free-trade also, and since neither free trade nor protection will produce the best economic effects under all conditions, it is only by the knowledge of such a law that any philosophic application of either policy is possible. If the conclusions reached in the preceding sections are correct, however, this law is already established, and we have a universal principle upon which a protective and consequently a free trade policy can be scientifically adopted. Briefly stated this law is : (1) *that competition can be economic only when it takes place between approximately equal competitors ;* (2) *that when there is any marked difference in the wage-level of the international competitors, such approximate competitive equality is possible only when the competition is based upon the higher wage-level of the higher ;* (3) *that no lowering of prices can cheapen wealth which does not result from diminishing the cost of production without lowering wages.*

Bearing these propositions in mind, we shall have no difficulty in seeing why a protective policy might promote industrial prosperity and social progress in America, and have the reverse effect in Austria, India, and Ireland. Nor will it be difficult to understand why America has more to fear from free trade with highly civilized England than with the less civilized nations of Asia and South America. And it will be equally clear why a tariff policy will not produce the same effect with a high-wage level in a small colony like Victoria with a million inhabitants, as in a large country like the United States, with sixty-five million of people.[1]

[1] See articles in *The Nineteenth Century* for September, 1888, and *Quarterly Journal of Economics*, October, 1888.

22

One of the arguments much relied upon by protectionists is that known as the " infant-industry argument." The burden of this argument is that industries should be protected in their early stages to prevent them from being killed by competition before they are fully established, the implication being that when they become well established they will be able to hold their own against the world.   For a time this idea was reluctantly accepted by anti-tariff people, but now that after having had protection for half a century and on the plea of " infant industries," a tariff is still demanded, the free-traders naturally ask " when do industries reach maturity ? "   They regard such reasoning as far more infantile than the industry, and insist that if there is any virtue in the protective principle, it should be applied in behalf of the weak against the strong and not in behalf of the strong against the weak.   Consequently, if protection can be justified at all, it is such countries as Russia, Turkey, Italy, Spain and the industrially weak countries of South America that need protection against the United States, and not the United States against them.

If the principle here laid down had been recognized, the obvious fallacy in both these positions would have been apparent ; and the talk about " infant industries " would never have been indulged in by the protectionist, and the free-trader's rejoinder about protecting the lower against the higher would have been too absurd for utterance.   It would then have been seen that the products of America do not need protection against those of England because the industries are younger, but because they are made under a higher civilization—a civilization in which the human element in production is more expensive. Hence, to permit the products of America to be undersold by those of another country, the lower cost of which results entirely from the use of lower-paid labor, would neither give cheaper wealth nor better social conditions.   It would also have been clear that this fact in no wise changes with age, unless either the wage-level of the lower-wage country rises, or the use of labor-saving appliances in the higher-wage country more than overcomes the difference.   Unless one of these things occurs protection will be as necessary at the end of a thousand years as it was the first six months, although both countries may have greatly advanced.

Indeed, the greater the advancement in both countries the greater will be the probability of their employing similar machinery, thus making the necessity of protection depend entirely upon the difference in their respective wage-levels, as is the case with America and England to-day. Therefore, when the tariff advocate asks for protection simply because the industry is young, and the free-trader opposes it on the assumption that the producers in a superior civilization ought to be able to economically compete with those in an inferior civilization, they both mistake the true economic gist of the problem. Social superiority, instead of making protection unnecessary, is the very thing which makes it necessary, provided it is *socially important* to retain or further develop the industry.

Nor is this peculiar to industry ; it is a general principle throughout society. In every phase of human relations, it is the higher that needs protection against the lower, and this because the latter will resort to methods of aggression and defence which the former cannot, for social or ethical reasons, afford to employ. Take, for example, the criminal laws. They are enacted to restrain the morally lower from injuring the higher ; it is to prevent the dishonest from plundering the honest, the malicious from assaulting the well-intentioned, that police courts and jails are instituted and armies maintained. Indeed, there is not a restrictive institution maintained in society which was not called into existence to protect the higher from the injurious effects of the lower.

It may be asked, if this theory is correct, why does not the American producer need a much higher tariff against the products of China, Russia, or South America than he does against those of England, since her wage-level much more nearly approximates to his own ? The reason for this is very simple. It is because the social chasm between America and those countries is so great, that the use of labor-saving appliances here more than makes up for the difference in the cost of labor in the respective countries. In China, for instance, where almost every thing is made by hand labor, the product per capita is so small, compared with what can be turned off by steam-driven machinery here, that it costs more to produce an article there with labor at 6 cents a day than it does here with labor at two dollars a day.

But if the labor-saving machinery of America were introduced into China, and operated by their six-cent-a-day laborers, then an immensely high tariff would be necessary in order to protect the high wage-level of America, because, in that case, while all other items of cost would be the same, the human element in the productive process would be many hundred per cent. dearer here than there. This is why England is a more dangerous competitor to us than China. True, the wage-levels of America and England are more nearly alike than are those of America and China, but the machinery of America and England is still more so. Indeed, it is because the machinery used in America and England is practically the same, that all the difference in their respective wage-levels is directly expressed in the relative competitive power of the two countries. What is true of England is equally true of France, Germany, and every other country, to the extent that they use similar machinery but cheaper labor than we do ; yet they may have very much cheaper labor, and still be practically harmless as economic competitors, so long as they use poorer machinery or hand methods.

Another error into which tariff advocates commonly fall, is in thinking that India, Ireland, or Russia would greatly improve their condition if they imposed a tariff against British products. Indeed, there are not a few Englishmen to-day who entertain a similar notion, and insist that England would be greatly benefited by adopting a tariff policy towards America. This is a mistake, for America's wage-level being higher than England's, we could not undersell her except by the use of superior methods, which either English producers would be forced to adopt or let American producers do the work, and in either case English laborers would have a net gain. If the better methods were adopted in England, she would have cheaper products without lower wages, which would be equal to a rise of wages. If America made the products, the English laborer could emigrate to America and obtain American wages.

The same is true with regard to England and continental countries. Competition between England and Russia would not injure Russia, because there are no economic methods employed in England which are not superior to those employed in Russia. Whenever Russia is undersold by England, her products will have to be made by English methods either in England or in Russia, and in either case the Russian people will be benefited. The only reason England is not injured to-day by competition with the countries in Continental Europe is precisely the same as that which prevents China from seriously injuring America, namely : that while her wage-level is higher, her machinery is so much superior to theirs, that it more than makes up the difference in the cost of production.[1] England has less to fear, however, from continental competition than we have, because their wage-level is nearer to hers than it is to ours, and to the extent that American and English machinery is adopted in continental countries faster than their wage-level approximates that of England, will their relative competitive power gain upon hers. In fact, unless the wage-level in continental countries rises very rapidly, it can only be a matter of time when they will occupy the same competitive position to England that she now sustains to America, in which case she will be compelled either to adopt a protective policy or surrender much of her manufacture to continental producers.

It will thus be seen that the seemingly inexplicable phenomena over which free-traders and protectionists have vainly contended, become perfectly explainable on the principle that international competition can only be beneficial when the competitors are approximately equal upon the plane of the higher. Therefore a protective policy is beneficial to a nation, only as affecting its relations with less civilized countries. While America may need protection against the machine-made products of all other countries, there is no country that can be permanently benefited by discriminating against the products of America. So too with England ; she may ultimately require a tariff against the machine-made products of all other countries but America, and so on. In a word, a tariff can only be of any permanent economic advan-

---

[1] According to Mulhall, 80 % of the productive energy in Great Britain is furnished by steam, while in continental countries steam only represents an average of 36 %. Consequently, the total cost of productive power per thousand foot-tons is 17 cents in Great Britain as compared with 27 cents on the continent. " This advantage enables us (England) as far as labor is concerned to undersell continental countries by 12 %, although our workmen's wages are almost double."—" History of Prices," pp. 54 and 57.

tage, to the extent that it protects the opportunity for industrial development afforded by a higher wage-level from the uneconomic influence of a lower wage-level and inferior civilization.

Section VII.—*The Effect of a Tariff upon the Price of Home Products.*

There is no objection urged against a tariff policy so much emphasized and so frequently repeated as the charge that a tariff is necessarily a tax—an oppressive burden upon the consumer. The free-trade advocates, especially in this country, deny that it is possible to improve the industrial condition of a community by any system of tariff legislation. They insist that at best it can only enable one class to gain at the expense of another.[1] Perry regards a protective tariff as an unmitigated curse, and says : "Political economy, denouncing it as the enemy of mankind, hopes soon to throw upon its loathsome carcass the last shovelful of cleansing earth."[2]

It will not, however, be difficult to show that despite the learning and dogmatism on its side, this mode of treating the subject is exceedingly superficial. The assertion that a tariff is a tax bears the stamp of the declaimer rather than the economist ; while seeming to say much, it actually says nothing. A tax is simply a contribution to the public treasury, and is one of the innumerable expenditures that social life makes necessary. The payment of two dollars for a hat or a pair of shoes is just as much a burden upon the resources of the citizen as is a tax of two dollars for the government.

Taxes, like all other kinds of expenditures, should be treated as an investment, the wisdom or unwisdom of which depends not upon its amount, but entirely upon whether it yields more in ultimate advantage than it costs in immediate disadvantage. This fact can be more easily determined in some cases than in

---

[1] "We deny that they can gain any thing from us, *on account of the law*, but what we lose ; we deny that the total gains to one part of society by this process can ever exceed the total losses of another part—*i.e.*, that the process can increase the wealth of the community ; we deny, finally, that our share of these hypothetical gains can ever be redistributed to us so as to bring back our first loss."—Sumner's " Protection in the United States," pp. 11 and 12.

[2] " Political Economy," p. 477.

others. For example, when one buys a steak, by the next meal time he can determine whether or not he received an equivalent for what he gave ; whether the satisfaction was equal to the cost. If he purchases a suit of clothes, however, the result cannot be so quickly determined. It will take several months to ascertain whether or not an equivalent was given and received. And if he invests in a farm or a factory, a still longer time is required to decide the wisdom or unwisdom of the purchase. The indirect and impersonal nature of governmental expenditures makes a still longer time necessary to determine the exact results.

In order to determine whether or not a tax is a good investment, we have to deal with general tendencies or with ultimate rather than immediate effects. For instance, if the wisdom of the expenditure involved in maintaining an army, navy, police force, were determined by the immediate effects at any given time, it would be regarded as waste. Nevertheless the expenditure necessary to enforce law and order is regarded as a good investment even by free-traders. It procures as good economic results as the expenditure for food, clothes, or shelter, since it is essential to their enjoyment.

The same is true of education, but the effects here are still further removed from direct observation, and consequently must be judged on a still broader general basis. There are in some countries, and indeed in some parts of this country, those who regard a tax for the public schools as an oppressive burden, an unjust exaction. But upon a broader view of the subject it appears that their general social safety, freedom, and well-being largely depend upon the intelligence of the great mass of the community in which they live, and this to a great extent depends upon opportunities for popular education. Experience has conclusively shown expenditure in public schools to be a good investment ; it comes back in better citizens and a higher civilization, which in turn supplies all the influences and conditions that make cheaper wealth and larger freedom possible.

In the same way must we estimate the wisdom or unwisdom of a protective tariff. In considering the effect of a tariff policy upon the price of home products, we must not consider alone the direct and immediate effect upon prices, but also the indirect and ultimate effect. It has already been pointed out that the test of cheapness is the ratio in which labor will exchange for wealth, things being cheap or dear according as a large or small quantity can be obtained for a day's labor. If home products can be undersold by foreign, solely because labor is cheaper abroad than here, the only result would be a readjustment of prices on the lower wage-level, with no advantage to anybody. Let us assume that a 20 per cent. tariff is necessary to prevent the home products from being thus undersold, that 20 per cent. would not in any sense be a tax upon the American consumer, because if that tariff were not applied, the wage-level would be commensurately lowered and a day's labor would purchase no more wealth than before. To say that under such conditions the home producer is enabled to add as profit on his whole product an amount equal to the tariff upon the foreign product, is to exhibit a striking unacquaintance with economic phenomena.[1] All that a tariff can do in such instances is to prevent a readjustment of prices on a lower wage-level. Prices however, would be governed by cost of production, according to the law before stated, just as if there were no tariff. The competition between home producers, together with the effort of the consumers to purchase at the minimum, will force prices down to the cost of producing the most expensive portion of the necessary supply. All who can produce at less than that, will obtain the difference as profit. Unless the cost of producing that dearest portion can be lessened by some other means than by lowering wages, it is utterly impossible to make any improvement by reducing price.

This much however, only applies to the direct and immediate effect, and is usually the only aspect which the advocate of *laissez faire* stops to consider. The permanent economic influence of a protective tariff upon the price of home products, however, is the indirect and ultimate effect rather than the immediate and direct. In preventing the products of dear labor from being undersold by those of cheap labor, the tariff protects the home market for the home producer. The economic effect of this, as already shown, is to promote the growth of manufacturing industries, and to concentrate population, which in turn creates a social environment that develops new tastes and habits, and these elevate the standard of living among the masses, and

[1] *Cf.* President Cleveland's message December 6, 1887.

consequently enlarge the demand for an increasing quantity and variety of products.

The necessary tendency of this is to develop a higher grade of social character and general intelligence, more inventive genius and improved methods of production, by which the cost and therefore the price of commodities is ultimately lowered without reducing wages. From the foregoing it will be seen that a tariff or any thing else which prevents a readjustment of prices on a lower wage-level affords protection to the opportunity for developing better productive possibilities through the use of labor-saving and wealth-cheapening methods. The effect of a tariff upon the price of home products, therefore, when applied according to the principles here laid down, is, first, to prevent a wasteful readjustment of economic relations on a lower wage-plane ; second, to protect opportunities for increasing productive possibilities and thereby make a readjustment of economic relations on a higher wage-plane necessary.

If space permitted it could easily be shown that, despite the frequent unseemly higgling and hauling to help local producers by absurd tariff schedules, this has been the general effect of the protective policy of this country. Take, for example, the cotton industry, to which reference has already been made. For reasons not necessary to explain here, the factory system had its rise in England, and by the close of the first quarter of the present century the use of steam-driven machinery, especially in the manufacture of cotton cloth, had become well established. At that time the cotton industry in this country was in its infancy, being mostly carried on in small factories run by water-power. The difference in the development of this industry in the two countries is clearly shown by the number of factories, amount of capital, etc., which, in 1830, was as follows :

	England.	America.
Number of establishments	1,151	801
Capital invested per establishment . . .	$147,680	$50,702
Number of spindles per establishment . .	8,108	1,556
Number of looms per establishment . .	87	41
Number of operatives per establishment . .	205	77
Weekly wages [1]	$2.51	$3.46
Price per yard	15½	17

[1] These figures represent for England (1833) the average weekly wages of 67,819 cotton operatives. And for America they represent the average wages of 31,471 cotton operatives in New England (1830).

It will be seen from the above that the English manufacturer had a double advantage over the American. In addition to having nearly half a century's start in the development of factory methods, by which he had acquired a much greater concentration of capital and more efficient use of machinery, he had an advantage of nearly 40 per cent. in the cost of his labor. No argument is necessary to show that under such conditions it was impossible to prevent our cotton cloth from being undersold by the English without reducing American wages fully one third. Nor would this reduction in wages have been limited to the factory operatives ; for even if the American manufacturer had imported English machinery free of duty, the higher wages of the bricklayers, masons, carpenters, painters, etc., would have made his building and general plant cost more than the English. It would have been necessary, therefore, to have reduced wages in all these industries to practically the same level as those in England, in order to be able to compete with the English manufacturer in our home market. To obviate this difficulty and make it possible for the American manufacturer to produce for the American market, a tariff was levied upon English cotton cloth. This, however, did not increase the price of the American product, as is commonly assumed, but it increased the price of the English product, thereby preventing the price of American cloth from falling to the English level, and making it unnecessary to reduce wages here in the cotton and several other industries. By thus putting the American producer on an approximate competitive equality with the English in the American market, an economic basis was furnished for the development of cotton manufacture in this country.

Nor did this tariff create a monopoly, by which the price of cotton cloth could be abnormally increased and fabulous profits obtained by the American producer. On the contrary, it prevented the English producer from monopolizing the American market through the use of cheaper labor. So long as the English producer, by paying lower wages, could undersell the American, there was no inducement for the American to take the risk of investing capital in improved machinery. But when this uneconomic advantage was removed and the competitors in the American market were put upon substantially the same wage-level, a strong incentive for developing superior methods was created, since their use became the only means of success.

With the rapid increase of population which our high wage-level stimulated the home market steadily increased, making a larger production necessary. This naturally led to a greater concentration of capital, the use of larger factories and better machinery, and the result is that cotton cloth, which could not be produced for less than seventeen cents a yard in 1830, can now be furnished at a profit for five cents a yard, while the laborer receives double the wages he did then.[1] The development of wealth-cheapening methods in the cotton industry, which the protection of the home market has made possible, will be seen by the following facts for England and America in 1830 and 1880 :

	England.		America.	
	1830.	1880.	1830.	1880.
No. of establishments .	1,151	2,671	801	726
Capital per estab. . .	$147,680	$140,292	$50,702	$275,503
Spindles per estab. . .	8,108	14,798	1,556	14,089
Looms per estab. . .	87	192	41	298
Laborers per estab. . .	205	180	77	228
Wages	$2.51	$4.66	$3.46	$6.45 [2]
Price of cloth per yard,	15¼	6¾	17	.07

It will be observed from the above that in 1830 the concentration of capital in the cotton industry was very much greater in England than in America, the ratio of capital to establishments being nearly three times as large, that of spindles more than five times, that of looms twice as great, and that of operatives nearly three times as great as in this country, while wages were 38 per cent. lower. But in 1880 their relative position is reversed. While in England the total capital invested had a little more than doubled, in America it had increased more than 400 per cent. In England, with the increased capital, the number of establishments had been commensurately increased, while in America the number

---

[1] See Part III., chap. iv., sec. v.

[2] The wages in this table represent Massachusetts and England for 1883. The average weekly wages for the whole period from 1872 to 1883 inclusive, in the cotton industry, were : in England, $4.60 ; in Massachusetts, $7.68—being 66.96. per cent. higher in Massachusetts than England. See " Massachusetts Labor Bureau Report for 1884," p. 419.

of establishments was actually reduced. Hence, in 1880 the amount of capital per establishment in England was $7,000 less than in 1830, while in America it was five times as large. The ratio of spindles to establishments only increased in England about 82 per cent., while in America they increased 800 per cent. The number of looms per establishment in 1880 had a little more than doubled in England, while in America they increased six-fold. During this period the number of operatives per establishment in England diminished from 205 to 180, while in America they increased from 77 to 228 ; and while wages in England rose $2.15 a week, in America they rose $2.99 a week. All this clearly demonstrates that the concentration of capital and the use of labor-saving appliances in this industry made greater progress in America than in England after the home market régime was inaugurated. This is further shown by the fact that the price of the product has been reduced more here, even with a greater rise in the wages, than in England. Consequently, so far as the manufacturing process is concerned, cotton cloth can be made cheaper in America to-day than in England, notwithstanding that wages in the same industry are 38 per cent. higher here than there.

Nor was the beneficial effect of protecting the home market in this instance limited to the cotton industry. The concentration of capital and development of large factories in the cotton industry naturally created a demand for machinery, which gave rise to various branches of home manufacture in the iron industry and the numerous industries involved in the building trades. With this growth of manufacture and diversification of employment, industrial centres became large cities, which furnished a steadily increasing market for the products of our food and raw material, producing population. This in turn necessitated railroads, which still further lessened the cost of production, diversified industry, cheapened travel, and thereby enabled the daily paper to penetrate the rural districts, and the country population to come into more frequent contact with city life ; and in other manifold ways developed the socializing influences of the nation, thus reacting upon the social life, standard of living, and wages of the laboring class.

Without attempting to follow the various phases of industrial development directly or indirectly resulting from the protection of the home market, it is perfectly safe to say that, with the advantage that England had in factory development, it would have been impossible to develop cotton and many other kindred manufacturing industries without the imposition of a tariff, or some other restrictive policy, unless we had lowered our wages to the English level. To have done that would have destroyed the incentive for emigration and thereby arrested the rapid increase of our population, which in turn would have commensurately checked the growth of our home markets, and thus necessarily have greatly hindered the development of many manufacturing industries. And if, without a tariff we had maintained our higher wage-level, not only our cotton cloth, but nearly all our manufactured products, would have been made in England, and we should have remained practically an agricultural people, and hence, in all probability, would now be a third- or fourth-rate nation, with a scattered population of perhaps from twenty to thirty millions, having smaller wages, less general intelligence, and therefore a lower civilization than England.

SECTION VIII.—*The Relation of Protection to Wages in Non-Protected Industries.*

One of the most plausible objections urged against tariff legislation is that it affords no benefit to those engaged in non-protected industries. It is insisted that in order to justify a tariff policy, its advocates are bound to show that it is as advantageous to those engaged in non-protected as in protected industries. Nor is this an unreasonable demand ; there can surely be no justification for any public policy which benefits one portion of the community only at the expense of another. That the theory of protection as hitherto presented has failed to fulfil this requirement can hardly be questioned by its most enthusiastic disciples. The protectionists unquestionably believe that the whole community is benefited by a tariff policy, but they have hitherto failed to explain how a tariff on the various articles of food, clothing, furniture, and the like, benefits the carpenter, painter, plumber, bricklayer, mason, engineer, compositor, and other domestic artisans. This is chiefly due to the fact that they have accepted the economic postulates of the *laissez-faire* economists, especially regarding wages, prices, and profits, thus·rendering a philosophic conception of the protective principle logically impossible. We have a striking illustration of this in Mr. Blaine's argument upon that point in his recent controversy with Mr. Gladstone. He said :

"He [Mr. Gladstone] sees that the laborers in what he calls the 'protected industries' secure high pay, especially as compared with the European school of wages. He perhaps does not see that the effect is to raise the wages of all persons in the United States engaged in·what Mr. Gladstone calls the 'unprotected industries.' Printers, bricklayers, carpenters, and all others of that class are paid as high wages as those of any other trade or calling, but if the wages of all those in the protected classes were suddenly struck down to the English standard, the others must follow. A million men cannot be kept at work for half the pay that another million men are receiving in the same country. Both classes must go up or must go down together." [1]

This statement, which represents the gist of the modern protectionist position regarding the economic relation of protection to wages, implies two assumptions, neither of which is correct: (1) that wages are directly increased by the tariff in protected industries ; (2) that through competition the rise of wages in protected industries brings the wages in non-protected industries up to the same level.

1. The idea that wages are high in protected industries because the tariff enables the manufacturer to obtain large profits, and hence to pay higher wages, is one of the most popular fallacies connected with the whole tariff discussion. Even if tariffs increased profits, that would not necessarily increase wages. Employers do not raise wages merely because profits are large. The increase of wages, except in rare cases, does not come through the generosity of the employer, but through the pressing demands of the laborer. Every laborer knows and every statesman ought to know that protected employers are as ready to reduce wages, as reluctant to increase them, and have as many strikes, as do unprotected employers. But the assumption that profits are larger in protected than in unprotected industries has no foundation in fact. Even if a tariff did at first produce this

[1] *North American Review*, January, 1890, pp. 47, 48.

effect, it would soon be destroyed by competition, as capital would leave unprotected to engage in protected industries, where larger profits would be obtained.

Had the economic law of profits been understood, no such assumption would have been made. It would then have been seen that if there is any competition between producers in the same market, the price of the commodity would tend to equal the *cost of producing the most expensive portion of the general supply.* If the cost of producing the dearest portion is lessened by free trade, the price will fall ; if it is increased by protection, the price will rise. But this change will affect the consumer's price, not the employer's profit. The profit in either case will represent the difference in the cost of production, increasing as the cost diminishes below that of the dearest competitor, a difference which neither free trade nor protection can affect.

2. Mr. Blaine's statement, that " a million men cannot be kept at work for half the pay that another million men are receiving in the same country," is also very unfortunate, as that is just what is actually taking place all the time. Coal miners, agricultural laborers, and many others are working every day in this country, in many instances for less than half the pay that many classes of workmen in the cities are receiving. And what makes this position still more unfortunate is the fact that the printers, engineers, bricklayers, carpenters, and others, whose wages are the highest, are employed in non-protected industries ; hence this cannot be the result of competition with the lower wages in protected industries. Neither is this difference in wages in the same country peculiar to nationality or to political institutions ; it is as great in America with protection and democracy as in England with free trade and monarchy, or as in Germany with protection and despotism. Instead of wages tending to uniformity in all industries in the same country, they tend to a greater diversity as industrial differentiation advances. The only sense in which wages tend to uniformity is in the same industry contributing to the same market.[1]

Nor is Mr. Blaine's statement, that " both classes must go up or must go down together," any nearer correct. Experience shows that they do not necessarily do any thing of the kind. For

[1] See chapter on Wages.

instance, in 1725 the wages of agricultural laborers in England were 5s. 4d. ($1.28) per week ; those of carpenters, masons, bricklayers, and other domestic artificers were 6s. ($1.44) a week.   In 1800 the wages of agricultural laborers were 11s. 5d. ($2.74) ; those of domestic artificers 18s. ($4.38).   In 1840 wages of agricultural laborers were 11s. ($2.64) ; of artificers 33s.[1] ($7.92). In 1877 wages in the London building trades were 42s. 9d.[2] ($10.26) a week, while in agriculture wages were about 13s. ($3.12) a week, being only 14s. ($3.36) in 1884.[3]   In a word, during the present century the wages of mechanics and artisans have increased more than twice as much as those of agricultural and other rural laborers.   The truth is, a protective tariff does not affect wages in any such manner as indicated by Mr. Blaine.[4] The laborer knows from experience that an increase in the tariffs on the particular commodity he produces does not yield any commensurate increase in his wages.   And to persist in telling him that it does, can only result in destroying his confidence in the economic advantage of a protective .policy. If working men are expected to take an intelligent interest in protection, a more rational explanation of its advantages must be presented.

[1] Wade's " History of the Working Classes," p. 166.

[2] Rogers' " Six Centuries of Work and Wages," p. 539.

[3] Mulhall's " History of Prices," p. 125.

[4] This argument clearly shows that the American protectionist has not yet outgrown the English demand-and-supply (wage-fund) fallacy, which is further shown by the fact that Mr. Blaine actually ascribes the rise of wages in England to the increased demand for labor here.—*North American Review*, January, 1890, p. 48.   If this were true why did not wages rise still more in Ireland, Germany, Italy, Bohemia, etc., from which countries the emigration has been much greater than from England, and why have wages risen as much in France, with almost no emigration, as in continental countries, where emigration has been the greatest ?   The truth is that voluntary emigration tends to check rather than promote the rise of wages, because it draws off the best laborers upon whom a rise in the wage-level depends.   It is only when the lowest laborers are exported that home wages are improved by the change.   That is why the condition of the laborers in any country can best be improved at home.   Hence the true economic policy is to develop the home market and diversify domestic industry instead of relying upon emigration as the means of relieving industrial distress. The true way to help the people of Russia, India, and China is to take our civilization to them and not to bring them to our civilization, and this can best be done by developing our own possibilities.—See section ix., p. 98.

Considered from the point of view here taken, however, these seemingly conflicting facts are easily explained. When we understand that the price of labor, like that of commodities, is governed by the cost of furnishing the dearest portion of the necessary supply, and that this cost is determined by the laborer's standard of living, which in turn depends upon his character and social environment, the whole subject assumes a new aspect. It then becomes apparent that no influences can permanently affect wages which do not operate upon the laborer's social life and standard of living. The only way a tariff can do that is by promoting the concentration and diversification of industry, thereby creating more complex social relations that, stimulate the growth of new desires and habits and a higher plane of living. Manifestly these influences operate just as much upon the laborers in non-protected as in protected industries. The non-protected printer, carpenter, and painter obtain just as much advantage from the social influences of a manufacturing city as do their protected neighbors, the hatter and cigar-maker. The wages of city mechanics are higher than those of rural laborers because their standard of living is higher, which is owing. to the more complex social conditions under which they live. It is only to the extent that a tariff promotes the development of these social conditions by protecting the home market that it influences wages in any industry. Upon the principle therefore that protection is economically beneficial only as it tends to develop the socializing influences of the nation, it is clear that its effect upon wages is not limited to protected industries, but that it effects equally the wages of all laborers to the extent that it directly or indirectly affects their social environment.

If it were true, as is usually assumed, that a tariff benefits the laborer through increasing the employer's profits and thus enabling him to pay higher wages, it would be true as is often urged that the non-protected mechanic has no interest in a protective policy. And so long as that view is taught by leading protectionists, we may expect to see the intelligent laborers in domestic industries, especially in our large cities, become free-traders. But from the point of view here presented their interest in a protective policy is quite as great and often greater than that of those employed in the most highly protected industries. With-

23

out the development of cities and manufacturing centres, as already shown, railroads, telegraphs and other industries, to say the least, would have been in a much less advanced state.[1] In which case the industrial and social environment of the great mass of mechanics would have been more homogeneous, hence a more simple social life and lower wages would have been inevitable, as is the case in small towns, rural districts, and non-manufacturing communities throughout the world. To the extent that a tariff policy has developed manufacture and the growth of cities, it has improved the social life and wages of laborers in *all* industries in those industrial centres, protected and non-protected. And to the extent that it has developed railroads and telegraphs, it has shortened the distance between farm and factory, and thereby increased the opportunities that force rural laborers into more frequent contact with the social influences of city life,—thus in its reflex action elevating the social life and wages of rural laborers. This explains why the wages even of agricultural and other laborers in isolating occupations are always higher in the immediate vicinity of cities and manufacturing towns.[2]

This view of the subject also enables us to understand why a tariff will not produce the same effect in a small community like an Australian colony, that it will in a large country like the United States, even though the wage-level is as high there as it is here. It is because the population there is too small to furnish a sufficiently large market to sustain the use of the most highly developed factory methods, without which the socializing environment necessary to raise the standard of living and the rate of wages cannot be developed.

There is one other fact that should be noticed before leaving this point. We are told that despite the improvements in machinery and the general advancement, the condition of the factory

[1] Witness India, Russia, and Turkey as compared with this country in these respects. There are six times as many miles of railroad in New York State as in all Turkey, and more miles of railroads in the United States than in all the rest of the world.

[2] This fact has been universally observed though very little understood. See "Wealth and Progress," pp. 160–163 ; Rogers' "Six Centuries of Work and Wages," pp. 171, 172, 180, 327, 535, 536. Also "Wealth of Nations," Book I., ch. viii. For similar facts in India see Buchanan's "Journey through the Countries of Mysore, Canara, and Malabar," vol. i., pp. 124, 125.

operatives of New England and the miners of Pennsylvania is no better, but in many cases is worse, than it was forty years ago, although the products of these industries are highly protected. There is some truth in this statement, and a great deal of error. In the first place, it is not correct in any general sense to say that the condition of the miners and factory operatives has not improved. It is true, however, that the condition of the laborers employed in those industries to-day, as compared with those of forty years ago, has not improved commensurately with the progress of the community. This fact is usually taken as conclusive evidence that, through some unjust manipulation of industrial forces, the laborers in these industries have been excluded from the beneficial effects of the increasing wealth and social advancement.

A little closer examination of the facts, however, will show that this conclusion is erroneous. Suppose, for example, that in a given business the laborers were intelligent Americans in 1850, but for some reason they all left it and their places were filled by Italians or Chinamen, would it be any test of the industrial and social progress of the laborers in the community to compare the wages, character, and intelligence of these Chinamen and Italians in 1890 with those of the Americans who were employed in that industry in 1850? Such a comparison would be rejected by any fair-minded investigator as unworthy of a moment's consideration. He would very properly insist that, in order to ascertain the improvement in the laborer's condition from 1850 to 1880, we must compare the condition of the *same* laborers. The wages and social condition of the Chinamen and Italians might have improved a hundred per cent., and still be no better in 1890 than were those of the American laborers in 1850. The only way to ascertain whether or not, or to what extent, the laborer's condition has improved, is to compare the condition of the American laborers in 1890 with their condition in 1850, and also the condition of the Chinese and Italian laborers in 1890, not with that of the Americans, but with their own condition in 1850.

Now this is precisely what has taken place in New England factory life. The operatives of forty years ago were mainly composed of native Americans, mostly children of the New England farmers. During this period the industrial history of

America has been unlike that of any other country in the world. Owing to our higher wage-level and the protection of our home market, manufacture and a variety of occupations increased much faster than did our native population. The consequence was a continuous stream of emigration to this country. The introduction of every new industry of a higher order naturally drew to it the more intelligent and characterful portion of the laborers from the grade below, their places being filled by the less competent. By this means there was an almost constant movement of laborers from the more simple to the more complex and artistic industries, and the less advanced laborers from other countries taking the simpler occupations. In the cotton industry, for example, as Americans moved up into the position of overseers, managers, or merchants, their places were taken first by English, next by Irish, and last by French Canadian operatives, so that to-day an American is scarcely to be found in the cotton factories of New England, except in the superior positions, many of the various grades of overseers, machinists, etc., being English or English-Irish. Therefore, if we compare the wages and social conditions of the spinner and weaver in New England cotton factories to-day with those of 1840, we are not dealing with the same class of people at all, nor even with the effects of the same civilization. The French or Irish operative may not be very much better off to-day than was the American who occupied the same position forty years ago, and yet his condition may have been improved several hundred per cent. The same is true of the miners of Pennsylvania, who to-day are largely composed of the poorest laborers from Continental Europe.

In order, therefore, to ascertain the progress that has taken place in the industrial and social condition of these classes of operatives, we must not compare their present condition with that of the American forty years ago, but with their own condition at that time. If we compare the condition of small merchants in New England to-day with that of factory operatives of 1850, or compare the condition of the English, Irish, and French Canadian operatives in New England and the miners of Pennsylvania to-day with what it was in England, Ireland, Canada, Scandinavia, Bohemia, or Russia thirty or forty years ago, the improvement will appear as marked as in that of any other class in the community. To overlook this is entirely to misapprehend the phenomena under consideration. These facts are not referred to here to give a rose-colored tint to the condition of these laborers ; on the contrary, I regard their condition, in many instances, as not only a disgrace but as a serious danger to our civilization.[1] They are referred to, only to emphasize the mistake of ignoring them in considering the effect of modern industrial influences upon the social condition of the laborers ; because it is only by recognizing all the facts in the case, that we can form any true estimate of the beneficial or other effects of any industrial policy. Hence it may properly be said that to the extent that protection has promoted the growth of manufacturing industries it has directly and indirectly improved the social condition and raised the wages of all classes of laborers in this country commensurately with the advance of the community.

SECTION IX.—*The Influence of Protection in the Most Advanced Countries upon the Progress of the Less Advanced.*

Perhaps the most specious argument employed in favor of a free-trade policy is that it is cosmopolitan in its character, that it rises above local, sectional, or even national considerations, treating all mankind as brethren, while protection is pre-eminently a local policy that endeavors to discriminate against the people of all other countries in favor of its own. It may be admitted that any policy which promotes the welfare of one country at the expense of another is essentially unphilosophic, and that the best policy for any country is the one whose beneficial effects are most universal. The economic character of a public policy, however, should never be judged by its immediate or temporary effect, but always by its permanent and ultimate influences. Measured by this standard, it is not difficult to show that the protective principle as here laid down is pre-eminently cosmopolitan in its character.

It may be regarded as a self-evident proposition that he who would help others must first develop the best in himself, since not to develop his own capacities is to limit his usefulness. The most altruistic effects are usually produced by efforts to broaden and

---

[1] See " Wealth and Progress," pp. 365–373.

elevate our own social life, because every addition to our own life embraces more of the efforts, interests, and well-being of others. In proportion as the interests of others becomes identified with our own, will our efforts be directed to promoting their welfare as much as our own. In other words, in proportion as we become socially interdependent do our efforts become altruistic and cosmopolitan. Indeed, it is only by increasing man's interdependence upon his fellow-man that the solidarity of the human race will ever be realized, and the altruism which shall make every man's happiness include that of all mankind become an established fact.

This is as true of nations as of individuals. The nation which would contribute most to the advancement of human progress must develop its own civilization. We might as well expect the weak to carry the strong, as barbarism to aid civilization. That nation which most completely develops its own industrial and social possibilities, creates the most improved methods of production. In this way it is not only able to obtain its own wealth cheap, but ultimately to produce many commodities at less cost than can be produced by the cheap labor of less civilized countries. Upon the principle that whatever undersells succeeds, the less civilized countries are compelled to adopt the superior methods. Thus the benefits of inventions which result from the development of a higher civilization are automatically transferred to the lower, and the socializing influences of improved methods of production become cosmopolitan.

This is clearly demonstrated by the adoption of various kinds of American machinery abroad, without the use of which many European products would have been undersold by ours. Nor are the benefits which more highly civilized countries confer upon the lower, limited to what is forced upon them by competition in commodities which they both produce. A still greater benefit arises from the introduction of new commodities, which more diversified tastes and more complex social life of the more highly civilized country bring into existence. As a demand for new commodities increases, labor-saving appliances are invented to reduce the cost of their production, until they can be sold in foreign countries at merely a nominal price. In this case the products of a higher civilization are not competing with those of a lower, but new products are being introduced into less civilized countries ; this stimulates a taste for articles they have not hitherto used, thereby introducing new elements into their social life. Just as fast as a demand for such new commodities is created, the social life is diversified, the standard of living is raised, wages are increased, and a market basis for new industries is established. This is what the diversified tastes and inventive genius of America have been doing in Europe and South America to an increasing extent during the last twenty years.

Another advantage of a protective policy is that it tends to make the economic selection of industries possible, thereby promoting the only conditions upon which free trade between nations can ever take place without injury to the higher-wage country.

The postulate, so frequently emphasized by the advocates of *laissez faire*, that nations, like individuals, should be enabled to adopt those industries for which they are best fitted, is unexceptionable. But in order to obtain this result, it is necessary to secure opportunities for developing the economic possibilities of the people. It should ever be remembered that the most effective economic force in society is human invention and not natural resources, as is commonly assumed. For reasons already explained, labor-saving inventions can be developed only under the influence of socializing and diversified industries. These conditions, without which a truly economic selection of industries is impossible, are what protection furnishes.

Although it may be possible for these conditions to exist without protection, history does not furnish an instance where such a thing has occurred. The way in which protection promotes this is easy to understand. In the first place, by raising the basis of international competition to the plane of the higher wage-level, it prevents the lower-paid labor of one country from being made the means of checking the growth of manufacturing industries in another. This secures a home market for domestic products and furnishes an economic basis for a diversification of socializing industries in the higher wage-country. The greatest incentive is thus furnished for developing the most economic methods of production. With concentrated capital, the use of highly perfected machinery, and the development of specialized industries, a truly economic selection of industries becomes possible. The conditions will then exist for determining what things a nation can most economically produce, by reason of its peculiar character, natural resources, and civilization.

When this point is reached, protection will be economically necessary only to the extent of preventing the substitution of simple for complex industries. It will then be to the advantage not only of that nation, but of the world, that it should devote its productive energies to those industries for which it has developed the best capacity, and to relinquish all others to countries for which they are better adapted. Just in proportion as this takes place, protection becomes unnecessary—*provided, however, that this change does not involve the substitution of simple for complex industries.* For example, if America becomes highly proficient in the manufacture of jewelry and relatively deficient in the manufacture of silk, capital will naturally go to the former and away from the latter industry. Foreign silk might then be admitted free of duty without injury to the American laborer. It will thus be seen that protection (as here considered) not only prevents a less civilized country from checking the progress of a higher, but by promoting the substitution of economic for natural (blind) selection of industries, it tends ultimately to make a mutually advantageous free trade possible.

Thus a protective policy is not necessarily narrow and exclusive, but, when philosophically applied, is a most truly cosmopolitan doctrine of industrial relations, because it tends first, to develop home industry and civilization without injuring others, and second, to automatically extend these beneficial results to all mankind.

Here, then, we have a truly philosophic and strictly economic basis for applying the protective principle both to foreign and domestic industrial relations. It consists in securing the present and promoting the future opportunities (incentive-creating conditions) for developing the highest industrial and social possibilities of a people, and may be briefly summarized thus :

Foreign—Applied to the industrial intercourse of nations, a
     true protective policy is to prevent the products of the more
     advanced countries from being undersold by the products

of less civilized countries, through the use of lower paid labor ; thereby securing opportunities for developing the best methods of production afforded by the larger consumption and higher social life of the more advanced country.

Domestic—Applied to the relations of individuals and classes within the nation, this policy is one to guarantee the safety of persons and property with the maximum amount of individual freedom, and to secure the education, leisure, and other like conditions, which tend to develop the best physical, intellectual, and moral qualities of the individual citizen.

The scientific application of this principle to the various phases of industrial, social, and political life is the true function of statesmanship.

CHAPTER IV.

THE PRINCIPLES OF ECONOMIC TAXATION.

Section I.— *The Economic Basis of Equitable Taxation.*

In the preceding chapter, taxation was discussed solely as an instrument of industrial protection and national development. It is now proposed to consider taxation as a means of obtaining public revenue. In order to determine how to obtain the necessary revenue with the least expense and the greatest equity to all classes, it is necessary briefly to consider : (1) the principle which should determine the individual's contribution to the state ; (2) the source from which the contribution should be drawn.

(1) The principle which should govern individual service to the state is a much debated one. It has been contended by some that a tax should be proportionate to the degree of protection furnished by the state. According to this view, if one class of property is exposed to more danger than another, its owners should pay a proportionately higher tax. The objection to this is that it would place the greatest burden upon those least able to bear it. Assuming taxes to stay where they are put, under this system the owners of coal mines, stone quarries, and land would be almost exempt from taxation, while those engaged in manufacture and commerce would have to pay very high taxes. Moreover, the very poor and helpless, who most frequently need the aid of the state in many forms and are least able to contribute, would be the most heavily taxed. Since the function of government is to protect and promote opportunities for increasing the well-being of the individual, the most equitable basis on which the individual can be called upon to serve the state, is evidently his ability to contribute without injury to him-

self. This idea is more or less generally recognized, as is shown in the frequent demand to have a heavier tax imposed upon commodities consumed by the rich than upon those consumed by the poor. And the frequent demand for taxing incomes above a certain amount, the exemption of wages and small homesteads,— all of which are efforts to make the rich contribute more to the public revenue than the poor, upon the principle that they are more able to contribute.

(2) From what source should this tribute to the state be drawn, or what is the best measure of an individual's capacity to pay without injury to his own well-being? It is commonly assumed that the ability of a citizen to pay a tax is proportionate to the property he owns ; this, however, is far from being correct. For instance, one may legally own a large amount of property which is so highly mortgaged as to make his ownership merely nominal. To tax such a man in proportion to his property would impoverish him, while the effect of a similar tax upon his neighbor whose property is free from mortgage would be relatively slight. One manufacturer with a large plant may, through a mere change of fashion or other social cause, be working at a loss, while another, with a similar plant, but who is unaffected by the fashion, may be making large profits.

Clearly, to tax the property of these two at the same rate would be to deprive the former of his means of getting a living, while from the latter it would take but a fraction of his surplus, and hence would in no way impair his present industrial or social status. Manifestly then a uniform tax upon product or property would not fall with equal weight upon all. In other words, the ownership of property does not constitute a correct measure of the individual's ability to contribute to the public revenue. There is but one source from which wealth can be taken with the certainty that it will not inflict a burden, and that is, surplus income, which embraces all the forms of rent, interest, and profit.

The reason this form of income can be taxed with the least burden to its owner is that it does not enter into the necessary cost of his living. The cost of the social well-being of all who participate in production being a part of the necessary cost of production is represented by wages and salaries, the surplus is what remains after these costs are defrayed. Consequently, although to pay a tax from one's surplus is to lessen one's wealth, it does not intrench upon the normal means of social well-being, and therefore inflicts the minimum amount of economic and social inconvenience. Clearly then, the extent of the surplus income is the measure of an individual's ability to contribute to the public revenue without injury to his own well-being. How then can taxes be levied so as to be drawn from the economic surplus of the community without disturbing industrial relations? This would be a very simple problem if the taxes would stay where they are put and were paid by those upon whom they are levied. But this is just what does not occur. In order therefore, to answer this question, it is necessary to consider the economic mobility of taxes.

SECTION II.—*The Mobility of Taxes and their Relation to Wages.*

To ascertain how taxes travel from one to another class in the community, and to find by whom they are ultimately paid, we have only to follow a tax from where it is levied to the place where it cannot be further shifted. For illustration, let us suppose that a tax is laid upon land ; the land being the source of all raw material, such a tax would affect all commodities in the first stage of their production. Upon the principle that a commodity cannot be continuously furnished for less than it costs, the tax will be added to the price of the product in the same way as wages and other items, and must be paid by the purchaser. If the article is wheat, the tax is thus transferred from the farmer to the miller. The tax being an inevitable item in the cost of the flour to the miller it is transferred by him to the wholesale merchant, and by him to the retail grocer, who in turn passes it on to the consumer. Manifestly unless the consumer can transfer the tax to some one else, he must pay it, because it is included in the price of his commodity in addition to all necessary costs.

This brings us to the most critical point of the subject. All writers of any standing recognize the mobility of the tax from the raw material to the consumer of the finished product. But it is generally assumed that the tax cannot be made to travel any further than the commodity in whose cost it is an item, and consequently whoever consumes the article ultimately pays the tax.

If we examine the matter more closely, however, we shall see that this conclusion is only partially correct. Whether or not those who consume the wheat pay the tax, will depend upon whether its consumption forms an item in any further series of production. Suppose, for instance, the wheat is consumed by horses that are employed in a brick-yard. The wheat in that case at once becomes an item in the cost of using the horse, which in turn is an item in the cost of the brick. This point is very important here, because it has a direct bearing upon whether or not the laborer ultimately pays the tax included in the price of the commodities he consumes.

The laborer, it should be remembered, exercises two functions One is social, and the other economic. As a social factor he is a consumer, and constitutes an important item both in civilization and in the market. As an economic factor, however, he is simply a productive force. In this capacity he affects the price of the product in precisely the same way as does any other force so employed, whether it be through the instrumentality of animals or machinery. Economically they all affect the cost and price of the product in the same way, namely, through the cost of procuring them. The cost of any productive instrument is what is consumed in maintaining its productive efficiency, and that cost must be replenished from the price of the product. Now, the cost of maintaining the productive efficiency of the laborer is his living. Whatever is necessary to that is a part of the price of his labor—wages,—and therefore becomes a necessary item in the cost of whatever he produces. Clearly, therefore, the more his living costs, the more expensive will be his labor. If his cost of living could be reduced, either by inducing him to consume fewer commodities or by lessening the cost of those he does consume, his wages could easily be lowered. The price of labor in Asia and continental Europe is less than in America because labor there costs less.[1]

For the same reason that the price of labor would fall if the cost of the laborer's living could be reduced, it must and will rise if the cost of that living is increased. Nor does it matter whether the increased cost is due to an increase in the amount of

[1] "Wealth and Progress," Part II., chap. vii., sec. i., pp. 162–167 ; also Brassey's "Work and Wages," pp. 88, 89, 94–96.

wealth he consumes or to a rise in the price of that wealth. Thus, during the American war, when the price of commodities was greatly increased through the inflation of the currency, wages soon moved in the same direction and fell again when the prices were lowered—as, indeed, they have throughout all history.[1] Clearly, therefore, if the price of a laborer's flour, sugar, coffee, clothing, and the like is increased by a tax, the result will be economically the same as if the higher price were due to the payment of higher wages to agricultural laborers, a rise in the rate of transportation, a failure of crops, or any other cause ; and if it becomes permanent it will result in his demanding and obtaining higher nominal wages.   The laborer would not gain any thing in well-being by such a rise of wages, but it would be necessary in order to furnish him the amount of well-being to which he had become habitually accustomed, and without which he would refuse to work.   In this way, therefore, the tax is transferred from the laborer to the employer.[2]   What is true of the laborer is equally true of all who receive stipulated incomes.

To whom, then, it may be asked, does the employer transfer the tax ?   Here the answer. is as before—to whomsoever he can. And if he cannot transfer it to anybody, he must pay it himself. He will of course utilize all the economic forces at his command to pass the tax to somebody else.   He may first try to make the

[1] "Wealth and Progress," pp. 148–156; also McCulloch's "Principles of Political Economy," p. 181.

[2] This fact was recognized by the early English writers, although, like many others of their best suggestions, it has been subsequently treated rather as an incidental than a primary fact.   Adam Smith says : " Such a tax must therefore occasion a rise in the wages of labor proportionable to this rise of price.   It is thus that a tax upon the necessaries of life operates in exactly the same manner as a direct tax upon the wages of labor.   The laborer, though he may pay it out of his hand, cannot, for any considerable time at least, be properly said to even advance it.   It must always, in the long run, be advanced to him by his immediate employer in the advanced rate of wages."—" Wealth of Nations," Book V., chap. ii., article iv., pp. 691 and 692 ; see also pp. 686, 693, 694, and 704.   Ricardo says : " There can be no permanent fall of wages, but in consequence of a fall of the necessaries on which wages are expended."—" Political Economy and Taxation," p. 75.   " A tax, however, on raw produce and on the necessaries of the laborer, would have another effect—it would raise wages."—*Ibid.*, p. 93.   " The effect of a tax on wages would be to raise wages by a sum at least equal to the tax, and would be finally, if not immediately, paid by the employer of labor."—*Ibid.*, p. 133 ; see also pp. 129, 136, and 141.

laborer pay it by refusing to increase wages, but here he will be met by the laborer's refusal to work, and, should he try to put it on the consumer in higher prices, he will only be repeating the circle, because the increase in the price will act as before upon wages, and he will have to pay out to the laborer what he has thus exacted from the consumer. In the last analysis, therefore, the only source from which the employer can pay the tax is his surplus or profit.[1] That being, as we saw in the last section, the true measure of the individual's ability to contribute to the public revenue without curtailing his own well-being, it is the most equitable basis of taxation. This brings us to the question how the employer replenishes his surplus from which taxes are finally drawn.

SECTION III.—*The Ultimate Effect of Taxation upon Profits and the General Wealth of the Community.*

If the conclusion reached in the last section is correct, and taxes finally come out of the surplus product, then it follows that either profits diminish as taxes increase, or that the employer has some means of replenishing his surplus. We know from experience that the aggregate amount of wealth taken in taxes tends to increase as society advances, and it is equally certain that the aggregate profits do not diminish. On the contrary, while there is a tendency to minimize the rate of profit per unit of product, the aggregate amount of surplus product in various forms unquestionably tends to increase. Clearly, then, there must be some means by which the employer can replenish his surplus when thus drained by taxation. How does he do it?

We have already seen that he cannot take it from the consumer

---

[1] Accordingly, any extra pressure of taxation is always first felt by the business portion of the community in the diminution of profits. Hence we always find the commercial class the first to protest against excessive taxation. For this reason no representative government, and few despotic ones, could suddenly increase the taxation of the country by an amount equal to the aggregate profits of the community, because such an act would practically be a seizure of the total surplus revenue, which would, in all probability, cause a revolution that would destroy the government. That is why, whenever an exceptionally large amount is to be suddenly raised by taxes, it invariably takes the form of a loan for a long period, thus extending the ultimate payment of a portion of the tax to future generations.

by raising prices, nor from the laborer by reducing wages. That he does not take it from either of these sources is further shown by the fact that contemporaneously with the increase of taxation, real wages have risen and the price of commodities has fallen. Manifestly then, the only way the producer's surplus can be replenished is by a new draft upon nature through increased production. Nor will it be difficult to see how this takes place, if we bear in mind the law of prices and surplus, previously presented.

Under this law, whenever productive methods are employed by which nature yields a greater amount of wealth for the same effort, all other demands upon the product being fixed amounts, the whole gain naturally flows to the contingent surplus of those who use the new methods. Consequently, all increase in the wealth of any stipulated income class in the community, whether it be through lowering prices or increasing wages, must be drawn from the contingent surplus of the producers. For instance when, by the adoption of more productive instruments, the surplus of the most successful producers increases, there arises a greater inducement to invest more capital in the enterprise, and thus increase production. In order to insure the sale of this increased production, it is offered at a lower price. If this reduction be ten per cent., the uniform price of the total product in that market will fall ten per cent. Manifestly this fall comes directly out of the profits of the producers, and all who were previously making less than ten per cent. profit will now have to leave the business or adopt the methods by which the reduction was brought about. Thus the additional wealth resulting from the increased productive efficiency first flows to the economic surplus of those producing the improvement, and then by competition, is transferred from the producers' surplus to the community in lower prices.

An increase of wages takes place upon the same general principles, and with substantially the same result, but it comes in a somewhat different way. A reduction in prices is a distribution of the surplus through the aggressive action of employers. An increase of wages is a distribution of the surplus by the aggressive action of laborers. As already explained, the enforced transfer from profits to wages compels the producer either to work without profit, or perhaps at a loss, or to adopt some labor-saving means by which more can be produced at the same cost. Thus the laborer's encroachment upon the capitalist's surplus forces him, under penalty of poverty, to make nature yield more wealth for the same effort, thus replenishing what the laborer has taken from him, and making the community absolutely richer by the amount to which wages have been increased.[1]

What is true of wages is true of any other form of increased consumption which adds to the cost of production. Taxation is precisely of this character. If 10 per cent. is added to the price of wheat or cotton by a tax, the mobility and ultimate economic effect upon profits and production will be identically the same as if 10 per cent. had been added to the cost by an increase of wages. The same economic power which would enable the farmer to add to the price of wheat an increase in the farm laborers' wages, and the miller, wholesale and retail merchant, each in turn to add it to the price of flour, and the mechanic, who consumes the flour, to add it to his wages, and thus ultimately take it from the employers' profits, will enable them to do precisely the same by a tax which increases the cost of production in the same way, no matter at what stage of the process it is levied. Taxation, like wages, is simply a form of consumption, and hence exercises the same influence upon profits and the general wealth of the community as any other form of consumption—namely, to increase the aggregate production, which added increment goes to replenish the source from which the tax was last taken—the employer's profit.

It will thus be seen that the entrepreneur does not pay the tax, in the sense of being permanently the poorer by it, any more than does the farmer, miller, merchant, or laborer. They each shift it on to the next purchaser of the product into whose cost it has entered. In the laborer's case, having become a part of the cost of his labor, it is charged to the employer in the same way. The employer, being unable to charge it upon any class of his fellow-men, is forced, by the impulse of self-interest, to exact it from nature, which he finally does in the form of a larger product. Therefore Professor Sumner's statement that "every

[1] Part II., chap. v., sec. iii. Also "Wealth and Progress," pp. 31, 32.

24

tax is an evil" is essentially false. A tax is not necessarily an evil any more than wages or any other form of consumption.[1] It will thus be seen that taxation properly occupies no such important position in economics as is usually ascribed to it. If the total consumption upon which the $300,000,000 of taxes in this country is expended were abolished to-morrow, instead of adding to our wealth, it would create an industrial depression in this and probably in several other countries, until, by enforced idleness and bankruptcy, production could be readjusted on the narrower basis to conform to the diminished consumption or demand. Were this relation of consumption to production properly understood, taxation would cease to be the hobgoblin of public affairs. The important question regarding taxation is not as to who shall pay the taxes, nor how much they shall be, but as to how they shall be expended. If a large amount of wealth is exacted from the community in taxes, and is squandered, then there would be no justification for a readjustment of economic relations which its production involves. If the tax revenue is used to repress any phase of social progress, as would be in maintaining a standing army, it is then a positive injury. Only when the wealth created by tax is used to further the social development of the people has it any economic or ethical justification. Upon what principle, then, should the public revenue be expended in order to justify its collection?

SECTION IV.—*The Legitimate Sphere of Public Expenditures.*

Since the public revenue is but the means by which government fulfils its functions, its expenditure is necessarily limited to the sphere of governmental action. We have already seen that the functions of government are essentially *protective, judiciary, educational*, and *impersonal* in their character. Clearly therefore, the sphere of public expenditures is properly limited to the promotion of those objects which may be conveniently grouped into two classes as the Static and the Dynamic functions of government.

---

[1] Whether or not a rise of wages or an increase of taxation will be beneficial will depend largely upon how it is expended, and this, in turn, will depend upon the influences by which it was brought about, but, in any event, it will cause an increase in production.

The static functions embrace all that is necessary to secure the community against a common enemy and to enforce the recognized system of social order as expressed in established institutions. This may require a large army, an extensive police force, and a numerous staff of judiciary and executive officers. The means necessary to sustain these instruments of public order should be supplied from the public revenue, for the obvious reason that it is the function above all others which can be best performed by the government, and without which it would be impossible for the individual to perform with safety and freedom any of the industrial and social duties of a civilized citizen. All expenditure for this purpose represents the price that civilization has to pay for guarding itself against the effects of barbarism, and should be reduced as rapidly as possible.

To accomplish this reduction involves the exercise of the dynamic functions of government. These relate to increasing the opportunity for developing all phases of individual capacity and freedom. Opportunity, as the term is here employed, is distinctively educational in the broadest sense of the word. Every thing is educational that brings man into more frequent contact with an increasing variety of social influences which tend to stimulate his wants and desires, sharpen his intelligence, and actualize the latent possibilities of his character. This embraces not only the elementary education furnished by the common school, which is of prime importance to citizenship, but it also includes the furnishing of clean, wholesome streets, good drainage, ventilation, and other sanitary requisites to wholesome domestic life, an abundance of public parks, gardens, museums, free lectures, reading-rooms, circulating libraries, and, above all, the leisure necessary to enable the masses to avail themselves of these and kindred educating and elevating influences. To the extent that these opportunities are increased will the intelligence and character of the citizen be elevated and the functions of the soldier, policeman, judge, and jailer become unnecessary. Consequently, to the extent that the public revenue is expended in performing the dynamic functions of the state will the amount required to perform the static functions diminish. This is the more important because every dollar that is consumed by the government in exercising its static functions involves so much production without any real increase in well-being,—it being all consumed in guarding what already exists. On the other hand, every dollar expended by the state in performing its dynamic functions involves an increase of production, all of which is a net gain in social well-being.

Therefore, instead of treating all taxes as an evil to be diminished, it is only the amount of the public revenue consumed by the government in performing its executive and police duties that can properly be so regarded. All that is consumed in extending the socializing opportunities of the people is a positive benefit and should be increased, especially as the increase of the latter is the surest way of diminishing the former. To oppose an increase of taxation for public improvements, in the name of economy, is a fallacy which cannot be too frequently exposed. It is just as important to have clean streets as to have clean houses, and the wealth consumed in the one contributes to civilization as much as that consumed in the other. The only question to be considered regarding such expenditures, is whether or not they can be more efficiently conducted by the government than by private individuals.[1] But that the wealth so consumed should be increased is sustained by all the interests of civilization, and those who oppose it are unconsciously or otherwise obstructing the movement of social progress as surely as those who oppose popular education and favor long hours of labor and low wages.

SECTION V.—*How can Taxes be Most Equitably Levied, Conveniently Paid, and Economically Collected?*

This proposition involves two questions : (1) How taxes should be levied. (2) What they should be levied upon.

1. There are two general methods by which the public revenue can be obtained—direct and indirect taxation. It is a peculiar feature in the history of taxation that those who are charged with the responsibility of raising the revenue and with the administration of government, usually prefer to obtain the revenue through indirect taxation. On the other hand, revenue reformers and social reformers generally advocate direct taxation.

Direct taxation is urged in preference to indirect, chiefly on the

---

[1] See Part IV., chapter ii., section iii.

ground that a tax is an evil which should always be minimized, and that if taxes were collected directly from the individual he would then realize how much he paid, and would therefore be more strenuous in his demands for a retrenchment of the public revenue. They insist that indirect taxation is simply a cunning device for making the citizen contribute to the public revenue under the guise of purchasing the necessaries of life, thus obtaining wealth from the individual which he would otherwise refuse to contribute. This position is based upon two assumptions : (1) that taxes are necessarily an evil to be minimized ; (2) that direct taxation affords each individual an opportunity of correctly estimating the amount he contributes to the public revenue.

In the first place it is an entire mistake to regard taxes as necessarily an evil. We have already seen that they simply represent the consumption of wealth in a public form, and have the same economic effect upon production, industry, and commerce generally, as does private consumption. And whether or not private or public consumption will be permanently beneficial to the community depends upon how such consumption takes place. To the degree that wealth is consumed in extending public improvements and enlarging the social opportunities of the people, it is both economically and socially a positive advantage. The assumption therefore that taxes are at best a necessary evil is not only erroneous in fact, but it is extremely mischievous in its effect, as it inspires opposition to expenditures for public improvements.

Nor is the idea that direct taxation enables each individual accurately to determine the amount he contributes to the public revenue any nearer correct. This is another of the numerous errors arising from a misconception of the law of wages. From what has already been said it will not be difficult to see that a direct tax upon the individual is just as mobile as an indirect tax levied upon the commodities he consumes. If a merchant can transfer a tax upon flour to the consumer, because it adds to its cost to him, he can also transfer to the consumer a tax upon his house or his horse for the same reason.

The same is true of the laborer. A direct tax upon his house or his wages or any thing in his possession, is simply so much addition to the cost of his living, and can be transferred through higher wages to the employer in precisely the same way as is his house rent, and the cost of his food, clothes, and other necessaries of life.[1] In many parts of England the different classes of local expenditure such as the "poor's rate," the "cemetery rate," the "highway rate," the "water rate," the "local-board rate," etc., are collected directly from each householder by the tax-gatherer in separate items, and often by different persons. These rates however, enter into the cost of the laborer's living, and have to be covered by his wages just as much as the amount of his grocery bill or his house rent, and are everywhere so recognized.[2] Where the rates and rents are high, as in London and other large centres, the wages in all industries are correspondingly higher than in localities where these items are low, which is one of the reasons why wages are always higher in large cities than in small towns and rural districts.[3] The economic mobility of a tax is in no-wise affected by the fact that it is directly or indirectly collected. Whether the taxes are gathered directly from the laborer in a specific sum, or indirectly through the enhanced price of com-modities, makes no real difference. In either case it enters into the cost of his living and the price of his service, and hence is ultimately transferred to the employer. Instead, therefore, of direct taxation enabling the laborer accurately to determine the amount he pays to the government, it has the opposite effect, and he is deluded into the belief that he is heavily burdened by pub-lic expenditures, whereas he actually contributes nothing except temporarily during periods of readjustment.

Moreover, the effect of direct taxation is pernicious in many ways. In the first place it creates a strong incentive for evading taxes, which is a standing inducement to dishonesty. So long as men believe that they are permanently impoverished by what they pay into the public treasury, they will endeavor to devise

---

[1] "Wealth of Nations."

[2] So manifest is this that where whole classes of laborers have to ride to and from their work, as in London and other large cities, the price of their fare is recognized as a proper cause for demanding higher wages, and in other districts where the employer furnishes the laborer's house rent-free, or the privilege of keeping a cow, etc., it is equally regarded as a legitimate reason for paying lower wages, and in such cases wages always are lower.

[3] "Wealth and Progress," Part II., chap. vii.

means to elude the tax-gatherer ; the " tax-dodger " is a well-known character.[1] In the next place direct taxation creates a strong feeling of dissatisfaction among the different classes in the community as to the justice or injustice of taxing or not taxing different classes of property. Hence the interminable controversy as to whether or not workingmen's homes should be exempt from taxation. It is held to be unjust to tax the work-ingman's home because that would be putting the burden upon those who are least able to bear it. But if they are to be exempt, at what point should the exemption be fixed ? To exempt home-steads at a given valuation would tend to encourage the building of houses within that valuation limit ; and that would be a decided injury, because it would act as a check upon the building of superior houses, and hence tend to stereotype inferior domestic conditions.

Again, whether or not all personal property should be taxed, and if not what kind should be exempt, is another point of con-tention. Some insist that productive property should not be taxed, because such taxation discourages industry, while others contend that to tax non-productive property is unjust, since it yields no income. And certain it is that every attempt to tax personal property encourages systematic misrepresentation and other fraudulent practices too numerous to recite.[2]

The same is true of income tax. This tax is assessed on the assumption that it draws the revenue from surplus incomes which would otherwise escape taxation. But when it is understood that in the normal course of economic movement all taxes are finally drawn from the surplus product, the force of such reasoning entirely disappears. So far from direct taxation being the model method of raising public revenue, therefore, it is essentially un-economic and demoralizing. It involves the maximum incon-

[1] In Boston for instance it has become an established practice among a large number of rich men to temporarily reside in Nahant, a small town a few miles from the city, where the local taxes are very light. By living there on the first of May, when assessments are made, they are taxed for Nahant instead of Boston. While they actually live in Boston, and obtain all the advantages of the large public expenditures there, they are only taxed according to the trifling expenditure in Nahant.

[2] See Prof. E. R. A. Seligman on " The General Property Tax," *Political Science Quarterly*, March, 1890.

venience, puts a premium on dishonesty, and tends to make the average citizen a persistent enemy of public improvements, without affording any compensating advantages. In short, direct taxation is defensible only in cases of exceptional emergency such as wars,[1] and even then but for the briefest period possible.

Since the public revenue must be directly or indirectly collected, it follows that all the reasons for objecting to direct taxation obtain in favor of the indirect. While it is highly important that the individual should always be fully informed regarding real burdens, it is quite as important that he be not deluded into assuming imaginary ones. Since the public consumption represented by taxation is not a permanent burden upon any class in the community, the public welfare demands that taxes should be so levied as not to have that appearance. Consequently, instead of making taxes as direct as possible, thereby giving them the most burdensome seeming, they should be levied with the greatest indirectness, so as to be as imperceptible as possible. To the extent that the individual ceases to be conscious of his contribution, and its exact amount becomes difficult to determine, will the incentive for the various forms of dishonesty and corruption for evading taxation disappear. And when an important public improvement is proposed which involves a large expenditure, the decision of the average citizen regarding it will be less likely to be neutralized by the feelings of his own inability to contribute his share. By removing this conscious personal element, the question of taxation will be considered solely with regard to its effects upon the community, thus removing one of the greatest obstacles to public improvements. With this view of taxation, all public expenditures of a protective, educational, opportunity-creating character (judiciously applied) would be regarded as an actual addition to the wealth of the community,

[1] The only reason for adopting direct taxation in case of war is that the surplus income is reached quicker by that means, but it is far more inconvenient and arbitrary ; and even in such cases it is more economic to borrow the necessary amount and let it be finally repaid out of the revenue indirectly collected. When it is thus furnished through the normal operation of economic law, it tends gradually to replenish the surplus from which it is drawn by increased production, and thus minimize, if not indeed obviate, the burden upon the community.

to be increased, instead of as at present being treated as a burden to be avoided at every turn.

2. Upon what class of property should taxes be levied is the question that remains to be considered. The important point to be considered in determining the class of property upon which taxes should be levied is how to obtain the greatest indirection of movement with the least cost of collection.

Manifestly a tax will have the greatest indirection of movement, and hence be most completely subject to economic law which passes through the largest number of hands and enters into the greatest variety of productive processes. To give a tax the greatest indirection, therefore, it must be levied at the point farthest removed from those by whom it will be finally paid. Since all taxes are finally drawn from the surplus product, they would necessarily be most direct when levied upon profits or other surplus, and conversely most indirect when levied upon the source of raw material. Upon the same principle that a tax upon surplus incomes cannot be shifted to any other class in the community, because it does not enter into the cost of production, a tax on raw material can be shifted in a multitude of ways before reaching any class of consumers, because it all enters into the cost of production, and becomes an indistinguishable part of the price of commodities. Clearly then, the greatest indirection would be secured by imposing a tax on real estate, especially on land. A tax upon land would of course be an addition to the cost of producing every species of wealth in the community.

It is equally clear that a tax upon real estate would be the most easy and inexpensive to collect. In the first place, it is the form of property that is most accessible, it cannot be concealed from the eye of the assessor ; hence it affords the least temptation for tax-dodging, or other dishonorable means of evasion. It is also the class of property whose value is most easily ascertained, because it is most frequently and permanently in the open market for sale or rent, either fact furnishing the basis for ascertaining its current value at any given time. This form of property has the further advantage of being immovable. The owner may leave the city, State, or country, but the real estate remains as accessible as ever. Another advantage in this form of taxation is that it avoids all the objectionable inquisitorial features involved in all direct, personal, and property taxes. There is no other form of property in society upon which taxes can be so easily and accurately assessed, so cheaply collected, and with as little intrusion upon the freedom of the citizen.

Nor can there be any complaint that such a tax would press unduly upon the landowner, because, so far as the income from the land represents the cost of service rendered in using it for productive purposes, the tax will all come back in the price of the product; and only that portion of the tax which falls upon the surplus as rent, interest, and profit will be untransferable and finally paid by the landowner, the equity of which no one can question. Nor can any legitimate complaint be made by those who advance the tax at any of the subsequent stages. In every case, so far as it affects the cost of economic production either in the form of the cost of raw material, tools, labor, or any thing whatsoever, it can be added to the price. Neither could there properly be any complaint about the personal wealth of the rich escaping taxation, because the tax having been laid at the source of economic movement, its *full* amount is included in the price of every thing they buy. Hence their only means of successfully avoiding taxation would be to forego consumption, which is to relinquish wealth and civilization. If taxes were thus levied, the rich jewelry, wardrobes, furnishings, and equipages of the wealthy would all carry their quota of taxation, and so far as they represented the stock of the manufacturer or merchant, or were included in the necessary cost of living of any who render productive service, the tax included in their price would be transferable as in all other cases ; that portion of these forms of wealth only which was supplied from surplus income would have finally to bear the tax. There certainly could be no justice in making an article, which has already borne its full quota of taxation in its economic journey to the consumer, yield a fresh tax each year after it leaves the sphere of economic movement. Such a tax must necessarily act as a direct check upon all new forms of consumption, especially among the wage- and salary-receiving class, and thus be positively inimical to the development of a high standard of living and social progress.

It will perhaps be objected that if taxes were all levied on real estate, and acted as an increase in the cost of raw material, the tax would fall the heaviest on those articles containing the largest amount of raw material. And since food and the coarser manufactured products consumed by the masses contain a much larger proportion of raw material than the finer products of manufacture and art consumed by the wealthy, the tax would fall much more heavily upon the poor than upon the rich. This is an objection which can be easily answered, if we bear in mind the law governing the mobility of taxes. It is true that in high-priced jewelry, pictures, books, and indeed the finer products of manufacture and art, the raw material forms the most insignificant portion of the cost. And if the tax represented in the price of such articles was limited to what is conveyed by the cost of raw material, it would indeed be very slight. The fact is, however, that the tax in such products enters mainly through the labor. Although the tax-bearing raw material in these products is very slight, that represented in the laborer's wages, which includes all that enters into his living, is very great, and as the high price of such products is largely made up of the cost of labor, they bear the tax levied upon all the raw material consumed by the laborer. The tax, therefore, in the finer products of manufacture and art will not be proportionate to the raw material they actually contain, but to all the raw material that has been consumed by every thing used in producing them. In other words, their contribution to the public revenue will be proportionate to their value as finished products, and therefore they represent the greatest instead of the least tax-transmitting power.

Another objection that will probably be urged against this position is, that a tax on raw material has the effect of adding to the price of the product not only the tax but also the profit upon the tax to those who advance it. This view has long been held by leading English economists.[1] According to this view, every time a tax is transferred it carries with it an added increment of

---

[1] Adam Smith says: "A tax upon those articles necessarily raises their price somewhat higher than the amount of the tax, because the dealer who advances the tax must generally get it back with the profit. . . . His employer, if he is a manufacturer, will charge upon the price of his goods this rise of wages with a profit, so that the final payment of the tax, together with his overcharge, will fall upon the consumer."—"Wealth of Nations," Book V., chap. ii., article iv., pp. 691, 692.

profit. Consequently, if it is transferred enough times, the amount of profit which is added to the consumer's price of the finished product by the tax will be greater than the tax itself. This doctrine is a logical part of the orthodox theory of profits, according to which the normal profits of the capitalists form a necessary part of the cost of production, and hence of the price of commodities. In stating this theory, Mill says : " And profit, we have also seen, is not exclusively the surplus remaining to the capitalist after he has been compensated for his outlay, but forms, in most cases, no unimportant part of the outlay itself." And after enumerating a long series of processes, in which the profits of each are compounded in the next, he adds : " All these advances form a part of the cost of production of linen. Profits, therefore, as well as wages, enter into the cost of production which determines the value of the produce." [1] Were this doctrine correct, it would certainly form an unanswerable objection to all indirect taxation, and indeed to indirect production also. Since every specialization and division of labor adds to the series of distinct profit-yielding processes, industrial improvements would serve to increase the power of the capitalist to add compound profit to the consumer's price of commodities.

Fortunately for civilization, however, economic law permits no such compound profit-making process. We have already seen that the price of the product in a given market tends to a uniformity on the basis of the cost of furnishing the dearest portion.[2] Consequently the profits of each producer can only be equal to the difference between his cost of production and that of those furnishing the dearest increment of the general supply, this increment being sold without profit. It is impossible therefore in any market, or at any stage of the productive process, to add the producer's profit to the consumer's price, since competition compels all who contribute to the same market to sell at the same price, which price is fixed by the cost of the no-profit producers. Consequently, if there is any profit, it must be obtained from nature through greater economy in production. It will thus be seen that the claim that taxes upon land or raw material must be repaid with a profit to those who pay them, is a pure phantom

---

[1] " Principles of Political Economy," vol. i., p. 568.
[2] Part II., chap. iv., pp. 125–128. *Cf.* pp. 205, 206.

which entirely vanishes in the light of the true law of economic prices, and with it disappear all the objections to indirect taxation, based upon adding compound profit to consumers' prices.

It will be seen that the question of taxation is much less fundamental than it is usually made to appear. Like the question of money, it is frequently employed to influence public opinion on a multitude of questions on which it has practically no bearing. Taxation is simply the consumption of wealth in a public form, and has no more economic effect than the same amount of wealth privately consumed. The only interest therefore the community has in the question is that the taxes shall be economically collected and wisely expended. If this fact is once clearly understood, the misconceptions in which the subject has been involved will disappear. Then the popular delusion that all taxes are finally paid by the laborer would lose its political utility, and the equally erroneous notion of Henry George, that to levy all taxes on land-values would abolish poverty and establish universal freedom, would at once be recognized as a mere social mirage. The only advantage in levying taxes upon land and real estate in preference to incomes and personal property is that the revenue can be collected from the former with greater ease, certainty, and convenience.

CHAPTER V.

BUSINESS DEPRESSIONS.

SECTION I.—*Economic Characteristics of Business Depressions.*

THERE are few questions upon which a greater variety of opinion exists than business depressions. They are ascribed to a different cause in every country, and often to as many different causes in the same country as there are phases of social reform, political parties, sectional or industrial interests.[1] Before any intelligent understanding of the cause of these social calamities can be obtained, it will be necessary to consider their economic peculiarities, and the industrial or other conditions under which they occur.

The first general characteristic of business depressions is that they are periods of exceptional industrial adversity. But there are two kinds of industrial adversity, whose characteristics and causes are widely different ; these are famines and business depressions. A famine is an actual scarcity of consumable wealth ; a business depression, on the contrary, is a relative plethora of consumable wealth. The first symptom of a famine is the failure to produce a sufficient amount of wealth to meet the existing de-

---

[1] The business depressions of 1873–1878 were attributed to over two hundred different causes by the various economists, capitalists, philosophers, and reformers, who testified before the Congressional Committee to investigate the subject. See reports of the Wright and Hewitt Congressional Committees on "Industrial Depressions," also the report of the United States Senate Committee on "Education and Labor," 1885, and the report of the Commissioner of Labor on "Industrial Depressions," 1886. Also report of Royal Commission (England, 1885) on the "Cause of Industrial Depressions."

mands of the community ; while the first indication of a business depression is the failure to find sufficient customers to carry off the existing supply of commodities. The economic distinction, therefore, between a famine and a business depression is that the former springs from a *scarcity of commodities* and the latter from a *scarcity of consumers.*

Nor do famines and business depressions both occur in the same countries. India, Egypt, and other less civilized countries, have frequently suffered severely from famine and consequent pestilence, as did also Europe during the Middle Ages,—thousands, and sometimes millions, died of hunger and disease,[1]—but they have no business depressions. America and the leading countries in Europe no longer have famines, but they have business depressions. Famines and business depressions are not only economically distinct, and occur in different countries, but the very conditions which promote the one tend to prevent the other. The very specialization of industry and development of science that have steadily diminished the possibility of famines, have brought into existence involved commercial relations and the factory system which make business depressions possible. Nor must business depressions be confounded with financial panics ; these are disturbances of another kind. A money panic may arise in the midst of business prosperity as at present (1890). Although, like any other social disturbance, a financial panic has a harmful effect upon the industrial community, it being purely a fiscal disturbance the evil effect is largely restricted to the speculative class. A money panic may be the final straw which reveals a business depression, but if the consumption of commodities is practically equal to the production it cannot produce one. Business depressions, therefore, may be characterized as periods of industrial adversity peculiar to machine-using countries, and arise from a failure to sell and never from an inability to produce consumable wealth.

Another characteristic of business depressions is that they are not local or even national in their movement, but that they occur with striking uniformity in all countries in which they occur at all. This will be seen by the following table, which shows the

[1] Mr. Cornelius Walford, F.I.A., F.S.S., in a paper published in the *Statistical Journal*, vol. xli., gives the history of 350 famines.

recurrence of business depressions in England, France, United States, Germany, and Belgium during this century.[1]

England	France.	United States.	Germany.	Belgium.
1803	1804	....	....	....
1810	1810	....	....	....
1815	1813	1814	....	....
1818	1818	1818	....	....
1826	1826	1826	....	....
1830	1830	....	....	....
1837	1837	1837	1837	1837
1847	1847	1847	1847	1848
1857	1856	1857	1855	1855
1866	1866	1867	....	1864
1873	1873	1873	1873	1873
1883	1882	1882	1882	1882
1885	1885	1885	1885	1885

By this table three facts are clearly indicated : (1) That business depressions are limited to machine-using countries beginning in England with the rise of the factory system. (2) That they have steadily extended to other countries as fast as factory methods of production have been adopted ; that is to say, as fast as they became manufacturing and commercial countries. (3) That business depressions have been practically uniform and international in their movement, and that all countries without regard to form of government, political institutions, physical or climatic peculiarities, when once afflicted are visited with every recurrence and almost simultaneously. With these facts before us regarding the nature and history of business depressions, we are in a position to intelligently consider the causes from which they arise.

SECTION II.—*Cause of Business Depressions.*

In order to warrant the conclusion that any circumstance is the cause of succeeding phenomena, it is at least necessary: (1) that it should be adequate to produce the effect ; (2) that it sustain some necessary relation to it. In seeking the cause of business depressions therefore, we must first eliminate from the problem all influences which are clearly insufficient to produce them. Among the hundred or more specific causes assigned for

[1] First Annual Report of U. S. Commissioner of Labor, p. 290.

the business depression of 1873 in this country were excessive speculation in railroads and real estate, inflation of the currency, high protective tariff, and the unnatural stimulus given to industry by the war.[1] But when we observe that none of these things occurred in England, and that still the industrial depression was as severe there as here, it becomes clear that these causes were insufficient to explain the facts. So too in the case of France. The fact that at the close of the war in 1872 France was compelled to pay an indemnity to Germany of five millards of francs in gold, appears at first sight to furnish a sufficient reason why she should have experienced a state of severe business depression and poverty in 1873. But when we observe that the depression was just as severe and protracted in Germany, where this colossal indemnity was received, as in France, from whom it was exacted, the virtue of this explanation disappears. Its inadequacy becomes still more apparent when we remember that although none of these circumstances existed in England, Belgium, and America, they all had business depressions equally severe and protracted. The same is true of causes assigned for the depressions of 1882 and 1885.[2] Without entering further into details regarding this class of causes then, we are abundantly warranted in rejecting them as wholly inadequate to account for the phenomena.

To what cause then can business depressions be attributed? A business depression can never occur unless the equilibrium between consumption and production is disturbed in such a manner as to result in a diminution of consumption as compared with production. The first symptom of an approaching business depression is the inability of producers to find customers for their whole product at remunerative prices. Manufacturers will con-

---

[1] "There had been a period of excessive speculation, especially in railroads and real estate, large failures following that of Jay Cooke, inflation of the currency, high protective tariff, large immigration, and the unnatural stimulus given to industry by the war, brought the monetary affairs of the country to a crisis, resulting in general distrust, fall of prices, apprehension, and all the train of evils which follow such crises."—"First Annual Report of the Commissioner of Labor," 1886, p. 60.

[2] For the cause of the depression in 1882 see "First Annual Report of the Commissioner of Labor," p. 76, and for a summary of the causes and remedies recommended, see *ibid.*, pp. 291–293.

25

tinue to produce wealth and will prosper so long as they can find a remunerative market for their wares, even though wars rage or governments are overthrown. Production being but the economic response to consumption, it is to the *influences which effect consumption that we must look both for the cause and cure of business depressions.* Nor is this all. Since business depressions are peculiar to factory conditions, and the market for factory-made products depends chiefly upon the consumption of the laboring classes, it follows that it is the failure of the laborers' consumption to keep pace with the capitalists' production—the failure of the home to grow as fast as the factory—that really produces business depressions. Here then we have a cause that is both adequate to produce the effect and necessary to it. So long as the consumption of the masses—*i.e.*, the wage- and salary-receiving class—increases commensurately with the productive capacity of the community, nothing can create a business depression ; and whenever this does not occur nothing can prevent one.

Why does the laborers' consumption periodically fall behind —the capitalists' production ? Is it a necessary part of the present productive system, or is it merely incidental to it ? The essential features of capitalistic production are specialization of labor, concentration of capital, and the use of factory methods. As already pointed out, these are essentially socializing in their influence ; hence, instead of being inimical to the growth of the laborers' consumption, they are characteristically favorable to it. This is also shown by the fact that all phases of social progress have advanced more in a single century under the factory or capitalistic régime than in any previous period of the world's history. And it may be added that this progress has been greatest in those countries where the factory system has most completely prevailed. Witness this country and England, as compared with the countries of Asia and Africa.

There is another feature of this industrial régime, however, which should not be overlooked. In proportion as the factory system improves economically, it tends to make the laborer more and more a specialist of some particular part of the finished product. Thus, the manufacture of a shoe is now divided into nearly seventy specified occupations, and cotton manufacture into eighty-six. In proportion as the laborers' employment is thus specified, the speed and quantity of machinery is increased, and the strain upon his physical and nervous energy intensified. With this concentrating and specializing tendency the piece-work system has been generally established, which places the laborers in severe competition with each other, and often results in overdoing.[1] Again, the use of improved machinery and the specialization of labor tend to diminish the necessity of a high degree of skill in the laborer. This leads to the employment of a large number of women and children in all branches of manufacturing industries; and, like the men, they too are forced to be automatic factors, their portion of the work being an indispensable part of the whole productive process. They have to labor the same number of hours, under the same constantly increasing strain and pressure, and under the same sanitary conditions as the men. The obvious effect of all this is to deaden the springs of ambition and check the growth of new desires and superior tastes and habits of life. The laborer whose energies are exhausted in the workshop is naturally impervious to more elevating and refining influences. His leisure moments find him physically tired, mentally dull, and hence morally and socially indifferent. The inevitable tendency of this is to cause him to gravitate towards the saloon rather than the reading-room, lecture-hall, or theatre for his instruction and entertainment. Persons who are subjected to such continued toil from childhood up, in the foul air of mines and the sweltering heat and stifling atmosphere of mills and factories, cannot be expected to develop the ambition and force of character necessary to inspire and elevate their domestic and social life. The effect of such conditions upon women and children is even more damaging than upon men. The employment of women, especially wives and mothers, in the factory tends to sap the very source whence the springs of social character arise. Just in proportion as woman is transferred from the home to the workshop is her in-

---

[1] So general is this that in nearly all factory employments it is necessary to have a large number, often 5 or 10 per cent., of spare hands, or substitutes, who take the place of those who are compelled to be absent a day or two at a time through sickness, or for a rest to prevent sickness, etc. It is not an uncommon thing for this, in a large proportion of cases, to average as much as one day in a week.

spiring, socializing, and humanizing influence in the domestic circle destroyed—a condition that will inevitably result in stereotyping the social life of the masses, and in checking the increase of their wealth-consuming capacity.

This relative diminution of consumption soon begins to show itself in the accumulation of the merchants' stock, which reacts upon the manufacturer, first in diminished orders for his *product*, then in a severe competition among producers for the contracted market, in which the smaller concerns are compelled to close, finally creating among the laborers enforced idleness, the most powerful factor of all in promoting business depressions. When the laborer ceases to have employment he practically ceases to be a consumer; for although in modern society he is not permitted to starve, he has necessarily to be supported by others, either in the form of indebtedness or charity. There is no one cause by which the aggregate consumption of the community is so rapidly diminished as by enforced idleness. Like a contagious disease, it rapidly increases its own power for evil. The actual restriction of the market resulting from enforced idleness still further limits the sale of commodities, rendering production unprofitable; this again results in suspending production and in further discharges, inevitably culminating in a business depression in which, through bankruptcy, the large capitalists absorb the smaller ones, and are thus enabled to wait till the lagging consumption again overtakes production. Every such ruinous adjustment is a temporary arrest of progress, and the more frequently it occurs the more permanent becomes its evil influence upon society.

Still another source of idleness is the use of improved machinery. Indeed changes in machinery are only improvements in proportion as they are labor-saving—*i.e.*, labor-discharging. Hence machinery that will discharge the most laborers is always adopted. This takes place most frequently when trade is most prosperous, and in countries where machine-using methods are most general. Nor is it possible, or even desirable, that this should be otherwise, since it is only through the use of improved methods of production that the drudgery of human labor can be reduced, the luxuries of life increased, and social well-being enhanced. Manifestly unless new employments are created as fast as laborers are discharged, enforced idleness and the recurrence of business depressions are inevitable.

It thus appears that while the factory system necessarily creates socializing conditions, it has been accompanied by influences which tend greatly to neutralize their beneficial effect ; but it it is not difficult to see that these neutralizing influences are in no sense a necessary part of the industrial system. While the various forms of industrial specialization tend to increase the draft upon the laborers' energies, it is not at all necessary that this should be inimical to his social advancement. There is nothing in the nature of factory methods which makes it necessary that their use should be physically and socially deteriorating. Bad ventilation and other unsanitary conditions, dangerous machinery, overdriving, the employment of young children, and long hours of labor are not essential to the factory system, any more than slave labor and the cat-o'-nine tails were an essential part of cotton-growing.

With increase of productive power and its accompanying pressure upon the laborers' resources should have come a commensurate increase in his leisure and opportunities for social improvement. The reason this has been neglected is entirely due to the mistaken social policy pursued by the employing class. For the same reason that the Southern slave-holder believed that slave labor was necessary to the cheap production of cotton and, consequently, to the prosperity of the planters, the modern employer has acted upon the erroneous assumption that cheap labor is necessary to his business prosperity. Accordingly he has resisted instead of promoting every effort to ameliorate the condition of the laboring classes, from the same motive that the Southern planter opposed the abolition of slavery. All other efforts to increase the social opportunities of the laborer have been resisted by the employing class as mischievous agitations, until they were made imperative by statute law or social custom. Indeed their whole attitude toward the labor movement in general has been one of persistent hostility. The experience of the last fifty years, however, has shown that in almost every instance they were entirely mistaken. It is now admitted that free labor is more productive and economic than slave labor ever was. And instead of the prosperity of the manufacturing class having been lessened by the various restrictions imposed upon their inhumane and uneconomic policy, it has steadily increased. The employer of to-day, with wages twice as high, hours of labor one fourth less, and the sanitary and social conditions of the laborer a hundred per cent. better, is more prosperous than were his predecessors fifty years ago.

Nor is this socially repressive policy due to any peculiar perversity of the employing class. They are not less humane and philanthropic than any other portion of the community, as their liberal contributions to charitable, educational, and other public institutions conclusively show. Their antagonistic attitude arises from a misconception of their economic relation to the laboring class ; and for this, the economic teaching of the period is responsible. The failure of the economist to recognize the revolution in the economic relation of the laborer to the capitalist which took place with the inauguration of the factory system, naturally led to the mistake of ignoring the economic importance of the laborers' consumption as the market basis for factory-made products. With this ante-factory-period view of the laborers' economic position, it naturally appeared to the employer that the true economic policy was to obtain his labor as cheaply as possible. Oblivious of the fact that the success of his factory as a mere money-making institution depends upon the character and wealth-consuming capacity of the masses, he has systematically regarded the laborers as merely so much productive force to be used to the limit of their endurance.

Under the influence of such doctrines, it is not surprising that the employing class should use every effort, industrial and political, to resist all endeavors to increase the social opportunities or raise the wages of the laborer.[1] Thus, through the influence of a mistaken industrial policy, the capitalist in the vain endeavor to increase his power to produce, by limiting the power of the laborer to consume, defeats the very object he most desires to accomplish, and instead of promoting his own permanent prosperity, he is continually planting the seed of business depression, enforced idleness, and bankruptcy. Thus business depressions, instead of being a necessary part of the factory system, are really the penalty which the employing class and the community have

[1] See "Wealth and Progress," Part III., chapters vi. and vii.

to pay for ignoring the economic and social advancement of the laboring classes as the real basis of industrial prosperity.

SECTION III.—*The Prevention of Business Depressions.*

It will be observed that business depressions are wholly a problem of the market ; and also that the market, while furnishing the economic basis for production, is a social phenomenon, having its rise in the *social life* of the people. Whether scientific production shall continually cheapen wealth and increase social well-being, or whether it shall create enforced idleness and business depressions, depends upon whether new employments are created as fast as labor-saving appliances are adopted. Production being the response to consumption, new employments can be created only as fast as new demands for commodities arise among the masses. This involves an important change in the general point of view from which the economic position of the laborer is regarded. In the first place it must be distinctly recognized as an irrevocable historic fact, *that with the inauguration of the factory system the economic relation of the laborer to the capitalist was radically changed, and that under modern industrial conditions the market for the capitalists' production finally depends upon the extent of the laborers' consumption ; hence business prosperity can be continuous only in proportion as real wages 'rise.* And it must be no less distinctly recognized as a fundamental principle in economics *that the cost of production is the controlling element in price movement, and consequently that the determining element in the price of labor (wages) is the cost of the laborers' living as determined by the standard of his social life.*

It should be remembered, however, that capitalists are not philosophers, nor have we any right to expect them to be. They are captains of industry, and as such are too busy with the administration of affairs to solve economic problems. Their function is to apply rather than to develop economic principles. The same is substantially true of the journalist. Although his position is that of an educator of public opinion, he is more like a manufacturer than a scientist. He is occupied rather with the popular presentation of accepted economic doctrines than with testing their validity. Like the capitalists, the ablest editors and

essayists rely mainly upon economists for their economic principles. It is to the economists, therefore, that we have a right to
look for the recognition and active propagation of the economic
truths underlying this important problem.

When the foregoing propositions are emphatically taught in
colleges and acted upon by capitalists, the first great step
towards a solution, not only of industrial depressions but of the
social problem will have been taken ; and the chief cause of antagonism between the laboring and the employing class will have
been removed. So long as the laborer and capitalist believe their
interests are economically antagonistic, unity of action to redress
social evils is almost impossible. If, however, the employing class
can be once made to realize (1) that there is no economic antagonism between the laborers' interests and their own, and (2) that
the initial point of industrial prosperity is not in production but
in consumption—not in the factory but in the home—not in profits
but in wages,—there will for the first time be a common agreement
as to the point towards which all efforts for industrial improvements must be directed, namely, *the elevation of the laborer's standard of living.* This fact established, the only question would be
as to the best means of promoting that end, since whatever would
do that would promote the welfare of the whole community.

It is not to be inferred from the above that an increase in the
laborers' consumption (real wages) is a simple matter that can be
arbitrarily accomplished by an official proclamation or a legislative enactment. On the contrary, the laborer's standard of living, being determined by his social habits, is a matter of relatively
slow development.

Although there is no immediate panacea for business depressions any more than for poverty, despotism, or other evils arising
from the lack of social character among the masses, there are three
ways in which their severity may be diminished and their ultimate elimination promoted : (1) negatively by lessening the ob-
structions to the social progress of the masses ; (2) positively by
constantly increasing the social opportunities of the masses ; (3)
by establishing an international business barometer by which approaching business depressions will be indicated sufficiently in
advance to enable their severest phases to be avoided.

    1. The greatest obstruction to the social progress of the masses,
26

as already pointed out, is the opposition of the employing class and their literary and legislative,allies. With the acceptance of the doctrine here indicated, there would naturally be a marked change in the attitude of the press and statesmen toward the social question, by which much of their opposition would be removed. In the first place, such men as Edward Atkinson, David A. Wells, and the leading commercial and political journals would no longer appear as the opponents of every proposition, legislative or other, for improving the laborers' social condition. Indeed much of their present attitude toward the social question would then be properly regarded as opposition to the public weal. The acceptance of this view would also further the same end by preventing a vast amount of misdirected effort at social reform, the futility of which often serves to strengthen the hands of the opposition. If it were clearly understood that nothing can promote business prosperity which does not directly or indirectly tend to elevate the laborers' social life, and make a larger consumption of wealth necessary, then the various social chimeras—such as land nationalization, socialism, and the like—would be discredited in advance as having no real bearing upon the question.

2. The disparity between the increase in the laborers' consumption as compared with that of the capitalists' production would be still more diminished, if the energy which has been constantly devoted to limiting the laborers' social opportunities were applied to increasing them. Then every proposition for improving the condition of the masses would be approached with the desire of adopting whatever feasible element of good it contained, instead of a determination to magnify all its disadvantages for the purpose of defeating it.

In order that the policy of increasing instead of restricting the laborers' consumption may be scientifically applied to the prevention of business depressions, it is necessary to have some means of knowing in advance the first indications of a business depression. It will be readily seen that if it could be correctly known that a movement towards business depression had set in, which if not arrested would inevitably bring a period of social disaster, all the wisdom of economists, statesmen, and capitalists would be applied to preventing its occurrence, and this could be done in two ways.

In the first place, if correct economic doctrine prevailed, efforts would at once be redoubled in all manufacturing countries to use every known legislative, personal, social, and industrial means of augmenting consumption among the masses. This would involve efforts to raise the laborer's standard of living, which of course means an improvement in his social condition. If such efforts were made in all machine-using countries as soon as the symptoms of an approaching depression appeared, it could always be weakened and in many cases obviated.

In the second place, if the consumption of the masses in the various countries could not be increased sufficiently to offset a threatened diminution in the market, the depression could be largely mitigated by a movement of capital. As soon as it was definitely known that the relative diminution of the market had set in, while established industries could not, without injury, curtail their production, the investment of new capital could and would be curtailed. By curtailing investments sufficiently in advance much new capital would be saved, and the shock to established industries would be greatly reduced.

Moreover, as business depressions generally arise from a disparity between consumption and production in certain lines of commodities, a proper knowledge of business phenomena would indicate in precisely what line of industry the disturbance existed, and thus enable a more economic direction to be given to new investments. By this means much of the capital that in such periods is wasted in America, England, France, and Germany might, and often would, be made to render a service to civilization by developing the social resources of South America, India, China, and other non-manufacturing countries. Is it possible then to establish such an industrial barometer; is there any means by which the early symptoms of a business depression can be surely indicated? I think there is.

Although the first symptom of a business depression is the failure of the producer to find a profitable market for his whole product, this may occur from causes which do not necessarily indicate a depression in business. A change of fashion for example, or the substitution of a superior for an inferior product through the use of better methods, may produce that effect in a specific industry. In that case however, the dulness in the old industry would be practically offset by the briskness in the new. Such a disturbance therefore will only be a temporary perturbation incident to the movement of capital and labor from one industry to another, and might indeed be a sign of business prosperity rather than adversity. But there is one fact in the industrial world which infallibly indicates an approaching business depression, namely, *enforced idleness.* There are many ways in which enforced idleness may be produced in machine-using countries, *e.g.*, by the immigration of laborers from non-machine-using countries, by discharges through the use of labor-saving machinery, or by the suspension of industry consequent upon a declining market. But from whatever cause or number of causes enforced idleness arises, unless it is arrested, an industrial depression is inevitable.

It is equally certain that nothing can produce a business depression of serious proportions which does not create enforced idleness ; indeed, so long as the laborers are all employed a business depression is practically impossible. Therefore, while enforced idleness may not be the initial cause of business depressions, it is one of the earliest and most infallible indications of it. Since a knowledge of the phenomena is a necessary prerequisite to scientific action, the first practical step toward prevention of business depressions, is the collection of statistics of enforced idleness. Nor would this be a difficult task, since the machinery for collecting industrial data is now fairly well established in most civilized countries. Statistics of enforced idleness not being of an inquisitorial nature, there could be no valid objection to their collection, especially as no class in the community would have any motive for withholding the information. In order that these statistics may have the utmost utility, the investigation should be authoritative, universal, and frequent.

To make the investigation authoritative, it should be undertaken by the state. Moreover, it is a work which peculiarly belongs to the government, because it is of universal importance, and can be performed more extensively, efficiently, and economically by the state than by the individual, especially in the less civilized countries. To give reliability to the data, the investigation should be as extensive as the factory system, including at least America, England, France, Germany, Belgium, Switzerland, Austria, Italy, and Spain.

These statistics should also be collected as frequently as possible, not less than once a year, and half-yearly or quarterly would be even better. Frequency of collection is one of the most essential requisites of idleness statistics, because it is only by a frequent collection of facts that the symptoms of an on-coming industrial depression can be observed in its early stages and hence the most efficient means of prevention adopted.

Such a body of data would furnish an inductive basis for the scientific application of economic principles to market phenomena, besides being invaluable in the treatment of all other phases of the social question. While it is not pretended that business depressions can be summarily abolished, it is indisputable that with full, frequent, and reliable statistics of enforced idleness in all machine-using countries, together with sound views regarding the economic relation of the laborers' consumption to the market, a great step would be taken towards their diminution and ultimate elimination.

CHAPTER VI.

COMBINATION OF CAPITAL.

It is a peculiar feature of the industrial history of society that every movement towards concentration or more complex association of industrial forces has always been viewed with alarm, and has had to encounter serious opposition from the community. The landed aristocracy saw with dismay the rise and growth of the mercantile class from the fifteenth to the eighteenth century, and accordingly used all their social and political power to harass and hinder the development of what to them contained naught but evil for society.

With the introduction of the spinning-jenny in the eighteenth century, this social alarm was taken up by the hand spinners. Their horror and indignation at the idea of a machine spinning eight threads where they could only spin one were such that they ransacked the home of Hargreaves, broke his machines, and drove him from his native county for inventing it. A similar alarm was raised in the first quarter of the present century by the hand-loom weavers against the introduction of the power-loom, and they went from town to town destroying the steam-driven machines. The small factory owners, who had encountered the violence of the hand laborers, subsequently raised a similar alarm against the corporation, and now small corporations, individual factory-owners, laborers, and non-commercial classes all join in raising a similar alarm-cry against trusts, syndicates, and other corporate combinations.

Perhaps the most remarkable feature in the attitude of the public towards industrial combination is their disregard for the lessons of history. The fact that in almost every instance the opposition to new forms of industrial organization has been a mistaken resistance to what finally proved to be a permanent benefit, seems to have almost no modifying influence upon their belligerent attitude. The opposition to trusts to-day is scarcely less intense than was that against the machines of Hargreaves and Arkwright a century ago.[1]

A very little reflection will show that this opposition to capitalistic concentration is as uneconomic and impolitic as is the crusade of capitalists against the combination of labor, and for substantially the same reason. The fallacy underlying both these positions is the assumption that an improvement in the condition of either is obtained at the expense of the other. The capitalist is opposed to labor-unions because he believes that a rise of wages involves a fall of profits ; and the public oppose the combination of capital because they believe that the large profits of a successful corporation are necessarily obtained at the expense of the laborer and the consumer.

In the light of the economic law of prices, surplus, and wages, as heretofore presented, the fallacy of such an attitude becomes apparent. When we once realize that profit is not added to the consumers' price, but that it represents a surplus produced by the use of superior instruments and natural forces, it is clear that the wealth of the capitalist is not drawn from the incomes of the other classes in the community, but from nature.[2] And so with the capitalist ; when he understands that a rise in wages is not a permanent tax upon him, but is ultimately replenished through an increased product—hence, like his own profit, is not drawn from his fellow-man, but from nature,—the ground of his opposition to labor combinations will disappear. Since neither the employing nor laboring class can permanently improve its condition by impairing that of the other, but only by increasing the product of nature, it will be obvious that neither one has any thing to gain by suppressing the combination of the other ; but, on the contrary, if combination will increase their economic power, everybody has an interest in extending and strengthening such combination.

[1] In 1888 a bill was introduced into Congress proposing to levy a tax of 40 per cent. on the products of trusts. In 1889 two other bills were introduced into the United States Senate, practically making trusts criminal conspiracies.

[2] Chapter on " Prices."

Without stopping to consider whether or not the trust form of combination is superior to any other, it may be laid down as a fundamental principle demonstrated by the history of industrial evolution, that the combination of capital is indispensable to economic progress. This consists in cheapening wealth as compared with labor. Capital and labor being the only two factors which enter into the cost of production, it follows that wealth can be cheapened only by increasing the productive capacity of capital. It is a fact too obvious and universal to need discussing, that an increase in the productive efficiency of capital is obtained by means of greater specialization and concentration, which increases as civilization advances. Of this, every successful factory, railroad, and steamship enterprise is a demonstration.

This much will be conceded by the most ill-informed anti-combinationist. But the objection commonly urged is that the gain resulting from this economy in production mainly accrues to a small class. It is insisted that this tends to create a double evil, by at once promoting industrial monopoly and political despotism. They assure us that wherever wealth is accumulated in the hands of a few, the poverty of the people, political corruption, and private immorality increase, and that intellectual, political, and national decay inevitably set in.[1] Although few arguments have more effect upon the public mind than this, there are none that reveal a greater lack of economic insight. It proceeds upon the assumption (1) that all accumulation of wealth in the hands of a limited class is injurious to the welfare of the community, and (2) that the concentration of capital necessarily destroys competition.

1. If we bear in mind the economic distinction between consumable and productive wealth or capital already referred to, we shall have little difficulty in seeing the error of this proposition. Whether or not the accumulation of wealth in a few hands will be beneficial or injurious to society, will entirely depend upon whether it is consumable wealth or capital that is accumulated.

No one acquainted with the subject will for a moment contend that concentration of consumable wealth in the hands of a small class is advantageous to the community. Since this class of

---

[1] See author's article on "Trusts," *Political Science Quarterly*, vol. iii., pp. 403-406.

wealth only ministers to human welfare when in the possession of the consumer, it follows that it can only yield the largest benefit to the community when it is most extensively distributed among the people.   With productive wealth or capital, however, the case is exactly the reverse ; its functions being solely that of a productive instrument, it can minister to human welfare only by producing consumable wealth.   Clearly therefore, whether or not capital is any advantage to its owner or to the public, depends entirely upon whether it is advantageously used in creating enjoyable commodities.   Since capital will only furnish consumable wealth to its owner in proportion as he can sell his products, its possession can only be advantageous to the capitalist when the consumable wealth it produces is generally and liberally consumed by the community.

It may be observed in passing that there is no tendency in modern society to accumulate consumable wealth.   On the contrary, the very prosperity of the community depends upon the constantly increasing consumption of consumable wealth.   When we speak of the accumulation of millions in the hands of a single individual or family to-day, it should be remembered that capital and not consumable wealth is referred to.   With the exception of a small amount personally consumed and dispersed in charities, the large fortunes of the Vanderbilts, Goulds, Astors, Rothschilds, and other millionaires are productively employed. Indeed, it would be regarded as the insanity of financiering to accumulate consumable wealth, because the only result of such accumulation would be deterioration and loss.   As shown in the preceding chapter, any tendency to prevent consumption from keeping pace with production, which is simply accumulating consumable wealth, surely leads to business depressions, and entails inevitably bankruptcy, and often ruin upon the owners of capital. Since capital can be of no advantage to its owner except when it is profitably employed in producing consumable wealth, and since it can be so profitably employed when its product is consumed substantially as fast as it is produced, it follows, as an economic necessity, that consumable wealth is most widely distributed where productive wealth or capital is most concentrated.   Thus we again arrive at the oft-repeated proposition that the prosperity of the capitalist finally depends upon the consumption of wealth by the masses.

2. The second objection is that combination of capital tends to destroy competition. If this assumption be correct, the power of competition will necessarily diminish as the combination of capital increases. Whether or not this has taken place can be determined only by the facts. In order to determine whether or not effective competition increases or diminishes with combination of capital, we have only to ascertain whether or not prices tend to press closer to the line of the cost of producing the most expensive portion of the general supply. Tried by this test, the assertion that the combination of capital necessarily tends to destroy competition will be found to be entirely erroneous.

There never was a time when economic combination was so great as it is to day, nor was there ever a time when competition was so fierce and unsparing—that is to say, when the margin between the cost of producing the dearest portion and the selling price was so small in such a large proportion of industries. Indeed, it is one of the chief indictments against the capitalistic system of production that it is a "competitive system." If we follow the combination of capital from the hand-loom weaver and the spinner of a single thread to the trust and syndicate, we shall find that the margin of profit per unit of product has steadily diminished—a fact which every business man knows. The reason for this is obvious. For instance, when the hand-loom weaver could only turn off forty yards of cotton cloth a week, a margin of a cent a yard would yield but an insignificant amount of profit. The profit on the product of fifty weavers would only be $25 a week, whereas the same margin on the product of fifty weavers to-day would yield a profit of $1,080 a week.

Much of the error in this connection is due to judging competition from the standpoint of the deposed or receding competitor. Thus, when the products of a small factory undersold those of a hand-loom, judged from the standpoint of the hand-loom weaver, competition was destroyed and monopoly established. Such however was not the case, as everybody now knows. What really took place was a readjustment of economic factors, made necessary by the introduction of superior methods, which resulted in transferring competition to a new plane, where its effectiveness was greatly increased. The same was true when the small factory was superseded by the corporation, and is true now when the corporation is superseded by the trust and syndicate.

It should be remembered that the influence of competition does not depend so much upon the number of competitors as upon the effectiveness of competition. Competitors may be very numerous and still competition be ineffective, as in the case of the hand-loom weavers. And conversely, competitors may be few in number and still be very effective, as is the case of large concerns to-day. One Macy furnishes more effective competition than a hundred small merchants with a few hundred dollars capital each. This does not mean that reducing the number of competitors will necessarily increase effective competition, but it demonstrates the fact that high competition is possible with a small number of competitors. Indeed, it is the severity of competition thus developed that has brought the trust and other forms of industrial confederation into existence.

That effective competition has thus increased with the increasing combination of capital, no one acquainted with the subject will dispute, but the alarm raised is ostensibly for the future. It is upon what trusts *may* do, and not upon what they *have* done, that the present opposition is based. It is said that the object of the trust is to monopolize the market. Even so ; there is nothing new in that. That has been one of the objects of every other industrial improvement. What motive could there be for introducing better methods and investing large capital, unless it would give the owner more advantage over existing competitors. To condemn an industrial institution because the object of its promoters is to undersell and supersede traditional producers and methods is economic insanity. It is not the motive of the capitalist but the economic effect of his action that must be determined in judging the social utility of industrial methods and institutions. Whether the capitalist acts as an individual producer, small factory owner, corporation, or trust ; whether he produces cotton cloth, shoes, or petroleum, conducts a railroad or publishes a newspaper, his motive is substantially the same ; namely, to obtain more wealth—" to make money." *Will it pay?* is the question upon which the doing or not doing in every sphere of industrial activity is determined.

The tone and politics of the newspapers are determined by that fact about as completely as is the form and quality of hats and shoes. Newspaper corporations have not invested hundreds of thousands and even millions of dollars in buildings, large and fast presses, automatic folders, foreign correspondence, special telegrams, high salaried editors and reporters, special trains for deliveries, etc., merely for the sake of furnishing the public with ample, early, and reliable news. This has all been developed by the effort of each to outdo his neighbor in the contest for obtaining public patronage—the market. It was only because this could not be done without furnishing a larger or a better paper at the same price—which nothing but a greater combination of capital and superior methods made possible—that the immense improvements in the daily paper have been produced. The same motive which has induced newspaper corporations to furnish a daily history of the human race for two cents, has given us our railroads, telegraphs, steamships, and other time-and-space-reducing and wealth-cheapening institutions, of which trusts are the most recent form. And the reasons for suppressing one will apply with equal force to suppressing the others.   ·

The opposition to the larger combinations of to-day will be found to have its root in the error which has characterized all previous opposition to productive integrations. The averagely intelligent antagonist to trusts will readily admit that all the evil predictions regarding the earlier stages of capitalistic combination were mistaken. He will also admit that the mistake consisted in the failure to recognize the increasing competitive power which the larger factory and corporation possessed, especially when accompanied by the daily press, the telegraph, and the railroads. The more intelligent now see that a multiplicity of competitors is not necessary to effective competition, having learned by experience that this may result in a great waste of economic power instead of a cheapening of commodities, and that competition is quite as effective, and far more economic, with a limited number of competitors. While they recognize the folly of assuming that any diminution in the number of competitors must weaken competition, they tenaciously insist that to permit the combination of capital to increase until the actual competitors are reduced to zero, must destroy competition. In other words, they insist that competition is impossible unless the competitors are actually present in the market.

The error in this view arises from overlooking the influence of potential competition. If we examine the subject from the standpoint of modern phenomena, we shall find that there is potential competition as well as actual, and that the economic effect of potential competition increases as its phenomena grow in complexity. The competitive power of capital will be found to ultimately depend not merely upon its actual presence, but upon its known availability at any given time and place. Consequently, the more intelligent and economically powerful competitors are, the more effectual will be their potential or possible competition, and *vice versa.* For example in the ante-factory period, with neither railroads nor telegraphs, the only capital known to be available was that visibly present ; hence, none other exercised any competitive influence in the market.

With the development of modern industry all this has changed. Electricity and steam have so diminished time and space, and concentration of capital has so increased the economic power of the producer, that now both capital and products thousands of miles away are economically available, and therefore exercise a positive competitive influence upon the market. Accordingly the wheat in India, Russia and Dakota, now exercises practically the same competitive influence in Liverpool as does that which is stored there, and solely because it is known to be actually available for the Liverpool market if the price rises high enough to warrant its movement thither. Thus through improved means of communication and transportation, products in the most remote parts of the earth exercise a competitive influence upon a market they may never actually enter, simply because it is known that they can be there if needed.

What is true of commodities is even more true of fixed capital, and as will readily be seen, potential competition or the power of the possible competitor increases as the combination of capital enlarges. Capital is proverbially one of the most sensitive things in the world. Although it will take great risks for large profits it will timidly recede at the sight of loss. There are many reasons why large combinations are more amenable to the influence of potential competition than small ones. Although more powerful, they yet have more at stake. The very fact that capital is cowardly makes it careful, and, since fear of loss next to hope of gain is the most powerful motive which governs its movement, the first condition to be secured is safety against loss. The greater the concentration of capital, the more serious and difficult this becomes.

It is a principle in economic progress that as the mobility of consumable wealth increases that of productive wealth diminishes, because the very means which promote the easy transfer of products involve a greater fixity of capital. In proportion as capital loses its mobility, the necessity of maximizing its economic utility in its existing form increases ; and when the concentration is very great, that becomes the only means of preserving it from deterioration. Take, for example, the Vanderbilt railroad system with its investment of $170,000,000 and 60,000 employés ; this is excellent property so long as it can be economically employed for its present purpose. If, however, it should be superseded by a superior system of transportation, the greater part of that property would be worthless, the capital invested being absolutely non-transferable. Such parts of the equipment as the rails, road-bed, engines, cars, and stations (representing nearly $150,000,000) which now have a full value as finished products, would in that case practically be reduced to the value of old iron. Three fourths of their value would vanish as completely as if the property were reduced to ashes.

If we bear in mind the fact that capital is simply an economic instrument whose decay can only be prevented by maintaining its productive utility, it will be manifest that in proportion as its concentration increases, the very life of capital depends more and more upon its wealth-cheapening efficiency. It will probably be replied that this may all be true so long as any actual competitors remain, but when the combination of capital has reached a point where the production of a given commodity is practically in the hands of a single concern this restraint will disappear, and prices can be indefinitely increased to suit a monopoly. Here is where the error of ignoring the influence of potential competition again shows itself. The very fact that capital cannot take wings and fly away, but is compelled to work where it is or perish, gives potential competition its greatest influence ; that is to say, gives the non-employed or less remuneratively employed capital its maximum price-reducing influence. It should never be forgotten that in a progressive society, where alone the greatest combination of capital is possible, two things are more or less constantly occurring: (1) the accumulation of wealth available for productive purposes, which increases as the margin of profit rises ; (2) the reduction of capital to no-profit uses, which increases as superior productive methods and management are adopted. From these two causes, which are as universal and constant as social progress, capital seeking remunerative employment is constantly increasing.

Hence this idle or unremunerative capital has the same economic effect upon productive capital that the wheat in India or Russia has upon that in Liverpool ; it is waiting for an opportunity. In the absence of legal restrictions, nothing will prevent this anxiously waiting capital from actually entering the field except keeping the margin of profit too small to warrant the risk. This of course involves the lowering of prices commensurately with the diminished cost of production, which is all the fiercest actual competition can do. It may be said that if new capital enters the field a monopoly will buy it up. But that takes more capital ; a million dollars invested in buying up a competitor is so much added to the cost of production, and directly diminishes profit. Clearly the million thus invested might just as well be surrendered to the community in lower prices. That this would be a safer and more economic method is manifest: (1) because lowering the price tends to increase the consumption of the commodity, extend the market, and make a still smaller margin of profit yield a greater aggregate return ; (2) because a new competitor is an unknown quantity, and may prove too strong to be bought up, in which case existing producers may be driven from the field, or have their profits reduced to zero. Since the least danger to existing corporations lies in *keeping out* rather than *buying out* new competitors, and since reducing prices alone can do this, it follows that the larger a corporation the greater is its interest in keeping prices low enough not to induce the organization of counter-enterprises to jeopardize its existence. It is thus evident that with economic freedom, the potential competition of available capital is essentially the same as if a new competitor were actually on hand. The fact that he *may come* any day has practically the same competitive influence as if he had *come*, because to *keep him out* requires the same kind of price-reducing effort that would be necessary to *drive him out.* Since the former always involves less risk and generally less cost than the latter, it is most likely to be adopted, in proportion as an intelligent understanding of economic movement prevails.

It is a great mistake to suppose that the investment of large capitals is specially desirable to the capitalist. On the contrary he avoids this as much as possible, always preferring to get along with the minimum rather than to use the maximum capital to accomplish any given result. Indeed to accomplish the greatest result with the least investment is the very art of economic production. Moreover, with every increase in the size of investments capital becomes more fixed, involved, and unwieldy, reducing margins and making it possible for great losses to result from very slight mistakes ; consequently greater expertness of management becomes necessary in every department of a colossal enterprise. Larger investments increase the risk of the capitalist and further outlay will be adopted only under the spur of some economic inducement—such as avoiding a loss, replenishing a diminished profit, or perhaps obtaining a still larger profit.

The economic movement of capital being governed by the law of increasing returns, it follows that capital will not (except by mistake) go into new industries. unless it can obtain a greater return per unit than it is already receiving. So, too, of concentration or combination ; capital will continue to concentrate only so long as it can obtain an increasing return per unit by so doing. When that ceases to be possible the motive for combination disappears ; and when the point of diminishing returns is reached self-interest is positively against further combination. That there is a point in any given state of society at which further concentration of capital will fail to yield increasing returns, and at which diminishing returns set in, cannot be doubted. Whether or not this point will be reached before the actual competing producers in the same market disappear cannot now be determined. Nor is this of any real importance since concentration will continue only so long as it will give increasing returns to the capitalist and cheaper products to the consumer. There is therefore no economic reason why the state should do any thing to limit the concentration of capital, since that will be arrested by the capitalist when it ceases to economize production and cheapen the wealth

of the community.   In other words, in the absence of legal restrictions economic law is more effectual in determining the equitable movement of capital than statute law can possibly be.

That this has been the general effect of the concentration of
capital during the present century is abundantly proven by the
fall of prices and rise of wages as shown by the increased purchasing power of a day's labor during that period.   The following table shows the average weekly wages and their relative
purchasing power in 200 staple articles for 1860 and 1885 : [1]

INDUSTRIES.	Number of branches.	1860.		1885.		Percentage of increase.
		Weekly wages.	Purchasing power.	Weekly wages.	Purchasing power.	
Arms and ammunition..........	12	$14.15	100	$13.15	119	19
Artisans' tools	10	8.45	100	11.45	174	74
Boots and shoes................	17	11.42	100	10.63	120	20
Carriages and wagons...........	7	10.47	100	12.80	157	57
Clothing	11	8.26	100	8.19	127	27
Cotton goods..................	86	6.50	100	6.45	128	28
Flax, hemp, and jute...........	15	4.63	100	6.46	180	80
Leather.......................	8	10.01	100	11.01	141	41
Liquors.......................	8	10.73	100	11.73	141	41
Machinery.....................	19	7.90	100	11.75	192	92
Metallic goods.................	10	9.07	100	11.25	161	61
Musical instruments............	8	10.94	100	12.94	152	52
Paper goods...................	18	8.63	100	7.63	114	14
Print and ·dye-goods...........	26	9.90	100	7.67	100	
Silk and silk goods.............	9	5.91	100	6.91	167	67
Stone........................	7	8.01	100	12.01	193	93
Woollen goods.................	58	5.38	100	7.90	189	89
Worsted goods.................	22	6.12	100	6.12	129	29
Carpetings....................	25	6.62	100	6.62	129	29
Building trades................	10	9.87	100	14.99	196	96
Average ....(Total 386)		8.64	100	9.88	150	50

This tendency is still more conclusively shown by the fact that
the fall in prices has been greatest in those commodities in
whose production there has been the greatest concentration of

[1] The wages in the above table represent 386 occupations in Massachusetts ;
the data for 1860 will be found in the Report of the Labor Bureau for 1884, and
those for 1885 in the Census Report for 1885 (volume on Manufactures).

capital, as will be seen by the accompanying table, which shows the purchasing power of weekly wages in commodities furnished by trusts and other colossal combinations for 1860 and 1890 :

Purchasing power of weekly wages.	1860.	1890.	Percentage of increase.
Cotton-seed oil, number of gals...	$18\frac{1}{100}$ [1]	$29\frac{98}{100}$	66
Sugar refined, number of lbs.....	$90\frac{9}{100}$	152	67
Freight New York to Chicago.			
First class...................	530 lbs.	1317 lbs.	148
Second class................	654 "	1520 "	132
Third class..................	822 "	1976 "	176
Fourth class.................	1309 "	2822 "	115
Telegraph messages, number of..	$8\frac{98}{100}$ [2] "	$31\frac{44}{100}$ "	283
Pretroleum refined, number of gals.	$107\frac{89}{100}$ "	$1086\frac{89}{100}$ "	907

It will be seen from the above tables that, although the general purchasing power of wages has greatly increased since 1860, the increase has been very much greater in those industries where the greatest concentration of capital has taken place. Taking 200 staple articles together, the increase is $53\frac{66}{100}$ per cent., whereas, in cotton-seed oil, it is 66 per cent. ; in sugar, 67 per cent. ; in transportation (all classes) together, it is 142 per cent. ; in telegraphy, 283 per cent. ; and in petroleum, 907 per cent. It should be observed in this connection that the figures for cotton-seed oil only extended to 1878, and that more than $\frac{11}{13}$ of the entire fall in the price has taken place since the trust was formed in 1884 [3] ; and also that the fall in the price of sugar during the last thirty years has all taken place since January, 1882.[4]

It may be said that the point has not yet been reached where actual competitors are reduced to none, and therefore the correctness of the theory here presented cannot be inductively verified. It is true that there are very few industries in which the actual competitors are not still relatively numerous. Nor is there any sufficient ground for concluding that the time will ever come

[1] The figures in this table are for 1878.

[2] These figures are for 1866.

[3] In 1878 the price of standard summer oil was $47\frac{84}{100}$ cents a gallon ; in 1883 it was $47\frac{8}{100}$ cents a gallon ; it is now (September 27, 1890) 33 cents a gallon.

[4] The average price of refined sugar in 1860 was $9\frac{1}{4}$ cents a pound. In January, 1882, it was $9\frac{3}{8}$, and in July $9\frac{5}{16}$ cents a pound.

when this will not be the case in a great majority of industries, but that in some industries production may practically be in the hands of a single concern is certainly within the range of possibility, since we have at least one instance of this kind already in the Standard Oil Trust. This concern comes nearer to having complete control of a given product than perhaps any other enterprise in the world. When petroleum was refined by small concerns, it was very poor in quality and very high in price. In 1861, when crude oil was only $1\frac{23}{100}$ cents a gallon, refined oil was $61\frac{54}{100}$ cents a gallon, making the cost of refining and transportation $60\frac{31}{100}$ cents a gallon. By concentration of capital and the improved processes of ten years, the price of refined oil was reduced to $24\frac{84}{100}$ cents a gallon. The oil was still both poor and dangerous to use, casualties from exploding lamps being of daily occurrence. This was practically as far as small concerns were able to carry the light-improving and price-reducing processes, and although the quality was poor and the price high the refiners' profits were small.

In 1872 the refiners formed a combination called the Standard Oil Company, which however did not include any considerable portion of the refiners until 1874, but by this concentration of productive power they were able to introduce various improvements otherwise impracticable. For example, before the organization of the Standard Oil Company, crude oil had to be transported from the wells to the market in small quantities, in barrels, tanks, etc. After the organization of that company, various methods of reducing the cost of transporting oil were adopted, which, about 1879, resulted in substituting for the railroad and other means of transportation, a general pipe line taking oil from the various wells and delivering it directly to the market. There are now two such lines reaching New York, with the capacity of 25,000 barrels a day. There is also one such line to the cities of Philadelphia, Baltimore, Buffalo, Cleveland, and Pittsburgh, and one is being constructed to Chicago. This was an undertaking absolutely beyond the power of any of the smaller corporations. Nothing short of a colossal combination was adequate to the task, which resulted in a saving of over 66 per cent. of the cost of transportation alone.

Similar savings in other departments, such as the manufacture of their various supplies, have been accomplished by virtue of the consolidation. Thus in 1872 barrels cost $2.35 each ; to-day the trust manufactures them for its own use at $1.25 each, a reduction of 47 per cent., or a saving of nearly $4,000,000 a year. In the cost of manufacture of tin cans, a saving of 50 per cent. has been made, the price having been reduced from 30 to 15 cents per can since 1874. As this company uses about 30,000,000 tin cans a year, that makes a saving of over $4,500,000 annually. The same is true of wooden cases, which in 1874 cost 20 cents each, while the company now manufactures them for itself at a cost of 13 cents each, being an annual saving of about $1,250,000. Similar economies have been established in the manufacture of tanks, stills, pumps, and other things used in the business. As a result of all this the price of the refined oil was reduced in eight years, 1872–1879, from $24\frac{24}{100}$ cents to $8\frac{8}{100}$ cents a gallon, or $66\frac{66}{100}$ per cent. Moreover, in addition to thus lowering the price, the quality of the oil was greatly improved by entirely eliminating the explosive elements and increasing its illuminating quality.

By these improvements in quality and reductions in price, the market for oil was greatly extended, and in 1880 a still further combination of capital was undertaken and the trust formed. This, as before remarked, included nearly all the leading refiners in this country, and therefore actual competition in this business was minimized.[1] Under these monopolistic conditions, according to the usual predictions, the price of oil might have been expected to rise, but the fact is that it continued to fall as will be seen by the following table :

Year.	Price of crude oil per gallon at wells.	Price per gallon of refined oil for export.
1880	2.24	9.12
1881	2.30	8.05
1882	1.87	7.41
1883	2.52	8.14
1884	1.99	8.28
1885	2.11	7.86
1886	1.69	7.07
1887	1.59	6.75
1888	2.07	7.50
1889	2.42	7.25

[1] The Standard Oil Trust refines about 75 per cent. of all the oil in this country.

. It will be observed that this fall in the price of refined oil is none of it due to a fall in the price of the crude oil which remained practically unchanged. This is the more surprising because improvements in the means of transportation and other processes had already been practically maximized, and, as will be readily observed, the possibilities for economy are very much less when the price has reached 9 cents than when it was 24 cents a gallon. Manifestly if the community is to receive in reduced prices the advantage of the limited improvements that remain possible and profits are to be maintained, economies must take a new direction. And this is exactly what has taken place.

During the last few years, and especially since the organization of the trust, a series of improvements has been developed by means of which what had been previously wasted is now converted into valuable commodities. In the refining of petroleum, after the illuminating oil is abstracted, there is a large residuum left which hitherto had only a fuel value. This formerly wasted material is now converted into naphtha, lubricating oils, paraffine wax, etc. In order to do this, however, expensive machinery and manufactories had to be constructed expressly for the purpose, which could only be profitably undertaken in connection with the most colossal processes of petroleum refining. Some idea of the extent of this may be formed from the fact that naphtha thus produced supplies more than two thirds of the public light of New York City, Brooklyn, and Jersey City because it is cheaper than gas. The price of paraffine oil also has been reduced by this means from 22 cents to $11\frac{1}{2}$ cents a gallon, and has been improved 50 per cent. in its lubricating qualities. In 1875 the standard for American paraffine oil by the commercial test viscosity was 100 seconds at a temperature of 70 ; it now tests 150, and its flash point, which in 1875 was 300, is 380.

Moreover, in 1875, paraffine oil could not be used for lubricating machinery without an admixture of from 20 to 50 per cent. of animal oil, while to-day it can be used without any animal oil. This is true of several other lubricants made from petroleum, especially cylinder oil. Even for railroad purposes this supersedes tallow and other animal lubricants, having the great merit of preventing corrosion by keeping the metal surfaces bright and clean. In 1875 the price of petroleum cylinder oil was $1.25 per gallon ; it is now only 35 to 40 cents. The price of black lubricating oils used for railroad axles was 15 to 18 cents a gallon in 1875, and to-day it is sold at 7 and 9 cents. The monthly sales of mineral lubricating oils were not more than 10,000 barrels in 1875 ; they are now nearly 70,000. Furthermore, the animal product of paraffine wax from petroleum was less than 6,000 tons in 1870, and this year the product is estimated at fully 20,000 tons, and the price has been reduced from 9 to 5 cents a pound. It may be added that the quality of this product has been so improved, that for candle purposes, especially in Great Britian, it has superseded tallow, stearine, products of palm oil, etc., and the price of candles has been reduced one half in consequence.

In addition to all this the trust has undertaken the manufacture of its own sulphuric acid, having need of a greater quantity of that product. Through improved processes introduced into the manufacture of this commodity the price has been reduced from a cent and a quarter a pound to eight cents a hundred pounds. By such means this trust has been able to give to the community in reduced prices the full benefit of all improvements in refining petroleum, and to obtain its profit from what formerly was mere waste.

Nor is this all ; the series of improvements, from the pipe line up, which have thus been developed through the increasing combination of capital, has since been copied bodily in Russia. Petroleum was discovered there long before it was known in Pennsylvania, but because of crude methods for developing it it was not much more serviceable to them than were the valuable mineral and agricultural possibilities of this country to the Indians. But after the development of these processes here, the combination of European capital took America's experience and discoveries to Russia, where oil is now produced by substantially the same process. It will thus be seen that the combination of capital in this industry has not only lowered the price and improved the quality of oil in this country, but has actually transferred that much of our civilization to Russia.

It may be said that this is not true of all trusts, but that some of these combinations have used their power to increase instead of to reduce prices. That there are men at the head of trusts

who mistake their true economic function will not be questioned
for a moment ; but to the extent that trusts are used for speculative instead of productive purposes—to create corners instead
of reducing the cost of production—will they fail to be a permanent advantage either to the community or to those undertaking
them. Corners can only be successful to the extent that they
can control a commodity for a sufficient length of time to force
its price up abnormally high. The concentration of productive
capital in trusts, railroads, syndicates, and the like, tends to
ultimately prevent this in two ways : (1) By increasing the
amount of product to such proportions as to make its permanent
control by a few persons practically impossible. (2) By increasing the facilities for communication and transportation so
that commodities can be readily obtained from any part of the
world.

Before the period of steam and the combination of productive
capital, although millionaires were few, corners were numerous
and relatively successful. With the development of the railroad,
telegraph, steamship, large factory, and trusts, however, corners
have become more and more impossible. This is shown by the
fact that during the last fifteen years almost every extensive
attempt to corner commodities has resulted in serious loss and
often ruin to its projectors. Witness Black Friday, and the ruin
of Keene in the wheat corner five years later, and the failure of
the copper syndicate last year, which came very near bankrupting
a number of the largest capitalists in the world and breaking the
bank of France.

The reason for the failure of these and many other efforts to
fictitiously inflate prices, is that the quantity of wealth produced
and the means for rapidly transferring it to any given point have
increased so enormously that to corner any staple product long
enough to accomplish the end desired is practically impossible.
Thus, so far from the combination of capital in production and
transportation being the cause of, or favorable to, corners, it
tends more and more to make merely speculative monopolies
impossible. The recent experience of the sugar trust and the
cotton-seed oil trust also illustrated the same tendency. The
combination of capital is strictly an economic phenomenon
subject to economic law, and when it is used for an uneconomic

purpose it is pretty certain to bring its own punishment. In other words, productive combination is in the order of industrial evolution, and any attempt to permanently restrict that movement is inimical to the best interests of a progressive society.

There is one fact, however, that capitalists would do well not to overlook—namely, that their safety in the future depends upon the economic use of their power. If they persist in the effort to employ the power of combination for uneconomic purposes, they will find themselves confronted by another and more summary kind of opposition than economic law presents. In proportion as the social condition of the masses improves and they become more informed and politically powerful, do they become sensitive about their rights, conscious of their strength, and indignant at any effort to trifle with their interests. Consequently, if capitalists fail to recognize this important fact and continue to trifle with the interests of the community by perversion of their industrial power, they may suddenly find themselves in the hands of an arbitrary political authority whose action may be even more unreasoning than theirs has been uneconomic. There is nothing which furnishes such a plausible basis for the demands of socialism to-day as the uneconomic conduct of the capitalist class. Whether industrial evolution and civilization shall be permitted to advance by increasing the wealth-cheapening capacity of capital, or whether society shall be forced into an experiment of socialism with its stultifying influences, will mainly depend upon the use made by the capitalist class of the economic power which society has conferred upon them.

CHAPTER VII.

THE COMBINATION OF LABOR.

THE combination of labor is the historic and economic accompaniment of the combination of capital ; it is as necessary to the wages system as the factory is to capitalistic production. In the preceding chapter we saw how uneconomic and short-sighted is the policy of those who oppose the concentration of capital. The unwisdom of this opposition is quite clear to the particular capitalists against whom it is directed. It was clear to small factory owners in the first quarter of this century ; it was obvious to the corporations in the third quarter of this century, and it is no less manifest to trusts, syndicates, and other colossal combinations of to-day. But singularly enough they are all tacitly or avowedly opposed to the combination of labor. The president of a syndicate, trust, confederated railroad, or telegraph system, can see the folly and inconsistency of the large newspaper, itself a gigantic corporation, railing against the combination of capital ; but he is apparently oblivious of his own inconsistency in opposing the combination of labor. This attitude can be explained only on the ground of mistaken notions regarding the subject. A little reflection will, show that every reason which obtained for the concentration of capital applies with equal force and for similar reasons to the combination of labor ; and that all the objections urged against the combination of labor are applicable to the combination of capital.

The standard by which all social institutions must be judged is their influence upon the welfare of the community ; nothing can permanently promote the industrial welfare of society which does not either reduce prices or increase wages. Since the economic effect of the combination of capital is shown in the price of commodities, and that of the combination of labor is shown in wages, the social utility of the former must be judged by its tendency to make wealth cheap—to reduce prices,—and that of the latter by its tendency to make men dear—to increase wages. We have already seen that, judged by this test, combination of capital is a great social benefit, and if we bear in mind the point of view from which the discussion has proceeded, we shall have no difficulty in seeing that the same is true of the combination of labor. Among the many objections to trades unions it is urged : (1) That they are un-American, because they were born in and belong to the monarchical institutions of the old world, and are out of place in a democratic republic ; (2) that they tend to destroy the right of individual contract, and thereby limit the laborer's freedom and industrial independence ; (3) that they tend to encroach upon the employer's right to manage his own business by preventing him from contracting for his labor with the laborers individually ; (4) that they cannot increase wages and improve the laborers' social condition, because they are contrary to natural law.

1. It is true that trades unions were not born in America ; neither were factories and railroads. If labor combinations are to be rejected in America because they arose in Europe, then the use of steam, the daily press, our literature, language, religion, and indeed our very civilization may also be rejected for the same reason. Of all the objections urged against the combination of labor, there are none more flippant and absurd than the fact that it was of old-world origin. Trades unions arose in England solely because capitalistic production and the factory system had their rise there. The combination of labor, like that of capital, is not a national but an economic institution, and must be judged entirely by its economic characteristics. To call an institution un-American because it did not have its birth in the United States, is to fail to distinguish between an economic principle and a geographical location. The truth or wisdom of a doctrine, institution, or policy, does not depend upon how or where it arose, but upon the social effect of its application.

2. The contention that trades unions destroy the right of individual contract and limit the laborer's freedom has a plausible seeming, but it is singularly superficial. If it be true that combination destroys the freedom of the laborer, why does it not

27

also destroy that of the capitalist. It will hardly be contended that capitalists who have steadily integrated into larger and larger combinations are less free than formerly; one great complaint against them is that they are having too much freedom. It is true that labor combinations have steadily increased during the last fifty years, and it is equally true that the laborers' industrial, social, and political freedom has increased more during that period than ever before.

Nearly all opposition to labor combinations is ostensibly for the laborers' benefit. As early as 1831, when the trades union asked Parliament to reduce the working time of the factory operatives in England from twelve to eleven and a half hours a day, the proposition was opposed on the ground that it would destroy the freedom of the laborer to work as many hours as he chose. And forty-five years later the same reasoning was presented in Massachusetts against the adoption of a ten-hour factory law. Edward Atkinson and others repeatedly pleaded against the measure on the ground of individual freedom, claiming that to limit the working day by law to ten hours was to deprive the working women (the law only applied to women and children) of their sacred right to make an individual contract to work as many or as few hours and for such wages as they pleased. Such reasoning implies that the factory women had previously enjoyed the precious boon of making individual contracts regarding their hours and wages. The fact is, however, that no such right existed; there was never a time since the factory system began when the operative of either sex could make any such individual contract; and prior to the factory system and the existence of trades unions the laborer had neither part nor lot in determining either his wages, hours of labor, or any other condition. Down to the fourteenth century the laborer was the property of his master. From the middle of the fourteenth to the close of the eighteenth century his industrial conditions were determined by statute law, in which he had no voice; and during the first half of the present century they were determined by the employer.[1] The right or expediency of con-

---

[1] During the reign of Edward III., Richard II., and the Fourth and Fifth Henrys, the law was chiefly directed to regulating the laborers' wages, food, clothes, occupation, and mobility, coupled with severe penalties for violation. And during the next four hundred years (1425–1825) this was supple-

sulting the laborer in such things is a matter of recent date; a fact which labor combinations have made possible and are fast making necessary.

The mistake in this attitude arises from a misconception of what constitutes freedom. As already observed,[1] freedom does not consist in the negative permission to do but in the positive power of actual doing. The essence of freedom is power, and the source of economic and social power is wealth. Nothing can furnish the motive to associate but the fact that association increases the power to obtain desired objects. The history of freedom is the history of progress, and the history of progress is the history of industrial, social, and political integration or combination. Every movement towards freedom is a movement towards greater economic and social interdependence between individuals. Interdependence involves mutual helpfulness, which in turn furnishes security of rights and the maximum freedom of action. The difference between freedom furnished by savagery and that secured by society is that the former affords the freedom to injure while the latter gives freedom only to help our fellow-man, and thereby benefit ourselves. If trades unions were inimical to the laborers' freedom we should find more individuality and freedom among unorganized than among organized laborers. The facts, however, are everywhere the reverse. In every country and industry it is the organized laborers who are the most characterful and progressive, and the most difficult to coerce or mislead, either industrially or politically. It is not correct therefore, either theoretically or historically, that labor combinations tend to destroy the laborers' freedom.

3. The complaint that trades unions invade the rights of the capitalist to control his own business, is regarded as the greatest grievance by the employing class. When discussing this point however, it soon becomes apparent that the phrase, " preserving the laborers' right of free contract " really means nothing but the right of the employer to insist upon making contracts with

mented by laws making it a penal offence for laborers to combine for the purpose of obtaining advance of wages, or for altering the hours of work." See Encyclopedia Britannica, vol. v., p. 181. Also, Rogers' "Six Centuries of Work and Wages," p. 399.

[1] See page 12. Also, " Wealth and Progress," pp. 131, 132.

laborers individually. A very slight acquaintance with industrial experience is sufficient to show that the reason for this is, that in so doing the laborer is less able to make contracts to his own advantage.

There is surely no principle in economics or equity which will not apply with as much force to the capitalist as to the laborer. If the capitalist has a right to object to the laborers acting collectively, the laborers have an equal right to object to the associated action of capitalists. In truth however, such an objection on the part of either is the very acme of absurdity, because individual action has been rendered practically impossible on both sides by the very constitution of the factory system. Everybody is now aware that associated capital is practically indispensable to successful production. No matter how desirable it might appear that each stockholder should directly participate in every transaction of the concern, such a town-meeting method is now utterly impracticable. That a considerable degree of associated and representative action is necessary for capital is generally admitted ; the individual contract system is literally insisted upon only for the laborer. All contracts for labor must take place between corporate capital and individual laborers. When the laborer purchases commodities he must buy *individually* from corporate producers, and when he sells labor he must sell *individually* to corporate purchasers.

This position is as illogical as it is impracticable. Fortunately economic law makes such an one-sided arrangement impossible. The very conditions which have made the combination of capital necessary, have rendered a practical uniformity in the price of labor necessary for the same work in the same shop. It is manifestly impossible for a concern employing several thousand laborers to make a special contract with each individual laborer as to the wages he shall receive and the hours he shall work. In the first place, a multitude of different rates of wages and other conditions would throw the whole concern into confusion. Every change of workman would be liable to involve a new price, and thus change the cost of producing the article. Since the labor of all the workmen is merged into a common product and sold at a uniform price, it would be impossible to know from week to week whether the selling price was above or below the cost of production. This difficulty would be further increased by the fact that the productive capacity of operatives greatly varies, especially where men, women and children all work at the same occupation. It was this fact, together with the desire to spur the workman to his maximum effort, that led'to the introduction of the piece-work system. It is needless to say that to have a special contract with each individual operative as to the price paid per unit of product is absolutely impracticable.

Still another obstacle to individual contract is the fact, that under factory methods the tools are all driven by a single power. This makes it essential to the economy of the process that there be a uniformity of hours in order that all may commence and stop at the same time, because it involves about as much cost to run the' machinery for a portion as for the whole number of operatives. Furthermore, since every department supplies but a fraction of the finished product, it is necessary that its quota should be furnished in a uniform proportion to all the rest, as any variation in this respect would be a disturbing hindrance to the whole concern. In other words, the workers in the seventy different branches in the manufacture of a shoe are simply integral parts of a continuous process, and therefore must all conform to a general system of operations. It is as impossible for each operative to make separate conditions without regard to the rest as it would be to make the cogs of a wheel of different length, breadth, or thickness, without regard to each other. Individual contracts therefore, regarding wages, hours of labor, or other working conditions, are absolutely out of the question under the factory system. Indeed, no practical business man would ever seriously entertain such an idea.

As a matter of fact, no such freedom on the part of the laborer to make an individual contract for himself, different from that under which his fellow-workman in the same shop or industry is working, is ever intended by the much-heralded phrase "freedom of contract." All that is really meant by this phrase is that the employer should have the freedom to take the laborers singly in order to make them jointly accept his terms. It simply means that in making a contract, the laborer shall not have the same right to be represented by the most competent of his class or craft that capital has ; but that each one, however ill-informed or incompetent to present his own case, shall be dealt with simply by the representative of corporate capital. Every time a laborer is induced, through ignorance or otherwise to accept inferior conditions, it increases the power of the employer to enforce similar terms upon others. Thus, while the uniformity of price for the same work in the same shop prevails, this method enables the employer to impose the maximum hardship and give the minimum pay that the superior men can endure, whereas if the laborers acted collectively, as the capitalists do, the more competent of their number could be chosen to negotiate the contract for the whole, thus preventing the inferior from being used as a means of destroying the contracting power of the superior. And since the contract made by the superior would always be as favorable or more so than that made by the inferior, the poorest laborers have every thing to gain and nothing to lose by associated or representative action. Any system of jurisprudence which should permit representation by counsel on one side and refuse it on the other, would throughout Christendom be pronounced as a scandalous violation of the principles of equity; yet this relation obtains between employers and employed in the most civilized countries, except so far as it has been rendered impossible by the power of organized labor itself.

As proof of the obvious one-sidedness of the individual-contract idea, it is only necessary to go into any large factory and read the printed rules which govern the conditions of employment. I have read scores of them. They are usually printed and posted up near the entrance of the factory, and they stipulate the various conditions of work the employers desire to impose. Sometimes these rules, miscalled contracts, appear to give the same rights to the laborer as to the employer. This, however, is usually followed by the qualification that in case of misdemeanor, inferior workmanship, or other cause, the laborer can be summarily dismissed, and of these things the employer is the sole judge. In short, these rules are formulated and enforced exclusively by the employer. And when a new laborer is engaged he neither hears nor sees any thing of them but the mere fact that they are posted up in the factory, and that he was not coerced into taking the position, is held to constitute a free contract, the conditions of which are legally binding, and are commonly so interpreted by the courts.

It may be replied that this is the only practical way of doing, so far as the employer is concerned. This is undoubtedly true ; but it demonstrates the impossibility of individual contracts ; hence the absurdity of objecting to labor combinations, on the ground that they destroy the laborers' freedom of individual contract. The right of individual contract means nothing, unless it means that every individual can make a contract for himself without regard to that of others. Experience has shown that such contracts are incompatible with a highly complex productive system. To the modern employer laborers constitute various parts of a vast productive machine, and hence must work in practical uniformity or not at all. This is not only true of the laborers in any given workshop, but it is practically true of the laborers in different workshops in the same industry, whose products compete in the same market. Thus it is the economic conditions of production, and not labor combinations, that have destroyed the feasibility of individual contracts ; and it is beyond the power of either laborer or capitalist, or both combined, to restore it without abrogating the factory system. Since both capital and labor now necessarily move in large aggregations, for organized capital to object to the existence of organized labor is manifestly as unjust as it is irrational and uneconomic.

3. Another objection urged against labor combinations is that they are uneconomic in their character and methods. It is insisted that they cannot increase wages because wages are governed by natural law, whose operation is beyond the influence of trades unions. That much of the conduct of trades unions has been uneconomic will not be disputed by any one familiar with their history. But it is scarcely less clear that this is mainly due to their acceptance of the capitalists' doctrine of wages, and not to any thing in the nature of labor combinations. This doctrine is that wages are regulated by the proportion between the demand for and supply of laborers, and consequently that nothing can increase wages which does not diminish the supply of labor, as compared with the demand. The supply of labor being determined by the number of the laboring population, any endeavor to increase wages except by limiting the population was held to be a futile attempt to suspend the operation of natural law.[1] A doctrine according to which wages could only be raised

[1] See Mill's "Principles of Political Economy," vol. i., p. 428 ; "McCulloch's "Principles of Political Economy," p. 174 ; Perry's "Political Econ-

by increasing the deaths or decreasing the births in the laborers' families was properly repugnant to them, though they were unable to answer it. While the laborers accepted the economists' theory, they rejected their means of applying it, and to their credit be it said, they endeavored to control the supply of labor without resorting to protracted celibacy or infanticide.

Moreover, they were constantly having object lessons in the application of this doctrine by the employing class. Supply and demand being regarded as the law of prices as well as of wages, the capitalists had practically to deal with the same problem. With this exception, however, that in their case supply involved the existence of commodities, in the case of the laborers it involved the existence of human beings. In acting upon this doctrine, the capitalists endeavored to regulate the price of commodities by withholding a portion of the product from the market—reducing the supply. This naturally led to corners and other forms of artificial monopoly, which are now recognized as social evils, especially as all such efforts are undertaken solely to increase the price of commodities.

That the laboring class should imitate the policy by which their masters had apparently been so successful cannot be a matter of surprise. They naturally tried to do with labor what the capitalists had done with commodities—namely, to limit the supply in order to increase its price, by withholding a portion of it from the market, which in their case is called a strike. Every strike for higher wages is simply the practical application of the doctrine of "supply and demand" to labor ; it is to the labor-market

omy," 1st. ed., pp. 122, 123. Also Wells' " Recent Economic Changes," p. 124. *Cf.* " Wealth and Progress," pp. 35–52. Nor can it be said that this doctrine has been discarded although its fallacy has been repeatedly exposed. The fact that Mill practically gave it up before he died, rendered the wages-fund form of stating it unpopular. But the doctrine that wages are governed by the relative demand and supply of laborers has continued to be taught by the most scholarly economists. Cairnes tried to rehabilitate it after Mill's conversion. Jevons reaffirmed it, and it is the essential idea in the most recent discussion of wages by German, Austrian, English, and American writers. And Marshall in his " Principles of Economics," (1890) which is characteristically the embodiment of the most recent discussion of the subject by continental and American writers, makes supply and demand the basis of all his reasoning on Distribution and Exchange.

precisely what a corner is to that of commodities. And yet this is precisely what economists have taught in theory and the capitalists have illustrated ,in practice. Thus the feature in the combination of capital which the public most oppose, and that in the combination of labor which the, employing class most condemn, is the logical result of the popular doctrines of prices and wages, and not a necessary part of industrial combination, either of capital or of labor.

We have already seen that the arbitrary and speculative feature of the combination of capital is the incident, and that its normal function is to increase the economic efficiency of production and reduce the price of commodities ; and also that the former is diminished and the latter increased as the progress of society advances. A very little consideration of the subject will show that this is equally true of labor combinations. Not only have the rise of wages and the general freedom of the laboring classes everywhere advanced with the growth of trades unions, but these organizations have been one of the most efficient means in promoting that end. The reason for this is obvious when considered in the light of the doctrine of wages already stated. When we realize that cost, and not the mere ratio between quantities, is the chief determining influence in prices, the importance of labor combinations as a means of raising wages is easily understood. Upon the principle that the cost of labor is high or low according to the simplicity or complexity of the social environment, it follows that whatever increases the laborer's social opportunities—*i.e.*, forces him into more frequent contact with an increasing variety of social influences, necessarily tends to increase his wages, and this is precisely what labor organizations do.

Isolation is social death. The poverty of the laborer's social life has always been the lack of social opportunity. For centuries the only opportunity for social intercourse open to the laborer outside of his meagre family circle and the church was the tavern. During the middle ages and practically down to the present century the church and the tavern or inn were the most prominent social institutions. Although the church was the centre of culture and refinement and furnished what there was of art and music, its attitude towards the laborer was always that of authority. It bade him obey under penalty of endless punishment. It afforded him little if any opportunity for social intercourse with his peers, where he could talk over his grievances on equal terms with those whose experience was practically like his own.

Social intercourse for the laborer, of a democratic character, was first furnished by the tavern. There the laborers, tired and heart-sore, with no industrial, social, religious, or political rights which their superiors were bound to respect, could meet over a mug of beer, relate their hardships to one another, and exchange sympathetic encouragement. By such social intercourse the laborers not only became more acquainted with, and interested in, each other, but the more intelligent and characterful among them were naturally inspired to suggest various methods for improving their condition and demanding new rights and greater freedom. Thus, by affording social opportunity, the tavern was one of the early instruments of social progress ; it may indeed be said to have been the birthplace of free speech for the masses.[1] What the tavern was to the early peasantry the trades union is to the modern laborer. Indeed, for the first half of the present century the trades union was really a differentiation of the tavern meeting. Instead of meeting in a general social way, they met for discussion and united action regarding their special industries.

The trades union tends to develop the intelligence and character of the laborers in many ways. In the first place it stimulates the study of industrial conditions, which involves a considerable amount of reading and general information, and also a close acquaintance with the industrial condition of their craft. The discussion of the various propositions which arise for consideration develops individual confidence, force of character, and a consciousness of industrial rights and social power, not only in those who actively participate, but in all who attend. In short, the trades union is a great educational institution ; it is the economic academy of the laboring class and is practically the only opportunity for industrial education they have ever had.

[1] The need of the tavern as a social resort will be better understood when we realize the fact that the first public meeting ever held in England for the open discussion of political rights did not take place till 1769. See Buckle's " History of Civilization," vol. i., p. 311. Also Hallam's " Constitutional History," vol. ii., p. 420. Cook's " History of Party," vol. iii., p. 187. Albemarle's " Memoirs of Rockingham," vol. ii., p. 93.

Moreover, the labor union is an important social centre ; in addition to furnishing the laborers with the means of a better knowledge of their economic conditions, it affords a degree of opportunity for social intercourse otherwise practically impossible. It is to the laboring class what clubs and other social institutions are to the wealthy. The social intercourse and activity thus created (which is frequently extended to their families and friends) necessarily awaken new tastes, wants, and aspirations. Nor is the influence of this limited to the personal character and home life of the members of the association, but the social rivalry between different organizations is equally pronounced. So strong is this that a class feeling often exists between trades as to their social position, the test usually being the wages paid in their trade and the financial strength of their organization. Thus, on all public occasions, they vie with each other as to which shall make the most opulent appearance. This social competition necessarily furnishes the incentive to new desires and ambitions involving a greater variety of social life and a more expensive standard of living.

The pressure of the increased necessities thus unconsciously developed makes a demand for an increase of wages necessary. This, of course, does not come suddenly ; it is felt first and most keenly by those who have been most susceptible to the social-izing influences and whose cost of living has been most increased. Their expenditure begins to press uncomfortably against their income, until finally they are unable to make both ends meet. Those who first begin to experience this hardship, being the most expensive of their class and usually the most intelligent and characterful, bring the matter before the union and advocate a general demand for an increase of wages. When this feeling is shared only by a few, they fail to carry their point..

Since it is impossible both from the nature of the factory system and the constitution of labor organizations to make special terms for individual cases, the only way for the most expensive laborers to secure an increase of wages for themselves is to obtain the same for their whole trade. Being thus compelled to rise together, or not at all, it becomes necessary to inspire their associates with substantially the same feelings and ambitions they experience themselves. To do this they are forced to argue questions over and 'over again, showing not only the necessity but the feasibility of their proposition. When they have succeeded in convincing twenty or thirty per cent. of the most characterful in their union of the wisdom of their demand, the remainder usually follow. With this united action of the whole class they invariably succeed sooner or later in obtaining the increase of wages or other improved conditions desired. All this is educational and socializing in its influence. It is through organizations which thus practically weld the laborers into a social class that the economic condition of the whole is improved by the efforts of a small but the most advanced portion.

It will thus be seen that trades unions are essentially economic institutions ; instead of being inimical to the laborer's interest and a menace to capital, they are a most important feature of modern society. For the same reason that nothing can permanently reduce the price of commodities, which does not diminish the cost of production, nothing can permanently advance wages which does not increase the laborer's cost of living. And upon the same principle that the combination of capital increases the facilities for diminishing the cost of production, the combination of labor increases the opportunity for increasing the laborer's necessities and cost of living. It is by their opportunity-creating influences, and not by their power to limit the number of laborers, that trades unions ever permanently affect wages. Of course they resort to strikes as a means of enforcing their demands when petitions and other more moderate forms of request have failed ; not because it limits the supply of laborers, but because a considerable portion of the laborers are acting under the pressure of a social necessity, which if not satisfied will involve a protracted social conflict.

It is commonly assumed that the conducting of strikes is the chief function of labor unions. This is as erroneous as it would be to say that the chief function of organized capital is to conduct lock-outs. Strikes are among the most reluctant and the least beneficial functions trades unions perform. It is indeed notorious that strikes diminish as labor organizations increase in extent and efficiency. It is a fact well known to those conversant with the history of labor organizations, that far more strikes have been prevented by the officers of trades unions than were ever inaugurated by them. It is, however, through their united efforts as industrial organizations and as the means of concentrating the political influence of their class to promote in a multitude of ways the improvement of their social condition, that the trades unions have done their best work. Take, for example, the reduction of the hours of labor; this they have persistently advocated for more than forty years, and in spite of the almost united opposition of the employing class, have succeeded in shortening the working time in almost every civilized country, in many instances from fourteen to ten and nine, and in some cases to eight, hours a day. It is due to their efforts that night-work for women and children in factories was prohibited, education for working children secured, and the truck system with numerous other degrading features of the factory system abolished. It may indeed be said that nearly all the improvements in the sanitary and social condition of modern workshops which have taken place during the last generation are directly or indirectly the result of the indefatigable efforts of labor combinations. The rise of wages is the secondary effect of these social improvements, which are simply so much added opportunity for individual development.

It is not pretended that these organizations furnish the only social opportunity the laborer enjoys; it is of course true that he obtains some share in the benefit arising from the general progress of society, but the degree in which he is thus benefited largely depends upon the social preparation he receives in his own special sphere. Suppose, for example, the mass of laborers continued to work in an unwholesome atmosphere under demoralizing conditions for twelve or more hours a day, and to spend their nights in dismal tenements, compared with which a very ordinary saloon is a wholesome attraction. The general culture of society would have but a very slight influence upon their social life. This much-needed preparatory social opportunity is what the trades union largely supplies. It does this first through the social intercourse and inspiration it directly furnishes within its organization, and next by its persistent efforts to modify the form of labor and diminish the amount of time the workshop shall exact from the laborer's life, and by increasing that which is added to it by leisure, and the general humanizing influences of society. Labor combinations, therefore, tend to promote the increase of wages in the most truly economic way possible, which is by stimulating the growth of the laborer's social wants and desires, and by promoting industries, education, and the possibility of united, intelligent action in economic and social affairs.

There is no force in society that can secure a permanent rise in wages unless the social necessity for it is previously developed. When strikes take place for an increase of wages, or any other object, before the demand of a considerable portion of the laborers has ripened into a necessity for it, they generally fail. It is always the most intelligent and characterful, whose habitual consumption presses the hardest against their income, who are the most cautious about entering upon a strike, and the most persistent in their endurance after the conflict commences. On the other hand, that portion of the class which has a little bank account or a mortgaged cottage, are the first to surrender when the real hardships of the struggle begin to appear. The reason for this, however, is not that they are inherently less heroic than the others, but that the advance in their standard of living has not outgrown their wages to the same extent. Consequently, the hardships arising from the insufficiency of their wages are less severe than those of the others ; hence their early surrender. In other words, their effort to obtain the advance is relatively weak because the consciousness of its necessity is relatively slight. And, conversely, those whose necessary expenditures press the hardest upon their incomes suffer the greatest inconvenience from the smallness of their wages, and hence will endure correspondingly great hardships in the efforts to obtain an increase.

It is, however, to the ill-advised strikes and other rash conduct of trades unions that we are usually referred as evidences of their evil influence. We are told that they are dictatorial, that they arbitrarily disturb trade and industry, destroy the profits of capital, and involve untold hardship upon the laboring class by loss of wages. It is, indeed, one of the favorite themes of the opponents of trades unions to foot up, periodically, how much the laborers have lost in wages through strikes, and to point out that they are the dupes of dishonest leaders.

This method of estimating the social and economic merits of labor unions is at once specious and misleading. Judged by such a standard, almost every great movement for social and political reform would have to be voted a failure. The Wat Tyler insurrection, the uprising of the Roundheads against Charles I., the Protestant Reformation, the Revolution of 1688, the French and American Revolutions, and our Civil War, all cost more financially than was immediately realized from them. But if the results of these struggles are estimated in their permanent effect upon social well-being, they were all great successes, yielding indefinitely more in benefits than they cost in sacrifice.

So it is with labor unions, notwithstanding their many mistakes. It is a great error to assume that, because a strike fails to accomplish the specific object for which it was inaugurated, the money and energy expended upon it are wasted. On the contrary, the educational effect of an unsuccessful strike on the employer and the public, as well as on the laborer, is often worth more than all it costs. But if these efforts are judged by their permanent effect upon the material and social well-being of the masses, they will have to be regarded as great successes even in a financial sense, to say nothing of the social and moral advantage resulting from the reduced working hours and improved industrial conditions they have secured. The increase of wages during the last forty years is many times greater than all that has been spent or lost through strikes since the dawn of the factory system. Indeed, the amount the laborers in this country and England have received through increased wages since 1850 is nearly equal to all they received during the previous fifty years. But what is still more important, all this gain will not only continue in the future without any further effort, but will furnish a powerful lever by which to obtain still greater improvement.

The laboring classes therefore are not permanently impoverished by what they pay into unions or lose in strikes. It should be remembered that their losses are only temporary, while their gains are permanent. Thus when they strike for an increase of wages or reduction of hours, if they fail to obtain that specific object their loss is slight, since their future wages are not reduced nor their hours increased on that account; but if they succeed they obtain a permanent gain. In other words, when they fail they practically hold their own, and when they succeed they gain forever.

That many strikes are unwisely inaugurated and badly managed would be readily admitted by those acquainted· with the
history of labor organizations.   Nor will it be disputed that dishonest men, or men otherwise conspicuously unfit for leadership, sometimes get at the head of labor organizations.   But is
this not true of every other form of social and industrial organization ?   Are capitalist organizations free from these charges ?
Do they not frequently act rashly and undertake enterprises in
which thousands of innocent confiding investors (often women,
children, and orphans) lose their little all ?   Have they not their
Grants and Wards, whose rash (or worse) conduct often disturbs
the whole commercial and industrial world, bringing bankruptcy
and ruin to large numbers ?

Cannot the same impeachment be urged with quite as much
truth against political combinations, social clubs, and even
churches ?   Would any one venture to say that because there
are dishonest railroad presidents and corporation treasurers, the
combination of capital should be prohibited, and because there
are dishonest and incompetent deacons and ministers church
associations should disband ?   Why should working men be expected to be more honest and wise than any other class in the
community ?   Why should perfection be demanded of them, when
liability to err is conceded to every one else ?   Since all other
social institutions are to be judged by their virtues, why should
labor organizations be judged only by their mistakes ?   Considering
their limited opportunities and the extent of the forces arrayed
against them, the wonder is not that the laborers have made so
many mistakes, but rather that they have succeeded at all.

Another characteristic of labor combinations, which should not
be overlooked, is the marked improvement in their methods of
dealing with industrial disputes.   In proportion as trades unions
become more complete in their organizations, and their members
more intelligent, they have become more rational and conserva-
tive in their attitude.   Whereas physical force, often involving
the destruction of life and property, was once their chief means
of warfare, they now mainly rely upon reason and facts as their
economic weapons.   Consequently we find to-day that in those
industries where trades unions are best organized and exercise
the greatest influence, strikes are fewest, wages are highest, hours

of labor shortest, and the relation between laborers and employers the most confidential and harmonious.

Trades unions therefore are not only legitimate, economic, and social institutions, but they are an integral part of the industrial organization of modern society. They are the economic counterpart of the combination of capital, and their existence and development are equally necessary to the harmonious development of society. It is an entire mistake, therefore, to regard trades unions as necessarily a menace to industry and social welfare; they are constitutionally important educational institutions, and whether they will be a power for good or for evil in society depends upon what they teach and how they teach it. Since labor organizations are the most effectual, and nearly the only means of furnishing the opportunities for economic education to the wage workers, instead of trying to degrade and suppress them, it is alike the interest and duty of both the employing class and the community to encourage their development and increase their usefulness. If capitalists would devote one tenth the means for helping labor unions to provide for more comprehensive and correct knowledge upon economic and social questions that they devote to opposing them, these organizations would become the source of sound economic education and the training schools for intelligent citizenship, instead of being the nurseries of industrial and social antagonism.

28

SUMMARY AND CONCLUSION.

In the preceding pages I have endeavored to discuss the general principles which govern the economic relations of society, and to indicate briefly their application to practical affairs. It will be observed that this treatment of the subject widens the sphere of economics, in that it applies these principles to society instead of limiting their application to *wealth* or *value*. Therefore instead of the principles of physical economics, which political economy has hitherto taught, we have the principles of social economics, a system which recognizes the tastes, habits, and character of man, as the source of all economic movement, and the development and perfection of man as the goal of social evolution. Since this is a departure from the traditional methods of discussing economics and involves the consideration of the whole subject from a different point of view, it may be well to briefly summarize the leading principles laid down in each of the four parts as follows :

Principles of Social Progress.—Social progress is here considered as a gradual movement of society towards a greater definiteness of economic and social relations, specialization of functions, and interdependence of individuals and classes, and an increase of wealth, power, and freedom for the individual, with a diminution of the arbitrary function of government. This movement has two characteristic phases, distinguishable as industrial and social. The former relates to the means of sustaining life, and the latter to the mode of enjoying life. The development of these two phases of progress in society is indicated respectively as follows : In economics by a movement towards the de-individuation and aggregation of productive force—both of labor and capital,—the individuation of management and responsibility, and the socialization of results in the form of more, better, and cheaper products. In society and politics it is indicated by a movement towards increasing the sovereignty of the individual and diminishing governmental authority. This produces two changes in the laborer's condition : one specializes and limits his economic function, the other generalizes and extends his individual and social function. Thus in proportion as the laborer's industrial individuality diminishes and he loses the economic power to employ himself, his social and political individuality increases, and he gains the power to control his employer ; and this power he will use to the detriment of existing interests and institutions if his well-being is neglected or impaired. Therefore as civilization advances, the prosperity and safety of the whole community depend more and more upon the industrial and social welfare of the laboring classes. The correctness of this view is sustained by universal history, which shows that civil and political freedom have everywhere followed the material prosperity of the masses, and this has everywhere been characterized by specialization of labor, concentration of capital, and private responsibility in industrial enterprise.

Principles of Economic Production.—Production is treated as the creation or increase of transferable utility. Since nothing has utility which does not serve human wants, effective desire or consumption is the cause of production. Industrial progress primarily consists in cheapening wealth, the test of which is the increase of material well-being obtainable for a day's labor. It is a universal law in economics, that productive efficiency is increased and wealth is cheapened according as natural forces are substituted for labor. Natural forces can only be harnessed to production by the use of capital, and capital can only be economically employed under conditions of increasing returns. Increasing returns are only possible with a relatively larger market, and this depends entirely upon the increase of consumption per capita in the community. Large consumption, which means high-priced labor, is one of the prime causes of cheap wealth.

Value is here treated not as the ratio in which things exchange for one another, but as the ratio in which wealth exchanges for service. Economic prices are high or low, things are dear or cheap, solely in proportion as a smaller or larger amount of them will exchange for a day's labor. A commodity at 50 cents in China, a dollar in Russia, or $1.50 in England, may be very much dearer than at $2 in America. To repeat this in another form, the economic status of wealth is determined absolutely by the ratio in which it will exchange for service as an *economic equivalent*. The basis upon which economic equivalents are determined is not *quantity* but *cost*. Therefore economic value or prices are not determined by the ratio between demand and supply, but by the cost of production. Under free competition in open market, the price of any given commodity tends towards uniformity, on the basis of the cost of producing the dearest portion of the supply in that market. Cost of production is determined not by the quantity of labor expended, but by the aggregate cost of labor directly or indirectly devoted to its production, and since large consumption induces the economic use of machinery, which saves labor and diminishes the cost of production, high wages promote low prices.

Principles of Economic Distribution.—The distribution of wealth is not a distinct economic function, but an inseparable part of the process of production. Economic distribution takes place in the form and order of wages (and salaries), rent, interest, and profit. Consequently, the social theories based upon the assumption that wages are determined by what remains of the product after rent, interest, and profit are deducted, as held by socialists, and practically supported by Jevons and Walker, are erroneous. Wages differ from rent, interest, and profit, in that they are economically *cost*, while rent, interest, and profit are *surplus*. Wages, being the price of labor, are determined by the same law as the price of commodities, namely, the cost of furnishing the dearest portion of the necessary supply, and are necessarily added to the price of commodities ; while rent, interest, and profit, being surplus, are not items in the cost of production by which the price is determined, hence do not enter into the consumer's price of commodities, so that prices are not higher or wages lower by virtue of rent, interest, and profit. The chief problem, therefore, to consider in connection with the distribution of wealth is *wages*. To increase wages is to increase the income of all who participate in productive enterprise, and this in turn extends the market for products, diversifies industry, and makes the various forms of surplus possible. In other words, the prosperity of all the other classes of the community finally depends upon that of the wage-receiving class. Consequently, the economic problem of society is not one of reducing rents, regulating interest, or abolishing profit, but it is a problem of increasing wages which finally depend upon the wants, habits, and character of the laboring classes.

Principles of Practical Statesmanship.—In applying the principles of economics to the practical affairs of society, it should be observed first of all that the functions of government are essentially of a *protective, educational,* and *judiciary* character. Therefore, while practical statesmanship has to deal with an infinite variety of circumstances, the machinery of government should be employed only upon the principle of protecting or enlarging the industrial, social, or political opportunities of the individual. This should be the test of every change in public policy of whatever character.

Applied to international relations, this principle involves whatever is necessary to secure to the people of a nation the opportunities for developing their highest industrial and social possibilities. This may take the form of protecting the people against forceful molestation by military invasion or an encroachment upon their political or territorial rights, or it may take the form of protecting them against an industrial invasion, in which the development of their home industries is menaced through the underselling of their products by those of lower-paid labor in less civilized countries.

Applied to domestic relations, the principle implies whatever is necessary to protect the individual in all the rights and privileges he now enjoys, and to increase in every possible way the opportunities for developing his character and capacity for assuming a still greater degree of individual responsibility and freedom in every sphere of life. In the first place, the policy of government should always be to encourage individual enterprise by securing the greatest possible freedom to capital consistent with business integrity and social safety. In other words, it should be the guardian of the interests of the community without assuming business responsibility. In the next place, it should not only protect the laborer's industrial and social rights, but it should employ all possible means for improving his industrial and social condition.

This is of fundamental importance : (1) because the laboring classes constitute the great mass of the community, and therefore most truly represent society ; (2) because under democratic institutions, public integrity, political and social freedom, depend upon the intelligence and character of the masses ; (3) because under factory methods of production material prosperity and social welfare finally depend upon the consumption of wealth by the laboring classes.

Thus it appears that, whether we consider the social question from the stand-point of the general progress of society, as indicated by the advance of personal, political, and religious freedom, or from the standpoint of industrial progress, as indicated by the development of labor-saving and wealth-cheapening methods of production and the more equitable distribution of the products of industry, as indicated by the increase of wages, or from the standpoint of practical statesmanship, as indicated by legislation, we find it all ultimately resolves itself into the problem of developing the character, individuality, and social life of the masses. When this fact shall become the accepted basis of public policy, the true economic relation of the laborer to the welfare of society will have been recognized for the first time, and one great step will have been taken towards the solution of the social problem.

Herewith is reached the end of our journey along the paths of industrial human development. Dimly lighted as it has been by the researchers and thinkers of the past, our way has been found only by closely following the light of facts. No theories have been allowed to stand against fact. No reasonings have been sustained in spite of fact. No propositions have been given credence contrary to fact. If novel and paradoxical conclusions have been reached, it has been in humble obedience to facts. If we have found the solution of many problems hitherto dark and tangled, it is fact that has unravelled the complexities of the subject. If many questions heretofore explained in tortuous methods difficult to follow have been given the guise of simplicity, it is because facts have been able to furnish a simple explanation.

That this book issues in a system of social development at once pleasant, profitable, and promising the greatest good, is agreeable to me, and should be to the reader. It may at first repel orthodox experts in political economy who have thought so long on the old dismal lines that nothing agreeable seems to them possible from the workings of economic law. Steeped in the dreary reflections of Malthus, Ricardo, Mill, and the rest, they may indeed reject with scorn any thing that opens a more cheerful view. But the world actually goes from good to better perpetually, despite their awful predictions. Men are richer, brighter, more virtuous and happy, wiser, stronger, and healthier than they ever were, and we have simply pointed out the principles that have brought them to this finish. The human race is on the road to better estates. Long ago it set out on its unknown and perilous journey. At the time when the first men learned to trust their brains instead of their muscles the march was begun, and still it goes on. Every day sees some new attainment of the human mind, some new conquest over its environment, and every day sees more and more men included in the general enrichment and enlightenment. The world becomes more peaceful, more industrial. The rewards of industry become greater ; the general comfort is increased ; the powers of production prevail ; education becomes more general and varied ; nature is subdued and harnessed ; political freedom waxes, civil broils decline, occupations are diversified, cities multiply, vast organizations are formed to contribute to human welfare, and machineries proffer their million fingers swifter than arrows, surer than muscles, more tireless than thought, to the workshops of mankind. There are formed the countless objects of human desire, most potent of all earthly forces. Steam drives the machinery, but human desire drives the steam. Out of man the movement springs, for him it labors, him it improves, and there is no limit to it. It has the nature of the infinite. The more it gets, the more it wants ; the more it does, the more it aspires to do ; the higher its advancement, the higher mounts its ambition.

Still no advantage is gained by magical methods such as those suggested by our modern dreamers of dreams, but all is accomplished by the well-known and powerful methods al-

ready at work among us—our present benefactors. No sequestra-
tion of the rents of land, such as Mr. Henry George is pleased
to advocate, has any share in the advance. How could it have,
when one sees that the more land there is to the person the
worse off all persons are ? The steppes and the untilled prairies
are the habitation of the idle nomad and the painted savage.
Miles of land per man, but no wealth. Men are richest where
each has least land, as in the teeming cities. " To every man his
own farm " is a motto of barbarism. Anti-poverty societies would
find plenty of land their death-warrant. It is to *escape* the bovine
monotony of farm life that men throng to cities and towns, where
intelligence is general and the resources of the individual enlarge,
where the interchange of human sympathies and criticism stimulates thought and develops civility, where, as in a beehive, socia-
bility supplants the dull hut of the lonely agriculturist, with whom
new thoughts are as rare as roses in January.

Nor is progress to be speeded after any such fashion as Mr.
Bellamy has pictured, nor by the methods advocated by socialists.
Work and system, organization and struggle for better materials,
more productive energies, wiser laws, clearer principles, nature
better understood and made more obedient, will always be the
real agencies of amelioration. And by the use of these means
more intelligently applied and more completely developed, the
human race may legitimately and soberly expect to reach the
goal of its most sanguine expectations. To reach it quickly the
main thing is to widen human desires. The true ideal is that
everybody should want every thing enough to be willing to work
for it and to get it, since this is the source and fountain of progress. No wants means no advance.

The first economic duty of society and government is constantly to stimulate desire. If the English in India could make
the Hindoo laborer.want more things, they could soon civilize
him up to their own standard. If the Russian peasants were not
content with so little, the development of Russia might run on at
equal speed with that of the United States. If our Indians could
only be made to want houses and steam machinery and good
clothes enough to work for them, the Indian problem would solve
itself in a single decade. If the Southern negro could be made
discontented with his slovenly hut, his scanty clothing and food,

the race problem would dissolve ; and if our own poorer classes could only be made to crave better homes, better amusements, better food, with better surroundings, the problem of poverty would soon disappear, since they would universally begin to get them.

To desire things is the first step in social progress, and this desire no sooner sets in with force than it begins to establish a new form of society. More wants means more factories, more machinery, cheaper products, our laborers more steadily employed, capitalists more comprehensive and adventurous. Enterprises on an ever enlarging scale are called for to produce the desired result,—enterprises surpassing in their extent all the trusts yet devised, controlled by individual management, under abler captains of industry than have yet appeared, and delivering cheaper products to be used by larger proportions of the people.

The laborer must become more specialized as a laborer, though more generalized as a man. His welfare must be seen to be the welfare of the community, because he is really seven tenths of the community, and his interest must be more and more considered by all classes, as carrying with it the welfare of the rest. When employers understand their true interest the stupid and stolid resistance which they have long made to his progress will give way to a genial and hearty co-operation in all that makes for his advantage. They will realize that in his advancement lies their own prosperity.

Then the future will be much brighter and happier, and larger numbers of men will succeed to a secure and pleasurable career. Since fifty years of devotion to industrial pursuits have wrought the wonders we know, and led mankind from the days of plague, pestilence, and famine, from general illiteracy, isolation, and superstition into the prosperity and progress of to-day, what will it be when a thousand years of intelligent progress have wrought out the possibilities of human development? When nature well understood and well harnessed to the supply of millions of human wants shall furnish the riches of her storehouse, abundance for all will be more easily obtained than is the little which the great mass of mankind now receives.

INDEX.

WEALTH AND PROGRESS.

A CRITICAL EXAMINATION OF THE LABOR PROBLEM.

BY GEORGE GUNTON.

12MO, 400 PAGES. PAPER, 50 CENTS; CLOTH, $1.00.

OPINIONS OF THE PRESS.

" Mr. Gunton has written one of the ablest works on a question of vast interest which has issued from the press in many years."—*Chicago Times.*

" It is a plain, practical, common-sense view by a sensible American, where every point is argued and a plain reason given for its adoption."— *Chicago Inter-Ocean.*

" The book is one of infinite suggestion and also of practical value."— *Boston Traveller.*

" No one can rise from the reading of ' Wealth and Progress ' without the profound conviction that it contains the first attempt ever made to put the claim for an eight-hour system on a truly economic and scientific basis."— *New York Star.*

" Mr. Gunton's work may be declared without hesitation to be the most notable contribution to the science since Walker's ' Wages Question.' "—*Political Science Quarterly.*

" The book contains a great deal of good sense, especially in its criticism of the one-sided views of the standard economical teachers."—*New York Sun.*

" The book contains an immense amount of exact information regarding all branches of the subject, and will be valuable as a book of reference to all students of the economical question."—*New York World.*

" Mr. Gunton has performed his task in a brilliant and masterly manner, and with a logical clearness and accuracy in argument that leaves scarcely a question of the truth and soundness of the position he has taken. The book is in many respects the most important, most thorough, and most satisfying that has been added to the literature of the subject."—*Boston Evening Gazette.*

" The author is very thorough, and contributes much valuable thought to the subject."—*Brooklyn Eagle.*

" The author presents a picture of the ' social crisis,' and develops his theory by historical illustration and demonstration. His presentation is fascinating and skilful."—*Boston Journal.*

" It is at once philosophic and eminently practical. It announces the natural laws which lie at the basis of the labor problem, elucidates them by historical data, and enforces their soundness with a logical cogency that carries conviction."—*Eastern Argus* (Portland, Me.).

" Mr. Gunton is the latest comer in the field, and he performs the job that he undertakes. We have never seen a neater piece of refutation than that to be found between pages sixty and seventy, wherein the George theory is particularly analyzed."—*Journal of Commerce* (New York).

" The practical experience of Mr. Gunton gives particular interest and value to his book, which in manner and matter would do honor to the most practised writer."—*Commercial Advertiser* (New York).

" It is the most thorough and comprehensive treatment of the labor question ever presented."—*Paterson Labor Standard.*

" The book is conspicuous for its close backing of all theory by practical demonstration."—*North American Review.*

" His book is the work of a sincere man and careful thinker, and deserves wide reading."—*Boston Post.*

" If any one cares to know what makes for human progress in the field of economics, here is the book of all books which America has ever produced." —*The Public* (Abington, Mass.).

"We commend Mr. Gunton's book as a calm and instructive argument, which is entitled to serious consideration, and he deserves the thanks of all sound economists."—*The American* (Philadelphia).

" Mr. George Gunton has done a real service in publishing his ' Wealth and Progress.' It is refreshing to read the utterances of a man whose talents and studies have fitted him for the work he has undertaken."—*Boston Advertiser.*

" If the arguments in this book could be taught in every high-school and college in the land, we might hope for a speedy settlement of the troublesome and knotty problems of the day."—*Public Opinion* (Washington, D. C.).

" It is the most noteworthy of recent American contributions to the economics of the labor problem. It will at once give its author an assured standing as a political economist."—*Chicago Dial.*

" It contains much originality of thought, boldly asserted and consistently maintained, and is presented in such pleasant and attractive form that much of it possesses the interest of a novel."—*Fall River News* (Mass.).

"We are impressed with the thoroughness of the author's investigation and the strength of his argument, no less than by the clearness and vigor of his style."—*Christian Advocate.*

" The argument of Mr. Gunton is supported by many facts well calculated to prove his theory."—*Chicago Herald.*

" It is a very remarkable book, and at the outset it will be very highly appreciated by those best versed in economic science."—*Sunday Tribune* (Minn.).

" 'Wealth and Progess' is a handsome contribution to the science of economics which is sure to command attention."—*New Orleans States.*

" It is a contribution to economical literature of marked value."—*Scientific Arena.*

" Mr. Gunton has brought to his task a large practical experience with industrial affairs, extended observation both in Europe and America, and close study of economic questions."—*San Francisco Bulletin.*

" The book is well written, and, while wholly opposed to socialism or the vagaries of Henry George's school, is yet strongly in the interest of the laboring classes."—*San Francisco Call.*

" It is one of the most comprehensive discussions of the labor question of the day."—*Buffalo Advertiser.*

" The subject is treated in a masterly manner, and will not fail to instruct and profit those who are interested in that all important theme.—*New Bedford Standard* (Mass.).

" We have in this volume the last contribution of science to the science of political economy, and, as it seems to us, the most valuable."—*Daily Herald* (Omaha).

" The present volume is clearly written, and is, to our mind, one of the ablest contributions which has of late been made upon the vexed subject."—*Buffalo Times.*

" 'Wealth and Progress' is a book designed to mark a new era in the history of political economy."—*Commonwealth* (Boston, Mass.).

" The author makes an exhaustive and able presentation of the subject, and his work is entitled to serious consideration."—*Syracuse Journal.*

" The book contains a large mass of valuable statistical information, and should be in the library of every student of the social problem."—*Labor Leader* (Boston).

" The author has produced a decidedly readable and suggestive work, giving good proof that political economy has become a study of prominent interest. He is no visionary socialist, but builds his propositions on facts and sound common-sense."—*The Moravian.*

" It will be readily admitted that he has in this volume made a valuable contribution to the discussion of one of the burning questions of the day."—*Washington Post.*

" We may fully commend it as presenting many aspects of the great question with remarkable force."—*Hartford Courant.*

" By none could such a work have been written but by a master of economic science, a thorough reader of statistics, a lucid and comprehensive thinker."—*Catholic Quarterly Review.*

" 'Wealth and Progress' will in time effect a revolution in what is known as political economy."—*Record and Guide* (New York).

ENGLISH NOTICES.

" Mr. Gunton is known in the United States as a hard student of economic questions, and as a writer of high ability. That character is fully borne up by his volume ' Wealth and Progress.' "—*The Scotsman.*

" Mr. Gunton throws fresh light on a much-discussed subject, and we cordially recommend his book to our readers."—*Belfast Northern Whig.*

" The work contains immense and laborious research, and is entitled to a thoughtful perusal and unqualified respect."—*Liverpool Post.*

" Mr. Gunton's book is a very important contribution to economic science, and deserves the most earnest consideration from all classes in the community."—*Literary World* (London).

" ' Wealth and Progress ' is certainly a work of great suggestiveness and usefulness. The practical value of its conclusion is undeniable. Its theory goes beyond explanation, and guides action—giving, indeed, a new scientific sanction to schemes of social amelioration hitherto taken in a spirit of vague philanthropy. He has gone far to achieve what economists and socialists alike have failed to do. He has developed a theory of wages in harmony with the social instincts and tendencies of to-day."—*Scottish Leader.*

" The performance leaves little to be desired for clearness of statement or for aptness of illustration."—*St. James's Gazette* (London).

" The idea is presented with clearness, and the arguments in its favor, as well as some of the objections to its practical workings, are ably stated."—*Morning Post* (London).

" The importance of the question, the ability, earnestness, and experience of industrial affairs which Mr. Gunton brings to the study of a difficult problem, entitle his work to respectful consideration. Mr. Gunton's book is very welcome, as it enforces from an economical point of view the great importance which must be attached to character."—*Charity Organization Review* (London).

" Mr. Gunton's book is written with great clearness and force of style and thought, and attacks two of the most long-standing doctrines in Political Economy—the doctrine of the wages-fund, and the determination of wages by supply and demand."—*The Spectator* (London).

For sale by booksellers ; or will be sent by mail, postage-paid, on receipt of the price, one dollar.

D. APPLETON & Co.   MACMILLAN & Co.

1, 3 & 5 BOND ST., NEW YORK   LONDON, ENG.

www.ingramcontent.com/pod-product-compliance
Lightning Source LLC
Chambersburg PA
CBHW031813270326
41932CB00008B/410